CONTROVERSY IN APPLIED ECONOMICS

CONTROVERSY IN APPLIED ECONOMICS

Edited by

Mike Campbell
Professor and Head of the Policy Research Unit
Department of Economics and Public Policy
Leeds Polytechnic

Mike Hardy
Head of School
School of Economics
Lancashire Polytechnic

Nige Healey
Senior Lecturer
Department of Economics and Public Policy
Leeds Polytechnic

HARVESTER WHEATSHEAF

New York London Toronto Sydney Tokyo

First published 1989 by
Harvester Wheatsheaf
66 Wood Lane End, Hemel Hempstead
Hertfordshire, HP2 4RG
A division of
Simon & Schuster International Group

Printed and bound in Great Britain by
BPCC Wheatons Ltd, Exeter

British Library Cataloguing in Publication Data

Controversy in applied economics.
1. Applied economics
I. Campbell, Mike, 1948– II. Hardy, Mike, 1949–
III. Healey, Nigel, 1957–
330

ISBN 0-7450-0463-6

1 2 3 4 5 93 92 91 90 89

To all our BA(Hons) Economics and Public Policy students, past and present.

CONTENTS

PREFACE

The central objective of this book is to provide a treatment of applied economics which explicitly approaches the field as contested terrain. It investigates the sources and nature of controversy within areas of applied economics in the context of the UK economy. This is a challenging prospect. Few, if any, other textbooks deal with controversy in applied economics in this direct fashion. All too often the tendency is to examine issues as if economics constituted a central, agreed body of thought, rather than a loose collection of competing perspectives.

The book adopts a systematic approach to understanding the nature of controversy. Chapter 1 establishes the 'core' themes and Chapters 2–12 then explore different areas of applied economics in the light of these insights. Finally, Chapter 13 draws some lessons for the future of economic science. The book is designed to meet the requirements of undergraduate students taking intermediate courses in economics, social sciences and business and will also provide useful supporting reading for students on a range of other courses.

The book has drawn on a team of specialists, all until recently colleagues in the Department of Economics and Public Policy at Leeds Polytechnic. The editors would like to thank these 'co-conspirators' in the enterprise, especially for their cooperation and patience during the preparation of the final draft. Our thanks, also, to the Department of Economics and Public Policy, Leeds Polytechnic and more recently to the School of Economics, Lancashire Polytechnic, for providing a stimulating and supportive environment in which to teach and write. Finally, our thanks are due to colleagues too numerous to mention, who commented on draft chapters at various stages in the preparation of this book.

Mike Campbell
Mike Hardy
Nige Healey

CONTRIBUTORS

Tom Burden is Senior Lecturer in the Department of Economics and Public Policy at Leeds Polytechnic. His research interests lie in the field of social policy and the state and he is author of several books in this area.

Mike Campbell is Professor in the Department of Economics and Public Policy and Head of the Policy Research Unit at Leeds Polytechnic. His research interests include methodology, local economic development and the state and he has published a number of articles and books in these areas. He is currently responsible for a wide range of research and consultancy projects under the aegis of the Policy Research Unit.

Mike Hardy is Head of the School of Economics at Lancashire Polytechnic and was formerly Principal Lecturer in the Department of Economics and Public Policy at Leeds Polytechnic. His main research interest is in the field of corporate organisation theory and he is presently responsible for a number of consultancies and research projects through the Local Economy Unit at Lancashire Polytechnic.

Nige Healey is Senior Lecturer in the Department of Economics and Public Policy and is closely associated with the work of the Policy Research Unit at Leeds Polytechnic. His principal research interests are UK domestic macroeconomic policy and international monetary economics. He has written a number of articles and books in these and related areas.

Roger Henderson is Senior Lecturer in the Department of Accountancy and Finance and Director of the Institute of Bankers' Courses at Leeds Polytechnic. He was previously with Lloyds Bank International and has a strong research interest in the UK financial system.

Terence Karran is Senior Lecturer in the Department of Economics and Public Policy at Leeds Polytechnic. He has a distinguished research background in the field of UK government and has written a number of books and articles in this area.

Bob Leach is Senior Lecturer in the Department of Economics and Public Policy at Leeds Polytechnic. He has written widely on local government issues and appears regularly on BBC radio and television to speak on this subject.

David Parker is Principal Lecturer in the Department of Economics and Public Policy at Leeds Polytechnic and Visiting Research Fellow at the Institute for Social and Economic Research at York University. He is currently engaged in a major research project on privatisation and regulation and has published a number of books and articles in this area.

Mel Powell is Lecturer in the Department of Economics and Public Policy at Leeds Polytechnic and Visiting Research Fellow at the Centre for Health Economics at York University. She is presently researching the economics of addiction and has written a book and several articles on this issue.

Richard Stead is Senior Lecturer in the Department of Economics and Public Policy at Leeds Polytechnic. His main research interests are in the business area and the application of new information technologies. He has written several books in this area.

Gerry Stewart is Senior Lecturer in the Department of Economics and Public Policy at Leeds Polytechnic. His research interests are primarily concerned with the growth of multinational corporations and, more recently, the economics of professional football.

John Sutherland is Associate Head of the Department of Economics and Public Policy at Leeds Polytechnic. His main research and teaching interests lie in the field of labour studies and he is currently engaged in a major project on the spatial pattern of unemployment in the United Kingdom.

1 · SOURCES OF CONTROVERSY IN APPLIED ECONOMICS

MIKE CAMPBELL

1.1 CONTROVERSY AND DISAGREEMENT?

1.1.1 Introduction

Most textbooks, and indeed most courses, present economics as if it were a relatively unified and coherent body of thought where there is broad agreement in our understanding of contemporary economies. Theories are presented and elaborated and, though more rarely, empirical evidence is presented which seems to demonstrate the solidity and validity of the current state of our economic knowledge.

Yet, contrary to the impressions given in such courses and textbooks, in reality there is no such unanimous agreement. There is no such consensus in economics. Even the most casual empirical review demonstrates a wide range of disagreement and controversy over economic issues. On almost every aspect of economic affairs economists can be found to argue contrary positions or to take an agnostic view. On television and radio, in newspapers and magazines, debate and contention flourish – not to mention the diversity of views emanating from economists advising differing political parties, pressure groups and professional organisations. In the more specialist and 'advanced' academic literature of the profession the existence of controversy is more obvious, for example, over privatisation (Kay and Thompson 1986), public expenditure (Heald 1984), or unemployment (Routh 1986). Indeed, popular wisdom on economic controversy is aptly reflected in what George Bernard Shaw is reputed to have said: 'If all the economists in the world were laid end to end they would never reach a conclusion.'

Let us take some recent examples. In 1981, 364 economists could be found to disagree with existing government macroeconomic policy, placing an advertisement to this effect in the national press: 'There is no basis in economic theory or supporting evidence for the Government's belief that by deflating demand they will bring inflation permanently under control and thereby induce an automatic recovery in output and employment.' There is disagreement here over what determines the level of output, the level of employment and the price level. A more recent article (Cobham 1984) identified four different economic strategies to deal with the United Kingdom's economic problems – each differing with regard to no less than 23 different policy issues ranging from fiscal policy and monetary policy to labour market and manpower policy; from competition policy to regional policy; from public expenditure to taxation; from the nationalised industries to international economic relations. Browning (1983) in a review of macroeconomic theory and policy identifies nine macroeconomic models of the economy whilst Cross (1982) sets out seven separate research programmes in macroeconomics. It is now commonplace to note the wide range of econometric models of the UK economy, including those of the Treasury, the National Institute for Economic and Social Research, the Bank of England, the London Business School, Liverpool University and Cambridge University, all of which generate different estimates of the economic impact of a wide variety of fiscal changes and all of which generate different forecasts for the UK economy (see, for example, Parliamentary Unit 1986 or Wallis 1987), as a result of different conceptualisations of the economic system, i.e., different understandings of how the system works.

Clearly then there do exist different views on economic issues amongst economists. Economics is a 'contested terrain' characterised by diversity, debate, plurality and controversy. Yet few textbooks reflect this range of disagreement. Hardly any actually set out and *examine* the controversies and those few that do offer an idiosyncratic partial examination of the causes of the disagreements (for example, Cole *et al.* 1983). This book by contrast explores these controversies in this chapter by seeking to *understand* the reasons for the existence of controversy. This then provides a lens through which to view the rest of the chapters of the book, each of which explicitly treats the relevant material as being contentious. The final chapter considers the terrain covered in the book and whether controversy and disagreement are likely to remain or to diminish over time to produce an agreed theoretical and empirical stance.

1.1.2 The issues

Applied economics involves the application of economic theory to real-world phenomena in an attempt to understand it better and explain it. It represents too the intersection of theory with reality. The question immediately arises, however, of how to decide which theory is 'best'. How reliable is our economic knowledge? How does it come about that economists can come to different conclusions? Can we decide what is true/correct and what is false/incorrect? How can we 'prove' which theory is right and which is wrong? How do we *choose* between theories? This issue of theory appraisal will be a constant theme of this chapter and raises difficult and complex issues, certainly much more so than the vast bulk of textbooks and journal articles would suggest. But, you may think, *why* is this such a problem? Economics is a clear body of theory and all that is required is to apply it to the real-world issue at hand. We can generate a hypothesis from a theory and test it against the facts. For example, from the theory of demand, we can hypothesise that when the price of eggs falls more of them will be bought. If this hypothesis is shown to be 'wrong', it will be rejected, if it is 'right' it will be accepted as reliable knowledge. So, over time, economic knowledge becomes more certain and controversies and disagreement disappear.

Let us leave aside, for the moment, the 'fact' that despite two hundred years of activity by economists such controversies have not yet disappeared. Leave aside too the attractive implicit proposition that *eventually* as our stock of knowledge gradually improves we will be in a position to understand fully the economic world based on safe, sure, secure knowledge. There still remains the problem that the pursuit of economic knowledge is not, unfortunately, so simple. There are serious *methodological* problems to be addressed in the pursuit of economic knowledge. An understanding of these should make us as economists more modest in our claims and more tolerant and respectful of those economists who 'disagree' with us and to respect colleagues in other social sciences who are more circumspect in their search for 'the truth'. This is necessary for, as we shall see, there is no 'algorithm of choice'. There is no universally applicable, agreed procedure for deciding which theory is best. This initially disconcerting truth will unfold in the coming pages, and will help us to understand the causes of controversy in applied economics. Such controversies are of much more than academic interest for they offer different understandings and interpretations of the economic world about us. One important consequence of this is that because there usually is no one agreed 'correct' explanation of economic phenomena, the decisions of organisations (firms, unions, individuals and governments) in being guided by *particular* explanations, may well be incorrect and, of even greater consequence, may lead to inappropriate policies and economic mismanagement.

The thrust of argument in this chapter, and indeed in the book, is that the economic knowledge we have is both provisional and contested. There are major philosophical, methodological and operational problems in improving our knowledge. In consequence economics in general, and applied economics in particular, is replete with controversy. Hence we believe it desirable both to adopt an approach to applied economics which treats the material in this way and to examine further the reasons for such controversy. The study of methodology provides a lens through which to view such debates and to examine the reasons why *applied* economics is no straightforward task.

The rest of the chapter proceeds as follows. In section 1.2, we discuss the difficulties encountered in trying to fit theory to facts and how this may mean that we cannot resolve controversy. In section 1.3, we discover additional reasons why disagreement is difficult to iron out, before, in section 1.4, considering a possible way of distinguishing between that knowledge we should retain and that which we should reject. Section 1.5, in contrast, briefly asserts that the search for agreement is not only impossible but undesirable. Section 1.6 considers three elements which ensure that controversy can never be eliminated from economics: the role of values, the difficulty in testing some assumptions, and the theory dependence of data. Section 1.7 examines the controversies that arise from the existence of alternative methodological approaches and hence competing perspectives from those considered hitherto. Finally, section 1.8 provides some concluding remarks. By the end of this chapter we should be in a position to understand better why it is that economists disagree and why controversy is endemic to the pursuit of economic knowledge.

1.2 THEORIES AND FACTS: METHODOLOGICAL ISSUES

1.2.1 Induction and verification

One way of beginning our search for knowledge about the world, one way of formulating a theory, is to start from the 'facts' of experience: 'facts' we can obtain by observation and the collection of empirical data. This knowledge is treated as objective in the sense that the economist as observer is an unbiased scientist in search of truth. Moreover, provided we collect a large number of observations under a wide variety of conditions, we can generalise from this data set to obtain a universally applicable law. So, for example, if we observe a large number of consumers, under a variety of conditions and for a large number of commodities, who respond to an increase in price by reducing consumption, we can generate a theory or 'law' of demand which states that demand is an inverse function of price. We have moved from observation to theory. This is the essence of the inductive approach. Moreover our knowledge continually improves as we collect increasing amounts of data about an ever wider range of economic phenomena. Furthermore, predictions (for example, when prices rise, demand will fall) and explanations (demand fell because prices rose) can be derived from such inductively generated theories through deductive reasoning (see section 1.2.2 below). As the latter is 'merely' the use of logic, these explanations and predictions are necessarily true for they are the logical consequences of the inductively produced laws or theories. Furthermore, as both the facts collected and the reasoning employed are objective, the approach is 'scientific', and thus beyond dispute.

However, this approach to securing knowledge is not immune from criticism. First, only observable facts count. We can construct theory only from data which can be observed, collected, measured and classified. We cannot then gain knowledge about what cannot be observed nor about phenomena where the facts have not yet been collected. Second, there is a logical problem with any approach which rests on 'verification', the search for confirming instances. Inductivists tend to generate such instances from the particular ones observed. Yet *no* amount of observations will, taking our example above, prove that *all* consumers have reduced or will reduce consumption when prices rise. But one observation of a consumer not behaving in this manner is enough to refute it. An infinite number of observations would be required before we could accept it, whereas one future observation will contradict it. Consequently, general laws cannot be justified through observation. Induction is not a secure basis from which to derive knowledge. This is known as the 'inductive fallacy'. Third, it is not possible to justify induction by attempting to demonstrate that successful predictions and explanations have in the past been made possible by inductively devised theories, for, as a moment's thought makes clear, this argument justifies induction by employing an inductive argument! Fourth, it does not offer precise guidance as to *when* we can generate a theory or universal law. What constitutes a sufficiently *wide* variety of conditions? And what happens if it has indeed been verified a large number of times, under a wide variety of circumstances, and then it is falsified by further observations? (Katouzian 1980). Finally, and as we shall see when we discuss the matter in detail below (1.6.3), data is not independent of theory. When observations are selected from the infinite number available some implicit theory is required /presumed in order to do so. There are then no objective facts that can be used to generate theory independently, as in the inductivist account, as the latter is involved in searching for the former. Consequently science cannot proceed from observations to theory as in the inductive approach. Should economics proceed in this manner there is enormous scope for controversy both theoretically and empirically. Similar problems arise should we attempt to verify or confirm theories according to the facts or should the derived explanations/predictions be so tested. Whilst there exists a range of problems in testing theories, to which we will turn later in the chapter and which also apply here, we can observe at this point that testing hypotheses/theories via verification cannot demonstrate their validity. It can only, and at *best*, show that they are not rejected, for we are not informed of the number of successful tests that would be required to accept them. In truth the number is infinite. Indeed a 'successful' test shows only that some aspects of the real world conform to the predictions. Confirming instances have been found, but there is no guarantee that other disconfirming instances will not or cannot be found. Yet, it could be suggested that much applied research in economics takes precisely this form, consisting of the active search for such instances and for the best fit for the particular period/place under consideration.

1.2.2 Falsification and the hypothetico-deductive method

There is, however, an alternative to the inductivist approach of gathering facts, generalising from them and then generating theories from which predictions and explanations are then deduced and tested. It is also an alternative to verification which, as we have seen, does not help us in distinguishing between true and false theories. The only element this alternative shares with inductivism is deductive reasoning. It is often referred to as 'the scientific method' and comprises two elements: the hypothetico-deductive method and the process of falsification.

Here a theory is formulated through starting with a series of *assumptions* which contain hypotheses about human behaviour (for example, firms maximise profits, knowledge is perfect and consumers are rational) and a set of definitions of the terms used. Logic is then applied to these assumptions and because it is infallible the process of deduction generates inevitably correct conclusions/consequences/predictions. Such conclusions are 'merely' the logical consequences of the assumptions that have been made. This is what is termed the 'hypothetico-deductive' method. It is most important to understand that a theory constructed in this way, and any hypotheses derived from it, consist solely of the logical implications of a set of assumptions. The only actual knowledge of the world contained within it is the assumptions. Now, given that, as we saw in the previous section, it is unacceptable to base these assumptions on empirical observation, they can only be, as Popper (1968) puts it, 'conjectures' or 'hunches', gained a priori. They may be subjective beliefs or even falsehoods. Consequently 'proving' a theory in this context only means tht 'under given assumptions it can be shown that . . . ' or 'If A and B then X then Y'. In no sense does it show that a theory is 'correct' or 'true' in relation to the real world.

Hence the crucial role in the generation of knowledge and in choosing between theories is played by the second element of the scientific method – 'falsification'. It is crucial to test the predictions of the theories by recourse to empirical data, for no *necessarily true* knowledge about the world is contained in the assumptions or the deductive logic. Knowledge is only gained by testing theories against facts. This is the only arbiter of theoretical disputes. Hence *applied* economics, and thus *empirical* work, is of paramount importance. But we already know from the previous section that we cannot demonstrate the truth of a theory through verification. So how does empirical testing proceed? Whilst we cannot show whether a theory is true we can demonstrate whether a theory is *false*. This then becomes the hallmark of real science: the development of propositions that can, at least in principle, be falsified by recourse to the facts through empirical investigation. So the search for knowledge becomes an endless attempt to falsify rather than verify existing theories; a ceaseless and ruthless process of conjecture followed by refutation where only the 'fit' survive. Whilst we can never definitely accept a theory as true we can reject those theories that are demonstrably, empirically, false. Instead of proving theories we disprove them. Moreover, in this context, what counts as explanations are really only hypotheses – testing them turns them into predictions. Note also that to the extent that values intrude into the analysis in the form of the assumptions (see section 1.6.1) because the validity of the theory depends entirely on its testing against empirical evidence, value penetration of theory ceases to be a problem.

The more falsifiable, i.e., the more wide ranging, are a theory's claims, the better, as it increases the possibility of falsification. Such events become the achievements of the development of economics, not (as with induction and verification) its lacunae. In order to be highly falsifiable, theories must be constructed and presented in such a way as to be clear and capable of precision. If this were not so, empirical tests would be unable to distinguish between results which falsify and results which corroborate the theories. Consequently, falsification has given enormous impetus not only to empirical testing but also to the development of mathematical formulation of theories, as well as the application of quantitative techniques, especially statistical techniques, in empirical tests.

1.2.3 Economics – a social science

Much controversy, however, arises over the extent to which this scientific method can be applied to the study of economic behaviour, which inevitably involves human agency. There are four main arguments here. First, human behaviour is unlike the behaviour of the inanimate objects of natural science in that humans are not passive but purposeful. Humans have both memories and an ability to undertake conscious action, and so respond to stimuli in a manner which is less fully *determined* by rules or 'laws' than the objects of natural science. This makes economic behaviour and its consequences in principle much less predictable (and explicable) and at least requires both theories/hypotheses and empirical evidence to be of a statistical nature, i.e., to allow of exceptions. At most it may mean that the effects of economic changes cannot be modelled to produce useful predictions at all, except on the basis of specifying very simplified, and possibly unrealistic, behavioural characteristics. Second, economic systems change more rapidly over time than 'natural' processes, as humankind consciously or unconsciously changes its behaviour, rules or institutions. In consequence the historical context within which hypotheses and theories are generated and within which empirical tests are undertaken becomes important. Thus the scope for universal (temporal or spatial) laws is diminished with the inevitable development of alternative theories which relate to different historical and institutional contexts. What is 'valid' for one time and place may not be so for another, or for ever. Third, controlled experiments (the crucial importance of which is considered in section 1.2.4) become extremely difficult, if not impossible. Holding all else equal in a dynamic, living, human environment poses considerable difficulties in setting up appropriate test conditions for the examination of both assumptions and predictions. Finally, some economists (see especially section 1.7.3) argue that economists have open to them a line of enquiry not open to natural scientists, through a knowledge of human behaviour gained through introspection and consequently that knowledge can be generated in this way.

1.2.4 When *ceteris* are not *paribus*

The well-known Heckscher–Ohlin theory of international trade predicts that nations with a relatively greater endowment of one factor of production, say capital, will export commodities which use relatively more capital and import those which use relatively more labour. Samuelson's development of it demonstrated that as a result of trade on this basis factor prices would equalise between the trading partners. Neoclassical labour market theory predicts that if the ratio of social security benefits to real wages increases then unemployment rises. Monetarist theory predicts that the rate of inflation is determined by prior changes in the money supply.

Economic theory contains many such predictions which are in principle falsifiable and in consequence can be tested so as to decide whether to retain, modify or discard them. In the Heckscher–Ohlin case there have been numerous such tests, including the famous Leontief test, which appear to refute the hypothesis. In the other cases there have been tests, some of which confirm the predictions and some of which do not. The issue here is, do such refutations falsify such theories/hypotheses and do such confirmations lead to our accepting them? We already know that the answer to the latter question is that they should not (see section

1.2.1) and, from our discussion of falsification (section 1.2.2) that the answer to the former question is that they do. Why then are falsified hypotheses/theories retained and, moreover, widely taught in economics courses?

One part of the answer to this question, and a major reason why controversy in economics is so difficult to eliminate, is that when theories are tested and, it appears, falsified by recourse to the facts, economists do not necessarily discard them. As we shall see below there are a number of possible reasons for this. The one with which we are concerned here is the so-called Duhem–Quine problem. This states that it is not possible to falsify an individual hypothesis because in a test we are actually testing it in conjunction with a whole range of 'auxiliary' statements including *ceteris paribus* clauses – we are testing several propositions at once. For example, the Heckscher–Ohlin theory actually predicts a particular pattern of trade *if* certain other conditions hold (e.g., the same techniques of production are used in the different nations; there is free trade; there is no factor intensity reversal; each factor receives its marginal product, and so on). Similarly neoclassical labour market theory's predictions about wages and unemployment depend upon assumptions about price flexibility, the response of labour to spatial wage variations, competitive conditions in labour markets, and so on. Monetarist predictions of the relationship between the money supply and the rate of inflation can only be tested by introducing a whole range of auxiliary hypotheses (see Cross 1982).

In other words, all tests are conditional on the *ceteris paribus* conditions obtaining, if we wish to conclude that an hypothesis is falsified or not. As we can see, however, all test situations in fact test a bundle of hypotheses so that if the predictions are falsified it is legitimate to conclude that it may be because one of the assumptions or auxiliary conditions, and we do not know which, is incorrect. Thus we can always save a theory from refutation by an 'immunising strategem' which protects the central hypothesis in the face of apparently contrary evidence. We may claim, quite legitimately, that *ceteris* were not *paribus*. Needless to say, this leaves plenty of scope for competition between theories and hence scope for considerable disagreement and controversy. It is clearly very protective of theory and implies that empirical evidence cannot be relied upon to provide crucial tests of theory appraisal and choice. When this is added to the additional difficulty in weeding out auxiliary hypotheses when we have to do without the possibility of controlled laboratory experiments (not to mention the occasional specification of hypotheses in textbooks without *ceteris paribus* clauses at all ('the imposition of a tax on a good will, *ceteris paribus*, increase its price'), which means it cannot be tested even in principle, we are forced to redouble our conclusion. Data do not and cannot bring theories down.

In any case, in practice, economics, at least as it is conventionally presented in textbooks, falls far short of the falsificationist ideal and is like 'playing tennis with the net down' (Blaug 1980). Economists do not always practise what they preach. What testing of theories there is, and there is relatively little presented and even less discussed in textbooks, tends to verificationism – the search for confirming instances. These are attempts to show that the real world conforms to the predictions for a particular period or spatial unit and is little more than verification. Few attempts are made to refute theory. Indeed, sometimes statistical analysis is undertaken first and only then is a hypothesis searched for to match the results. On other occasions, for example, a variety of forms of an equation expressing a hypothesis is used and the one which yields the best fit for that particular set of observations is selected and the others discarded. Step-wise regression seems, to the present writer, the *reductio ad absurdum* of this approach.

It is worth considering too the implications of the 'unity' of explanation and prediction in the scientific method which we mentioned in section 1.2.2 above. The only difference between the two in this approach is that the former comes after, the latter before, events. However, successful prediction through empirical tests does not necessarily imply explanation, for the former requires only good correlation between variables. Though, for example, a strong empirical relationship between the money supply and inflation may allow us to *predict* changes in the rate of inflation from changes in the rate of growth of the money supply, it does not give us an *explanation* of the rate of inflation – certainly if verification is being practised. Even with falsification, the failure to falsify the relationship proposed in the hypothesis only shows that hypothesis and test results are consistent with one another. This is because of the notion of *causality* embedded in the scientific method, where causation refers to the constant conjunction of different events in time and space. Here the prior event (the change in the money supply) is the cause and the later event (the change in the rate of inflation) the effect. There is no *necessary* connection between them, no mechanism guaranteeing the relationship (see section 1.7.4). Indeed there is no way of distinguishing between alternative theories, each of which poses a *different* set of underlying, necessary relations between inflation and the money supply. For example, changes in *both* may be caused by different exogenous variables, they may have independent causes, and the relationship may be statistical only; or both may be caused by a third single exogenous variable. Indeed, strong test results are not only consistent with all these possibilities but also that the *chain* of causality runs from inflation to the money supply rather than vice versa, reversing the definition of which variable is dependent and which independent.

Finally, there are a number of technical difficulties related to economics as a social science, that arise from the statistical nature of corroborating theory with empirical evidence. To examine these technical issues and the problems they pose requires a study of 'econometrics', which cannot be attempted here. However, it is important to note two things. First, that an important source of controversy arises because all predictions are probabilistic (i.e., allow exceptions) and thus economists require principles of when to reject a hypothesis as false or not. Particularly when observations are samples, hypotheses can be accepted/rejected with different degrees of confidence. For example, it may be accepted at a 5 per cent level of significance, giving a one in twenty chance of it being incorrect. Clearly there is scope here for disagreement over what constitutes an appropriate degree of verification or falsification. Second, in trying to capture the extent of the relationship between the variables hypothesised in a theory, regression techniques are used to identify the statistical nature of the relation between the dependent variable (in the above example the rate of inflation) and the independent or explanatory variable (the money supply). Few economic relationships are so simple however and in consequence multiple regression techniques aim to capture the independent effects of a number of explanatory variables. Problems arise, particularly with time series data, of serial correlation (interdependence of data at different points in time) and multicolinearity (interdependence between the explanatory variables). Whilst there are technical solutions to these problems, different levels of technical expertise and understanding between economists provide scope for a wide variety of results and degrees of their acceptance. With multicolinearity in particular we are left unclear as to which of the explanatory variables has the key determining role in the model, as it is hard to disentangle determinants from concomitants and cause from concurrence (Green in Green and Nore 1979). Anyone who doubts the extent to which statistical testing can generate rather than resolve controversy is referred to Chapter 10 in this book on the monetarist/Keynesian controversy; the long-running saga of the consumption function (see Green in Green and Nore 1979); or the history of the Heckscher–Ohlin theory of international trade (see Edwards 1985), as examples. Few, if any, key economic questions have (or can be) settled by appeal to the facts. The wary reader will note, however, the writer's use here of verification/confirmation rather than falsification and may wish to consider how one could undertake a convincing attempt to falsify/refute his proposition!

1.3 PARADIGMS AND CRISIS IN ECONOMICS

We have, so far, come across many reasons why economics remains a contested terrain of theories and evidence; many reasons why the scientific method cannot offer simple, objective criteria for theory choice. There are, however, other reasons why disagreement is so difficult to iron out. It has been argued (see Kuhn 1970 and, for a summary, Chalmers 1982 or Caldwell 1982) that the way science progresses is far more discontinuous than the incremental process implied in section 1.2.2. Kuhn points to the revolutionary character of progress where entire theoretical approaches are abandoned and replaced by other, incompatible, approaches. In periods of 'normal' science, scientific development is governed by a single 'paradigm', 'the constellation of beliefs, values, techniques and so on shared by the members of a scientific community' (Kuhn 1970) where work is devoted to the articulation, development (attempt to solve 'puzzles' that arise) and applications of this accepted approach. The approach itself is not questioned or criticised. Failure to resolve puzzles is a problem *for* the scientist not *of* the paradigm. Such failures are seen as anomalies rather than falsification of the paradigm. Controversy is limited to attempts to resolve the anomalies, either theoretically or through empirical tests.

However, these anomalies may become more numerous and increasingly perplexing, and resistant over time to attempts at their resolution. Particularly if these anomalies strike at the fundamentals of the paradigm or relate to a pressing social need (for example, unemployment), the paradigm may experience a crisis which deepens if a rival paradigm emerges to challenge it. In such a period there is no agreement on values, beliefs, techniques or the questions to be asked within the scientific community until the new paradigm is established together, then, with a new set of questions, puzzles, techniques, beliefs and values. For example, one could think of the marginal revolution (the transition from classical political economy to neoclassical economics) and the Keynesian revolution as periods of crisis, revolution and ultimate succession of one paradigm by another. One could also, possibly, consider the present state of economics as one of crisis, as yet unresolved, where paradigms are competing for 'hegemony' within the economics profession – a struggle for acceptance between Austrian, Marxist and post-Keynesian approaches (to name but three) with the dominant neoclassical–Keynesian synthesis (see section 1.7). Conversely, one could consider such competition for intellectual supremacy within the profession as characteristic of Kuhn's period of 'pre-science'.

According to Kuhn the choice between theories in periods of crisis, necessary if it is to be resolved and a new period of 'normal' scientific discovery to ensue, cannot be objective, logical or rational. This is because the choice is between incompatibles with different methods, world views and languages as well as standards of theory appraisal. They are *incommensurable*. Intense methodological debate, resulting from methodology being paradigm specific, ensures no 'scientific' criteria for choice. Consequently the contest between paradigms becomes a social process, a process of subjective judgement likened to a '*Gestalt* switch' or religious conversion.

In reality such complete conversion from one paradigm to another is very rare in economics, with a 'dominant' rather than 'hegemonic' paradigm being more usual. Indeed it can be argued that the dominant paradigm in economics is the 'market' paradigm, which in that sense has never changed; there has been no revolution in economics.

But why are economists, and for that matter other social scientists, reluctant to modify or discard theories which fail to conform to the facts? Why are paradigm changes so difficult to achieve? We already know that one reason is because there are no objective criteria to decide the question of theory choice. But there are other reasons, which Kuhn's analysis hints at. Earl (in Eichner 1983) suggests that it arises because economists are committed not to the discovery of truth but to career development and individual enhancement. Given that progress through the academic hierarchy is dependent on one's acceptance by other (often older) colleagues in appointment and promotion committees and that the volume of research papers and articles produced is a key criterion for promotion, conformity, conservatism and prowess in the conventional wisdom becomes important. Critics or the unconventional can face contempt or even reprisal. Katouzian (1980) similarly points to the question of power and authority within the profession, in grant-awarding bodies, in journal editorial boards, and so on. These are powerful ways in which the extent and nature of controversy is controlled, yet which provide no mechanism for its resolution, save authoritarianism. Wiseman (in Wiseman 1983) argues that, in addition, economists (like others) are reluctant to accept the obsolescence of the stock of intellectual capital they have painstakingly built up over the years. Theories and techniques acquired through undergraduate and postgraduate education, years of teaching and research practice, are retained despite their 'refutation'. In addition an aversion to risk, the fear of the new (where other members of the profession from the challenging paradigm already have a head start in the 'new' theory, methods and literature) is a powerful incentive to a lack of innovation. This is particularly so if the new is not susceptible to mathematical expression or econometric sophistication. There are several among us who have heard colleagues protest that they are unable to accept a particular alternative to their received wisdom as it is tantamount to a repudiation of their professional teaching and research practice.

Finally, it is worth pointing out that controversy tends to be greatest in periods of severe economic problems, in so far as the dominant wisdom is unable to fully account for, or resolve, the problems. (See, for example, Cole 1983 or Edwards 1985.) It is noticeable that controversy in economics appears to have been considerably less during the post-war boom years of the 1950s and 1960s than it is today.

1.4 RIVAL THEORIES: A CRITERION FOR CHOICE?

So far we have argued, *inter alia*, that controversy cannot be eliminated either through induction, verification or falsification; and that theory choice is ultimately a result of the psychology and sociology of the profession, augmented by external economic and possibly political pressures. However, before proceeding in the next section to identify further sources of controversy in economics, we pause to consider a possible alternative to (some would say synthesis of) those views above associated with Popper and Kuhn. Lakatos (see especially Latsis 1976) has argued that whilst it is impossible to falsify individual hypotheses and theories, it *is* possible to test a whole cluster of interconnected theories – what he calls a 'scientific research programme' (SRP). The rationale for this is twofold. First, unlike naive falsification which does not specify the number of times we need to attempt falsification in order for it to be preferred, and which is riven with the Duhem–Quine problem, this sophisticated falsification allows of comparison between theories regarding their different degrees of falsification. Hence the decision is not an absolute one of theories to facts but a relative one of theories to facts to theories. Theories are not tested in isolation but in relation to each other. Second, and implicit in our first point, is the recognition that there exist rival, competing SRPs (similar to Kuhn's paradigms) and theory choice therefore involves an assessment of their *relative* merits. Unlike Kuhn, however, these SRPs coexist throughout time and must be explicitly considered. This, of course, widens the scope of economic discourse and explicitly incorporates competing 'research programmes' as legitimate fields of enquiry.

Each SRP comprises two elements. First, a rigid 'hardcore' of coherent propositions and assumptions which are treated as irrefutable 'by the methodological decision of its protagonists' and not subject to test and falsification. This is the 'negative heuristic' which stipulates the base assumptions and methods which cannot be modified – to do so is to withdraw from the SRP and move into another. This 'hardcore' will map out the programme for research within the SRP. Second, there is a 'protective belt' of auxiliary assumptions and propositions, which is flexible and contains a 'positive heuristic' or guidelines for developing the SRP. It is these auxiliary hypotheses which are subject to test and thus to falsification. In order to compare rival SRPs, the judgement of superiority is whether a programme is 'progressive', that is, it predicts new facts through amending its protective belt so as both to increase the range of testable predictions and generate evidence of them being corroborated, or whether it is 'degenerating', that is, it is amended and added to in such a way as to reduce its range of testable predictions and resort to ad hoc procedures, 'immunising stratagems', to defend itself from falsification by empirical evidence. Degenerating SRPs, in this manner, give way to progressive SRPs. Cross (1982) offers one of the few attempts to divide theories on this basis in his exposition and appraisal of seven varieties of macroeconomic thought, ranging from fundamentalist Keynesianism to the new classical macroeconomics. Whilst it seems that this approach has considerable merits, not least in the potential it has for reducing disagreement in economics, it does require a substantial knowledge of rival SRPs. To this end it requires a proliferation in the analysis and appraisal of rival programmes in the economics literature and teaching before an adequate assessment is possible. Without such a pluralist commitment the existence of separate SRPs merely constitutes a dialogue of the deaf with distinct non-communicating research programmes in existence. It requires an extension of the 'contested terrain' before it can be reduced. Whilst this appears desirable, whether it could be achieved was discussed in section 1.3. Even if it were, there would remain a problem in their relative appraisal. How much time must elapse before we can agree that a SRP has degenerated? There is no clear criterion.

What seems therefore, with hindsight, to be offered here is more controversy rather than less.

1.5 ANYTHING GOES?

Feyerabend (1975) would welcome such a development. He has proposed an 'anarchistic' theory of knowledge. Attempts to evaluate theory against objective criteria are not only impossible (a view the reader may be increasingly coming to share) but undesirable and even dangerous. They are *impossible* not only for the reasons given above but because methodological criteria are not applicable independently of theory. Methodological positions, like theories, are not comparable because of what one might call the 'theory dependence of methodology' (see section 1.7). Thus different theoretical systems (paradigms, SRPs or schools of thought) are 'incommensurable' and as such there is no rational basis for choice between them. This is so because the meaning and interpretation of concepts depend on the theoretical context in which they occur (e.g., capital, competition); because each theory has its own set of concepts and categories incommensurate with those of others (e.g., liquidity preference, accumulation); and because theories may not share the same observation statements (e.g., profit). They are *dangerous* because such a procedure leads to the elimination of theories. Because all theories have something useful to say about the world, this reduces the stock of knowledge available. In particular it leads to the reduction of empirical content both because every theory has its own independent empirical content and because facts are theory dependent.

Consequently it can be argued that theory proliferation is superior to theory elimination. Pluralism rules. Theory choice is inimical to scientific progress. This does not mean that it is impossible to compare theories, but it does mean that evidence must be related to theory *in its own terms*, not through a universal method, for the latter approach leads to other 'paradigm' standards being imposed on others. Ultimately, however, we are unable to make choices in any other than an ethical (political?) way. To summarise, the principle here is 'anything goes!' In other words 'everything stays!' It is a plea for academic tolerance . . . and academic freedom. It may however also be interpreted as a recipe ensuring that the wheat is never separated from the chaff!

1.6 CONTROVERSY REVISITED

1.6.1 Values

We saw above in section 1.2.2 that had falsification been possible the influence of subjective values in the construction of hypotheses/theories would be unproblematic as they would be weeded out through empirical testing. However, as falsification is now in doubt as a method of theory appraisal, the possibility that values may intrude in economics provides potential scope for enormous disagreement within the subject. It will become clear in this section, we hope, that economists cannot be entirely separated from their environments or thought-conditioning either with regard to observation (a point treated further in section 1.6.3 below) or the development of hypotheses a priori. It is not possible for economists to develop theory or undertake empirical work that is value free (see especially Katouzian (1980) and Lessnoff (1976)).

However, we can distinguish between 'positive' statements, about what is, from 'normative' statements, about what ought to be. An 'ought' statement cannot be derived from an 'is' statement without introducing a value judgement. So provided we neither *move* from a positive to a normative statement nor stray outside positive economics, values need not intrude. However, as ever, economics is not quite so simple.

First, there is the issue of objectivity in constructing theory and collecting evidence. Knowledge, as has been seen, can start either from the facts (inductive reasoning) or a priori (from the mind). It it starts from the latter this is, by definition, subjective and prior to observation/experience. If it starts from the former there is the problem of the theory dependence of data. Data are not randomly observed; they must be searched for, using criteria to select what is relevant. Consider the disagreement over what/who constitutes the 'unemployed'; how many people are in this category and the constant changes to the 'official' definition of the unemployment statistics. The criteria too are logically prior to experience. Moreover once selected, facts on their own reveal nothing. They have to be processed by empirical methods, themselves a product of the human mind and between which there is a choice. Even the simple reporting of observation will be value impregnated. For example, do we observe/classify the IRA and/or the ANC as freedom fighters or terrorists?

Second, given the problems of testing theories, the actual construction of theories and the predictions made from them take on an extra importance. So it can be demonstrated (i.e., logically deduced from a set of assumptions) that a decentralised market system, provided it is left unhindered to operate freely, will generate an optimum allocation of resources. From this it further follows that attempts to interfere with such a system will generate inefficiencies such that an optimum allocation is not achieved. There is not a problem of deriving 'ought' from 'is' statements here, but clearly there is implied a stipulated norm of behaviour. Moreover, to obtain such a prediction a whole series of assumptions have to be made which, one could legitimately argue, constitute ethical positions (e.g., the consumer is sovereign and social preferences are the sum of independent, individual preferences). What is more they are generally not falsifiable either (see 1.6.2).

Third, and this is even more contentious, it could be argued that economics is 'ideological' in the sense that it is a set of ideas which support the dominant form of economic organisation (Cole *et al.* 1983).

Fourth, the focus of economics, or at least of the major economics textbooks, is usually given as that of efficiency – 'economics is the science that studies human behaviour as a relationship between ends and scarce means which have alternative uses' (Robbins 1935). This itself constitutes an ethical bias as it focuses on one set of social objectives whilst relegating others to moral (unscientific?) judgements on which we cannot make statements, unlike efficiency questions which can be objectively discussed. Moreover it ignores the variety of SRPs coexisting within the subject.

Fifth, and to an extent related to the previous point, economics cannot escape the intrusion of values by a focus solely on means and taking ends as given. As we have already seen, concepts of relevance to the former, like equilibrium, not only describe a certain state of affairs but imply its desirability. The concepts are replete with evaluation. But moreover to be indifferent to ends is itself a moral judgement. Such 'moral nihilism' implies that economics will be the handmaid of any power/interest that is in control of the ends. To ascribe irrelevance or indifference to ends is dangerous in any social context. Finally, some economists explicitly state that they are in the business of ends, and therefore values, as well as means. Some do practise 'political' economy. For example, according to Hayek:

> Economics has never been the product of detached intellectual curiosity about the why of social phenomena, but an intense urge to reconstruct a world which gives rise to profound dissatisfaction.
>
> (Hayek 1933)

In other words, it is valued impregnated.

1.6.2 The assumptions problem

We have established above that choosing between different theories on the basis of empirical validation of their *predictions* is difficult, and in consequence a convergence of views between economists and between different theories on this basis is unlikely. Another possibility however is to test the *assumptions* of a theory against empirical reality. Some economists do not accept this as an appropriate test of a theory (for example, Friedman (1953) and Machlup (1978)) arguing, in instrumental fashion, that the proof of a theory lies solely in its predictive success. For them therefore the option of testing assumptions does not exist.

For those who do attempt empirical validation of assumptions two additional problems arise. First, and to the extent that it is actually possible to decide whether an assumption is empirically correct, the substitution of more 'realistic' assumptions for the more simple abstract ones usually encountered in economic theory (for example replacing 'firms seek to maximise profits' with 'firms seek to maximise managers' utility') makes precise prediction less easy and thus increases the difficulties of testing the predictions against reality. Hence it is not surprising that assumptions are rarely chosen to define an interesting or realistic problem but rather to define a solution (Heathfield and Hartropp 1983). Second, what counts as realistic? Because deciding on this involves confronting the assumptions with observation, we run back into the problem of the theory dependence of data to which we have referred on several occasions and which is fully examined in the next section. Beyond accepting that 'the abstractions used in formulating economic theory today are peculiarly inappropriate to the economic system they purport to represent' (Eatwell 1986), deciding on what those real representations of reality should be depends on which theoretical stance one adopts (see section 1.7).

Third, and most important, some fundamental assumptions are untestable. The central assumption in mainstream theory is the 'rationality postulate', that is, that individual economic agents have preferences which are well ordered, consistent and stable and seek to maximise their own individual objective function. Such a postulate is however not falsifiable. To take some examples: the assumption that consumers maximise their utility is consistent with almost any pattern of observed behaviour; the assumption of consumer sovereignty, implying that the satisfaction of human wants is the purpose of economic activity, cannot be established as inferior/superior to the assumption that the purpose of economic activity is the accumulation of capital; the assumption of autonomy in individual preference formation; assumptions about the state of information of expectations, and so on. Hutchinson (1978) has argued that we cannot even test the law of demand as we are unable to check the initial conditions of tastes, the prices of other goods, price expectations and so on. Certainly a core assumption like the law of diminishing returns is untestable as it is operationally unquantifiable. All it asserts is that marginal returns will decline 'eventually'.

The only alternative to addressing the empirical validity of assumptions, apart from the Friedmanite view, is to develop them a priori. To this we will return in section 1.7.3.

1.6.3 The theory dependence of data

If facts, the data collected against which are to judge the truth/falsity of theories/hypotheses, are *not* independent of the theories to be tested, then falsification of theory through confrontation with the facts is not possible. If falsification is not possible, rival theories and the controversy that goes with them will persist. Indeed the claim that data are not independent of theory, especially if combined with the difficulty of separating values from theories, produces interdependencies between values and facts; between facts and theories; and between values and theories, which undermine the entire basis of the possibility of an objective, neutral, empirically based economics and pave the way for an alternative 'political economy' approach to economic affairs, whether of an Austrian, a Marxist or another variety.

So how can it be argued that test data are theory (and value) impregnated? The argument begins from the assertion that different observers do *not* see the same thing. The classic example is the image beloved of psychologists which can be seen as either a vase or the faces of two women. The observation 'chosen' will depend on what one expected to see, based partly on previous experience. The 'same' data can be presented in different ways – witness the alternative representations of the map of the world presented by the Mercator or Peters projections. The argument is then that the observer cannot be completely detached from what is observed because she/he is looking through a filter of expectations and experience partly constructed by the theory (explicit or implicit) to be tested. Relevant data can only be chosen in the light of some prior conceptualisation. Selection of data implies a prior formulation of a problem. Without it, we would be unable to know what to observe. Data, and the interpretation of that data, cannot be fully separated. For example, consider unemployment data and how it is presented and disputed from different theoretical positions. There are no theory-independent unemployment data, just as there are no theory-independent data on the personal distribution of income or strike behaviour. The measures, the classifications, the definitions and the sources required just to 'describe' phenomena are theory dependent. As Sen (1984) argues, 'any conscious act of description contains some theory.' Or Myrdal says (1958): 'Facts do not organise themselves . . . questions must be asked before answers can be given. The questions are an expression of our interest in the world, they are at bottom valuations. Valuations are thus involved already at the stage when we observe facts.'

A further implication of this line of argument is that since observation statements are theory dependent and thus fallible when theories/hypotheses are falsified, it is quite legitimate to reject the data rather than the theory. Consequently, for this reason alone conclusive falsification is not possible.

1.7 COMPETING METHODOLOGIES AND PERSPECTIVES

1.7.1 Frames of reference

In this section of the chapter we seek to examine those sources of controversy in economics that arise from the existence of fundamentally different methodological approaches and perspectives. Hitherto, we have examined the sources of controversies that arise from within the dominant methodological approach in economics. This approach can, for the sake of convenience, be called 'the scientific method' or, better, 'the positivist/empiricist method' and is used throughout mainstream, orthodox economics. Here we explore the controversy that arises because of the existence of alternative perspectives which can be separated from the mainstream and from one another, with regard to both their views of the world and their methodologies. A full consideration of these perspectives and methodologies cannot be undertaken here for reasons of space. However, it is our intention to consider the ways in which their approaches to economics are distinctive from the mainstream, so that we are able to provide an account of this additional, and substantial, cause of controversy within economics.

That there exist such alternatives to the mainstream is rarely obvious from textbooks and not always obvious in economics courses. However, as with methodological questions, there exists a specialist literature positively bristling with alternative approaches. In one of the few non-specialist and explicitly comparative books to do so, Cole *et al.* (1983) distinguished three 'schools of thought' or frames of reference: subjective preference, cost of production, and abstract labour. Unfortunately this conflates Austrian economics (1.7.2) with mainstream neoclassical economics and also distinguishes between schools of thought solely on the basis of the theory of value to which they subscribe. Cole *et al.* then, rather functionally, attribute these to the different 'interests' within the economy and society – subjective preference to the owners of capital; cost of production to managers and the organisers of production; and abstract labour to the working class. They further associate these respectively with the political perspectives of conservatism, social democracy and socialism.

None the less, despite these weaknesses it does firmly establish the existence of different perspectives. Dow (1985) in her analysis of macroeconomics, establishes the existence of four schools of thought, mainstream, neo-Austrian, post-Keynesian and Marxist, on the basis not of theories of value but of methodological differences which incorporate different views of the world. As this chapter and book focus on methodological differences as sources of controversy we shall, with one amendment, adopt a similar classification for the purposes of our presentation. Before so doing, however, it is important to recognise that the differences between them are substantial. Lichtenheim (1983), for example, in examining mainstream, post-Keynesian and Marxist approaches, shows that they differ with respect to the economic sphere analysed (respectively exchange, distribution, production); the focus of attention (respectively allocation, reproduction and accumulation); the primary factors or units of analysis (respectively individuals, classes, classes); the concept of value (respectively subjective, objective and rooted in the technical structure of production, objective and rooted in the social relations of production); the source of profit; the purpose of theory; institutional assumptions; relations between economic agents; and policy stances. The variety of sources of controversy here is clearly considerable.

1.7.2 Neo-Austrian economics

Neo-Austrian economics, which is currently undergoing considerable resurgence in modern economics, is different in scope and method to mainstream economics in many respects. We have seen how mainstream economics develops its assumptions, theory and hypotheses either from observation (induction) or from conjectures which are falsifiable through empirical tests. The neo-Austrian approach instead is to begin from the establishment of a priori axioms, which are considered to be self-evident, and to proceed by deductive logic to their inevitable consequences. These axioms are not open to empirical refutation. In consequence propositions derived logically from them are also not open to refutation; they describe the implications and effects of ordering economic behaviour on the basis of fundamental characteristics of human action. If 'reality' does not conform to theory, the implication is not to amend the theory (for it is based on the intuitively obvious character of human behaviour) but to amend the real world to reflect appropriately the necessary, and desirable, logic of human action:

> if contradiction appears between a theory and experience, we must always assume that a condition presupposed by the theory was not present or else that there is some error in our observations.

Clearly the specification of the assumptions are crucial, for they are taken to be true a priori unlike the conjectures of the falsificationist approach, and the application of deductive logic to them renders 'testing' of their implications against empirical data unnecessary, and thus the problems faced by falsificationists otiose. The theory is explicitly normative and as such constitutes 'political economy', fully accepting both the theory dependence of data and the value dependence of theory.

As soon as we acknowledge the existence of conscious purposive, choosing, interacting individual economic factors we have the basis of economic knowledge, neo-Austrians argue. When people are free to undertake the voluntary exchange that inevitably results from conscious human action and we add to it the a priori facts of maximising individual gain through the discovery of information, we can deduce the economic consequences of it.

A second distinctive feature of this approach is its 'subjectivism'. Knowledge and understanding can only be gained through introspection, through the private experience of individuals. Consequently, the individual's valuation is the focus of study. Because everyone is unique and choice is subjective then no mechanical interpretation of events is possible. Indeed as this is the foundation of economic knowledge there are no objective, directly observable facts. In consequence one cannot apply the methods of natural science to economics, or the human condition generally, and thus prediction too is ruled out. Knowledge of the future is unpredictable because behaviour is uncertain and has unintended consequences. The focus is on explanation and understanding.

Third, an extreme version of methodological individualism is employed where all propositions are reduced to those about individuals. All other propositions which seek to attribute choice or action to aggregates are inadmissible for only individuals undertake purposive action.

Finally, and a logical implication of this approach, decision-making is regarded as subjective and, to varying degrees, occurring under conditions of uncertainty and ignorance, unlike in mainstream economics where it is regarded as objective and perfectly well informed. Markets constitute the process of information discovery, not a set of equilibria. Hence the focus is on learning and acquiring information through markets, not on the static properties of the conditions for efficient resource allocation.

After all, it is axiomatic that markets offer an efficient mechanism for transactions between individuals. For example, for neo-Austrians with regard to industrial organisation, 'power' and 'profit' are not a function of size, concentration or the degree of monopoly as in mainstream theory, but rather they lie in the unique knowledge that market actors possess. Disequilibrium rather than equilibrium is the focus, as the former offers opportunities, the latter none.

The neo-Austrian research agenda and the means of undertaking it are clearly different from the mainstream. Moreover, once the a priori self-evident axioms are accepted and providing there is no error in deductive logic, the arguments of the neo-Austrian are immune from criticism.

1.7.3 Marxist economics

The Marxist theoretical and methodological framework differs in a variety of respects from the mainstream and from the neo-Austrian approach. First, it is argued that theoretical categories, concepts, economic behaviour, relations and economic 'laws' are not universal. They are historically specific to the particular organisation of the economy and society under examination. Second, the focus of attention is the dynamics of development of different modes of economic organisation and the 'laws of motion' that govern their operation. It is not concerned with resource allocation and indeed tends to assume that markets operate in a reasonably efficient manner with regard to agents' responsiveness to price signals. Third, the actions of individuals are not independently formed, rather the social division of labour generated out of, say, the organisation of a capitalist economy structures the roles of economic actors. Thus there is no such thing as 'free' exchange, 'voluntary' contracts, 'free choice', but rather class relations, engendered by the ownership of means of production in the hands of a specific class, ensuring that workers must sell their labour power to capitalists in return for a wage under conditions of structural inequality. There is an objective conflict of interest rather than the harmony of the market between capital and labour.

Fourth, and most important, Marxist economics distinguishes between analysis conducted at the level of (market/exchange) appearances and that conducted at the level of (production/social relations) essences:

> All science would be superfluous if the outward appearance and the essence of things coincided.
>
> (Marx 1970b)

Explanation is the objective, rather than prediction, and explanation not in the sense of the empirical regularity and association of occurrence between observable variables but in the sense of establishing the *necessary*, underlying connections between things. The aim is to uncover the underlying structures and mechanisms that generate observable phenomena. This clearly requires postulating the existence of unobservable entities and processes, a procedure considered metaphysical by some and certainly non-scientific by the falsificationists, because the existence of these is not subject to empirical refutation. This type of explanation also involves a different notion of causation from that with which we are familiar in this chapter so far. Causation here is not a relation between discrete events (increasing money supply causing an increase in inflation) but is used rather in the sense of the structure and mechanisms in the economic system which are capable of producing, have causal powers which allow them to produce such an association. In other words, reality is not as it appears. In order to discover it we must uncover the underlying mechanisms that produce phenomena. For example, to establish the real relations between workers and capitalists (employers) we must go beneath the level of the market transaction to the underlying inequality of the relationship uncovered in the social relations of production. To establish the causes of crises we must go beneath the immediate causes of falling investment, expectations and 'animal spirits' to the motors of accumulation and the balance of class forces.

This involves going 'back' to the defining characteristics of capitalism, or any other economic system, examining the structures so formed and the mechanism they generate. It proceeds by starting from the essential but simple and abstract formulations of the system (for example, wage labour and other basic features of a pure capitalist mode of production) and successively in stages moving towards more complex and concrete formulations of the structures, relations between them and mechanisms generated until one can reproduce the actual composition of the real economic system. This method of successive approximation produces 'tendency laws' right up to the point where the actual composition of the system is reproduced and clearly implies that the actual effects or outcomes at the level of appearance are contingent rather than necessary. Their falsification against empirical reality is, therefore, not an appropriate test of the theory. In any case because of the conscious capacity of classes to respond to unfolding economic conditions in a non-predetermined way, there are no predictions of the theory to be tested. On 'scientific' grounds, the theory is irrefutable . . . a situation not dissimilar to the neo-Austrians.

1.7.4 Post-Keynesian and institutional perspectives

Somewhat less developed and somewhat less coherent methodologically and theoretically, are two further perspectives adding to the diversity, richness and controversy of modern economics. *Post-Keynesian* analysis regards the economic system as essentially unstable and focuses on the institutional structure of economies and how it changes over time to generate new sources of instability. In particular there is concern to examine the role of large organisations (monopolies) and how through their price-setting behaviour they affect the macroeconomy. There is concern to capture adequately the 'micro-foundations' of the macroeconomy. They focus too not only on the micro–macro interface but the distribution–macro/micro interfaces, examining the effects of the growth of monopoly on the distribution of income and the distribution of income on conflict and macro stability.

The *Institutionalists* tend to examine the economy at the level of institutions, rather than individuals or classes. Their primary concern is to describe accurately and concretely the actual nature and behaviour of companies, unions, government and so on, showing how the specific institutional structure affects economic behaviour. As such, they clearly reject abstraction, prediction and rationality, preferring descriptive realism and behavioural accuracy. The approach is dominated by empirical detail, devoid of deductive reasoning though not of inductivism. They explicitly refuse to recognise distinctions between facts/values or ends/means, being interwoven in a narrative with an ethical commitment in the study of institutional change and power relations.

Clearly, in this section we have been unable to do full justice to the subtlety, variety and sophistication of the variety of competing perspectives in economics. However, it is hoped that we have done enough to make the essential point that one significant cause of controversy is the very existence of alternatives to mainstream theory, which are embraced by a large number of economists throughout the world.

1.8 FREE TO CHOOSE?

This chapter has sought to establish reasons for the existence of controversy in economics and to provide a lens through which to view the controversy displayed both in the different areas of economic knowledge covered in the rest of the chapters in this book and, indeed, in any material the reader may come across in courses and reading. It should not, of course, be expected that the following chapters will address controversy in the same manner as each other, nor that they will address all of the sources identified here. For one thing different areas of economics are more or less amenable to different aspects of the sources of controversy identified here, and for another this expectation would be tantamount to missing a central point of this chapter. Economists disagree, both the authors of the chapters in this book and the authors of the works on which they are reporting . . . not least about the reasons for their disagreement!

We have established a veritable cornucopia of reasons for the existence, and persistence of controversy. Indeed it may seem remarkable to the reader now that there is scope for any agreement and consensus among economists. An understanding of methodology has helped us to understand the reasons for controversy though whether it can be of assistance in a search to eliminate it and to discover the truth is another matter. The theory choice problem, it appears from this chapter, is insoluble. We have been unable to establish agreed, objective criteria to choose the 'best' theories. As Chalmers concludes for the natural sciences:

> There is just no method that enables scientific theories to be proven true or even probably true . . . there is no method that establishes scientific theories to be conclusively disproved either.
>
> (Chalmers 1982: xvi)

We may be free to choose between theories but it is very difficult to make the right choice. What applies to the natural sciences is even more applicable to economics. Thus methodological and theoretical pluralism is to be welcomed. It is to be hoped that courses and books become less rigid in scope, method and variety of approach over time, if only because it is quite possible that all approaches have something useful to say and that they may operate as useful correctives to each other, providing complimentary rather than competing insights into the complexity that is economic society.

FURTHER READING

Few individual sources cover the range of material dealt with in this chapter though Pheby (1988) is the best single introduction to the field. However, four books which cover many of the issues raised in the first six sections of the chapter are Chalmers (1982), Caldwell (1984), Katouzian (1980) and Blaug (1980). All can be strongly recommended. Other useful references are Whynes (1983), Campbell (1981) Chapter 1 and Wiseman (1983). On the problems of social science, see also Eichner (1983); on paradigms and crises see Keat and Urry (1982); on scientific research programmes see Latsis (1976) and Cross (1982).

With regard to competing methodologies and perspectives, for a general overview, see Pheby (1988) again, Rowthorn (1980) Chapter 1 and the excellent Wolff and Reisnick (1987). Then try Cole *et al.* (1983) and Dow (1985). On the neo-Austrian approach see Littlechild (1985), Shand (1984) or Green (1987). On Marxist economics see Keat and Urry (1982), Fine (1975) and Harrison (1978); on the Post Keynesians see Sawyer (1986) or Lichtenheim (1983); on the institutionalists see Seckler (1983) or Whynes (1983) Chapter 3.

2 · ENTERPRISE IN ECONOMICS

A guide to policy

RICHARD STEAD

2.1 INTRODUCTION

Enterprise may be broadly defined as the creation of new business: it is the sale of goods or services to new groups of buyers. The products in question may be either ones which have already been on sale in other markets or items which are wholly new. The best-known instances are, perhaps, inventions like Henry Ford's automobiles or Clive Sinclair's home computers. Nevertheless it must be recognised that technological innovation is but one form of entrepreneurship: the work of seeking out new markets for existing products or even new customers within established markets could all be legitimately included.

Enterprise is a matter of some importance. For the economy at large, it engenders change (Burton 1983) – the formulation of new business plans, the growth of new organisations and markets, the creation of new products, the development of new industries, and so on. For many economists, entrepreneurship is the engine that powers the development of the modern economy. Like so many concepts in economics, the topic is attended by controversy. The fundamental issue is how the idea of enterprise can be incorporated into economic theory. This chapter examines the approaches of two schools of economic thought: neoclassical economics, which allocates but a peripheral role to enterprise, and Austrian economics, which affords it central importance. The chapter proceeds to examine how this theoretical controversy gives rise to conflicting economic policies towards matters such as monopolies or the welfare state. The discussion moves on to review the controversies which relate to the position of small firms in the economy, and attempts to show how these issues exemplify differences between economists in terms of both theory and the interpretation of empirical evidence. The first task, however, is to examine a little more closely the nature of enterprise itself.

2.2 ENTERPRISE AND INFORMATION

The basis of enterprise is alertness to market information (Kirzner 1973), that is, to information about the prices of goods, services and factors of production, the existence of unfulfilled demand and the possibilities of meeting demand by new or cheaper sources of supply. Recognition of these data creates possibilities for entrepreneurs to act in various ways. For example, an entrepreneur may perceive that transactions are failing to be concluded simply because of ignorance on the parts of buyers and sellers. There may be a dearth of some product in one part of the market, with consumers offering high prices and yet failing to obtain the goods in question. At the same time, in another part of the market, there may be oversupply, with stocks of goods standing unsold. If the simultaneous existence of these two situations were unknown to the buyers and sellers in the different parts of the market, it would be open to an entrepreneur to intercede, buying products from the oversupplied area and selling them in the area with the shortage. This form of enterprise is called 'arbitrage', and it serves to ensure that all goods offered find buyers. Arbitrage thus helps markets to clear, that is, to attain equilibrium.

A more far-reaching form of arbitrage involves the switching of resources between markets. An entrepreneur may notice that the factors of production needed for the production of, say, carpets are available in the textile industry at prices which are lower than those ruling in the carpet industry. The entrepreneur could then hire resources from the textile industry and set them to work to produce carpets which – as long as prices remain unaltered – could be sold at a profit.

Finally, an entrepreneur may identify or even anticipate changes in the conditions of demand and supply, that is, consumer tastes, technology or the costs of resources. (These are also known as 'market givens'.) Changes in these factors open up possibilities for an entrepreneur to modify existing products, to produce new ones, to develop new production techniques or to exploit lower-cost sources of supply. (In practice, of course, these various strategies may be difficult to distinguish.) This form of enterprise differs from arbitrage in two respects. First, rather than moving a market towards its equilibrium, it serves to disturb equilibrium. Second, it involves not merely buying and selling but the creation of new products, organisations or markets, that is, innovation. To distinguish it from arbitrage, this form of enterprise may be termed 'Schumpeterian' enterprise after Joseph Schumpeter, the economist who emphasised the role of innovating entrepreneurs in promoting economic development (Schumpeter 1952 and Loasby 1982). The reason for the breadth of the definition of enterprise at the opening of this chapter should now be apparent: it had to include both arbitrage and innovation.

Risk-taking is intrinsic to enterprise. The accuracy of an entrepreneur's assessment of changes in tastes or technology or the extent of unsatisfied demand can never be proved until the products finally reach the market. Entrepreneurs are thus compelled to marshal their resources – financial, organisational and technological – on the basis of *conjecture*.

The reward for enterprise is profit, which arises from the difference between the costs of the products and their selling prices. It is often supposed that profit accrues to the owners of capital, that is, the owners of a business. More properly, of course, the reward of capital is interest. The confusion arises because entrepreneurs usually own (all or part of) their businesses and thus receive profit and interest together. This fact should not, however, prevent economists from making the important distinction between these two categories of factor reward.

2.3 ENTERPRISE VERSUS EQUILIBRIUM

The first controversy pertains to the relative importance that should be accorded in economic theory to the ideas of enterprise and equilibrium. The issue arises because markets cannot both be in equilibrium and provide scope for enterprise at the same time. In equilibrium, all goods offered for sale are purchased and there is, by definition, no possibility of arbitrage. Nor, as long as market givens remain unaltered, is there any scope for marketing new products or exploiting new technology. There is thus no possibility of exercising Schumpeterian enterprise either. It is only when buyers and sellers are failing to meet or when the conditions of supply and demand are changing that entrepreneurs can play a role (Kirzner 1979).

It is plain that economists face a simple choice. Theories must be constructed on the basis of one of two rival assumptions – either that markets are generally in stable equilibrium or that entrepreneurs are active. The choice would, naturally, have to be consistent with other questions such as the phenomena which economists wished to analyse, the kinds of evidence which they were prepared to accept and the types of theories and explanations which they sought to develop. Thus the choice between enterprise and equilibrium involves, for any individual economist, a decision between competing schools of economic thought. The two groups of economists which contest most directly the issue of the relative importance of the ideas of equilibrium and enterprise are neoclassical economists, who stress the former, and Austrian economists, who emphasise the latter.

Neoclassical economics is the economics which is most familiar to students of the discipline, the introductory textbooks being largely given over to its exposition. This theory is used to explain the relative prices of different goods and services such as, for example, the (hypothetical) fact that hair conditioner costs twice as much as a cup of coffee in a café. This is because, the logic of neoclassical economics suggests, first, consumers value the former twice as highly as the latter, while, second, resources which are twice as valuable are needed to produce it. In short, hair conditioner is twice as *scarce* as cups of coffee. Similar kinds of explanation could be offered for the relative prices of other products, the relative rewards of factors of production, the exchange rates between national currencies and so on.

The commitment to explaining prices obliges neoclassical economists to make two important assumptions. The first, already noted, is that markets are generally in equilibrium. This is necessary because relative prices are explained as being the outcome of underlying forces like consumer tastes and the costs of resources, that is, the conditions of supply and demand. The only prices which fully reflect these forces are equilibrium prices, for non-equilibrium prices could clearly be influenced by a whole range of extraneous factors. Non-equilibrium prices are therefore excluded from the discussion by the assumption that markets are in equilibrium.

Second, neoclassical economists find it necessary to assume that buyers and sellers have perfect information. This is because prices can only reflect the underlying conditions of supply and demand if economic agents – buyers and sellers – are aware of those forces. Thus, in the example above, the proposition that consumers value hair conditioner twice as strongly as coffee can only hold if consumers are familiar with both products. If hair conditioner were a completely new product, it could hardly be argued that its price reflected the strength of consumer preferences.

These two assumptions – that markets are in equilibrium and that economic agents are endowed with perfect information – are naturally related. Perfect information is most likely to be found in markets where business follows the same course from year to year, that is, markets that are in equilibrium. Conversely, markets which are in disequilibrium – perhaps as a result of the launching of new products or shifts in consumer preferences – are likely to be characterised by limited information: consumers will necessarily be unfamiliar with the new goods on offer, or producers may be uncertain about the new trends in tastes and what new products will find favour. Since the creation of new products is an instance of enterprise, these considerations serve to underline the antithesis between equilibrium on the one hand and enterprise on the other.

The school of thought which places the mechanisms and consequences of enterprise – rather than prices – at the centre of attention is Austrian economics. This body of theory takes its name from its early development in Vienna in the late nineteenth century, though today it is naturally no longer confined to one country. Austrian economists stress that consumer tastes and producers' costs cannot be taken as given but must be discovered by entrepreneurs offering new deals, trying out new lines of goods or experimenting with new productive techniques. While acknowledging that enterprise in the form of arbitrage may tend to move markets towards equilibrium, Austrians argue that market givens change so rapidly that the process is unlikely to be completed before it is set in motion once again. Schumpeterian enterprise, furthermore, can be expected to disturb any equilibrium which has been attained. The economy is thus, according to Austrians, perpetually in flux. The process of adjustment is never completed: market givens must not only be discovered, they must be rediscovered continually.

The activity of establishing market givens is, of course, the work of the entrepreneur. By trying out new products, new approaches to marketing and new technologies, entrepreneurs are able to discover the truth – or otherwise – of their assessments about the conditions of supply and demand. For Austrian economists, enterprise is akin to a series of experiments which improve an entrepreneur's understanding of consumer preferences, the capabilities of new equipment and so on (Boland 1982: 168–9, 175–87). Thus a notable point of contrast between neoclassical economics and Austrian economics is their differing assumptions about human knowledge. Neoclassical economists, as noted above, assume that people have perfect information. Austrian economists, by contrast, make the assumptions, first, that economic agents have limited information and, second, that they – or, at least, the entrepreneurs among them – *seek continually to extend that information*.

An important aspect of enterprise from an Austrian perspective is the point that the plans and products of one entrepreneur can readily be superseded by those of a rival. No sooner has one entrepreneur cut his prices or remodelled his product to appeal to contemporary tastes than a competitor will announce even more attractive prices or reveal an even more modern design. Entrepreneurship, in other words, is intrinsically competitive.

It should be noted that the Austrian conception of competition differs radically from the neoclassical view. For Austrians, competition consists of the perpetual modification of the price and design of products. It is, therefore, a process. Neoclassical economists, by contrast, perceive it in purely static terms. For them, competition is measured by the number of firms in an industry or market and the share of total sales accounted for by the largest firms. Thus an industry with many small producers would be described as competitive, while one in which the biggest five firms took most of the sales would be said to be 'concentrated' or, if there were but one firm, 'monopolistic'. For Austrians, however, the important evidence on which to decide whether an industry were competitive or monopolistic would relate to the ability of new entrepreneurs to enter the market. Even if a corporation were the sole producer of an item, Austrian economists would argue that, in the absence of any legal restraints, new entrepreneurs could be expected to follow the pioneer and eventually offer similar products to consumers (assuming, of course, that such a course of action were profitable). In Austrian eyes, the fact that one firm is the sole source of a product does not indicate that the process of competition has ceased to operate.

The theoretical controversy over the concept of enterprise turns ultimately upon the competing merits of neoclassical and Austrian economics. The claim of neoclassical economics is that it provides an explanation of relative prices, while the advertised advantage of Austrian economics is that it offers a description of the processes of competition and change. Equally, both schools tend to be less competent in explaining phenomena which lie outside their respective spheres of interest. It is not, of course, our purpose here to adjudicate on this issue but simply to note that the relative emphasis to be placed on the principles of equilibrium and enterprise is a matter of ongoing debate.

2.4 THE POLICY DEBATE

The second controversy, which follows from the first, relates to the differing approaches to policy which are generated by the above two schools of thought. These relate primarily to microeconomic policies such as the regulation of monopoly, public ownership of industry and the provision of welfare services. These are taken in turn after a brief review of the organising themes of policy which derive from the two schools.

The key concept of neoclassical economics for policy purposes is the idea of the optimum allocation of resources (Lipsey 1979). This is the allocation of resources which matches consumer preferences as closely as possible. It is to be attained, the argument runs, by the free play of supply and demand in competitive markets. There are, however, some caveats to this conclusion, namely, there must be no monopolies, external costs or external benefits. (External costs are costs which are imposed, without compensation, on other parties – pollution is the classic example. External benefits are benefits which are conferred free of charge on others, like the advantages of faster travel which are bestowed upon motorway users. The two categories may be termed collectively 'externalities'.)

In consequence of these arguments, neoclassical economists tend to endorse a general policy stance of *laissez-faire*. They also support Free Trade, that is, the policy of allowing overseas producers unhindered access to the home market, on the grounds that this enhances competition. At the same time, however, their perceptions of the problems of monopolies and externalities make them ready to sanction state intervention to control or to compensate for these phenomena.

Austrian economists, while sharing neoclassical economists' broad approval of competition, have no corresponding confidence in the ability of the state to effect any improvement in economic affairs. This belief stems from their view that the economy is generally in a state of flux rather than of equilibrium, implying that no optimum could ever be identified. All that can be hoped for from an Austrian perspective is the promotion of *flexibility* in the economy. State agencies, by their very nature, can never be as quick to respond to economic change as private entrepreneurs, and for this reason Austrian economists favour policies which give the maximum control of resources to the private sector.

These contrasting approaches to policy lead to markedly different attitudes on specific issues as the following examples show.

2.4.1 Monopoly policy

The converse of both schools' approval of competition is naturally a condemnation of monopoly. The neoclassical case is that a monopolist will tend simultaneously to overcharge and to undersupply his customers. In consequence, the outputs of monopolistic industries are therefore lower than they would be under optimum conditions: resources are misallocated. Neoclassical economists tend therefore to take the view that governments should both break up existing monopolies and prevent the formation of new ones by regulating mergers between firms, and hence look with broad approval upon the 'anti-trust' laws which are to be found in most western countries.

The Austrian criticism of monopoly rests not upon the misallocation of resources but upon the possibility that enterprise may be thwarted. Whether this is the case depends upon the barriers to entry on which the monopoly is founded. Indeed, the concern of Austrian economists lies not so much with the monopolist as with the underlying entry barriers.

These Austrians divide into two categories. First are entry barriers which are the product of normal commercial tactics such as the public image which a product can acquire through advertising. Barriers of this type can, Austrians argue, be overcome by the very means by which they were established. In the case of advertising and product differentiation, all that is required is that a rival product with a sufficiently attractive design and the support of an appealing advertising campaign be placed upon the market. Similarly, any monopoly which is based upon a technological lead can be superseded by other innovations. For example the American railroad monopolies of the late nineteenth century were overthrown (over the course of decades) by Henry Ford and the other entrepreneurs who developed the automobile industry. For Austrians, trust-busting is to be undertaken not by courts of law but by enterprise. Indeed, the more that monopolists exploit their customers, the greater is the incentive for entrepreneurs to assault their positions. Moreover, the prospect of having one's business broken up may deter entrepreneurs from undertaking new, large-scale ventures. It follows that many Austrian economists oppose anti-trust legislation.

The other class of entry barriers are those which owe their origin to the state, such as the route licences which were at one time issued to British long-distance bus operators. These reserved the right to run buses over designated routes to the licensee alone, who thus had a monopoly. Another instance is the practice of having work like cleaning, vehicle maintenance and laundry services for public authorities undertaken by in-house departments rather than by private firms. The critical point is that barriers of this nature cannot be broken down by entrepreneurial business tactics. From an Austrian perspective, the problem with these barriers is that they prevent private enterprise from being exercised. Entrepreneurs are debarred from entering into competition with the monopolist, while the monopolist himself loses all incentive to experiment with new technologies and products because his position is secure. Austrians accordingly favour a policy of 'liberalisation' or 'deregulation', that is, of demolishing state-created entry barriers by ending route licences, opening state services to private contractors, and so on.

2.4.2 Natural monopolies and public ownership

The formation of large companies can frequently be justified on the grounds that such organisations are able to realise economies of scale. For example, it would be inefficient to have more than one company selling natural gas in any one neighbourhood. Instances like this are termed 'natural monopolies', and they clearly pose problems for policy-makers in that the price of efficiency can be the formation of a monopoly.

One way of resolving this dilemma would be to control the prices which natural monopolies are allowed to charge. Thus in the United Kingdom and the United States, privately-owned companies selling natural gas, telecommunications services and so on are supervised by regulatory agencies. An alternative approach would be to take the industry into public ownership. To justify such a move in economic terms, it is necessary to argue that the transfer of ownership from private to public hands will, of itself, make no difference to costs and productivity. In other words, it must be assumed that costs are given and can easily be ascertained. This assumption is of course entirely consistent with the neoclassical view that economic agents have perfect information. Although economists of the neoclassical school are by no means committed to nationalisation, the economic arguments which can be deployed to support public ownership derive from neoclassical thinking.

Austrian economics, by contrast, provides no analogous support for the public ownership of industry. Indeed, the logic of Austrian economics suggests three grounds for strong opposition to the idea. Two stem from the particular form which nationalisation has taken in the United Kingdom, while the third relates to the very principle. First, the public corporations which ran the UK nationalised industries were in many cases given the sole rights to perform those services. No one, for instance, can mine coal in the United Kingdom without the permission of British Coal. Regulations like these are clearly state-based barriers to entry. Second, the public corporations were themselves limited to certain kinds of activity. British Rail, for example, was charged with providing rail services and was in effect forbidden to experiment with, say, express coach services on converted tracks. Thus the enterprise of the corporations themselves was restricted.

The third and most general objection to public ownership stems from Austrians' rejection of the idea that costs and demand are both fixed and known to the managers of the industries. Rather, Austrians argue that these must be discovered by entrepreneurial experimentation. Once found out, moreover, they must be rediscovered in the light of changes in market givens. There is therefore an unending need for experimentation with new products, services and technologies, that is, for enterprise. The problem with publicly-owned corporations, however, is that such enterprise will necessarily be lacking for the simple reason that there is no incentive to call it into play. Since the ownership of a public corporation is vested in the state, no individual has the possibility of making profits legitimately from its efficient operations. As a result, the industry will become progressively more wasteful and bureaucratic (Burton 1983). In short, Austrians' objection to public ownership is that enterprise is smothered.

In the light of these arguments, it is scarcely surprising that Austrians generally approve of the policy of 'privatisation' whereby public corporations are sold to private shareholders. While these sales frequently mean the replacement of a public monopoly by a private one, Austrians are content to argue that, with the ending of legal barriers to entry, technological changes will in the long run allow other entrepreneurs to find ways of breaking into these markets.

2.4.3 The welfare state

In most industrial countries, health care, education and social security absorb a substantial proportion of the national budget. They also provide a further locus for controversy over enterprise. The economic justification for the free public provision of these services is that they generate positive externalities, that is, that their consumption provides benefits both for the direct consumer and for other members of society. For example, higher education is argued to help graduates to secure better employment and at the same time to enhance the productivity of the economy at large. Thus the total value of higher education exceeds its value to the immediate consumer. The clear implication is that consumption of these 'merit goods' (or rather 'merit services') should be stimulated by making them available at a zero charge.

The assumptions underlying these arguments are similar to those upon which the case for public ownership of industry was based. Among them are the critical ideas that the costs of providing the services in question are independent of whether the service is provided by a public authority or by the private sector and that these costs can be readily established without any practical experimentation. These ideas, which are plainly neoclassical in origin, are naturally subject to criticism from the Austrian school.

The Austrian case against state-funded public services turns on their alleged effect on enterprise. This is argued to operate in three distinct ways. First, large-scale state services necessitate high rates of taxation which are held to undermine incentives to seek promotion or to undertake new business ventures. Second, the agencies like hospitals and universities which receive state funds have no incentives either to use resources efficiently or to respond to changes in consumer preferences. For example, hospital doctors may find it more rewarding in terms of prestige and promotion to undertake heart transplant operations rather than hip replacement operations which could help far larger numbers of people for the same cost (Bosanquet 1983). Again, university research may be devoted to topics which the staff find stimulating but which are of little relevance to society at large.

The third Austrian objection to state-funded welfare services relates to what may be termed the 'cultural climate'. Austrians argue that state provision of welfare services like pensions and council housing removes the incentive for people to take responsibility for their own affairs. Austrians therefore see the welfare state as a 'nanny state' which stunts personal responsibility. The cultural climate that Austrian economists would prefer is an 'enterprise culture' in which the risking of personal wealth in business ventures is common practice.

In place of state-funded welfare services, Austrians would prefer agencies to receive their funds directly from their clients. University research, for example, should be financed by industry, so ensuring its relevance to business needs, while pensions should be provided by the medium of private saving and investment. Hospitals which received their money from patients rather than the state would thus be forced to perform the operations for which there was a patient-felt need rather than those which suited the surgeons. Above all, the obligations to search continually for new ways of using resources more efficiently and to be attentive to consumer demand, that is, to be entrepreneurial, would be placed upon organisations which had hitherto been insulated from these pressures.

As an intermediate stage, Austrians believe that funding for hospitals, colleges, and so on should cease to be automatic. Rather, the payment of public funds should be related to their performances. Colleges, for example, could be given contracts by central government to run particular kinds of courses, with their income being dependent upon the satisfactory fulfilment of the contracts. Institutions would then have the incentive to compete with each other in finding lower-cost ways of delivering their services and in offering more attractive types of service. Where possible, Austrians argue, institutions should seek funds from sources other than the government.

Austrians recognise of course that these market relationships may not always be sufficient. One problem is that the poor may find themselves unable to afford certain services. Such a problem could be met, Austrians argue, not by providing a free service for the whole society but by subsidising the particular groups of needy people. Another problem is that some people, given the choice, may decide – simply on the grounds of preference – not to educate their children to a socially acceptable standard. The Austrian reply is that while governments may legitimately desire everyone to consume a product or service (such as education to the age of 16) there is no necessity either for that service to be paid for by taxpayers or for it to be provided by public agencies. Austrians argue that welfare services, like most others, can be better provided by the private sector acting under the direction of profit-conscious entrepreneurs. For example, most governments take the view that motorists should be insured, yet it is rare for insurance cover to be provided by publicly-owned insurance companies. Rather, consumers are free to choose their policies and insurers are forced to engage in competition. Austrians would argue that this competition ensures that motor insurance is both cheaper and more varied than it would be if provided by a state agency. Indeed, the thread which runs through Austrian attitudes on all the policy issues discussed is a desire to minimise the role of the state (Bosanquet 1983).

The objections which could be lodged against these policies are not difficult to see. With regard to industry, the Austrian approach implies a willingness to tolerate a monopoly for as long as it takes an entrepreneur to find the technology which will throw the market open. Since this process could take a generation, it is not clear that such a policy stance would command universal assent. One objection to a policy of turning the welfare services over to private fee-charging firms – that the poor could be deprived of access to health and education – has already been noted. Another is that educational and health care institutions could find themselves reducing the quality of their work in order to cut costs. There is, in consequence, continuing debate among both economists and the public on these issues.

2.5 SMALL FIRMS

Another major controversy which stems from the dispute over the importance of enterprise relates to small firms: their role in the economy, the policies which government should adopt toward them and the effectiveness of those policies. Here the emphasis falls not so much upon theory as upon the differing constructions which may be placed upon empirical evidence.

As a subject for both research and policy, small firms were largely ignored for many years, interest falling principally upon large-scale business organisations. Indeed, in the 1960s, the British government deliberately assisted manufacturing companies to merge into larger units. It was partly to balance this preoccupation with larger companies that the same government established, in 1969, the Bolton Committee 'to consider the role of small firms in the national economy, the facilities available to them and the problems confronting them' (Bolton 1971: xv).

Reporting two years later, the Bolton Committee found that, although their importance had tended to decline, small firms were a useful source of new competition and innovation in the economy (Bolton 1971). The Committee also observed that small firms were the 'seed-bed' which produced the large businesses of the future. It went on to recommend that small firms be given special consideration in terms of taxation, planning regulations, the filing of statistical returns and the provision of advice and, possibly, of finance. A government minister, the Committee felt, ought to be given responsibility for coordinating policy toward small businesses (Bolton 1971). These recommendations, however, were largely disregarded: neglecting Austrian perspectives on economic affairs, policy-makers gave little consideration to small firms for eight years.

Events took an abrupt turn in 1979 when Mrs Thatcher's first Conservative government entered office with a pledge to assist small firms. Among the policy initiatives taken was the Business Expansion Scheme (BES), which allowed investments in small firms to be offset against income tax, effectively subsidising such investments by between 30 and 60 per cent. Second, the Loan Guarantee Scheme encouraged banks to advance money to small firms by reimbursing them for any losses which they incurred through the failure of the businesses concerned. Third, Enterprise Allowances were given to unemployed workers who started new firms. Previously, anyone who undertook such a venture would have lost their unemployment benefit even though the business might have been running at a loss. Together with the steps recommended by Bolton, and a range of other measures, this amounted to a commitment of some magnitude. Indeed, by 1985 the main policy measures alone – the EAS, the Small Firms Loan Guarantee Scheme and the BES – were costing the Exchequer over £200 million per year (HM Treasury 1986; Inland Revenue 1986).

The government was, at the same time, successful in inducing other organisations to adopt a more positive approach to small businesses. The Stock Exchange, for example, set up the Unlisted Securities Market, on which small companies could sell their shares under less onerous conditions than those normally in force. For example, less information had to be disclosed to investors and a shorter trading record was required. (In 1987, a 'third market' with even fewer conditions was initiated.) The net effect was to make it easier for new firms to raise finance. Similarly, a 'venture capital' market was set up by investors who were willing to lend 'risk capital' specifically to new enterprises, while many large industrial firms began to engage in 'corporate venturing', that is, the practice of investing in promising new firms. Established firms also came together to develop 'enterprise agencies' which offered advice to new businesses on a local basis. The 'enterprise boards' of the former metropolitan county councils (Merseyside, Greater London, West Yorkshire and the West Midlands) also continued to provide investment finance, while local authorities and universities began to construct 'science parks' to foster the growth of technology-based enterprises.

The policy – which has parallels in many other industrial countries – rested upon several ideas. First, it was believed that small firms were the principal source of new jobs, and that the formation and expansion of new firms was the only effective answer to unemployment. Second, it was thought – by the Bolton Committee, among others – that small firms were important sources of innovation. There was, furthermore, the feeling that small businessmen and women were particularly entrepreneurial. In particular, it appeared to be the view of the government that the act of establishing a new business involved the very quintessence of enterprise: that the founders of new businesses were necessarily more entrepreneurial than the directors of large, bureaucratic corporations (Lloyd, 1986). At the same time, government spokesmen were content to propagate the idea that their policies were successful in increasing the number of small firms in the economy. The evidence supporting the above ideas is at best ambiguous.

2.5.1 Small firms and employment creation

The primary research relating to the United Kingdom for the argument that small firms create employment was undertaken by Gallagher and Stewart (1984). Building on work by Birch (1979) for the United States, the researchers examined data taken from a credit-rating agency for the manufacturing sector from 1971 to 1981. They found that 31 per cent of gross new jobs (that is, jobs in newly created firms and in expanding firms) were provided by firms employing fewer than 20 workers, while firms with fewer than one hundred workers accounted for 52 per cent of gross jobs. Firms in the larger categories, however, made markedly smaller contributions.

Several problems with the research were discussed by Storey and Johnson (1987). One arose from the fact that the data covered only 25 per cent of firms with fewer than 20 workers. Gallagher and Stewart had estimated the employment trends for the whole of this class by simply scaling up by a factor of three the data for the firms covered. This procedure would only have been legitimate if the 25 per cent were representative of the remainder. As Storey and Johnson suggested, the data could well have been biased toward expanding firms since unsuccessful ones would be less likely to disclose information to a credit-rating agency. The job-creating trends of small firms could thus have been overstated.

Another problem was that the agency's coverage of the small firm sector improved between 1971 and 1981. The later data thus counted as new openings firms which had been in existence for many years but which had simply registered for the first time. This effect would also have exaggerated employment creation by small firms.

Attention was also drawn by Curran (1986) to the fact that Gallagher and Stewart did not assess the *net* job gains in each size category, that is, they ignored closures and employment contractions. The view of the Minister for Small Firms (Trippier 1984: 388) that the research 'reveal[ed] that small firms will continue to increase their share of the labour market' is notably more generous than Gallagher and Stewart's own observation: 'our results must be interpreted with some caution' (Curran 1986: 34).

2.5.2 Small firms and innovation

The contribution of small firms to innovation is equally difficult to establish. Problems are created by the paucity of data: there is neither an accepted definition of an innovation nor any reliable statistical record. While it is possible to measure the employment of qualified engineers and scientists (QSEs), to assess expenditure on research and development (R&D), to count patents and to interview businessmen about past innovations, all these procedures are open to objections of various kinds. For example, employment of staff or the expenditure of money reflects inputs into the innovation process, rather than the completion of successful innovations themselves. Similarly, only a small fraction of technical innovations are patented, while interview methods often contain bias.

Data problems notwithstanding, the Bolton Committee attempted to assess the role of small firms in the process of industrial innovation. Supporters of the view that the small firms' contribution was significant were able to take heart from the Committee's finding that the share of small firms in innovation was rather greater than their share in R&D, implying that their R&D was rather more efficient than that of larger firms. They also observed that the flexibility of small firms could contribute to the process of innovation by permitting innovators to develop their ideas outside the confines of a corporate research laboratory.

Other evidence to the Committee was, however, less flattering to the small firm sector. It showed that small firms in manufacturing employed fewer QSEs, undertook less R&D and accounted for fewer important technical innovations than their share of manufacturing output would have warranted. Much of the evidence was provided by Freeman, who drew on an investigation of 1,200 industrial innovations in the United Kingdom between 1945 and 1970 (Freeman 1974). He found that, whereas small firms (defined as those with fewer than 200 workers) accounted for 25 per cent of manufacturing employment and 21 per cent of output, they had produced only 10 per cent of the sector's significant innovations. Defining a 'traditional' strategy as one of simply refusing to innovate, he went on to observe that 'The innovative small firm is the rare exception, not the general rule. For every small firm engaged in . . . innovation, there are . . . hundreds which follow a "traditional" strategy – the peasants of industry' (Freeman 1974: 218). Given the problems of both collecting and interpreting data in this area, it is hardly surprising that most research is inconclusive, allowing protagonists on both sides to find evidence to support their cases.

2.5.3 The success of policy

The question of whether government policy toward small firms has been successful has also occasioned some debate. The Department of Employment claims to have assisted 220,000 people through its Enterprise Allowance Scheme (EAS) (HM Treasury 1987) by March 1987. Since 90 per cent of participants go into business by themselves (rather than in partnership with their fellows), this seems to imply that some 210,000 enterprises have been started through the scheme. The BES is also claimed (Inland Revenue, 1985, 1986) to have helped to start 1,100 new enterprises as well as promoting the growth of a further 389 established ones.

The success of a policy, of course, is to be judged not in terms of activity but of results, that is, in terms of the number of firms in the economy. It must, however, be borne in mind that the population of firms is constantly changing, with the total population of firms experiencing birth and death rates of about 8 per cent per year (Customs and Excise 1986: Table 8). (Growth in the stock of business units occurs because the birth rate usually exceeds the death rate by a small margin.) New firms, moreover, have even higher rates of failure: in manufacturing, only 60 per cent of new businesses survive for more than three years and only 30 per cent last more than ten years. Firms, in other words, are ephemeral beings, with the consequence that the impact of a policy of assisting their formation must be expected to diminish over the years. Of the claimed 200,000 or so extra businesses founded between 1979 and 1987, therefore, only a falling proportion could be expected to remain in existence at any later date, a fact which future research into the success of policy must take into account.

The principal difficulty in assessing the effectiveness of policy is that the two most accessible indicators give conflicting readings. First, the number of self-employed workers rose by over 630,000 between 1979 and 1985. Although this might seem to indicate that the policy had been successful, it must be remembered first that over those six years the number of employees in employment fell by some two million, and second, that many firms have been transferring staff from the status of employee to that of subcontractor. In other words, the changes recorded may be more apparent than real in terms of the creation of new, independent enterprises. Moreover, half of the increase in self-employment predates the commencement of the EAS, which only began in 1984.

The second indicator is the total number of businesses registered for the payment of VAT. The growth in this total is shown in Fig. 2.1. The graph shows that the number of businesses rose by 150,000 or 11.3 per cent in the six-year period 1979–80 to 1985–6. Although substantial, this is not significantly different from the growth of 130,000 or 10.9 per cent recorded for the six-year period 1973–4 to 1979–80. In other words, despite the battery of policy measures and the expenditure of some £250 million per year, the rate of growth in the number of business units remained very close to its trend. Evidence of the existence of an additional 200,000 or more new enterprises is absent.

The conflicting evidence from the two indicators can be reconciled by reference to the fact that VAT is paid only by businesses with turnovers in excess of a certain threshold. (In 1987, this figure was £21,300.) The net effect of policy may thus have been the creation of firms which were below the limit. Should this have been the case, the policy of assisting small firms has indeed been meeting with success: it has created firms which are diminutive.

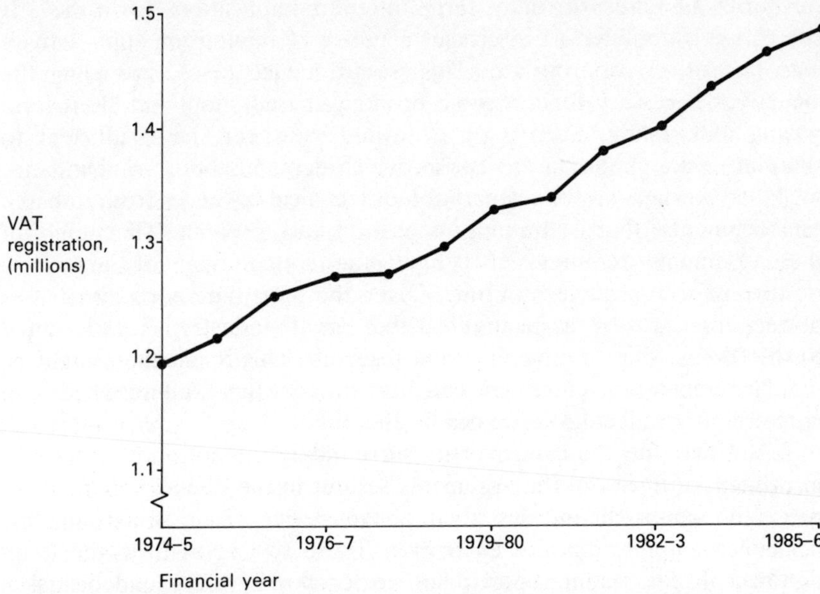

Fig. 2.1 Growth in the total number of businesses registered for the payment of VAT. *Source*: Reports of the Commissioners of Her Majesty's Customs and Excise.

2.6 CONCLUSIONS

The controversies over policies toward enterprise and small firms have been characterised to a degree by confusions over terminology. Three instances merit attention. First, Storey *et al.* (1987: 8) noted that in growing literature on the subject, small firms had been defined in some forty different ways. Few of these definitions, moreover, take account of the markets in which firms operate. Although ICI, GEC and the Rover Group (now part of British Aerospace) may appear to be large in the context of the UK economy, they are small compared to the firms with which they compete.

Second, it must be noted that enterprise is not confined to the founding of new businesses. While such activity is plainly entrepreneurial, so too is the action of executives in existing companies in exploiting new technology, developing new markets or transferring production to new locations. New business, in short, should not be confused with new business*es*. In a competitive world, of course, there are powerful arguments in favour of policies which stimulate the former. The case for subsidising the creation of new business organisations is, by contrast, rather less self-evident.

Third, the precise form of enterprise which is the subject of policy has never been clarified. The importance of this point is that the various categories of enterprise may carry different implications for policy. If enterprise is confined to arbitrage, a policy of minimising state activity may be entirely appropriate. This would reduce taxes, providing the incentives necessary for a flexible economy based simply on short-term buying and selling. Such a policy would, however, be insufficient to stimulate Schumpeterian enterprise, which demands both an abundance of skilled workers and the generation of technical advances from research establishments, that is, training, education and research. The supply of these elements requires, of course, the commitment of large-scale resources for long periods of time. Given the short time-horizons of most businessmen, it is by no means clear that private industry is ideally suited to the sponsorship of education and research. This implication might be that Schumpeterian enterprise can best thrive when well supplied with human and intellectual resources by the public sector.

Taken over all, the controversies surrounding the notion of enterprise in economics illustrate the arguments set out in the opening chapter. At root, the controversies described above derive from two competing principles: equilibrium and enterprise. These two ideas form the foundations of contrasting approaches to economic theory, neoclassical economics and Austrian economics. It is clear that these two schools of thought are what Lakatos would describe as 'scientific research programmes', in so far as both schools of thought have their respective 'hard cores' of ideas which are not to be challenged. In each case, the hard core is a conception of the psychology of economic decision-makers. For neoclassical economists, decision-makers are perfectly informed and are thus able to make markets move swiftly to equilibrium. For Austrians, economic agents have information which is not only restricted but is falling rapidly out of date as circumstances change. In this context, those decision-makers who are entrepreneurs are able to try out their ideas with a view to making profits.

The controversies over policy follow from these conflicting theoretical approaches, with Austrians desiring to minimise the role of the state and neoclassical economists more ready to justify public intervention. While these views relate to the differing theoretical positions on equilibrium and enterprise, it is clear that they are also infused with contrasting social values and beliefs about political priorities (Hayek 1962). It is also clear that statistical evidence can often bear more than one construction. It must therefore be recognised that the clarification of definitions and the presentation of research findings can under most circumstances only serve to elucidate the differences between approaches to economic theory and policy. Given the irreducible role for individual judgement in these matters, the topics of enterprise and small firms will continue to be contested terrain.

FURTHER READING

Kirzner (1979) provides an invaluable introduction to the idea of enterprise and to the contrasts between Austrian and neoclassical theories, although it does, perhaps, tend to concentrate upon the role of the entrepreneur as arbitrageur. For an exposition of the role of the entrepreneur as a disequilibrating force, see Schumpeter (1952), while Loasby (1982) provides a useful summary of different conceptions of entrepreneurship. Hayek (1962) and Bosanquet (1983) discuss the political implications of Austrian approaches to economics. Lloyd (1986) is a readable popularisation of the proposition that new, small, high-technology firms are qualitatively different from large, bureaucratic corporations. Storey *et al.* (1987a), (1987b) take a less sanguine approach.

3 · 'MERGER MANIA'

Making sense of corporate acquisitions

MIKE HARDY

3.1 INTRODUCTION

> The stock of literature on mergers has in recent years grown even faster than the number of mergers, though the stock of knowledge on this subject reveals little growth.
>
> (Gort and Hogarty 1970)

It was difficult not to agree with Gort and Hogarty's observation in 1970. In the late 1980s it remains correct. There is little indication in the extensive literature on mergers which has appeared since 1970, to suggest that either the stock of knowledge has grown significantly, or that the merger phenomenon, *per se*, is better understood.

Merger transactions include all amalgamations of two or more independently operating units, whether integrated or not as a result, under some common control. They may take the form of acquisitions, consolidation or combinations of already large firms. We will not seek to differentiate between types within the confines of this chapter unless otherwise stated, and, hence, will use the terms merger and acquisition synonymously.

Studies of the merger phenomenon predominantly serve two masters. The most influential of these in the literature is public policy towards the dominant firm and monopoly power. Mergers affect shareholders, employees and consumers; they impact upon the rate of technological innovation and, over time, can redefine the economic structure of communities. The size and frequency of contemporary merger transactions may even determine the capital investment plans of the economy as a whole. Mergers in the United Kingdom, as elsewhere, have led, over the past 30 or so years, to a substantial concentration of the control of assets in all sectors of the economy. The public policy concern is centred on the question of whether, if left unregulated, the economy will become increasingly dominated by large conglomerate firms.

A second direction to the study of merger conduct serves the needs of firms themselves, in particular the needs of corporate strategists. These significant players within the corporate economy require, increasingly, better information and better understanding of the merger process, whether for self-aggrandisement or self-defence.

The literature on mergers, then, serves these two perspectives, quite apart from the general and continuing interest of academic economists, and others, to explain the observed behaviour of business firms.

Even if economists, as a group, were desirous of resolving the different and sometimes contradictory explanations of merger conduct, and of producing a single, non-controversial received wisdom, the complexities and diversities of merger transactions may well produce insuperable obstacles.

First, one of the more fundamental problems in the literature concerns the confusion between explanations of *why* mergers occur, and explanations of *when* they occur. Indeed, the substantial literature which seeks to explain mergers by reference either to the cyclical conditions in the economy, or to the prevailing 'climate' in the financial and stock markets (for example, Prais 1976 and Kuehn 1975), makes capital of blurring the distinction. Mergers are events with two dimensions: motivation and timing (Scouller 1987). It may be that we can learn about trends in merger activity, periods of intense merger 'mania' for example, by studying the interaction of these two dimensions, but it might equally be the case that studies which fail to distinguish clearly between the two dimensions, in turn fail to advance the understanding of either. An understanding of why the UK economy experienced merger booms in 1968, 1972 and from the mid-1980s, may well not add significantly to our understanding of why firms engage in merger transactions in the first place.

Second, most mergers are governed by multiple objectives. Several actors are involved in the play; this is particularly the case in the contested bids which so characterise mergers in the 1980s. Quite apart from understanding why the owners of firms try to acquire other firms, or why hired managers seek to buy assets on behalf of widely dispersed and usually absent owners, reasons must be found to explain why owners, or managers, prefer to sell rather than remain independent. Further, and for the great majority of cases, merger transactions for the control of assets are conducted on behalf of shareholder-owners whose role remains a passive one. In many cases even hired managers are bypassed by the activities of middle-men, 'merger professionals'. These 'acquisition specialists' (Davidson 1985) operate in a territory that is separate from any decision that a firm might take to merge, and separate from the economic consequences of merger.

Third, most studies are premised upon an economic rationality assumption. Business conduct is assumed to be driven by clearly defined objectives. Many so-called 'motives' are proxies for real reasons, and indeed, objectives need not remain consistent over time. As a result, even the richest and most elegant multi-aspect models in economic research may not be good models of merger behaviour.

Finally, research on motives for merger is far from complete. Many motives have yet to be examined and will remain unclear as long as the available data are less than perfect or research continues to rely on case-by-case examination. Importantly, many motives lie outside the rationality assumption framework: it may be that sociopolitical explanations enhance understanding rather better than do economic-technical ones (Goldberg 1983).

3.1.2 Chapter objectives

This chapter does not seek, directly, to add to the stock of literature on mergers, but rather it seeks to explore further the nature and context of the controversy within existing work. Section 3.2 reviews the data on merger activity. Section 3.3 considers competing explanations of the motives for merger, and reviews the discussion on timing. Section 3.4 discusses the issues raised for firms and business strategy and considers the degree of confusion which prevails in the UK public policy towards mergers. Section 3.5 concludes by considering briefly the changing nature of merger within the modern corporate economy.

3.2 MERGER ACTIVITY IN THE UK ECONOMY

3.2.1 The period up to 1965

Reviews of the historical development of mergers in the United Kingdom point towards the 1960s as a watershed (Hannah 1976; Hannah and Kay 1977). Until that time mergers had accounted for a small share of the total investment spending by UK firms, even though some individual industries had become more heavily concentrated as a result.

By the end of the 1960s, however, merger transactions were generally the dominant influence on industrial structure. Newbould (1970) reported that by 1970 more than one-third of firms quoted on the London Stock Exchange in 1960 had disappeared as a result of merger transactions; Hannah (1974) shows that between 1957 and 1968, 38 per cent of all quoted firms disappeared through merger. In comparison, up to 1950 the main cause of company disappearance was liquidations (Hughes and Singh 1980).

Mergers were in evidence in earlier years. A first major peak in activity appeared around the turn of the century, when multi-firm amalgamations, mainly horizontal in nature, sought to reap the benefits of large-scale and monopoly power. The impact of limited liability legislation and the growth of stock exchange quotations acted as the main facilitators. The 1920s witnessed a second acceleration in merger activity, generating the doubling of the average size of UK firms during that decade, and a significant increase in market concentration. In general, merger transactions throughout the period 1930–60 remained at a relatively low profile.

This period up to the mid-1960s was characterised by a relative lack of attention to merger by economists. The predominance of the horizontal merger within industrial sectors growing in concentration, created little controversy in the literature. Data on mergers were desperately inadequate, but a more powerful reason was the relative ease with which merger strategy, as observed, could be explained away. Given that most of the financial constraints had been reduced by the emergence of a more malleable capital market, the creation of large enterprises, with the accompanying concentration and centralisation of capital, was explained away with the monopoly and technological rationale (see 3.3.2). Indeed, much more attention was paid in the emergent literature on large firms, to the management and coordination problems which resulted.

Hannah's study (1974) observed that less than 1 per cent of mergers in the 1920s and 1930s involved diversification of any significance, a figure which rises to 9 per cent in Utton's study (1979) of the assets acquired in all mergers between 1954 and 1965.

During a period, then, when the great majority of merger transactions involved horizontal and vertical integration, these were argued to be consistent with the traditional, *post hoc* explanations of monopoly power and economies of scale. Firms in pursuit of profit merged to increase market share or to reduce costs by operating on a larger scale. Conglomerate firms, formed by merger, were the exception and seen as special cases (Hindley 1970).

3.2.2 1965–83

In sharp contrast, this period witnessed considerable merger activity. It is during this period that merger transactions become a norm for business strategists, and in which UK public policy adopts an increasingly active role in monitoring merger movements.

The Monopolies and Mergers Act of 1965 introduced vetting and referral procedures for those merger transactions involving assets of £5 million or more, or where monopoly power, defined as one-third of the supply of a good or service, would result. These criteria were later revised respectively to £15 million, by the 1980 Competition Act, and a 25 per cent share, by the 1973 Fair Trading Act.

Table 3.1 UK merger activity 1965–88, industrial and commercial companies

Year	Number of mergers	Amount paid 1985* (£m)	Index (1963=100)†	Conglomerate (%) ‡
1965	1,000	3,295	146	7
1966	807	3,077	140	7
1967	763	4,928	216	4
1968	946	11,145	362	7
1969	846	5,794	201	9
1970	793	5,730	238	22
1971	884	4,255	164	30
1972	1,212	11,023	357	50
1973	1,205	5,197	213	22
1974	504	1,749	141	33
1975	315	806	64	19
1976	353	1,064	79	27
1977	482	1,690	117	32
1978	567	2,159	146	23
1979	534	2,763	187	28
1980	469	2,087	155	31¶
1981	452	1,447	107	27
1982	463	2,569	178	32
1983	447	2,608	150	26
1984	568	5,806	294	—
1985	474	7,091	309	—
1986	696	14,185	420	—
1987	1,125	14,563	—	—
1988‖	1,224	20,050	—	—

Source: Green Paper (1979, Annex D.), Business Monitor MQ7 Series, and adaptations from Clarke (1985) and Scouller (1987).
*Expenditure at 1985 prices from DTI.
†Index reflects the amount paid in current prices deflated by the FT 500 Ordinary Share Index.
‡Proportion of proposed mergers by value of acquired assets considered by the Mergers Panel 1966–83.
¶Figures from 1980 are affected by changes in the vetting criteria hence are not strictly comparable with earlier years.
‖Provisional.

Public policy attentions, notable in the 1978 Green Paper and the annual reports of the Director of the Office of Fair Trading, also generated a much more comprehensive and more detailed empirical analysis of merger transactions.

The data in Table 3.1 show that, albeit with some variations, since 1965 there has been considerable merger activity, both in the number of transactions and in the value of the amount paid for acquisitions. Even if we accept the view that the paucity of data from earlier years generally understates the merger phenomenon at that time, the period from the mid-1960s presents a completely different climate in the corporate economy, and a significantly distinctive context for examinations of the merger process. Mergers as both threats and opportunities become much more significant influences on business behaviour.

In addition, the period shows a change in the character of merger activity. Conglomerate diversification, for example, as Table 3.1 indicates, accounted for a significant share of those mergers reviewed by the Mergers Panel between 1970 and 1983.

3.2.3 Merger booms and the 1980s

Such was the increase in the frequency and extent of merger transactions post 1965 that commentators began to discuss the notion of 'merger-mania', with activity concentrated into defined, short bursts. As was suggested in section 3.1, explanations of merger conduct in these boom years tend to emphasise the 'when-to-merge?' rather than the 'why-merge?' factors. Within an historical perspective, what is important is that an inherent tendency to engage in merger transactions of all types is more in evidence after the mid-1960s than before.

Table 3.1 shows that in terms of the number of transactions within the industrial and commercial sectors of the economy, the years 1965, 1968 and 1972 are boom years, with a reported level of transactions above a thousand in each case. When measured by the value of the amount paid for acquisitions, the years 1968, 1972 and the period from 1984 onwards witnessed at least a three-fold increase in the amount of activity when compared to a 1963 base level.

Most recently, it is apparent that the economy is locked into the largest and most sustained boom in expenditure on merger in British history. By the third quarter of 1986, expenditure on acquisitions by UK firms had been at a high level for three consecutive years. At current prices, between 1984 and the third quarter of 1986 some £23,834 million of expenditure on acquisitions took place, almost twice the total spent during the 11 years since the previous expenditure boom of 1972. 1986 itself was a record year, with in excess of £20 billion worth of take-over bids reported in the first quarter alone.

These boom years may share common magnitudes, but should be seen as very different sets of events. Booms are exceptional periods and may be caused by exceptional circumstances. The concentration of explanations on observations of boom years may well add to controversy in the subject rather than to improved understanding.

Apart from the intensity of activity rates, the period from the mid-1980s shares little in common with earlier boom years. The period has heralded a change in the character of the merger process. Just as the rise in significance of the conglomerate merger in the 1960s brought into doubt previously held explanations based on the pursuit of monopoly power and scale economies, this changing character provides further complication for the development of satisfactory explanations of the process.

Three such changes stand out: first, as Table 3.1 indicates, the recent high levels of expenditure on mergers were not initially accompanied by historically high numbers of merger transactions, as was the case in 1968 and 1972. The merger wave of 1984–6 was characterised by relatively few very large transactions. The top five mergers in 1985 together accounted for almost 40 per cent of expenditure in that year, whilst in the first three-quarters of 1986 two mergers alone accounted for 45 per cent of recorded expenditure. Evidence for 1987, however, does show a significant increase in both the number and value of merger transactions.

Second, the 1980s have witnessed significant developments in the financing of merger transactions, changes which have important implications for the nature of the merger process itself. Mergers are paid for, in the main, by a mixture of cash, new equity and new debt. The sheer scale of the most recent transactions has made cash reserves a much more improbable source of acquisition finance. At the same time, the successful issue of new debt and equity will depend, largely, on the underlying buoyancy of the financial markets.

As Scouller (1987) shows, merger-financing relies increasingly on new equity, 64 per cent of expenditure on mergers in 1986 compared with an average of some 40 per cent since 1970. Similarly, debt-issue for 1986 was at its highest level since the 1972 boom, at 20.6 per cent of expenditure on mergers. Such observation of individual years, however, disguises longer-term trends in merger-financing.

Further, and more permanent, developments are the changes in the qualitative aspects of financing. The first of these is the rise of the merger intermediary, willing and able to develop new and creative forms of financial packages. The second is the growth of employee-shareholding, supported, again, by new types of debt. The former injects a major new variable into the merger process which links the frequency of merger more closely to the state of the financial environment, whereas the latter represents a trend towards the replacement of public equity with private debt, illustrated by the growth of so-called management 'leveraged buy-outs'. Both have implications for the firm and for public policy to which we shall return.

The third change in character concerns the sectors of the economy involved. Although manufacturing continues to dominate, there has been a marked shift towards the tertiary sector, especially in distribution and financial services. Office of Fair Trading data indicate that between 1983 and 1985, 60 per cent of all acquisition proposals were in the financial sector. In the same period, over one-half of all proposals were for diversified mergers, and UK firms became major buyers of non-UK firms. There has also been a marked growth in the purchase of whole independent companies in preference to inter-firm sales of subsidiaries, and the arrival of a distinctly modern phenomenon, that of firms purchasing, or at least bidding for, firms of greater size than themselves.

Overall, these developments may be more or less in evidence during given bursts of merger activity. Clearly, no sector of the economy, nor any particular type of firm has special significance. Merger transactions are now accepted as commonplace business practice and, as such, have transformed the industrial, commercial and financial environment. Once the tactic of the cavalier business entrepreneurs, mergers are now the territory of established and successful firms, as well as emerging and relatively small 'bidders'. No firm is immune, all firms are potential targets.

3.3 THEORIES AND EXPLANATIONS OF MERGERS

3.3.1 Sources of controversy

We can identify two approaches to merger behaviour in the theory of the firm – the traditional approach and the managerial approach.

The former approach is based on market failure. Mergers are seen as a vehicle by which firms exploit capital market imperfections in order to gain monopoly power in the product market. The tradition predicts that mergers are profitable, and that waves of mergers threaten the efficiency of markets and call for state intervention and regulation. In addition, and in contradiction, the approach also sees some virtue in 'failed' markets, if rationalisation results in a more efficient allocation of resources.

The managerial approach adopts the early work of Berle and Means (1932) by recognising managerially dominated, multi-owner firms. Managers use acquisitions to maximise the size of firms, often at the expense of the owners' wealth. Managerial firms, then, engage in merger transactions even where the marginal cost of acquisition is higher than the marginal increase in the value of the firm. Dispersed owners, as a result, are expected to earn lower than normal returns; mergers, then, should not necessarily be expected to result in enhanced profitability.

As merger transactions are so diverse in character, and given that the relative frequency of different kinds of merger changes continuously, it may not be surprising that little accord exists in either theoretical or empirical studies. Theories and explanations of merger behaviour are a heterogeneous and differentiable collection within which contradictory conclusions appear.

First, there is the difference, referred to earlier, between 'why-merge?' and 'when-to-merge?' explanations. When overlooked, this difference gives rise to the emergence of proximate causes, which may explain better the event itself rather than any underlying cause of the event. This applies equally to micro-studies of mergers in particular sectors, for example, studies of the national or international economy.

Second, whereas some studies have sought to develop uni-causal explanations, many economists have deliberately avoided the search for a general theory of mergers. As a consequence, studies of merger, like many issues in applied economics, have been greatly influenced by implicit normative assumptions. Neoclassical theory, for example, expects mergers to enhance the efficiency and profitability of firms, and as a consequence emphasises the characteristics of the firms which are predicted to be acquired. Managerial theories, the theory of Marris (1964) in particular, focus on the interests and characteristics of the acquirer (Sawyer 1985).

Third, an important division in the literature is between those explanations whose roots lie in assumptions about perfect information and environmental certainty, and those which explicitly recognise imperfections in information and the lack of certainty in the real world.

Fourth, while some studies place the merger transaction at 'centre-stage', others interpret mergers as incidental by-products, mere instruments used to achieve more fundamental objectives such as firm diversification, innovation or growth. For these, mergers may not be inevitable, but some kind of action on the part of the firm is.

Fifth, there exists a great variety of methodologies employed in the development of explanations. These give rise to large disparities in the relative feasibility of empirical testing. Explanations which emphasise defensive manoeuvring by firms, or mergers as 'fleeting opportunities' (see section 3.3.6) are difficult, if not impossible, to test within formal models susceptible to formal statistical estimation. Others, conversely, retain both the elegance and formality required to allow rigorous testing, often at the cost of limiting the scope and range of the discussion. Differences in results may also arise from the differences in techniques employed, or differences in periods examined.

Finally, there is a more subtle distinction between explanations which consider merger within the context of rational business strategy and long waves in the development of capitalist enterprise, and those which view mergers as more transitory transactions, fleeting opportunities which are seized within very short decision horizons by alert entrepreneurs. For these latter theories, the decision to merge is made on a much more speculative basis, where success, however measured, depends as much on luck as on design.

These are not mutually exclusive issues, and they appear in many different combinations throughout theoretical and empirical studies of the merger phenomenon. In many ways the literature is rich because of this variety of starting-points and approaches, but we may conclude that, as a result, controversy is as endemic as the forces at work which will maintain merger activity as a permanent feature of the corporate landscape.

With these issues in mind, we will continue by considering briefly the 'best-travelled' of the explanations for merger conduct. Section 3.3.2 considers merger for monopoly power or for economies of scale; 3.3.3 considers theories of economic disturbance; 3.3.4 examines managerial motivations; the impact of oligopoly and uncertainty is discussed in 3.3.5; a 'fleeting opportunity' approach is considered in 3.3.6; and 3.3.7 discusses issues of timing.

3.3.2 Monopoly power and technological rationale

Explanations based on the traditional, neoclassical theory of the firm are framed within the context of profit-maximisation. The incentive to merge, for whomsoever controls the firm, is provided, within that tradition, by the probability of synergistic gains. The effects of merger, then, are predicted to be 'multiplicative', where successful mergers reveal the benefits of increased market power, measured by the share of sales in the market for a given good or service, or the accruals of cost savings associated with economies of large scale. Synergistic gains imply that post-merger profitability is greater than the profit expectations had no merger taken place.

Traditional theory is designed to predict the responses of firms to changes in relative prices, and the analytical assumptions adopted of owner-entrepreneurs seeking to maximise utility in a certain environment offer the prospect of a 'general theory' of merger.

Empirical studies, however, at best, suggest the effects of merger are 'additive', and at worst they are both contradictory and inconclusive. Studies which measure potential synergistic gains by the effects on profit either examine the different characteristics of acquired and non-acquired firms (Singh 1971) or compare the performance of acquired firms with that of their acquirers (Newbould 1970; Singh 1971). The results are much influenced by the time-periods studied and the methods and definitions adopted, but, in general, they record little significant impact of mergers on profitability. Similar results are reported by Mueller (1980), from comparative studies made on the consequences of mergers across seven countries.

The evidence on scale economies indicate that such benefits may be a necessary feature of merger, but by themselves are not a sufficient justification. Indeed, studies have not identified the existence of significant economies of scale arising from merger transactions (Hughes and Singh 1980).

Where merger in pursuit of synergy might make sense for the predominant horizontal and vertical acquisitions, conglomerate diversifications which do not exhibit the more obvious monopoly power or technological rationale are more difficult to accommodate.

In addition, there are other consequences arising from observations that acquirers may not profit from acquisition. The great variety of evidence, and the lack of conclusive results are, themselves, central sources of continuing controversy. Merger transactions tend to result, almost by definition, in a net transfer of wealth from the owners of acquiring firms to the owners of the acquired. Thus satisfactory explanations, within a traditional framework, need also to consider the motives of those acquired. Again, traditional theory adheres to its economic rationality assumption. Owner-entrepreneurs, it is argued, are faced with finite lifetimes and if without heirs, are confronted with a three-cornered choice: they can recruit professional managers, who would not necessarily manage the firm in the best interests of the owners; they can dispose of the firm in a piecemeal way, which may have a negative impact on the market value of the assets; or they can sell the firm as an entity. A reasoned choice would involve a comparison between the price received with the projected value of the firm as a continuing entity incorporating a loss of owner control.

One of the more important studies was that of Gort (1969). Gort found that mergers had little to do with either monopoly power or economies of scale. His study found no significant relationship between mergers and markets dominated by a few, large firms, nor where high barriers to entry or slow rates of growth were in evidence. Similarly, he failed to find significance in the rate of change of the average size or absolute numbers of firms.

3.3.3 Economic disturbances and business cycles

Following the 'disappointing' evidence on synergy, in relation to the validity of traditional theory, and still in search of a general theory, Gort argued that mergers occur because of differences in the valuation of assets between buyers and sellers. In other words, both buyers and sellers expect to gain as a result of the merger, since they hold different expectations about future income streams and about stock market prices associated with those streams. His theory of economic disturbances argues that the differences in asset valuations, as indicated by bid and offer prices of quoted company shares, were caused by technical change, relatively high levels of security prices and rapid rates of industrial growth.

His work is significant for two reasons. First, it focuses on the relation between mergers and stock market activity, and second, it is consistent with more recent studies of conglomerate merger centred on entrepreneurial behaviour (see Hindley 1972).

There is broad agreement in most studies that there exists a close relationship between mergers and levels of stock market activity (see Nelson 1959; Maule 1968), though there is less agreement about the importance of business cycles.

It is clear that the capital market is an important proximate factor in merger movements; mergers require financing, and mergers can, for example, allow a capitalisation of expected profits which may be attractive, if in part distributed, to the market professionals who arrange and foster corporate 'marriages'. It is more probably the case, however, that stock market trends explain better the timing of mergers.

3.3.4 Managers and mergers for growth

Developments in the theory of managerial capitalism (Penrose 1959; Marris 1964) adopt an alternative, overriding business objective – that of maximising the rate of growth of the firm. Mergers are viewed as instrumental in achieving rapid firm growth rates. Such an approach is based on the argument that large firms are now controlled by professional, salaried managers with discretion over conduct. As such, firms are assumed to be run for, and on behalf of, managers who exploit their freedom from direct owner influence, and pursue goals other than profit.

Within this framework, Penrose suggests that the greatest obstacle facing a growth-seeking management team, is that management's capacity to grow by internal means alone. Merger can, in part, increase the level of the management constraint.

Two explanations of mergers are developed in this tradition. First, on the supply-side, manager-controlled firms, by usurping shareholder interests, are likely to have lower stock values, and, in consequence, offer the prospect of an above-average rate of return for an acquirer. This will increase the likelihood of being acquired, and represents a well-recognised constraint on manager conduct.

Second, on the demand-side, managers seeking fast growth are likely to place a lower valuation on potential acquisitions. Mueller (1969) suggests that a growth-maximising management will be faced with a 'boundless set' of potential acquisitions, all with prices below their present value to the management team. This increases the likelihood of mergers.

Testing these explanations is problematic as it is difficult to separate findings from exogenous factors affecting stock market valuations, and business expectations in general (see Reid 1968). Mueller concludes his study by asserting that conglomerate merger, where no obvious synergy can result, is difficult to explain by other than a growth-maximisation hypothesis.

The notion of a 'managerial' revolution is highly controversial and rests on the validity of two propositions: first that a separation of ownership from control does exist, and second, that where it does, the objectives of 'managers' and 'owners' are both different and divergent. Additionally, it relies on managers having real, unconstrained freedom to act. Campbell argues that 'these propositions have been grossly overstated and that the goal of profitability remains paramount' (Campbell 1981).

3.3.5 Uncertainty and the costs of rivalry

This set of explanations shares two common and interrelated characteristics. First is a concern to examine the relationship between mergers and changes in an uncertain environment. Second is the argument that mergers can only be fully understood in the context of large oligopolistic firms. By merger, it is argued, large firms can gain measurable commercial advantage by reducing the costs of oligopolistic rivalry in an uncertain world.

Newbould (1970) suggests that merger transactions are deliberate defensive strategies by manager-controlled firms concerned with minimising the impact of environmental uncertainty. His key source of uncertainty is the level of competition in markets, so, within given markets, increases in the numbers of mergers directly increase uncertainty for those firms not involved. Mergers will take place, according to Newbould, when the desire to merge, which is positively influenced by rising uncertainty, is accompanied by the management ability to merge, which is reduced by uncertainty. Uncertainty increases management caution, and rising numbers of merger transactions increase to cost of acquisition. Newbould's approach is useful when examining a rising rate of merger activity rather than mergers themselves.

Aaronovitch and Sawyer (1975) emphasise the cost of oligopoly rivalry. Large firms, in oligopoly markets, incur high costs, perhaps by holding excess production capacity or in development and marketing strategies. Oligopolistic interdependence increases the importance of these costs for the firm. In simple terms, these costs diminish as rivalry diminishes, and increase as environmental uncertainty increases. In common with Newbould, they see the intensification of international competition after 1945 as the major economic disturbance. This caused large firms to seek greater control over their markets through acquisitions. As the costs of rivalry impact upon the firm rather than at plant level, diversification by merger would also be expected. In their view, mergers are a natural strategy of large firms, making the recorded trend towards increased concentration and centralisation of capital inevitable.

Such theories are plausible, i.e., consistent with empirical data, given market trends in the last 40 years or so, but almost impossible to test. Newbould used business optimism among managers as a proxy for uncertainty and produced highly significant results for the period 1967–8. Aaronovitch and Sawyer found a significant relationship between the observed growth of multinational corporations together with movements in international trade and merger activity.

3.3.6 Fleeting opportunities

The explanations considered so far emphasise rational economic behaviour by merger participants, and assume such behaviour is feasible and not exceptional. In the case of Aaronovitch and Sawyer, the rationality is not of individuals but of the capitalist accumulation process itself. They fit comfortably into a vision of a corporate sector which makes plans and takes decisions, albeit in a less than certain world, over longer, rather than shorter, time horizons. Such explanations observe merger transactions as business strategies, with managers or owners making predictable, or at least explainable, choices from a range of strategic options.

An alternative view reflects an interest in mergers as 'fleeting opportunities'; opportunities which are taken up in response to a particular set of circumstances. This approach is argued to provide a greater correspondence between ideas and the results of empirical studies. In addition, this approach draws a much closer relationship between the 'why-merge?' and 'when-to-merge?' discussions.

Those who control assets, be they managers or owners, are under constant pressure to act. Taking a dynamic view of the competitive process, whether under oligopoly domination or not, suggests that firms face continuous uncertainty. This may shorten decision horizons for those firms whose market influence is insufficient to guarantee market control over time. The greater the intensity of local or international competition, for example, the greater is the pressure for the controllers of firms to act. The fear of the consequences of inactivity may be a greater motivating force than the rationale of the activity itself.

Two forms of structural pressure to act are popular in the literature (see Mueller 1980; Goldberg 1983). First, the pressure facing firms as they approach, or reach, the end of a product or process life-cycle; second, given that managerially dominated firms prefer to retain earnings over time, an accumulation of excess undistributed profits may provide irresistible pressure for action.

An opportunity to merge may appear to offer an immediate response to such structural pressures; mergers can provide, instantly, new product lines, additional managerial experience or, simply, more information. Regarding accumulated earnings, mergers are investment opportunities. These will be 'fleeting' opportunities as their availability is rarely restricted to a single buyer or seller, and as cash-rich firms, or ones which are performing below par, they are themselves vulnerable to acquisition.

More significantly, a systematic and time-consuming planning of acquisitions, or of the willingness to sell, may not be feasible as this may 'telegraph' intentions to the market and thereby change the dimensions of the opportunity by, for example, driving up the acquisition prices or inviting competitive bidders to the scene. This approach, then, draws heavily on the others, but stresses rapid and imperfectly-informed behaviour. As a result, it detaches merger behaviour from singular and clearly defined business objectives and highlights the vulnerability of merger transactions to 'bandwagoning' behaviour in which mergers become the 'flavour of the month'. Thus, mergers may be purely or partially speculative responses to general structural pressures, and reading implications into the measurements of the result of such mergers becomes relatively meaningless.

3.3.7 Timing: 'when-to-merge' explanations

Explanations of why firms merge when they do are less controversial. Studies of the timing of merger transactions are, however, limited in their contribution to general explanations of mergers. First, by definition, they eschew direct examination of the underlying business motivation by assuming that firms will merge whenever they are able; as a result, second, they concentrate on those conditions under which firms are more, or less, able to engage in merger transactions.

Most of these studies are extensions of the economic rationality, utility-maximising approaches, even though they appear as new and competing explanations. They differ from other explanations in two respects; these explanations of mergers and merger frequency are characterised by an attentiveness to the external environment in which firms operate, and they use as their base observations of merger activity, and build explanations around these events.

Inevitably, in the context of recent UK experience, there is much interest in the bursts of activity recorded in 1968, 1972 and from 1984 (see Prais 1981; Scouller 1987). Three interrelated factors lie at the centre of analysis; the prevailing macroeconomic conditions (essentially business optimism), government policy and the financial environment of firms.

Studies of 1968 and 1972 suggest that the frequency and extent of merger activity is strongly related to movements in the business cycle. Similarly the boom of 1984–6 is associated with recovery from the deep recession of the late 1970s. In these cases, evidence indicates that the business optimism associated with rapid growth rates creates an environment in which firms appear more likely and able to engage in merger transactions. Additionally, when capacity utilisation in the economy is increasing, again associated with fast growth rates, firms seeking fast growth in their own capacity may look to merger. Finally, rising profits improve the ability of firms to finance acquisitions, and associated increases in share values improve the availability of debt finance.

Discretionary government policy towards competition and taxation is also cited as a strong influence on merger behaviour. UK merger law has been fairly benign, especially with regard to conglomerate mergers, and the great majority of merger transactions proceed unhindered by government. In 1986, of the three hundred cases reviewed, a mere thirteen were referred to the Monopolies and Mergers Commission, of which, it is estimated, one in three will be cleared (Borrie 1987).

Similarly, changes in taxation laws, especially those which reduce incentives for investment, may have encouraged the purchase of existing assets in the form of existing companies, rather than new capital formation. Prais (1981) argues that the Corporation Tax changes in 1965 encouraged the use of profits to buy firms rather than to distribute profits. It may be, as we have indicated already, that managers did not require much encouragement.

Studies of the financial environment of firms, however, argue this to be the key determinant of mergers, at least of their timing, in the United Kingdom. Institutional factors dominate Prais's study of large firm evolution (Prais 1976). First, Prais observed that UK banking practices encourage large firms to replace equity with debt, and to use the debt for acquisitions. This willingness of the banking sector to provide debt for merger transactions appears as a key variable. It is combined, in most recent experience, with an increased inventiveness on the part of financial institutions, to provide the massive funding required for the contemporary large and hostile bids.

At the same time, successful firms, with relatively highly valued shares, appear quite willing to accept the debt burden, even in years of relatively high real interest rates, to acquire less successful firms whose market values may be low compared to asset value, particularly replacement asset value.

Although these observations are consistent, to an extent, with the 'mergers for growth' and 'the costs of rivalry' analyses, they imply that the real motives for merger are concerned with consolidatory strategies of firms. As such, the underlying considerations by firms appear to be those concerned with general industrial restructuring. The ability of firms to engage in acquisition strategies is a function of institutional perceptions, viz., stock market reputations. These are less predictable and highly volatile, and determined by a complex combination of factors.

Studies of timing emphasise, above all else, the role of managers and merger intermediaries and provide a confusion of implications for public policy towards the merger phenomenon.

3.4 THE POLICY DILEMMA

3.4.1 Public policy issues

Public policy towards merger in the United Kingdom is controversial in its own right. This is partly as a result of the competing views about the role of government in the economy as a whole, and partly the consequence of the lack of a clear understanding of the causes and effects of merger.

Merger policy is inseparable from government's general concern about dominant firms, both in the context of individual industrial sectors and within the economy as a whole. As such, merger is an important issue for both competition policy and industrial policy.

Within competition policy, government attention is focused on static efficiency, and the market failure which results from the exercise of excessive market power by large combinations of assets. Merger transactions lead, with certainty, to the acquisition of economic power and the potential of monopoly power abuse. Competition policy, then, is reactive to market failure, and is predicated upon the assumption that the protection of competition will ensure that markets work efficiently.

Industrial policy, in contrast, has different objectives, and is concerned primarily with dynamic efficiency, or the ability of the economy to produce output efficiently and competitively. In this context, mergers offer the possibility of real resource savings when more efficient combinations of assets might yield the benefits of lower costs or of greater innovation in products and production technologies. Larger firms, resulting from mergers, may be more able to initiate and apply research and development, more likely to invest in new capital formation, or be better equipped to compete in international markets.

Industrial policy, then, may be proactive, with government concerned, *inter alia*, to promote the most appropriate industrial structure for international competition, or to generate desired regional distributions of industry.

At a theoretical level, *a priori*, a static efficiency perspective may favour an anti-merger stance by government, whereas a concern for dynamic efficiency may actively encourage industrial restructuring by merger. This potential conflict in policy objectives is sharpened by the lack of a clear explanation of mergers, and by the absence of clear evidence of their effects.

A second issue for policy concerns the choice between a structuralist and a behavioural approach within either a competitive or an industrial policy framework. A structural policy can prevent or promote the emergence of a dominant firm; prevent the abuse of monopoly power, or promote the efficiency gains associated with large scale. A pragmatic merger policy in this vein would seek to assess the costs and benefits of merger on a case-by-case basis.

Alternatively, a behavioural policy approach would aim to modify firms' conduct through continuous regulation. Thus, for example, a merger policy may not adopt an anti-trust stance, or require the breakup of large firms by divestment, but would ensure through price and profit-rate regulation that any efficiency gains resulting from increased concentration were realised by the economy at large.

3.4.2 Policy conclusions

The last official review of merger policy in the United Kingdom (1978) reflected on the controversial nature of merger literature and evidence and concluded that the most appropriate policy response was to take a neutral stance, which assumed no preconceptions about the desirability, or otherwise, of merger. In reality the stance adopted is both neutral and confused. It is neutral in the sense that, philosophically, the policy is not premised on the assumption that a competitive economy is necessarily desirable. It is confused because of the multiplicity of approaches adopted.

Both neutrality and confusion result from the complexity of the merger process discussed above, and because of the great variety of merger with which policy has to deal. The pragmatic assumption that there may be both costs and benefits associated with merger is, in part, the consequence of the lack of conclusive or clear explanations and evidence. It also reflects the general uncertainty and non-predictability of merger conduct which is central to the changing characteristics of merger transactions.

The absence of a satisfactory explanation has led to the development and implementation of an administratively popular, though unwieldy, case-by-case approach, driven most recently by the single criterion of competition. Within this it is recognised that mergers can both enhance and frustrate competition, and that the potential conflict between competition and industrial policy may be reduced when competition is defined broadly to include potential and real rivalry from overseas (see Borrie 1987).

Current UK policy also acknowledges that economic power may result from merger irrespective of the consequences for the degree of monopoly, though it remains relatively unclear about the growth of conglomeracy and the broader issues of the acquisition of economic power in general.

What is clear is that the long period of relatively benign merger policy has resulted, by the mid-1980s, in heavily concentrated industrial, commercial and financial sectors of the economy.

3.4.3 Current policy debates

The important conclusion from the lack of clear explanations of merger transactions, together with the realisation that current policy has little to say about conglomerates, may be that a fundamental change in government policy is required.

First, policy may cope better with mergers were the onus of proof shifted so that the merging firm or the potential acquirer was required to demonstrate the potential and expected benefits, and provide satisfactory responses to all suggestions of potential detriments.

Second, given existing levels of industrial concentration, a policy of required divestment might be introduced by which large and powerful firms would be required to shed particular subsidiaries or interests. This would, of course, have the effect of increasing the supply of possible acquisitions.

Such approaches may reduce the problems for policymakers of competing and contradictory analyses of merger transactions, as they would be less dependent on an *a priori* understanding of the causes and effects of mergers.

3.5 CONCLUSIONS

3.5.1 The development of ideas

Mergers are events which require explanation because of the considerable and varied effects they impose on firms, industries and the economy as a whole. They are events, however, which defy simple explanation, whether such explanations are designed to serve the business strategist or public policy.

No general agreed theory of mergers is in evidence. Instead, there exists a series of partial, often contradictory theories which claim to explain particular types of merger transactions involving, perhaps, individual firms, and employing different philosophical and methodological frameworks. Neoclassical theory of the firm concentrates on the rational pursuit of profit, whereas the managerial tradition emphasises the priority of growth and security. The 'cost-of-rivalry' approach concerns itself with the rationality of the capital accumulation process, rather than the role of individual agents. Some examine buyers, some sellers, whereas, as we have seen, others record the impact of environmental factors.

At one level, however, the search for satisfactory explanations has developed more than a mere stock of literature. Traditional theory, based on the economic rationality assumption, within the framework of utility maximisation, generates plausible predictions that horizontal and vertical integration follows the pursuit of monopoly or technological advantage.

Conglomeracy is explained away by the rational search for synergy and replacement markets given finite product life-cycles. Where multiplicative gains are not in evidence, and where managerial objectives are assumed to replace those of owners, merger is explained away as consistent with growth maximisation.

These approaches to the merger phenomenon have been further developed to accommodate alternative empirical observation. The relation between mergers and financial markets is recorded, and the role of 'acquisition specialists' noted. Similarly, domestic merger activity is related to the intensification of international competition over the past forty years.

In general terms there is today a richer understanding of the impact of global uncertainty and the consequences this has for large and vulnerable oligopolies. The 'cost-of-rivalry' approach recognises the reality of modern economies dominated by large diversified corporations who seek greater security through increased control over their environments. This implies that mergers are an inevitability in modern corporate economies, and may suggest that issues of timing, the when-to-merge explanations, have greater application for business strategists and public policy.

3.5.2 Unanswered questions

The changing character of merger transactions, over time, presents particular problems for the development of satisfactory explanations. Acquisitions have further increased the size and diversity of already large firms. Vertically integrated, multidivisionalised firms have replaced owner-entrepreneurs. Investment decisions are increasingly subject to managerial, rather than capital market, control. Decision-making is more heavily bureaucratised and centralised, and geographical centres of control over economic resources have shifted. These represent new building blocks for theories of business conduct.

Merger transactions themselves have become accepted and expected business practice. At one time acquisition was an exceptional tactic, cautiously used, whereas within contemporary corporate economies take-over is an ever-present threat and opportunity from which no firm is immune.

Mega-mergers and hostile, contested bids dominate the current merger scene. Their prevalence affects the merger process, as defence and consolidation become an important strategy for managers and owners alike. Such mergers are developing managerial insights; influencing corporate behaviour. Similarly, divestments are an increasing proportion of mergers, indicating, perhaps, a desire on the part of corporate controllers for more manageable operating units.

As the merger transaction becomes more complex, so the search for explanation becomes more difficult.

FURTHER READING

Two of the more substantial and comprehensive reviews of merger behaviour, in an international context, are to be found in Mueller (1980) and Goldberg (1983). Cowling *et al.* (1980) provides a thorough investigation of the impact of mergers upon efficiency and monopoly power in the United Kingdom. For a discussion of mergers and business strategy, see Sutton (1980). Aaronovitch and Sawyer (1975) offer a compelling study of the extent, causes and consequences of merger activity, relating it to the growth of concentration in the United Kingdom. For a revealing discussion of mega-mergers in the United States, see Davidson (1985), and for a topical account of the 1980s merger boom in the United Kingdom see Scouller (1987). Recent developments in the economic analysis of firms are ably discussed in Clarke and McGuinness (1987). Finally, for a succinct review of both theory and evidence see Sawyer (1985).

4 · THE IMPACT OF MULTINATIONAL ENTERPRISES

A blessing in disguise?

GERRY STEWART

4.1 INTRODUCTION

A multinational enterprise may be simply defined as an 'enterprise which owns and controls income-gathering assets in more than one country' (Dunning 1971:16). MNEs engage in foreign direct investment (FDI) – that is, investment in enterprises overseas – which involves establishing a productive capacity (via a subsidiary or branch plant) in at least one foreign country. MNEs are, therefore, distinguishable from firms which either trade abroad by exporting domestically produced output or engage in portfolio investment – buying shares in overseas companies with the aim of participating in ownership (and profits), but not control.

Few issues have generated more controversy in recent years than the debate surrounding the impact of MNEs. Although there exists a widespread consensus that MNEs act as 'engines of structural change' and transmit change across national boundaries, opinion remains sharply divided on the geographical distribution of the resulting costs and benefits. With MNEs accounting for a larger share of the United Kingdom's gross national product, employment and balance of payments than in comparable western economies, the debate is of special significance to UK policy-makers.

This chapter examines this debate in the light of the methodological issues raised in Chapter 1. Section 4.2 provides the descriptive background, charting the growing importance of MNEs in the UK economy. Section 4.3 then reviews the major theoretical contributions to our understanding of MNEs and FDI and finally section 4.4 uses these perspectives to try and assess the impact of MNEs on the UK economy.

4.2 MULTINATIONAL ENTERPRISES AND THE UK ECONOMY

MNEs vary considerably in size and in the spread of their operations. Many operate in only a small number of countries and in terms of their share of total world FDI such firms are relatively unimportant. The dominant forces in the world capitalist economy are the truly *multi*nationals whose activities span upwards of 20 countries. Such giant firms, less than 5 per cent of all MNEs, account for at least three-quarters of all foreign affiliates and about the same percentage of all FDI.

FDI has grown rapidly since 1945 both in absolute terms and in relation to other economic aggregates, such as the visible trade, domestic investment and real output of the world's most developed capitalist economies (OECD 1981). Furthermore, although the rate of trade and output growth slowed in the late 1970s as the capitalist world economy fell into recession, FDI remained more buoyant than domestic investment, suggesting that MNEs have been better able to adjust to the less favourable economic circumstances and that they are becoming increasingly important forces in changing the shape of world economic development.

In terms of its share of global FDI, the United Kingdom is a major source country, never occupying a position lower than second in the world ranking (after the United States). In simple numerical terms, it is currently estimated that about 1,500 parent companies in the United Kingdom manage between them some 10,000 subsidiaries and branch plants overseas. There is a strong correlation between size and the extent of multinationality. Some 60 per cent of UK MNEs have overseas assets of less than £1 million, which represents a mere 1.7 per cent of total overseas assets. Conversely, just thirteen MNEs account for 35 per cent of total UK FDI. Similarly, the number of overseas affiliates varies systematically with size. The largest MNEs control an average of 107 subsidiaries and branch plants, the smallest an average of less than two (Dicken 1986).

The United Kingdom is also a major recipient of FDI, competing with the United States and Canada for the second position in the world ranking of most important host country. Again, activity in the United Kingdom is concentrated in relatively few foreign MNEs. The largest one hundred foreign MNEs account for about 60 per cent of the total inward investment.

Thus, 'the UK is, par excellence, a two-way international investor' (Dunning 1985:13). Generally speaking, UK MNEs invest more overseas than foreign MNEs invest in the United Kingdom. The ratio of outward to inward direct investment has, however, been declining sharply since the era of UK dominance of world industrial activity and trade. It fell from 33 : 1 in 1914 to 15 : 1 in 1938, reaching 8 : 1 by 1971 (Dunning 1985). Table 4.1 shows the current position.

Table 4.1 Net direct investment overseas 1980–6 (£m)

Year	Outward	Inward	Ratio O/I
1980	4,924	2,541	1.94
1981	6,093	2,932	2.07
1982	4,109	3,027	1.35
1983	5,402	3,386	1.59
1985	8,828	4,421	1.99
1986	10,895	5,275	2.06

Source: British Business.
Note: 1984 data are excluded here because there was net inward disinvestment in that year and for the purposes of calculating ratios is distorting.

In terms of its geographical distribution, *outward* FDI from the United Kingdom historically (pre-1914) reflected both the United Kingdom's industrial dominance and its imperial position. The inter-war depression and the increasingly protectionist policies of the major industrialised economies, however, forced UK firms to concentrate investment in the more receptive countries of the empire. The latter continued to be the main destination for UK FDI well into the post-war period, such that by 1962 over 70 per cent of UK direct investment stocks was located in the Commonwealth, much of it in the so-called 'white dominions' of South Africa, Canada, Australia and New Zealand, with only 12 per cent and 9 per cent respectively in Europe and the United States (see Fig. 4.1 (a)).

Figure 4.1 (a) and (b) shows the changing pattern of outward FDI since the early 1960s. The Commonwealth and South Africa have continued to receive a sizeable proportion of UK FDI, but a fundamental reorientation has occurred as UK firms increasingly sought to build, develop or protect their market positions within other advanced economies. By the early 1980s, the relative share of UK investment in the Commonwealth had declined significantly. Instead, European Community (EC) countries (with a 21 per cent share) and the United States (with 28 per cent) were becoming the main hosts to UK MNEs.

The EC assumed greater importance for UK MNEs, firstly when the United Kingdom attempted to join in the 1960s and later in the immediate aftermath of entry in 1973. In the first eighteen months of membership, eight hundred new affiliates were created. In contrast, the United States has always been an important destination for UK MNEs, but its attractiveness increased in the 1980s. This was due to the cheapness of dollar-denominated assets (the dollar was very weak 1980–2 and since 1985), the faster rate of growth of the US economy and the domestic restructuring by US companies which allowed UK companies to acquire an increasing stake in existing US industry (DTI 1986).

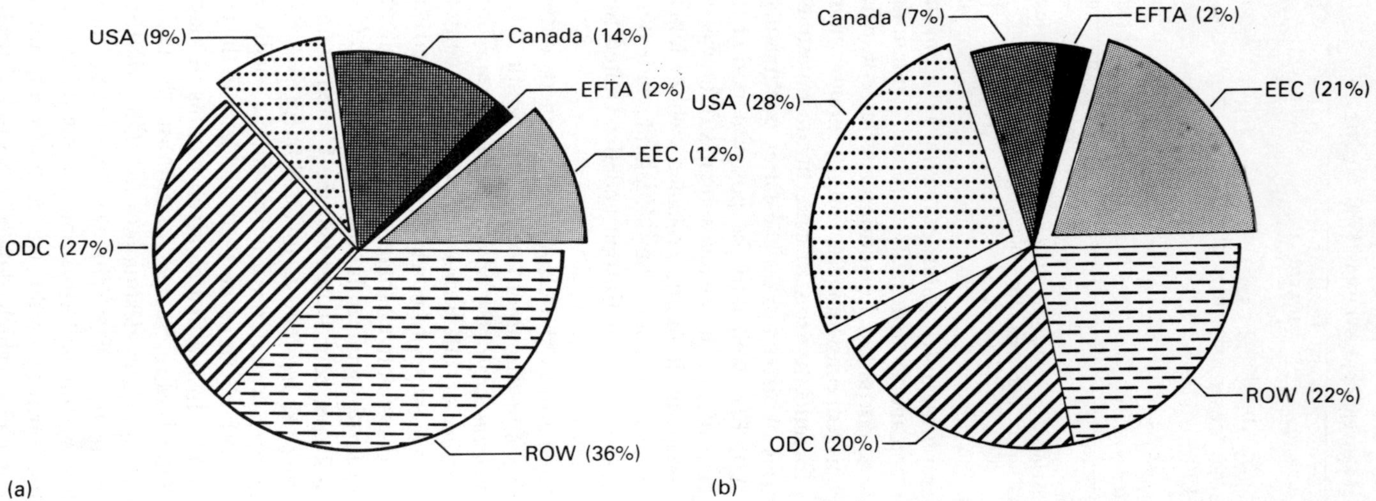

Note: Denmark, Irish Republic, Greece, Portugal are in EEC in all years.

Fig. 4.1 (a)UK outward direct investment stock by main area 1962. (b)UK outward direct investment stock by main area 1981. *Source: British Business*, 3 July 1987, pp. 35–9.

Figure 4.2 (a) and (b) shows that the United States is also by far the most important source of inward FDI. In 1962, US-owned MNEs were responsible for nearly two-thirds of the total stock of FDI in the United Kingdom. The United Kingdom is attractive to United States MNEs because it provides an environment with similar language, legal and commercial structures; the United Kingdom is also an important market in its own right and offers a gateway to the Commonwealth and latterly the EC. The United Kingdom has thus accounted for a disproportionate share – over half in many years – of US FDI in Europe during the post-war period.

Although the United States remains the dominant source of inward investment, with well over half of the total stock of inward FDI, its share of total inward FDI has declined in recent years as EC companies have increased their presence in the United Kingdom. Also largely as a consequence of EC entry and the fear that other member countries would erect barriers to their exports, the Japanese have begun a wave of FDI in Europe with the United Kingdom receiving the highest single share (Rapoport 1986; de Jonquieres 1987). The Japanese are now being followed by a number of MNEs from other smaller, though rapidly developing countries, of the Far East.

The sectoral composition of outward FDI has historically reflected its geographical destinations. In the earlier years when the colonies accounted for a relatively high proportion of total FDI, the emphasis was on services and the extraction of minerals and raw materials. Manufacturing, as a proportion of the total, only began to increase when much of the services investment, especially in transport and public utilities, was nationalised by newly-independent countries.

As the destination of outward FDI became increasingly European and American, so manufacturing rose to pre-eminence. Between 1962 and 1978 outward FDI by UK manufacturing firms grew at twice the rate of such investment by non-manufacturing MNEs (Dicken 1986). More recently, however, there has been a shift away from manufacturing back towards investment in the service sector (see Table 4.2).

As far as inward FDI is concerned, manufacturing has traditionally been the most important sector. Nevertheless, as Table 4.2 shows, its importance has also declined in recent years. This is partly due to the rapid investment in North Sea oil in the mid-1970s (the effect of which is not fully recorded in Table 4.2) and, more recently, the sharp rise of FDI in the financial sector, particularly by US and Japanese MNEs (DTI 1986).

Despite the fact that the flow of FDI in the primary and service sectors has increased in importance, manufacturing remains the largest and most important sector for outward FDI, though less so in recent years for inward FDI. There is, however, an important difference in the kinds of

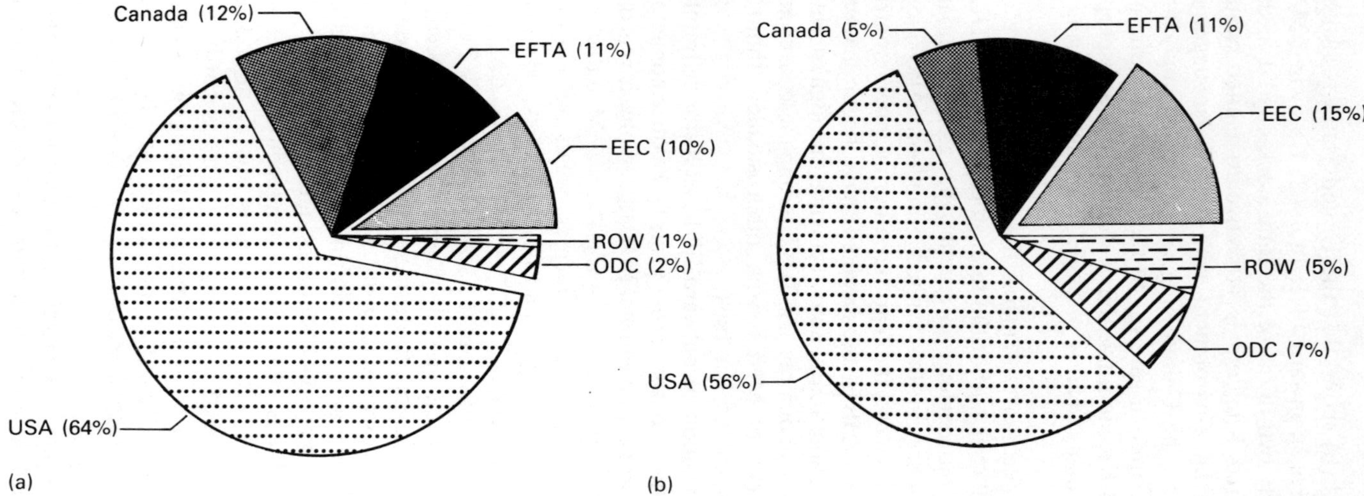

Fig. 4.2 (a)UK inward direct investment stock by main area 1962. (b)UK inward direct investment stock by main area 1981.

Table 4.2 Net outward and inward FDI in manufacturing and non-manufacturing

Year*	Outward (£m)			Inward (£m)		
	Manuf.	Non-manuf.	Manuf.(%)	Manuf.	Non-manuf.	Manuf.(%)
1980	1,426.9	1,963.8	42.08	1,472.6	1,068.3	57.95
1981	2,646.8	2,024.4	56.66	265.2	714.5	27.06
1982	1,579.1	542.7	74.42	194.9	942.3	17.13
1983	2,126.4	1,333.7	61.45	999.3	1,064.1	48.42
1984	2,100.3	3,828.2	35.42	1,056.0	−1.301.7	†
1985	2,984.1	6,610.1	32.17	952.9	3.377.9	22.00

Source: *British Business*, 3 July 1987, pp. 35–9.
*Figures for 1980–3 exclude oil companies.
†Data are excluded here because there was net inward disinvestment in that year and for the purposes of calculating percentages is distorting.

manufacturing in which UK MNEs and foreign MNEs invest. For example, only two industrial sectors, 'food, drink and tobacco' and 'chemicals' account for over half of all UK outward FDI, whereas inward investment by foreign MNEs is much more widely dispersed. Furthermore, if manufacturing is divided into 'high, intermediate and low' technology sectors, the United Kingdom has tended to invest overseas in the last while playing host to the first (Dunning 1985). This may have important implications for the impact of inward and outward FDI on the UK economy.

4.3 THEORIES OF MULTINATIONAL ENTERPRISE

Having charted the growth and changing nature of MNEs in the context of the UK economy, section 4.4 attempts to evaluate the impact which inward and outward FDI has had. Central to this analysis is the nature of the theoretical perspective adopted and this section therefore outlines the two most popular theories of MNE behaviour.

4.3.1 Neoclassical theory

This perspective adopts the broad framework of traditional micro-economics and combines elements of the theory of the firm, capital theory, location theory and international trade theory. It seeks to identify the conditions necessary for successful FDI, starting from the presumption that profit-maximising firms in perfectly competitive market situations can hold competitive advantages only temporarily, since in the longer term they would be competed away. Once this has happened, because MNEs incur 'distance' costs – cultural, commercial, legal and language disadvantages not suffered by domestic competitors – they would then be at a competitive disadvantage and be forced out of the market. It follows that FDI must be a product of market imperfections, which are a source of advantage to MNEs, enabling them to more than compensate for 'distance' costs.

Three sets of advantages are important to the firm considering FDI. The first concerns the range of assets or competitive strengths that are unique to the firm itself and which can be transferred across national boundaries. These 'ownership-specific' advantages include size and the scale advantages associated with access to capital, research and development (R & D) facilities and the possession of patents and managerial skills.

The possession of such mobile resources does not, of itself, lead to FDI since they could just as easily be exploited from a home base by exporting finished products embodying them. MNEs' preference for overseas production suggests that the advantages are more profitably exploited by combining them with a second set of 'location-specific' advantages. These are immobile and unique to a particular location, but available to all firms producing in that location. They include natural resources, labour of a specific kind, particular market and industrial structures and host government policies with regard to, *inter alia*, taxes, subsidies and import controls.

Even this combination is insufficient to justify FDI. A licensing agreement between a foreign firm possessing the ownership advantages and an indigenous firm able to exploit the locational advantages would be a suitable alternative. To explain the preference for FDI therefore, a third source of advantages is introduced via the concept of 'internalisation'. This refers to the practice whereby a firm brings under its own ownership and control (i.e., internalises) a range of transactions which would otherwise take place in less efficient and more uncertain external markets. Internalisation is advantageous to the extent that it reduces the cost of these transactions, ensures a more regular supply of primary and intermediate products at prices dictated by the firms' internal mechanisms, reduce risks (e.g., that the licensee may eventually set up in competition with the licensor), avoids arbitrary government policies (on imports for example) and helps to create entry barriers.

The above factors have been used to explain the changing pattern of FDI in the United Kingdom. For example, foreign MNEs are said to possess ownership advantages over their UK counterparts in the production of high-technology goods which they then exploit from a UK base. Evidence for this is two-fold. First, a high proportion of UK imports consist of high-technology goods (Panic and Joyce 1980), thereby demonstrating foreign firms' comparative ownership advantages in the production and sale of such goods. Second, the aforementioned heavy foreign participation in the more technology-intensive sectors of UK manufacturing indicates that some of these firms may also find it profitable to combine their ownership advantages with the locational advantages of a UK production base and internalise their operations by producing in the United Kingdom.

4.3.2 Marxist theory

An alternative and conflicting perspective on the nature of the MNE emerges from a more radical school of thought. Basically Marxist in nature, this approach advocates a different level of analysis from the aforementioned. Whereas the traditional, neoclassical approach views the capitalist system as a function of the aggregated behaviour of individual firms with given characteristics, which make decisions on production, trade and investment according to the given characteristics of countries, Marxists argue that the capitalist system acts as a coercion upon firms. Corporate behaviour, it is claimed, is determined by the necessities of ensuring survival within the constraints of that system. The most appropriate level of analysis of MNEs and the growth of international production, therefore, is that of the capitalist system as a whole.

Briefly, the dynamics of capitalist development are such that individual capitalists, competing in the search for greater profits, are compelled to accumulate more and more capital and to continually lower production costs by using more advanced and efficient techniques, by achieving economies of scale and generally by intensifying and increasing their control over the labour process. A number of important consequences follow. First, there is a tendency for capital to become concentrated in fewer hands as the more efficient firms survive and prosper and the less efficient capitulate. Second, as the forces of production develop, restructuring takes place both between and within industrial sectors and within individual firms. Third, firms develop a flexibility and mobility both industrially and internationally in order to respond to changes (however temporary) in relative profit rates between sectors and locations. Global flexibility also serves to weaken worker resistance to the restructuring of production and the increasing managerial control over the labour process which such restructuring facilitates.

From this perspective, MNEs are the inevitable consequence of world capitalist development. They emerge as the most dominant force of production within the capitalist system and are seen to dominate and exploit their hosts (especially less-developed countries) and to create a process whereby the latter are dependent upon them for income, employment and technological development (Hymer 1972). In this, they are openly encouraged and supported by their own governments which, in their attempt to maintain economic prosperity at home (by ensuring access to foreign supplies of raw materials, for example), are pressurised into preserving an international trading and investment system which facilitates MNE expansion. On occasions, the state itself may actually become the MNE. UK governments, for example, have been majority shareholders in British Petroleum and Italian state-owned oil MNEs. ENI and IRI rank fourteenth and seventeenth respectively in the list of the world's largest 100 industrial companies (Fortune 1985). Hence, MNEs are viewed as the modern agents of imperialism. No longer is it necessary for large powerful countries to dominate their smaller weaker neighbours by political and military means. This can now be achieved by the economic expansion of FDI.

The empirical validity of both the neoclassical and the Marxist perspectives is difficult to assess. Undoubtedly, evidence exists of increasing concentration and centralisation of capital, much of it by acquisition (e.g., see Young and Hood 1980; DTI 1986; Atkins 1988), as does evidence of locational flexibility (Hood *et al.* 1982). Similarly, case study evidence on individual MNEs and their treatment of host governments, including that of ITT, Lonrho, Chrysler (UK), Lockheed and the 'seven sisters' oil companies (Hood and Young 1979) is suggestive of dependency and domination. And British firms have been 'accused' of preferring FDI in imperial and semi-protected markets to embarking on a path of confrontation with their workforces over large-scale restructuring of industry (Kilpatrick and Lawson 1986).

Prima facie, such 'evidence' appears supportive of the Marxist perspective. There are, however, problems in so concluding. The evidence is not, for example, inconsistent with the neoclassical perspective that firms behave according to a calculus of ownership and locational advantages. Nor is there any necessary causal relationship involved in the finding that foreign participation and concentration are correlated (Fishwick 1982). Similarly, the case study evidence cited above is not proof of the existence of imperialism nor that MNEs are the agents of such. In all the above cases, there exists a difficulty in separating cause and effect.

As explained in Chapter 1 (section 1.7.3), however, the Marxist approach is not one which necessitates an association of occurrence between observable variables. Rather, the need is for the establishment of the underlying connections between the structure and mechanisms which generate both observable and unobservable phenomena. The Marxist perspective is, therefore, important in that it takes us away from a narrow focus on purely economic relationships and on the specification of such in market terms with their implicit assumptions of harmony and interest, rather than the social relations that underpin them. It assesses MNE activity in political and social as well as in 'economic' terms. Furthermore, by focusing on dominance, exploitation and dependency, it raises issues which must be taken into account in any comprehensive assessment of the impact of FDI.

4.4 THE IMPACT OF MULTINATIONAL ENTERPRISES ON THE UNITED KINGDOM

Measuring and evaluating the impact of MNEs is extremely complex. Using such measurements to test the varying hypotheses and theories of MNEs is even more problematic. Two major difficulties militate against any precise assessment of the costs and benefits involved. First, there is the difficulty of identifying the most appropriate criteria for assessing the contribution FDI makes to an economy. Such criteria may vary between countries, within a single country over time and between different sectors within one country at any given point in time. Thus, any one or a combination of economic, social or sovereignty factors may constitute a valid set of criteria for assessment purposes. Needless to say, the differing perspectives disagree on the most 'appropriate' set of criteria. The Marxist approach favours an examination of the impact on classes and on power relations, whereas the traditional, neoclassical approach, adopting a unitary frame of reference, prefers an examination of FDI on the economy as a whole.

Second, even assuming an agreed set of criteria, there is the 'counterfactual problem' of evaluating the effects of FDI net of the effects that would have occurred had the resources used by the investing companies been differently employed. (To what extent would indigenous firms have made better use of the resources allocated to incoming MNEs? Would an export-led strategy have been preferable to outward FDI?) Undoubtedly, such methodological difficulties serve to heighten the controversy over the impact of FDI. In what follows, analysis is restricted to a consideration of the short-run effects of FDI on selected aspects of the UK economy, namely the balance of payments, employment, technological development and industrial relations.

4.4.1 Balance of payments effects

The neoclassical perspective tends to assess the impact of FDI on the balance of payments within the context of international trade theory. To the extent that MNEs combine resources across national boundaries to produce more efficiently, there are potential gains to be shared between the MNE itself, source and host countries. If an MNE makes a net positive contribution to the balance of payments, which is greater than that of uni-national firms, they are therefore judged to benefit the country concerned.

The Marxist perspective focuses on exploitation by MNEs, as they move funds around the world (by profit repatriation, excessive payment of royalties and management fees, and 'transfer pricing') for currency speculation and profit declaration purposes, thereby depriving both source and host countries of revenues. Exploitation also occurs when MNEs employ low-wage labour, primarily in less-developed countries but also in the United Kingdom itself (Fine and Harris 1985). Emphasis is less on the existence of a short-term net positive contribution to the balance of payments and more on the longer-term effects of MNE activity and the distribution of the gains from such.

As aforementioned, the validity of the Marxist perspective is difficult to test, partly because the available empirical 'evidence' in this case focuses mostly on the relationship between MNEs and less-developed countries. That which exists for the United Kingdom is almost wholly conducive to an analysis only of the neoclassical approach and its value is seriously questioned by Marxists, arguing that the statistics disguise the 'real' effects of FDI. This should be kept in mind in any overall assessment of the impact of MNEs on the UK economy.

The balance of payments effects of inward and outward FDI can be separated into three main categories. First, and most straightforward, there is a 'capital account' effect, namely the net effect of inward and outward capital flows to finance direct investment. Second, there is an 'invisibles' effect, which is the net effect on current account of interest, profits and dividends paid by UK and foreign affiliates to their parent companies. As shown in Table 4.1, outward flows have always exceeded inward flows such that the net effect on capital account is generally unfavourable for the United Kingdom. This, it is argued, is partly offset by the favourable current account effect, which reflects the fact that UK earnings from overseas investment exceeds those of foreign firms' repatriation of funds to their parents (Stopford and Turner 1986).

The most recent outward capital flows and invisible earnings from profits, interest and dividends of UK firms and those of foreign firms operating in the United Kingdom are given in Table 4.3. In fact the table shows that the net effect on current account from invisible FDI-related earnings is also negative. Taken together, the cumulative net effect from both flows is a massive deficit of £10.5 billion for the period 1980–5. There are, however, other invisible items which must also be taken into account, for example, royalty payments and payments for management services and the branch plants' share of head office expenses. Stopford and Turner (1986) argue that these provide a significant offset to the negative flows highlighted in Table 4.3.

Third, there is the 'trade effect' – the net effect of flows of exports and imports of goods and services which are a direct or indirect result of FDI. This is much more difficult to quantify. It necessitates an estimation

Table 4.3 Financing effects of outward and inward FDI, 1980–5 (£m)

	1980	1981	1982	1983	1984	1985
Net capital outflow*	−1,757	−2,639	−423	−1,238	−1,043	−4,025
Interest, profits, dividends received	+1,294	+1,514	+1,272	+1,790	+2,839	+3,008
Total out	−457	−1,125	+849	+552	+1,796	−1,016
Net capital inflow*	+1,851	+341	+370	+1,016	−2,590	+596
Interest, profits, dividends† paid out	−1,183	−1,322	−1,314	−1,261	−3,926	−3,664
Total in	+668	−981	−943	−244	−6,516	−3,068
Net balance	+211	−2,106	−94	+308	−4,729	−4,084

Source: British Business, 3 July 1987, pp. 35–9.
*Figures for 1980–3 exclude oil companies.Total investment less unremitted profits; includes equity and loan capital.
†Dividends remitted abroad, branch profits (assumed all remitted home), and interest paid on inter-company debt; includes associated companies.

of the extent to which outward FDI stimulates or replaces exports (or encourages imports) and whether inward FDI stimulates or replaces imports (or generates exports) to a greater extent than would have been achieved by British firms operating from a purely domestic production base.

Much of the available evidence on the trade effect suggests an overall positive effect in the United Kingdom's case. On outward FDI, for example, firms with larger proportions of their assets abroad have higher export propensities than do firms in the same industry with smaller foreign asset ratios (Dunning and Pearce 1981). The explanation for this seems to be that operating abroad not only provides better market information to the domestic base, but it also provides a 'captive' export market for spare parts and semi-processed goods that continue to be produced in the United Kingdom. The value of such 'investment-pull' exports (estimated at one-quarter of total exports), plus an allowance for initial capital goods exports, are thought to have yielded £1.5 billion in 1983 (Stopford and Turner 1986).

The evidence is not all one-way, however. Although export propensities appear to have risen with increasing foreign assets, they might have risen even faster had reinvestment in better products and processes taken place at home. Sometimes such an export-led strategy was ruled out in favour of the easier option of FDI because the latter was 'the way the industry was going' (Stopford and Turner 1986). This point takes on added significance when one notes the evidence that stay-at-home British firms have recently begun to reassert their export abilities, in many instances more aggressively faster than MNEs (Business Monitor M4 1981). Second, the export gains from FDI may be offset by imports back to Britain by overseas subsidiaries (Panic and Joyce 1980). Finally, the positive trade effect has diminished in recent years. Whereas exports directly attributable to FDI grew faster than the national average up to 1977, they have declined faster thereafter (Stopford and Turner 1986).

On the inward investment side, exports from foreign-controlled subsidiaries are proportionately even more important. Again captive exports are significant, since they could not have been replaced by domestic alternatives. Valued at £5.3 billion in 1983, these exports are almost as large as those for all British MNEs (Stopford and Turner 1986). Yet again however, the foreigners' overall export success is only part of the story. For one thing inward investment is concentrated in export-prone industries and relative to UK firms in the same sectors the foreigners' performance is less impressive. Indeed, direct comparisons in mechanical engineering have shown that British firms have a higher export propensity (Solomon and Ingham 1977).

Second, foreign firms often have higher import ratios than equivalent British concerns. This is especially significant in the motor vehicle and electronics sectors. According to Stopford (1986) an 'absolute minimum estimate places these imports at over £3bn per year at 1983 prices'. The same source concludes, however, that such imports would have been even higher in the absence of the foreigners' output, since it is unlikely that domestic companies could have filled the gap. Finally, as in the case of outward FDI, trade gains directly attributable to inward FDI are diminishing. Though foreign-controlled captive exports grew much faster than all non-oil exports up to 1977, they declined faster thereafter. Between 1977–83, these exports declined in real terms by 22 per cent compared to a national decline of only 13 per cent (Stopford and Turner 1986).

Overall, Stopford and Turner (1986) conclude that the net effects of inward and outward FDI result in 'a substantial bonus compared to the size of the annual surpluses or deficits on current account'. It is also pointed out, however, that official reporting practices internationally differ to an extent that renders interpretation extremely difficult. Indeed, it has been suggested that US reports of UK FDI there exceed British versions by as much as $5 US billion!

4.4.2 Employment effects

For many, the most important issues in the debate on the impact of the MNE are those concerned with employment. For the neoclassical analyst, the concern tends to be purely about the creation or destruction of jobs. Again a comparative methodology is adopted, the focus being on the job creation effects of MNEs relative to their domestic, uni-national counterparts. The Marxist approach is also concerned with employment levels, but questions are also raised about the type of jobs created, the job conditions and the degree of job security attached to those that are created, especially where there is a heavy regional dependence on such.

The precise effects are difficult to determine. Comparing the employment records of different categories of manufacturing companies, Stopford and Turner (1986) point to a loss of over 600,000 jobs in UK MNEs over the survey period 1972-83. Whilst a comparison with their uni-national counterparts displayed little difference (i.e., a 32 per cent reduction in both), the fact that during the same period these MNEs created 200,000 jobs overseas (Stopford and Turner 1986) appears to condemn their home employment record. However, Stopford and Turner point out that prior to 1978 the relative rate of job loss in British MNEs as compared to domestic enterprises was slow and that the faster rate of decline thereafter may simply be a reflection of the fact that MNEs were cushioned by their overseas earnings up to 1978 but found the pressures to rationalise that much greater in the post-1979 recession. Second, sectoral comparisons suggest that where British MNEs have been strongest (e.g., in chemicals and food) their home record has been at least as good as that of purely domestic firms. Where they have been weakest (e.g., in engineering) the adjustment costs have been felt to a much greater extent. Third, many of the overseas jobs resulted from acquisitions and were not therefore 'new' to the employees.

Such arguments do not completely exonerate MNEs, however. Capital invested overseas is not available for investment at home. Second, the superior pre-1978 employment creation performance of British MNEs compared to domestic companies is also exaggerated by domestic acquisitions. The net employment effect is less than it appears. Third, the method of analysis adopted in the above exercise is seriously flawed. Comparing the performance of MNEs with domestic companies is only legitimate to the extent that the operations of each is independent of the other.

> It is more plausible either by oligopolistic power within a sector or by employment effects across sectors that MNEs will determine the place of domestic producers and pass on the employment effects of their own operations.
>
> (Fine and Harris, 1985:106)

When measured in terms of employment levels, the record for inward investment over the same survey period appears to contrast sharply with the performance of UK companies. Though employment declined after 1978, gains up to that point were sufficient to lead to a net increase of

Table 4.4 Manufacturing employment change in Britain by nationality of ownership, 1975–81

	Percentage changes			
	1975–8		1978–81	
	Foreign-controlled	UK-controlled	Foreign-controlled	UK-controlled
Employment change in surviving plants	+5.89	−0.96	−14.60	−15.70
Employment lost by closures	−2.60	−3.08	−7.30	−6.04
Employment gained by new opening	+0.86	+0.86	+0.46	+0.20
Net change	+4.15	−3.18	−21.44	−21.54

Source: *British Business*, 26 November 1982.

80,000 over the decade as a whole. In terms of employment stability, the situation is more complex. Some of the 80,000 jobs were created as a result of new arrivals and a sufficient period of time has not yet lapsed for a judgement of this nature to be made on these. At the national level, and restricting the analysis to a comparison of existing plants over the period 1975–81, the superior performance of foreign MNEs is again apparent. This can be seen in Table 4.4.

At the regional level, however, the 'retreat' of foreign MNEs is well in evidence. For example, between 1976–81, severe job losses occurred with the partial and sometimes total closure of large and often long-established companies in Scotland, including Timex, NCR, Massey-Ferguson, Goodyear, Singer and Hoover (Hood and Young 1982). Although others have opened up there in the 1980s, particularly in the electronics industry in what has come to be known as 'Silicon Glen', as Stopford and Turner (1986) point out, 'this new wave of investment has still to prove it will have more staying power.'

The employment creation benefits of inward FDI also have to be tempered by considerations of the type of jobs created. There is a genuine concern that MNEs tend to generate a low rate of highly skilled and managerial jobs; rather the tendency is to create low-skilled routine assembly-line jobs in 'screwdriver' plants which are highly cyclically sensitive. A more recent cause of concern is the female bias in employment creation especially in the rapid expansion of the electronics sector in Scotland (Hood and Young 1982). Both tendencies could be a direct consequence of the geographical segmentation of high- and low-order occupations created by MNEs centralising the former in the parent plant and the latter in overseas branch plants.

4.4.3 Technological effects

Balance of payments and employment issues are inextricably linked to those of technological development. The latter, embodied in new products and production processes, may improve international competitiveness thereby stimulating economic growth and employment. The creation of new products and processes through sustained R&D is, however, a high-cost, high-risk strategy undertaken only by those, like MNEs, with the resources necessary to finance such activities. The neoclassical approach focuses upon MNEs as transmission agents of new technology, to the extent that it is available to MNE affiliates at low or zero cost and may, thereby, become more widely diffused throughout the economy as domestic competitors emulate the best practices of MNEs. The focus, therefore, is on the extent to which UK MNEs operating overseas learn of new technologies for transfer home and whether foreign MNEs operating in the United Kingdom improve the competitiveness of the UK economy by importing the same.

In contrast, the Marxist approach not only questions the extent to which the transfer of technology takes place, but also the costs of such transfer in monetary and non-monetary terms (e.g., whether the economy becomes technologically dependent upon and dominated by a few domestic or foreign MNEs and whether this results in a loss of sovereignty), the purpose of the introduction of new technology and the appropriateness of the technology when transferred. The last is mostly of concern in the context of an examination of the relationship between MNEs and their 'underdeveloped' hosts and will not be considered here.

Undoubtedly some transfer of technology takes place whenever a MNE operates outside its home economy, in the simplest case by the employment and training of the local labour force. But the benefits will only be diffused throughout the wider economy to the extent that the technology is made available to potential users outside the MNE. This can occur through direct 'linkages' with indigenous firms acting as component suppliers, through an increase in the human capital of those involved in the research projects of the MNE (who may subsequently set up their own firms) or through a 'demonstration effect' on other indigenous suppliers or competitors.

The empirical evidence, however, is inconclusive. On linkages, for example, IBM claims to have 1,100 suppliers within the United Kingdom and Sony has also built up strong links with British component suppliers. On the other hand, the extent of local supply links of foreign electronics plants in Scotland remains small and the import propensity of MNEs tends to be higher than average (McDermott 1979). Similarly with R&D, the United Kingdom appears to have been successful in attracting research from the pharmaceutical companies (Brech and Sharp 1984), whilst electronics giants Hewlett-Packard has joined IBM and NCR in setting up research facilities in recent years; yet such examples appear to be exceptions to the general rule that R&D activities tend to be located at the parent plant (Hood and Young 1976). Finally, the demonstration effect is, by its very nature, difficult to measure.

In any case, to the extent that a transfer of technology does take place, it has to be paid for. Branch plants remit payments to the parent in the form of royalties and service payments (i.e., management expenses, branch companies share of head office costs and commission for work done). In the years 1973–83, foreign MNEs in the United Kingdom transferred some £2.9 billion to their parents overseas. The costs of technology transfer may be felt in other ways. Most important among these are the twin issues of dominance and dependence. Briefly, the argument is that if the high technology sectors of an economy are dominated by foreign firms, the rate of technological progress of such sectors and probably the vitality of the entire host economy, which may lose its potential for self-generating growth, will become dependent upon and therefore subservient to, the dictates of overseas decision-makers.

Past experiences have caused UK governments to show some concern in this regard. US-owned electronics MNEs like Texas Instruments, Motorola and National Semiconductor have been 'accused' of supplying outdated technology to British equipment manufacture. Such concern led to the formation of the indigenous supplier of integrated circuits, ICL. More recently, the issue of technological dependence came to the fore in the political debate surrounding the take-over of the Westland Helicopter Corporation by the US concern, Sikorsky, and in the proposed sell-off of the United Kingdom's last volume vehicle producer, Austin-Rover, to the US MNEs Ford and General Motors.

In questioning the purpose of the introduction of new technology, the Marxist approach goes beyond the neoclassical approach's intuitively obvious rationale that firms apply new process technology purely to increase productivity and efficiency and thereby reduce costs. Marxists argue that increased productivity could be achieved simply by intensifying production and/or prolonging the working day. The likelihood of labour force resistance to such a policy leads management to introduce new technology as a mechanism for cheapening and de-skilling labour, the purpose being to effect a transfer of control over the labour process from labour to management. Having achieved this aim, management are in a stronger position to reduce costs and increase profits. The nature of this argument renders it impervious to empirical testing by statistical techniques whether in the context of MNEs or of uni-national companies. It is, none the less, an argument which gains wide currency in trade union circles and must be considered in the light of MNEs' propensity to transfer technology worldwide.

4.4.4 Industrial relations effects

Inter alia, an economy's performance, as reflected in its balance of payments position, the level and stability of employment and the rate of technological progress affects, and is affected by, the performance of the industrial relations system in the country. To the extent that MNEs adopt policies that are distinct from those of uni-national companies, this has to be taken into account when assessing the overall impact of FDI on the economy. As elsewhere, however, the issues are clouded by theoretical and empirical controversies.

The Marxist perspective sees the very nature of the MNE as creating specific problems for its employees. In general, MNEs are said to possess attributes which provide them with bargaining powers in excess of those normal in capital–labour relations. This includes: the sheer size and global flexibility of MNEs, which enables them to relocate production facilities in the event of a subsidiary's performance failing to meet expected standards; access to finance which enables the company to withstand disruption to production resulting from an industrial dispute; and an ability to circumvent disputes by 'dual sourcing', thereby ensuring output levels are met from a non-strike-bound plant. These attributes are used to 'divide and rule' the labour force into an 'international division of labour', thereby reducing the otherwise collective bargaining power of labour and lowering labour costs. In addition, and with particular respect to a host country's labour force, MNEs are said to import 'alien' industrial relations practices, which are again designed to weaken worker resistance. This includes centralising all key decisions, including those on industrial relations matters, at the source country's headquarters, such that the remoteness of decision-making frustrates labour in its attempts to bargain in good faith with the company; refusing to recognise a trade union for bargaining purposes; refusing to follow established bargaining procedures; and the withholding of information necessary for bargaining purposes.

The empirical evidence adduced in support of this perspective tends to be either case study based or anecdotal. Thus, the International Labour Organisation (1976) refers to 'union concerns' over MNE threats to relocate production in the face of 'unreasonable' wage demands. Ford (ILO 1976) and Goodyear (Gennard 1972) were accused of attempting to break strikes in the United Kingdom by sourcing their UK market with output from their other overseas plants. Anecdotal examples abound of MNEs (primarily US-owned) which have consistently refused to recognise British trade unions for bargaining purposes, concentrating recruitment on 'uncontaminated' young women (who are not, and have not been, members of trade unions nor subject to their influence) for assembly-line operations (Gapper 1988). There are also numerous references to complaints by trade union leaders of the difficulties they have in dealing with remote management (Forsyth 1972; Hamill 1984).

The neoclassical perspective suggests that far from MNE status weakening the bargaining power of organised labour, there are good reasons to suppose that such power will be strengthened. Since MNEs are created by a process of internalisation, with the company becoming a closely integrated global entity critically dependent on the internal flow and exchange of finished, semi-finished and intermediate goods, they are acutely sensitive to the possibility of production disruption. Further, the constraints on an MNE's ability to switch production activity, especially in the short term, are considerable. Transference, set-up and production loss costs are such that MNEs are unlikely to relocate as a result of short-term industrial relations problems or marginal changes in relative labour costs. The (multidivisional) type of organisational structure typically favoured by MNEs is also said to encourage the decentralisation of functions, including those of industrial relations (Stopford and Wells 1972).

The supposed vulnerability of MNEs in this regard is seen to be a major determinant of their policies of high wages and fringe benefits (Gennard 1972; Steuer and Gennard 1971) and may result in there being an even greater awareness and concern with personnel and industrial relations function in the organisation, inclusive of trade union recognition (Purcell *et al.* 1987). Similarly, with respect to the import of alien industrial relations practices, MNEs have been viewed as 'pace-setters' in developing practices which provide the flexibility needed for maintaining competitiveness in an era of rapid technological change and increasing international competitiveness. Prime examples include productivity-bargaining at Esso's Fawley plant in 1960 (Flanders 1964); Ford's bonus schemes specifically designed to reduce short-term disruptive stoppages (Incomes Data 1979); and more recently the plethora of Japanese industrial relations practices, such as single-union agreements, no-strike agreements and pendulum bargaining, all of which could be regarded as leading to a diminution of industrial conflict and, as such, evidence of 'good' industrial relations.

Apart from the problems involved in establishing whether industrial conflict is higher or lower in foreign-owned than in domestically-owned plants, some studies have reached conflicting conclusions partly because of a period-specific or regionally-specific bias (Steuer 1973 and Forsyth 1972 respectively), whilst others remain inconclusive, finding the incidence of strikes greater in some measure but lower in others (Enderwick and Buckley 1985). It is debatable whether an analysis of industrial conflict provides a yardstick by which we can measure 'good' industrial relations or whether this has a 'beneficial' or 'detrimental' effect on the economy and on the power relations consequent upon this. As in all other aspects examined, the observation of 'beneficial' or 'detrimental' effects will be defined by the perspective adopted.

4.5 CONCLUSIONS

MNEs are an increasingly important world phenomenon. This chapter has sought to analyse the impact they have on the UK economy, a prerequisite of which was a description of the nature of such enterprises, their role in economic activity and the factors which give rise to their peculiar organisational form. In all aspects of the analysis, from the definition of MNEs to the perceived impact which FDI has on the UK economy, controversy has reigned. The major starting-point of this controversy is the adoption of competing perspectives. To quote Stopford (1986), 'how one looks at the problem and how one values each of the various parts has much to do with the conclusions reached.' No attempt has been made to evaluate the validity of either perspective examined, nor has a prescriptive approach been adopted. Rather, it is hoped that an understanding of the sources of controversy (as set out in Chapter 1) is intrinsically valuable. Students and policymakers of all kinds and at all levels are considerably better informed in the conduct of their own analyses by an awareness of the extent to which they, or others, adopt – implicitly or otherwise – a particular perspective.

FURTHER READING

There is a wealth of literature on all aspects of MNEs. For topics not covered in any detail here, readers are directed to the following sources: Cowling and Sugden (1987a), for a discussion of the importance of broadening the definition of MNEs to consider companies which although not formally part of the organisation are nevertheless subject to its control; for an articulation of the neoclassical approach, see Buckley and Casson (1976) or Dunning (1979). For the Marxist approach, the collection of readings in Radice (1975) or Cowling and Sugden (1987b). Hood and Young (1979) contains chapters reviewing both perspectives.

Whilst restricted to a host-country viewpoint and from a narrow theoretical perspective, Dunning (1981) usefully considers the analytical problems of conducting a 'tool-kit' approach to an examination of the costs and benefits of FDI. For a discussion of the public policy dimension, see: Stopford and Turner (1986), especially Chapters 8, 9 and 10; Dunning (1985); or Cowling and Sugden (1987b). Dicken (1986) provides a useful analysis of 'global shift' in the textiles and clothing, iron and steel, motor vehicle, and electronics industries.

5 · HEALTH AND HEALTH CARE

Should we take the economists' medicine?

MEL POWELL

5.1 INTRODUCTION

Health economics has been described as the application of the 'discipline' of economics to the 'topic' of health (Williams 1979); as the use of a set of distinct theories, concepts and techniques to a set of defined problems, phenomena or policy issues. The specific application of orthodox economic theories to health care began in the 1960s (Feldstein 1967, Lees 1961), developed throughout the 1970s (Cooper and Culyer 1973), and gained greater acceptance in the 1980s (McGuire 1988 and Teeling-Smith 1987). The theories are largely those of welfare economics and the issues mainly focused on health care. The dominant approach is through expected utility theory within the positivist/empiricist method of orthodox neoclassical economics.

Marxist theorists have also examined the role of health in the capitalist process of accumulation (Doyal 1979 and Navarro 1976). This type of political economy framework sets the provision of health care against the changing needs of capital in sustaining and legitimising the productive and reproductive capacity of labour. However, the challenge to orthodox theory has been treated as part of controversy at the level of general scientific methodology, and not as part of controversy within health economics. By contrast, the views of the New Right theorists have generated an element of controversy over the future structure and finance of the National Health Service (Green 1986). The methodology of health economics is not being challenged, rather the underlying value structure of individual choice is being reasserted. As a result, mainstream applied health economics has continued to develop along two lines: the expansion of normative welfare theory to encompass the analysis of health (for example see van der Gaag and Perlman 1981) and the development of applied positive economic techniques for policy evaluation and option appraisal in health care. (See Drummond 1980 and Warner and Luce 1982.) The key elements of current controversy have therefore arisen at the interface of normative theory and positive application.

From the outset, the application of neoclassical economic theory to health provision has proved both problematic and controversial. In order to apply the normative model of welfare economics, economists have had to devise cardinal measures of non-marketed intangible benefits. Measures such as Quality Adjusted Life Years (QUALYs) are overtly value laden and difficult to assimilate within the framework of 'positive' theory. The techniques adopted remain at the margin of orthodox theory. A further problem arises because most consumers lack the information needed to make rational decisions on health. Doctors or suppliers act as agents to determine demand. Economists have responded by creating models which explain the loss of consumer sovereignty and rationality in order to retain policy relevance. Controversy has therefore arisen between health economists over the most appropriate method of reconciling theoretical concepts with observed data, over the definition of the relationship between equity and efficiency in health, and over the potential for separating normative from positive analysis.

Early analysis in health economics centred on macroeconomic distributional issues relating to the allocation of public funds. Focus has shifted since the 1970s towards microeconomic questions about the efficiency of resource allocation within constrained budget health care. A more recent addition to the current emphasis on resource efficiency is found in studies appraising expenditure on prevention rather than treatment (Russell 1986). A number of health economists now argue that efficiency and policy should not be judged through macro or global measures such as expenditure, length of stay or bed occupancy in hospitals, but in terms of microevaluation of services delivered (Maynard and Ludbrook 1981). In addition it is argued that moral judgements are being made in the decision to advocate clinical efficiency over economic efficiency, which have not been justified. The policy prescriptions of economists have, not surprisingly, generated controversy among the medical profession and among politicians over the required level of public expenditure and methods of financing and providing health care.

This chapter begins with an outline of the principal topics in applied health economics (5.2) and an introduction to the problems confronting mainstream analysis. The main elements of controversy are then identified and considered in more detail (5.3). The derivation of controversy in health economics is then examined in relation to the problems of applying theory and the concepts introduced in Chapter 1.

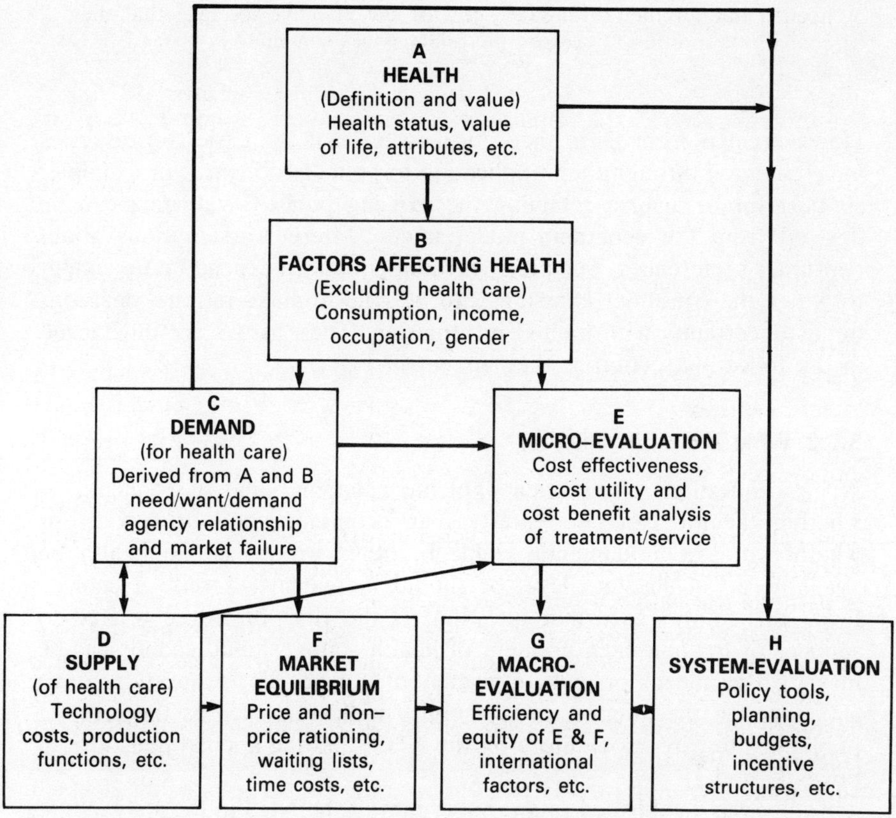

Fig. 5.1 The structure of health economics.

5.2 PROBLEMS IN THE ECONOMIC ANALYSIS OF HEALTH

5.2.1 The structure of health economics

The positivist/empiricist methodology of health economics is set out in Figure 5.1, which displays the principal subjects of analysis within health economics and the connections between underlying theory and applied analysis. (The diagram is widely used in the teaching of health economics and was devised by Alan Williams at York University.) Boxes A,B,C and D contain the theoretical construction of economics applied to health. Boxes E,F,G and H contain the main areas of practical application. The relationship between the two elements is summarised by Culyer (1987), who suggests that most health economists would treat the content of boxes A,B,C and D as instrumental:

> needed not for their own sake, but for the effective leverage that they enable one to bring to bear on the policy issues contained in boxes E,F,G and H.
>
> (Culyer 1987:18)

However, it is from these theoretical issues that the basic controversies have emerged through their application to policy problems. For example, support for or against retaining the existing public/private mix can be derived from the economic model under different assumptions about consumer preferences. The policy recommendations depend on the extent to which the consumer is assumed to be able to make rational decisions under uncertainty with limited information. These issues are introduced in the following section as they appear in Fig. 5.1.

5.2.2 What is health? (box A)

A basic question raised when applying economic analysis to health is whether 'health' can be treated as an economic good or service, or whether it is a fundamental right. In other words, should health be available at an absolute level or should individuals exercise a choice? From this follows a further question. Is the right of choice related to services or to some measurement of health status; should economists be investigating means or ends, efficiency or equity? These questions have a bearing on the intepretation of policy indicators such as the level of public health care expenditure on the NHS, and the applied questions in boxes G and H.

Equity was established as a primary aim of the NHS in the 1944 White Paper which states:

> government . . . want to ensure that in future every man, woman and child can rely on getting . . . the best medical and other facilities available: that their getting them shall not depend on whether they can pay for them or on any other factor irrelevant to real need.
>
> (HMSO 1944:5)

The ideological foundation of the NHS is based on universal access and service according to need rather than demand. Access to health care is not related to efficiency through market willingness to pay or ability to pay. This approach is mirrored to some extent across all developed countries as shown in Fig. 5.2. Although the United Kingdom spends a relatively small proportion of national income on health relative to other developed countries, a high proportion of that spending is in the public sector. The Conservative government's review of the NHS financing and organisation reflects the political ideology of market efficiency. There is a belief that public expenditure on health is both difficult to control and inherently inefficient or costly at any given level of health care. It is argued that any increase in expenditure on health as a proportion of GDP should arise from an expansion of the private sector. However, it

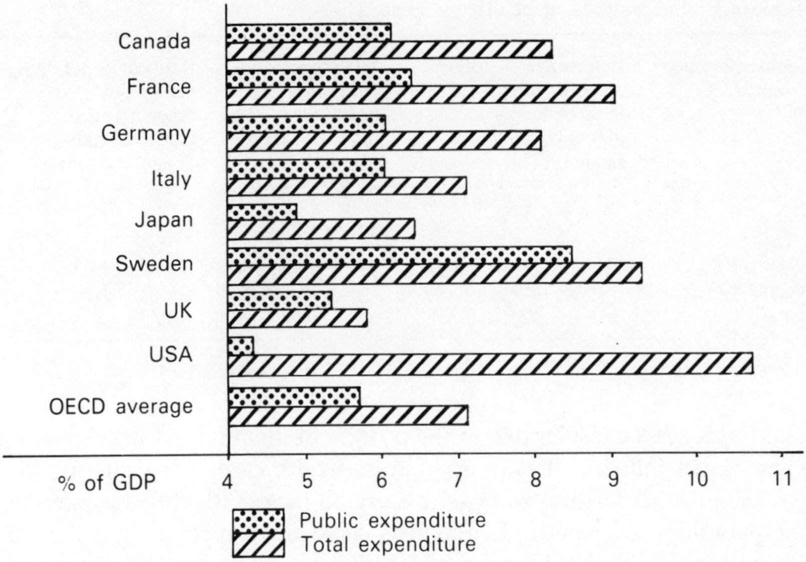

Fig. 5.2 Health spending in OECD countries as % of GDP. *Source*: OECD financing and delivering health care (1987).

is not immediately clear that an increase in private sector inputs (expenditure) would raise outputs (health indicators). For example, the United States spends nearly twice as much on health as a percentage of GDP than the United Kingdom, but still achieves worse rates of infant mortality and life expectancy (OECD 1987).

Most economists agree that the efficiency of the NHS should be evaluated in terms of output measures of health rather than inputs. However, they disagree on methods of measurement and the appropriate incentive mechanisms for achieving efficiency. For example, the New Right approach seeks to increase private provision through insurance and allow the price mechanism to allocate services (Green 1986). Those who support the NHS principles have devised within-service mechanisms to increase efficiency without privatisation. Those who wish to 'measure' efficiency have devised innovative health status measures, the most controversial of which is the QUALY index. Even within the latter group there is controversy over the method of evaluating quality and quantity of life, and the relative importance of equity in valuing health status (Jones-Lee 1982 and Broome 1985).

5.2.3 What influences health other than health care? (box B)

Health is a normative value-laden concept, difficult to measure within a positivist framework. The influence of other disciplines concerned with

Table 5.1 Inequalities in health by social class

Socioeconomic group (SEG)	Percentage of total reporting either limiting long-standing illness or acute sickness	Percentage of health care expenditure	Ratio of expenditure per person reporting ill to that for SEGs V and VI
I and II	14.8	18.8	1.41
III	19.4	20.5	1.17
IV	36.7	34.6	1.05
V and VI	29.1	26.2	1.00
Total	100.0	100.0	

Source: Le Grand (1978: 130).

health has been considerable in the process of identifying (or delineating) what factors influence health apart from health care. For example, diet, gender, income, leisure, work, stress are all factors identified as affecting the pathology of health. Economists have developed a model of the demand for health as a function of health care and non-health care factors where non-health factors are largely consumed under market conditions (work, smoking, sport, drinking, etc.) (Grossman 1972). The rational well-informed individual can therefore choose a desired level of health care against consumption of those goods which affect health at the margin. One implication of this approach is that the achievement of equality in health rather than efficiency may involve altering tastes and incomes through policies which affect both willingness and ability to pay.

Some evidence suggests that equality in health status and health care utilisation has not been achieved. The Black Report (1982) identified marked inequalities by class gradient in both the standards of health and service utilisation after 30 years of NHS provision. The authors called for a policy related to 'total' health rather than a service-oriented approach, because non-health care factors such as smoking and education affect inequality. In another study, Le Grand (1978) used General Household Survey data to investigate inequalities in health and utilisation by social class. From results such as those shown in Table 5.1, Le Grand concluded that the lower social classes have a higher incidence of ill health (similar in distribution to other classes) but receive a relatively smaller proportion of health care expenditure. However, a subsequent study by Le Grand and Rabin (1986) showed a reduction in inequality since 1931, measured by the Gini coefficient of age at death. Macroeconomic factors such as growth and unemployment have also been associated with health (Brenner 1977), together with lifestyles, poverty and class determination.

Economists who model demand for health care must make assumptions about the route of causality and the interdependence of non-health care factors on health care utilisation. The implications for policy are diverse.

If consumers are assumed to be able to choose lifestyles and health care to balance out their expected utility from health, a minimal level of government intervention in health and social policy is justified. Equally, the constraints of unequal income may limit the achievement of equal health. But how much inequality is desired by preferences and how much is forced by the ability to pay? There is no agreement about the type of equality desired, access, utilisation, health status, etc., or the level justified within the economic model.

5.2.4 The demand for health (box C)

Following Grossman (1972), most economists now model the demand for health as a stock of human capital, so that the demand for health care is derived from the demand for health. Empirical work has therefore included the modelling and estimation of the production function for health (Stern 1983), as well as the demand for health care and the demand for hazardous goods such as alcohol and tobacco (Godfrey 1986). Although most economists agree that market failure on the demand and supply side exists, the two main models of the demand for health care reflect different opinions as to its importance and the degree of inefficiency resulting. Grossman assumes that the individual consumer has sufficient information and knowledge to make decisions about consumption which affect health. The individual demand for health care is represented as a bridge between perceived current health state and the preferred or expected level at any time.

A more problematic model is the 'needs' approach which introduces the asymmetry of information between the patient and doctor (Williams 1978). If patients have insufficient information and defer decisions about their demand for health care to their doctor, doctors become the judge of needs rather than demands. The agency relationship that results separates the allocative mechanism from consumer sovereignty. The agency relationship can lead to a situation where the doctor creates demand to increase profits, leading to a quantity demanded in excess of the efficient level. In a private system based on insurance, rising costs can be spread across all individuals in the form of increased premiums. However, in the state system 'supplier-induced demand' may still arise through pressure from drug companies, advertising, and the pursuit of career advancement. There is controversy over the extent and importance of this issue of market failure for modelling the demand for health care.

Welfare economics has provided the theoretical basis for justifying public provision of health care because of significant market failure in demand. The concept of external benefits from the public provision of health or the 'caring' externally has been developed by modelling altruism as an externality (Arrow 1974; Collard 1978). This notion has been extended to examine the role of charitable provision or what Titmuss (1970) called the 'gift relationship', with particular reference to the provision of blood. The extent to which the market failure model of externalities can be used to explain 'collective' or 'social' provision is an important element of current controversy.

5.2.5 The supply of health (box D)

Economic theory has been more widely used to investigate the supply of health care in those countries with a large private sector. In the United Kingdom econometric analysis has been limited by a paucity of theoretical models. Analysis of the health care industry is complicated, even under public provision, by the multiplicity of institutions and personnel. For example, health care is provided not only by dentists, osteopaths, family care and charitable institutions, but also through education and the social services. There is no clear definition of the boundaries of the health care industry for empirical analysis. Supply estimation has therefore concentrated on factor substitution in staffing, and on efficiency and economies of scale in hospital provision. (See Wagstaff 1987 for a review.)

Emphasis in the American literature has leaned towards aspects of insurance and pricing together with the efficiency of different delivery systems. There is an ongoing debate over the cost implications of a move from 'guild free choice', where insurance leaves the patient free to choose supply source, to 'market free choice', where consumers can contract with known suppliers (Enthoven 1985). A variety of new systems of delivery are now in operation in the United States in which the patient contracts with providers to effect cost control. Economic debate in the United States has influenced opinion on types of reform in the NHS, particularly on the adoption of internal markets.

Supply models must also account for the agency role over consumer sovereignty and the potential for supplier-induced demand. Models of supplier activity assume that doctors would make rational profit-maximising decisions under a fee-for-service situation (with insurance), and thereby shift demand. However, it is also possible that supply and demand are not independent. For example, if suppliers aim to provide maximum health care for a given desired income and price is set exogenously, an increase in the number of doctors will lead to more demand as doctors must generate greater utilisation to reach desired income. Not only is the model sensitive to the assumption of price exogeneity, but it also highlights the problems inherent in any attempt to identify an optimal level of the supply of health care.

Most economic models of health care assume that the result of the supply of health care is an improvement in health, all other things being equal. However, there is considerable controversy over the accuracy of epidemiological information and the effectiveness of different health care treatments. Uncertainty affects the ability of doctors to improve health. Doctors may give treatment to those who do not require it or to those who would die or deteriorate despite treatment. Most therapies carry their own risk of additional illness, adding to the initial information problems. The controversial concept of doctor-induced disease is discussed by Illich (1976) not only in its clinical form but also as a social and cultural effect. The development and testing of both demand and supply models is therefore dependent on the questionable validity of health measures, experimental procedures, data reliability and interpretation.

5.2.6 Market analysis and cost-benefit analysis (boxes E and F)

The components of market analysis are mainly empirical, concerned with non-price rationing since the impact of price mechanisms in the United Kingdom is limited (Culyer and Johnson 1986). Two main theories have been contested. One approach explains non-price rationing and the level of market provision according to supplier decisions by doctors and different concepts of need (Cooper 1975). The opposite approach is based on consumer theory relating waiting-lists to the individual value of time (Culyer and Cullis 1976).

By contrast, there has been a mass of research on methods and techniques for evaluating health policy and programmes. The difficulties involved in measuring intangibles in health have led economists to develop alternatives to the full monetary evaluation required in cost-benefit analysis. In cost-effectiveness analysis, benefits are assessed as physical units. The use of measures of health status as benefits has become known as cost-utility analysis because the measures are derived from consumer preferences (Drummond 1986).

5.2.7 System evaluation and equity (boxes G and H)

Both the areas of planning and monitoring and system evaluation have received limited attention. The lack of adequate models in demand and supply and the development of evaluative techniques at the microeconomic level have diverted attention to other areas. Most debate has emerged from proposed methods of reducing inefficient bureaucracy in the NHS by introducing internal markets (Akehurst *et al.* 1988). Among the most controversial proposals are those of a voucher system similar to the case for education, the introduction of Health Maintenance Organisations (HMOs provide all health care for a regular prepaid fee), the fee-for-item-of-service approach and allocating purchasing power to doctors in health care (Teeling-Smith 1984; Robinson 1988). The impact of these proposals on policy depends upon the extent to which government perceives the policy of equity from the provision of universal services (restricting total costs) as separable from the decision to maintain a state monopoly. If the decisions are separable, government could allow doctors or regions to buy and sell services within or outside the public sector (Enthoven 1985).

The connection between equity (equal access) and measures of economic efficiency has also remained unresolved in attempts to develop criteria for allocating regional budgets from the centre. In 1976, the Report of the Resource Allocation Working Party (RAWP) devised a formula to create a more equitable reallocation of total resources between health regions over a long-run adjustment. The formula was intended to measure regional need by setting targets for region expenditure adjusted for population and standardised mortality rates. It was designed to increase equal opportunity of access for those at equal risk. However, the formula applies only to hospital and community care service budgets and treats each country within the United Kingdom separately. A review of the formula in 1987 made no fundamental changes. Some economists have recommended a wider application of the RAWP formula to increase both efficiency and equity (Birch and Maynard 1988). They argue that the current formula is limited to achieving equity of inputs rather than outputs and cannot account for differences in the efficiency of different hospitals, nor for the increasing burden of care on family practitioner services.

Economists who adopt a microallocation approach to investigate the balance between efficiency and equity, argue that the long-run factor affecting unequal provision is the disparity in efficiency between regions. An alternative approach would of course be to seek to improve the mobility of patients between regions rather than to seek to equalise access in all regions. Efficiency would require that the transaction cost of mobility is not greater than the loss of efficiency generated by creating equality between regions. The choice of policies proposed by economists can be grouped along a range from better use of the market mechanism, reorganisation of the NHS structure to the introduction of simulated market conditions.

5.3 THE PRINCIPAL AREAS OF DISAGREEMENT

From the outline given above, many areas of controversy can be identified in health economics, some of which are common to all areas of applied economics. There are, however, a few key conflicts which are specific to health and closely related study. These are the problems of externalities, supplier-induced demand, value of life and quality of life measures. Each of these is discussed in turn below. The nature of the controversy and the implications for policy relevance are examined in the light of ideas introduced in Chapter 1.

5.3.1 The market failure debate

According to mainstream welfare economics, the identification of Pareto-relevant externalities, certain types of informational failure and the existence of monopoly power, can provide theoretical reasons for government intervention and rules for policy-setting. Health economists have followed the methodology in order to provide an explanation for the public provision of health care. Controversy over the efficiency of state provision relative to private provision therefore depends upon the interpretation of what is or what is not a relevant form of market failure in health.

On the demand side, the most frequently cited elements of market failure in health care are ignorance about health and quality of care, the irregular and unpredictable consumption related to uncertainty, the occurrence of moral hazard and adverse selection in insurance, and the existence of external costs generated by the interdependence of utility in health. Economists have debated the relevance and extent of these issues in the health market and the degree to which non-market institutions will arise to increase efficiency in the absence of state provision. For example, uncertainty can be reduced by market insurance schemes and ignorance reduced by provision of health information. Adverse selection can be minimised in insurance by compulsory insurance schemes which need not be state run, and moral hazard reduced (inasmuch as it is deliberate) by financial penalties on premiums (Arrow 1963; Pauly 1968).

Of the elements of market failure identified above, the debate over the importance of externalities best illustrates the nature of controversy. Culyer and Simpson (1980) review the debate in terms of three phases. The dominant view in the 1960s was that externalities in health service provision were trivial or not Pareto relevant. A few economists argued that externalities were relevant but not significant, so that state provision would not raise welfare (Lees 1967). Both views can be countered by the argument that the positive investigation required to establish the non-relevance of externalities had not been undertaken. More importantly, Culyer and Simpson argue that the non-relevance of externalities implied that mainstream economics could not explain the existence of the NHS. Public provision must therefore result from mistakes or collective irrationality, which is unsatisfactory.

By the 1970s some economists had begun to argue that the externalities were relevant and generated through the consumption of medical services. Culyer and Simpson identify two broad approaches. In the first, associated externalities are derived from actual levels of inequitable health care consumption leading to a support case for selective rather than universal subsidies. In the second, externalities are derived from the difference in levels of consumption between people, leading to the conclusion that the method of provision must ration high levels of demand and make provision cheaper at low levels of demand. However, neither of these approaches could explain the existence of the state structure. As the economic model could not explain the existing structure of the NHS, it was inferred during the 1970s that the system was inefficient or required an alternative structure. The aim of reducing bureaucratic inefficiency lies at the heart of attempts to restructure the NHS.

The most recent change of emphasis in externality analysis emerged with Grossman's model linking externalities to health status rather than health care alone. Health status externalities result from the divergence of health for some groups from a minimum or average desired level. Public concern arises over medical care because of its impact on health status. The innovation provided a theory-consistent explanation of public provision. It also provided wider scope for explaining and evaluating government intervention in factors affecting health status such as prevention and housing. Mooney (1986) argues that the caring externality is about health status and utilisation. It cannot therefore justify the actual aim of the NHS, that of equality of access. Margolis (1982) has developed a model of individual choice based on two utility functions: a conventional selfish utility (which includes externalities), and one where utility is derived from the process of participation in group activities. The second utility function accounts for the potential reduction in utility that could arise from an altruistic act under the normal utility function. The individual makes an optimal choice based on equalising marginal utility between these two functions. Mooney suggests that state provision will arise in societies where people prefer group to selfish actions in health care. This explanation relies upon assumptions made about the separability of utility into selfish and group determinants. Otherwise it reduces to the externality model.

The example of the externality debate highlights the progress and development of economic theories in response to the need to explain existing structures. Despite the fact that the concept of externality from the provision of 'health care' failed to explain the existence of the NHS, the theory was not rejected or falsified. Instead the focus of attention was shifted to a wider concept: 'health'. State provision of health care can then be shown to be more efficient than cash benefits. The provider of health care, the taxpayer, wishes to reduce the externality felt from unequal health. If cash benefits are given, the receiver may spend them on consumption which is detrimental to health. This action reduces the utility of the giver. However, when the nature of the gift is large relative to the individual recipient, (as in the NHS), the externality argument can

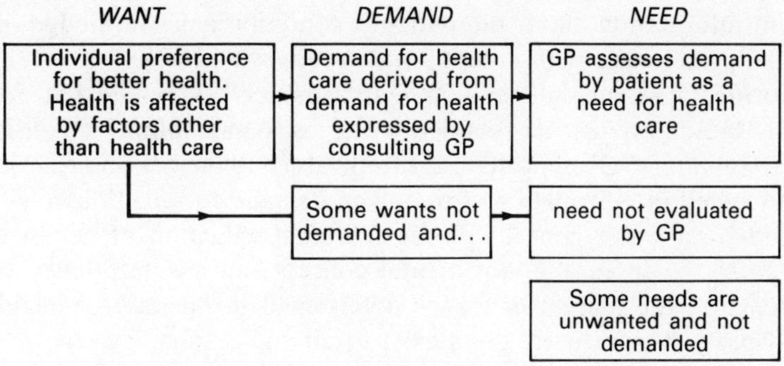

Fig. 5.3 The relationship between want, demand and need. *Source*: Mooney (1986).

be used to explain state services. The underlying assumptions of the neoclassical model of individual preferences are retained in this explanation of 'collective' action as they are in the Margolis model. However, neither model can be falsified because the underlying assumptions about utility cannot be tested against objective data.

5.3.2 The impact of supply induced demand

On the supply side, the provision of health care is characterised by a monopoly of knowledge, by limited professional entry, by the absence of the profit motive and, most importantly, by the agency relationship between doctor and patient. As noted earlier, this element calls into question the relevance of the basic assumption of consumer sovereignty. If the assumption did not hold, individuals could be dissatisfied with the correct policies. The theoretical relevance of economic analysis in health policy is then lost or substantially reduced. Economists have attempted to resolve this issue by modelling a rational relationship between demand and need.

Cooper (1975) expressed the relationship between want, demand and need as uni-dimensional and causal from want for better health, through demand in seeing a doctor, to need as assessed by the doctor. Mooney (1986) elaborates by adding an additional route direct from wants to needs (undemanded wants), and by separating needs into three types as shown in Fig. 5.3. He cites the example of a patient who may want treatment but not demand it because of ignorance, a patient who may want and demand but not receive treatment, and a patient who needs treatment but who does not want or demand treatment because of ignorance. The agency relationship therefore becomes the rational consumer's response to uncertainty with a limited set of information. This model operates efficiently if the doctor has adequate medical knowledge, relevant information about the patient's condition and knowledge of the patient's preferences with regard to alternatives and risk.

A form of rational information search model lies behind the agency model. Rationality can be retained if the consumer follows a consistent behaviour pattern, given preferences for health and the risk and transaction costs involved in information search. The demand for health care is then replaced by a wider concept of the marginal valuation of health care. Need to the economist is not a total concept, an absolute level, but a preference at the margin of choice determined in the case of health by a third party. Opportunity costs exist to all choices made at the margin which implies that all needs cannot be met (Williams and Anderson 1975). Mooney (1986) argues that the agency relationship becomes efficient when the 'autonomous externalities' are insignificant. An autonomous externality would exist if a personal right such as the freedom to choose becomes a generalised sentiment such as 'people should cope for themselves'. When this type of externality is strong, consumer sovereignty will increase. Several problems arise from the use of the agency model. The patient allows the doctor to act as an agent because the transaction costs involved in obtaining information on high technology medicine are prohibitive. When the treatment is life saving, the agency model may function well as demand is likely to be highly inelastic for life-saving technology. However, a large proportion of medical care is used to relieve pain or incapacity for temporary conditions or chronic ailments. These conditions create extensive halfway technologies (Thomas 1977), or treatments which improve quality of life but do not modify the progress of disease. In these cases, the patients may be the best judge of their needs in terms of their quality of life. The agency relationship fails to represent patient preference when treatments do not alter quality of life, or indeed reduce quality of life. As a result, the agency relationship can lead to uncontrolled increases in health care costs.

An efficient agent should take into account the opportunity cost of treatment to the patient. However, if the patient will not make a choice based on the full social cost of treatment, does efficiency require that the doctor should assess all costs? In the agency role, the doctor follows medical ethics based on clinical judgement and need only consider total utility from the patient's need for health care. Economic efficiency requires the doctor to make a decision at the margin based on social costs and benefits. The extent to which the decision criteria used by doctors are likely to deviate from economic criteria will depend on the efficiency of the agency relationship. It may also depend upon the proportion of decisions made by doctors which relate to quantity of life (life and death decisions), rather than quality of life. Consumers may be quite rational in making decisions based on total benefits rather than marginal benefits when faced with a discrete choice between life or death. In these circumstances, patients may place no value on equity considerations or costs at the margin.

The development of the agency relationship model has aided the retention of mainstream economics in health policy analysis by verifying the assumption of consumer sovereignty in the face of potential falsification. There is no way of testing the assumption of rationality or consumer sovereignty in relation to health. Falsification of the demand or valuation model can only be tested in relation to data which are largely unobservable. For example, medical ethics disallow the use of testing or control comparisons of treatment. Doctors must therefore rely upon treatments which have untested outcomes. Data relating the utilisation of services and the incidence of disease are subject to the interpretation of the doctor as well as the economist. As a result, health cannot be uniquely identified by either the doctor or the patient under the theory of the agency relationship. It is impossible to test even the relatively simple positive prediction that doctors can shift the demand for health care.

5.3.3 The value of life and health status measurements

An ongoing debate in health economics has resulted from attempts to apply cost-benefit analysis to evaluate health policies and programmes. Many economists agreee that comparative evaluation is appropriate but disagree over the method of estimating shadow prices for intangible benefits such as the value of life and health status. There are two aspects to the debate: the availability and accuracy of epidemiological data (relating to the incidence and causality of disease), and the methodology adopted.

Benefits derived from medical treatment and primary prevention are treated as improvements in health or years of productive life saved. Life saved can enter an economic valuation as a cost or a benefit, depending on the nature of alternative option or opportunity cost taken into account. For example, the benefits of smallpox vaccination include saved lives, but the costs include deaths resulting from vaccination. Three types of methodology appear in the literature for shadow-pricing the value of life. To comply with neoclassical theory, the valuation should be derived directly from consumer preferences. The main approaches are the following:

1. Implied-valuation.
2. Human capital valuation.
3. Willingness-to-pay valuation.

The implied-valuation method is based on the economic rationale of revealed preference, so that subjective valuations can be deduced from physical choices or actions. If government does not take a decision which could save a life, for example, the value of life must be less than the expenditure forgone and vice versa. This methodology aims to extract values from past decisions. The willingness-to-pay approach developed by Jones-Lee (1982) attempts to extract a value of risk from an individual by asking how much they would be willing to reduce the risk of death. By far the most widely used approach to valuing life is the human capital method which relates the value of life to productive capacity over a lifetime. The result is an estimated present value of the future stream of lifetime earnings, discounted over the expected working life. This type of valuation cannot value non-market production such as housework or family health care.

Some attempts have been made to use the implicit-value technique on the differential accepted by workers as danger payments for risky work to proxy the value of life (Fromm 1985). However, the assumption of linearity between the probability of death and the willingness to pay to reduce the probability of death has been criticised. Culyer and West (1979) use Mishan's criticism to show that someone might accept £200 to compensate for an increase in risk from 0.001 to 0.002, but not accept £200,000 for the certainty of death. Mishan's (1971) suggestion was that the willingness-to-pay approach should be based on decisions *ex ante*, before any certainty is known, using the notion of compensating variation. Compensating variation measures the minimum income that someone will accept to endure an increased risk of death. It is this factor that ties the willingness-to-pay approach to economic theory. However, it can still be argued that *ex ante* decisions do not reflect *ex post* values with regard to life lost and the welfare associated with certain death.

The human capital approach is used to estimate the value of life-years lost for those who have died in any year, assuming earnings are a proxy for output lost. The methodology is relatively simple to apply and is used in medical cost-of-illness studies which value the resources lost from disease. Costs are calculated as the direct medical costs plus the indirect medical costs of associated disease and death, plus non-medical costs such as those of the fire and police services (Godfrey and Powell 1987). However, estimates of total resource costs from disease in any one year cannot be interpreted as potential savings or potential welfare gains because the opportunity cost has not been taken into account. The methodology is therefore inappropriate for cost-benefit analysis.

The application of normative cost-benefit analysis in health is founded on the development of measures of the valuation of life. There is a basic moral judgement involved that human life can be valued at the margin. Attempts to unite measures with theory by introducing individual preferences have largely failed. However, the use of the human capital approach has continued. This can be partly explained by the focus of policymakers on total expenditure and costs of health care. It can also be viewed as a practical alternative to more theory-consistent measures when data on preferences are unobservable. Economists have more recently begun to side-step the issue of measuring the value of life by developing physical measures of the quality of life lost.

Any NHS development requiring capital investment over £5 million is subject to formal cost-benefit appraisal. As cost-benefit analysis in health care has become more acceptable, the techniques for measuring benefits have become more sophisticated. Physical measurement of benefits as life-years lost is crude because it does not account for differences in quality of life gained by treatment. Ten years of life confined to a wheelchair in constant pain are unlikely to be equivalent to ten years of mobile life free of pain. In addition, because the measure of life-years lost is a measure of lost production, it cannot be related to the outcome of health care, which is health status. Williams (1981) argues that the appropriate methodology for cost-benefit analysis (as cost-utility analysis) of health care is to compare changes in resources used in care with changes in health status.

The aim is to devise a measure of health benefits which will not reflect an individual's ability to pay. Williams defines the search as one for an 'uncontaminated' and 'cardinal' set of relative values of health status incorporating an egalitarian weighting principle. The first requirement is an ordinal ranking of health status devised from individual preferences. This might be devised by using a questionnaire to determine patients' preferences for different states of mobility and pain for example (Rosser 1983; Torrence 1986). These ranks are then assigned cardinal values which determine whether two days of pain are equivalent to one day of twice as much pain. To move from an individual measurement of health status to an aggregate measure requires a judgement about the relative benefits of a year of healthy life between individuals. The egalitarian principle adopted in most measures is that a year of healthy life gained is the same for all individuals.

Despite the fact that health status measures are derived from consumer preferences and are therefore theory consistent, the development remains controversial. Health status measures are likely to be combined with measures of resource use which are contaminated by the consumers' ability to pay in cost-utility analysis (Williams 1981). For example, increased income after treatment may be compared to health status benefits gained. Williams concludes that social values must determine the weights which policy decision-makers attach to non-health benefits. The question that remains is whether these values are represented in individual preferences or are imposed on individuals by independent policymakers. Can questions of efficient allocation of resource be separated from distributional questions? Is positive evaluation separable from normative evaluation?

As a result of the search for better or more theory-consistent measures of health benefits, economists have adopted different approaches to distributional questions in cost-benefit appraisal. Those who emphasise the importance of externalities have placed the source of distributional issues within individual preferences, making equity an element of efficiency. Those who emphasise the 'need' approach have replaced individual preferences with those of experts or third parties. Distributional issues are therefore determined separately from individual preferences. Yet again, the basic assumption of consumer sovereignty and the supremacy of individual preferences cannot be tested against either approach. Economic theory takes consumer preferences as a datum and to some extent these are observable. However, if moral preferences are separated from consumer preferences, the theory cannot be tested because morals are not observable. Any attempt to rely on 'revealed-preference' models in values must incorporate the use of theory-laden data.

5.4 CONCLUSIONS

The application of welfare theory to health has resulted in controversy relating to the applicability and policy relevance of welfare economics. First, the application has identified a case where the basic behavioural assumptions of economic theory may not be relevant. Economists have responded by extending the mainstream theory to accommodate the behaviour of individuals in their choice of health care dependent upon different assumptions about individual ability to use limited information. Because these assumptions cannot be tested, a needs-based model cannot be identified as preferable to a human capital choice model. The failure of the economic model to explain state provision of health services has been corrected by the adoption of an extended market failure model based on caring externalities or group utility. The method by which individual preferences are converted into social or collective actions also remains untestable as are any policy recommendations derived from the health models.

Economists have relaxed and modified the market assumptions of the neoclassical model to widen its predictive and explanatory power in application to health. However, at each stage of modification, the theory becomes more difficult to test whilst appearing to better represent observed data (see section 1.6.2, Chapter 1). For example, the agency model is based on an assumption of long-run rational behaviour over the use of information by both patient and doctor. Apparently irrational behaviour can be explained by invoking the *ceteris paribus* clause under choice in a short-run disequilibrium state. If it is impossible to falsify the elements of the neoclassical health model, the values underlying the development in theory remain uncontested. There can be no objective economic theory of health if there are no objective data. Measures such as the quality of life are overtly normative because they involve introducing assumptions about equity which cannot be tested. Data on the incidence of disease are constructed as a result of medical judgement and social construction. Data on the outcome of treatments are judged by third parties rather than the recipients. As a result, there are no objective criteria on which to judge the value of different policy models or the results of normative cost-benefit analysis.

From the point of view of the 'scientific research programme' discussed in Chapter 1 (page 30), the basic assumptions of consumer sovereignty and rationality can be seen as the hardcore of economic theory. Normative welfare economics and its applications form part of the protective belt which has been constantly revised to protect the hardcore elements in the face of non-conforming observation and the competing medical research programme. The growing body of econometric analysis in health economics is used to test the predictions of modified models and also forms part of the protective belt. Econometric results are used to evaluate positive or empirical facts such as values for income, elasticity of demand for health care and the size of economies of scale in hospital services. However, it is difficult to gauge whether the research programme is progressive or deteriorating. Economists have expanded the number of theories for testing, but these can only be tested by recourse to the same set of theory-laden data. The notion of economic efficiency is, however, challenging the criteria for choice traditionally adopted by the medical profession.

The current political debate over the future of the NHS in the United Kingdom reflects many of the elements of controversy within health economics. New Right proposals emphasise the ability of individuals to choose their health status and their demand for health care. The market is assumed to be efficient in its allocation of health between individuals. Health is assumed to be an economic good. Public provision will inevitably lead to increasing levels of expenditure because costs are not included in supply decisions. Defenders of the NHS assume that the market inefficiently allocates resources but that public expenditure acts as a systematic constraint on costs. Internal mechanisms can be adjusted to increase the efficiency of the non-market institution. An expansion of private provision will not halt the expansion of expenditure. Equity is an element of consumer choice which is inefficiently recognised by private provision. These models cannot be judged on objective criteria.

Controversies within the neoclassical framework applied to health result from the abstraction of analysis from a social definition of health. They occur at the interface of normative theory with positive measurement because the nature of health is socially determined. The central controversy over the role of equity in health has led to developments such as the Margolis model which incorporates not just the utility associated with the consequences of choice, but also utility from the process of choice itself. Margolis (1982) suggests that his model forms part of positive analysis and can therefore bridge the gap between normative theory and positive analysis. But process utility involves measuring moral and social choice about equality of access to health rather than the consequent utility of economic actions. These elements of controversy cannot be resolved within the neoclassical framework. They relate to the social structure and therefore the political economy of health.

FURTHER READING

For a general introduction to mainstream health economics see McGuire, Henderson and Mooney (1988) and Mooney (1986). Further discussion of the issues raised by specific economists can be found in the edited volumes by van der Gaag and Perlman (1981) and Teeling-Smith (1987). The Journal of Health Economics and the Journal of Social Science and Medicine are also useful sources. For those students looking for an introduction to cost-benefit analysis, Drummond (1980) covers the methodology and Drummon *et al.* (1986) examines applied examples. Economic measures of health status and the quality of life are discussed in two edited texts by Culyer (1983) and Teeling-Smith (1983). The classic econometric studies by Feldstein (1967) and Grossman (1972) are worth consulting. The development of externality theory in relation to charities, altruism and morality can be followed in Sen and Williams (1982), and medical ethics in Veatch (1980). For an introduction to a Marxist analysis of health see Burden and Campbell (1985), Chapter 7, and for further analysis see Doyal (1979) and Navarro (1976). The New Right approach is outlined in papers produced by the Centre for Policy Studies and the Institute for Economic Affairs.

6 · PUBLIC CONTROL OF NATURAL MONOPOLY IN THE UNITED KINGDOM

Is regulation the answer?

DAVID PARKER

6.1 INTRODUCTION

Economists have long recognised the likelihood of market failure in situations where a private firm has a natural monopoly. To avoid this outcome, in the United Kingdom the predominant regulatory method has been public ownership. But some other countries, notably the United States, have adopted a different approach, preferring to restrict private monopoly abuse through government regulation while retaining private ownership. Since 1979, as part of a more general programme of privatisation, UK policy has switched from public ownership to introducing a regulatory framework for control of natural monopolies on the US model. In the quest to raise efficiency and in a belief that state-owned enterprises are highly inefficient, the Conservative government has concluded that '. . . even where competition is impractical privatisation policies have been developed to such an extent that regulated private ownership of monopolies is preferable to nationalisation' (Mr John Moore, Financial Secretary to the Treasury, 17 July 1985).

This chapter reviews the controversy which surrounds transferring state monopolies to the private sector as regulated private monopolies. Initially, in section 6.2 the nature of natural monopoly is considered. The discussion then proceeds in section 6.3 to state ownership and privatisation, and then in sections 6.4 and 6.5 to the literature on regulatory failure and the system of regulation currently being adopted in the United Kingdom. Consideration is given to alternatives to both state ownership and state regulation in section 6.6. The chapter concludes by suggesting that private ownership combined with state regulation may not provide the best solution to market failure under natural monopoly.

6.2 THE NATURE OF NATURAL MONOPOLY

Broadly, a natural monopoly exists when a single firm can produce the total output of an industry more cheaply than a number of competing firms (Sharkey 1982). It is therefore related to the nature of an industry's cost function and hence the technology used and to the level of total output. It is possible for a single firm to be most cost efficient at low output levels but for competition to be feasible if demand increases. Also, changes in technology may make a previously competitive industry naturally monopolistic or make competition feasible where in the past monopoly has been most cost efficient.

In the single-product firm natural monopoly is closely related to the concept of economies of scale. Economies of scale may be technical (arising from spreading high fixed costs over a large output, e.g., costs relating to the laying and use of gas pipelines), managerial (spreading managerial overheads) or transactional (networking economies). However, in multi-product industries economies of scale are neither necessary nor sufficient for natural monopoly as it is the composition of output as well as the scale of output which determine costs. Economies of scale in the production of separate products may be less important than cost complementarities in supply, where an increase in one output in a firm reduces the incremental costs of producing other outputs. Such 'economies of scope' may arise from the sharing or joint utilisation of tangible and intangible inputs, such as capital or know-how, in the production of a number of outputs (Panzar and Willig 1981). For example, on the railways track and other infrastructure are used by a number of different rail services, thus spreading fixed costs over higher output levels.

Formally, a natural monopoly in a multi-product enterprise occurs when the production cost of a weighted average of a set of output bundles, $q_a, \ldots, q_n$, is produced more cheaply in one firm than in several so that the cost function is subadditive[1], i.e., the monopolist produces a vector of outputs $q_m = q_1, \ldots, q_n$ and:

$$C(q_1, \ldots, q_n = q_m) < C(q_1,O) + C(O,q_2) + \ldots + C(O_1,q_n) \quad \text{for all } q \leqslant q_m$$

However, it is important to appreciate that while such cost conditions define natural monopoly, they do not necessarily guarantee that where they exist an industry will be populated by one firm. It is possible that a number of firms could exist in the industry, even though it would be desirable on cost grounds to produce the whole output in one firm. In such cases the monopoly is said to be 'unsustainable', because, while the total output is produced most efficiently under monopoly, subsets of total output can be produced at lower cost in separate firms. This will mean that groups of consumers will have an incentive to switch to a supplier willing to supply only their needs at lower cost (Baumol *et al.* 1977). Also, it is possible for an industry to be a monopoly, though monopoly is not most cost efficient. The monopolist maintaining its position by, for example, predatory pricing and investment tactics. Therefore, the existence of a sole supplier is not in itself sufficient evidence that an industry is a natural monopoly.

However, where natural monopoly does exist it is advantageous for one firm to produce the industry output, provided the well-known disadvantages of monopoly can be avoided, notably high prices and inefficiency. Monopolies are notorious for abusing their market power. Therefore, the controversy surrounding natural monopoly today is concerned with how to reap its cost advantages while preventing monopoly behaviour which is welfare reducing.

6.3 STATE OWNERSHIP AND PRIVATISATION

In the post-war period down to the 1980s in Britain, the predominant view was that public utilities were natural monopolies and should be state owned. The mail has been a state service since the sixteenth century and telephones were taken over by government in 1912. From the nineteenth century municipal authorities took a major stake in the development of gas, electricity and water supplies. However, it was under the 1945–51 Labour government that the railways, gas and electricity were nationalised as state monopolies and later, in 1973, most of the water industry was reorganised into ten public enterprises.

Nationalisation occurred for many reasons unrelated to natural monopoly. But it was often defended on the grounds that public monopoly was superior to private monopoly. In particular, the Labour Party argued that state ownership was the best way of preventing abuse where there is monopoly, by removing a powerful interest group, shareholders, who could be expected to pursue maximum profits. State ownership, it was argued, facilitated effective regulation of monopoly by bringing the monopoly directly under the control of government and by substituting a public interest objective for profit maximisation.

The practice of nationalisation from the 1940s, however, has not borne out such optimistic expectations. According to critics, nationalised industries have operated inefficiently, leading to high prices for consumers and frequent subsidies from taxpayers. Costs have risen because of damaging political interference in commercial decision-making, excessive wage increases for employees, managerial disillusionment and bureaucratic self-seeking. It is claimed that there are inherent weaknesses in state ownership and that private ownership is more efficient because of the profit motive and bankruptcy constraint on management, both of which are absent in the public sector. Although it has been argued that competition in the product market rather than ownership may be more important in determining efficiency (Millward and Parker 1983), some economists believe that private monopolies are superior to public monopolies because of a capital market constraint. In the private sector shares are traded and, therefore, there is a constant threat of take-over by new management which creates incentives for existing management to maximise efficiency (Friedman 1982; Littlechild 1986). By contrast, public sector managements are immune from take-over because there are no tradeable ownership rights in state concerns.

Also, there has been growing controversy about the existence and extent of natural monopoly in the industries served by state firms. Nationalised industries are often protected from competition by legislation, but there appears to be no cost reasons why coal mining, for example, should not be competitive in Britain. Equally, a number of economists have argued that parts of the public utilities operations could be beneficially opened up to competition, including electricity and gas production, telecommunications trunk networks and equipment and the provision of certain postal and rail services (Beesley and Littlechild, 1983; Vickers and Yarrow, 1985). But while the Conservative government since 1979 has introduced a major programme of privatisation, it has so far fought shy of a major restructuring of monopoly utilities.

Although the government has explored ways of introducing some competition into telecommunications and gas supplies, these utilities have been privatised with their monopoly powers almost intact. In so far as the industries are natural monopolies this is defensible on efficiency grounds. However, the failure to restructure also stems from the successful opposition of the management and workers of public utilities to the loss of their industry's monopoly. A smooth and successful transfer to the private sector needs the cooperation of management and workforce so government has been reluctant to alienate them. In addition, a monopoly industry is worth more when sold because the sale price capitalises potential monopoly profits. This may well have been a further reason for not restructuring. The government has been keen to raise finance from privatisation sales to set against public expenditure and to facilitate tax cuts.

6.4 REGULATORY FAILURE

One goal of privatisation is greater managerial freedom from political interference, yet more freedom for management of monopolies may lead to monopoly abuse. Therefore, denationalisation of monopolies in the United Kingdom in the 1980s has been coupled with the introduction of a regulatory structure to replace direct regulation of the industries by government department under state ownership. The form of regulatory regime introduced is discussed in detail in section 6.5. But first, it is useful to consider the operation of regulation in the United States. The system of regulation there, which has a long history, is not dissimilar to that being introduced in the United Kingdom.

In the United States regulation is undertaken at federal, state and local level and takes a variety of forms, but the common objective is prevention of monopoly abuse, especially discriminatory treatment of consumers and excessive profits, while at the same time providing incentives to produce. In recent years, however, drawing upon experience of how regulation actually operates in the United States, economists have identified inefficiencies caused by regulation, which must be balanced against any benefits regulation brings. In terms of the theoretical perspectives discussed in Chapter 1, the literature on US regulation is firmly within the neoclassical paradigm. It is assumed that firms attempt to maximise profit when free of state-imposed constraints and that individuals pursue their own utility. As observed in Chapter 1 this approach is in itself controversial. Nevertheless, the literature provides interesting insights into the possible consequences of regulation in the United Kingdom. It can be usefully divided into that part which deals with regulatory distortion of output, prices and investment and the literature on 'regulatory capture'.

6.4.1 Regulatory distortion

At its simplest, suppose that there is a profit ceiling imposed by regulation so that the firm is unable to benefit in terms of higher profits from efficiency and innovation. In such circumstances we would expect the firm not to introduce cost savings. If regulated firms are not permitted to increase profits by reducing costs but must pass on all savings in lower prices, why bother to be enterprising? One effect may be to create incentives for firms to operate off their production frontiers, overemploying all inputs, with managers slacking and labour and capital underutilised. Another manner in which costs may not be minimised is if firms are operating on their production frontiers but not reacting optimally to input prices, leading to overuse of one factor of production compared with another.

Over the last twenty years economists researching regulation have been especially interested in this possibility and a number of detailed models have been developed. Each model depends upon the specific assumptions made about the form regulation takes. Under a 'cost markup' method of regulation, where the profit ceiling increases with all costs, a marginal increase in spending on one input adds as much to the profit ceiling as a marginal increase in spending on another input. The equilibrium rules for employment of factor inputs are altered from the normal marginal product to price ratio ($MP_a/P_a = \ldots MP_n/P_n$) by exactly the same proportion.

However, where one or more of the productive inputs is excluded from the regulatory constraint, a regulated firm is likely to use more of a given factor of production which enters into the constraint compared to factors which do not. One example is the method of regulation found in the United States in industries with low capital–labour ratios, e.g., bus transport, postal services and trucking, in which prices are regulated by a mark-up over operating costs. When operating costs rise firms are permitted to increase their prices, which reduces the incentive to control operating costs compared with fixed costs. The result is overemployment of labour and less use of capital.

But most attention in the regulatory literature, since a seminal study by Averch and Johnson in 1962, has centred upon the opposite possibility, overemployment of capital, which can result where 'fair' rates of return (profits as a return on capital) are set directly or indirectly through permitted prices. It is this form of regulation which tends to be found in industries such as gas, electricity and water in the United States and is also found in parts of Europe, especially West Germany. The regulator attempts to achieve a rate of return higher than the cost of capital, to create incentives to invest and produce, but at a rate less than would be achieved in the absence of regulation (otherwise the regulation would be ineffective!). The monopolist then maximises profit subject to this externally imposed constraint, which takes the general form:

$$\text{Max: } (s - r)K$$

where K = the capital stock (asset base); s = allowed rate of return; r = unit cost of capital; $s > r$.

The firm increases its use of capital as the 'fair' rate of return is lowered from the level of monopoly profit towards the cost of acquiring capital. Since total profits now vary according to the amount of capital used, but are unaffected by labour use, the result is overexpansion of the firm's asset base to a level which would not be optimal in the absence of regulation.

This result can be shown diagrammatically. In Fig. 6.1 the profit-maximising output for the natural monopolist is p_1q_1. The capital stock is optimal since short-run and long-run marginal costs and short-run and long-run average costs are equal at output q_1. Suppose, however, that a profit constraint is introduced, which when incorporated into the short-run average cost curve shifts it from $SRAC_1$ to $SRAC_1R$. Profit at output q_1, which is still the profit-maximising output as marginal cost is unaffected, is above the regulated amount and hence the monopolist has an incentive to expand output by increasing capital stock. This will rise until the SRAC

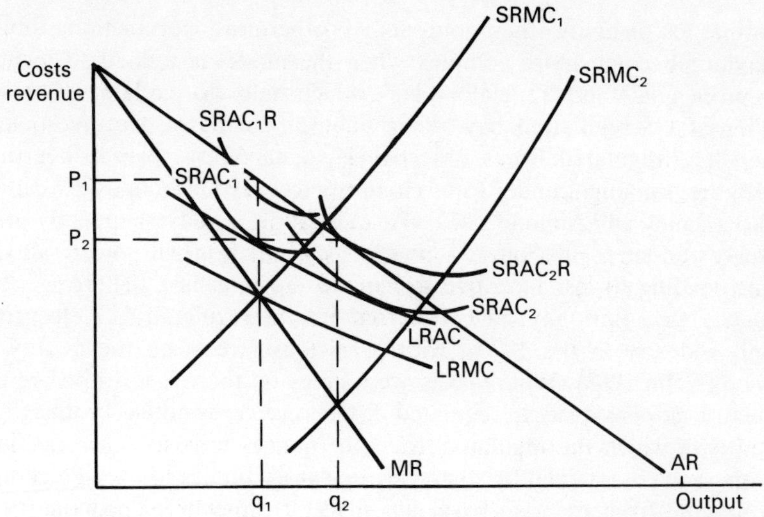

Fig. 6.1 The Averch–Johnson effect. *Source*: Utton (1986: 193).

($SRAC_2R$ which includes the profit constraint) equals the average revenue (AR). Profit is now equal to the regulated maximum and output is q_2 and price P_2. However, at this output long-run marginal cost is greater than short-run marginal cost ($LRMC > SRMC_2$) and short-run average cost ($SRAC_2$, which excludes the profit constraint) is greater than the long-run average cost (LRAC). The firm's capital stock is therefore no longer optimally adjusted to the output q_2; more specifically the capital base is overexpanded. There is employment of more capital and less labour than is consistent with minimum costs at any given output (Utton 1986).

The rate of return regulated firm will not only have an incentive to overinvest, it follows that it will prefer to own rather than lease assets where leased assets are not part of the regulated asset base, even where this is not the least-cost strategy. Also, the Averch–Johnson model has been extended to show that rate of return regulation distorts pricing structures reducing allocative efficiency, with controls on prices leading to excessive competition in other variables such as service levels and marketing (Douglas and Miller 1974; Finsinger *et al.* 1985). In addition, where a utility serves more than one market and profit is regulated in only one of the markets, the firm will have an incentive to charge as high a price as competitive conditions allow where profit is not regulated. Regulatory constraint thus distorts the firm's operations from what would otherwise be the profit-maximising path and it may lead firms to use surplus funds in an attempt to dominate unregulated markets. This is a possibility that has clear implications for UK privatised monopolies now allowed to diversify their outputs. Furthermore, predictions about behaviour become more complex when the model is refined to include non-profit goals and 'regulatory lag', which helps to explain why some studies of US regulation have been unable to confirm overinvestment. Where the regulated firm's objective is to maximise sales rather than profit, the firm might under some circumstances favour labour over capital inputs (Bailey and Malone 1970). Also, a failure to adjust speedily price increases under regulation at a time of cost inflation will lower rates of return leading to less incentive to expand the rate base. There is some evidence that this may have occurred in the regulated US electricity supply industry in the 1970s, with pernicious effects on the quality of service (Kahn 1983). Where costs are falling and there is a lag before the regulator adjusts prices, regulated firms receive windfall profits. The speed with which the regulator reacts to changes in costs of production, and the powers retained by some US regulatory bodies to exclude certain investments from the rate base, has made it difficult for economists to predict precisely the likely effects of regulation. Nevertheless, there is broad agreement that in the United States regulation distorts outputs, inputs and prices, and reduces allocative and productive efficiency (Joskow and Noll 1981).

6.4.2 Regulatory capture

The fact that regulatory effects are difficult to model accurately is partly due to the way in which regulatory agencies behave. In the United States they are usually staffed by an impressive array of lawyers, businessmen, accountants, economists and politicians. But they are often understaffed to obtain the amount of information necessary to regulate effectively and therefore become dependent upon data from the regulated enterprises themselves. If the regulator had perfect information, any wasteful investment by the monopoly would be disallowed in the rate base on which regulated profits are determined. But in practice there are important information asymmetries between regulator and regulated and inefficiencies may be concealed. An inability to regulate private companies effectively was an important reason why utilities, such as gas and water, were taken into public ownership in Britain (Millward 1986). Where governments own industries they may have superior information about outputs and costs to regulate effectively. Equally, however, governments may lack incentive to use this information to maximise social well-being; preferring instead, for example, to manage industries in the pursuit of political support and the utility of state bureaucrats (Niskanen 1973).

There is also the theme of whether regulators will pursue the 'public interest' (however defined) even when adequate information to regulate effectively is available. A number of economists have studied the process of regulation and question whether regulators are disinterested parties simply correcting inequities and inefficiencies in markets. Regulation may be subject to 'capture'. From a public interest perspective regulators are expected to operate at arm's length from their industries, providing an objective assessment of performance. But while regulators may start with good intentions, in 'regulatory capture' literature the regulator is soon drawn into controlling market entry and becomes too closely identified with the interests of the regulated utility.

In the United States, major regulatory bodies such as the Civil Aeronautics Board, the Federal Communications Commission, the Federal Energy Regulatory Commission, the Interstate Commerce Commission and the Federal Maritime Commission have all been criticised at one time or another in the post-war period for being too close to the industries they were regulating and neglecting the interests of consumers. For example, the Interstate Commerce Commission, the oldest federal regulatory agency in the United States, was set up in 1887 to regulate railway tariffs because of pressure from rail users concerned about monopoly pricing. However, by the 1930s the Commission had switched to protecting the railways by defending railway charges from the new competition from trucking. By the 1960s the Commission was regulating railway rates to protect trucking companies. There is similar suggestion of 'regulatory capture' in the way that local traffic commissioners in the United Kingdom limited competition in favour of existing bus operators prior to liberalisation of the market in the 1980s. The lesson seems to be that as regulatory regimes evolve they lose sight of their original objectives. In addition, a number of US studies have revealed the extent to which personnel switch during their careers between regulatory bodies and regulated monopolies, increasing the likelihood of 'regulatory capture'. Between 1960 and 1975 30 per cent of people appointed to nine regulatory commissions came from the industry they were to regulate; and of 85 commissioners who left agencies in that period, 32 became employed in a regulated firm within five years (Weidenbaum 1981).

A somewhat different if allied argument to 'regulatory capture' has been put forward by the American economists Stigler (1971) and Peltzman (1976), Stigler argues not that regulatory bodies are set up to pursue the public interest and are later 'captured', but that from the outset: 'as a rule, regulation is acquired by the industry and is designed and operated primarily for its benefit' (Stigler 1971:3). Now known as the 'economic theory of regulation', to distinguish it from the literature on 'regulatory capture', its central thesis is that regulation is not introduced to benefit consumers but to benefit the regulated producers by limiting competition. A good example may be world-wide airline regulation which restricts entry and allows airlines to obtain higher prices in an industry which is naturally competitive rather than monopolistic. This argument cannot explain all cases of regulation, however, for in some cases consumers were the driving-force for its introduction in the face of opposition from the industries concerned (American railways in the nineteenth century) (Posner 1974; Wilson 1980). Nevertheless, it usefully draws attention to the fact that regulation is sometimes designed to cause rather than cure 'market failure'. The general conclusion from this theory and the 'regulatory capture' literature is that while regulation may appear to exist to defend the interests of consumers, in fact it may stifle competition and raise costs by protecting the monopoly of existing suppliers.

Whatever the source of regulation and its precise effects on allocative and productive efficiency, regulation clearly involves significant resource costs to balance against any benefits. Estimating the overall burden is subject to considerable error. But one estimate puts the direct costs alone of operating the 56 major federal regulatory agencies in the United States (covering wider issues such as safety and health as well as particular industries) at $5.8 US billion in 1979; while the total administrative and compliance costs of regulation may amount to the upper end of estimates of welfare loss from monopoly (Weidenbaum 1981; Utton 1986). At the same time, the benefits are unclear. In the United States natural monopoly regulation is criticised for (a) promoting inefficiency; and (b) ineffectiveness in protecting consumers. Therefore, regulation of monopoly in the United States is surrounded by considerable controversy regarding its purpose and consequences. This is an important conclusion at a time when the United Kingdom is substituting private regulated companies for monopoly enterprises.

6.5 UK REGULATION

In the United States in recent years, because of the history of regulation, there has been a movement away from directly regulating industries towards promoting competition. For example, since 1977 airlines and trucking have been deregulated and telecommunications has been opened up to competition. However, by contrast the British government has resorted to preventing monopoly abuse by introducing a new tier of specially created regulatory agencies (the exception is airports where there was an existing regulatory body, the Civil Aviation Authority). These regulatory organisations, like their US counterparts, administer price controls, ensure licence compliance, police anti-competitive behaviour and handle complaints.

However, some economists familiar with the US experience doubt whether regulation will have its desired effect. They argue that in the absence of competition, private firms may perform little better than nationalised monopolies. This suggests that the government has wasted an opportunity to restructure industries such as telecommunications and gas (Kay and Thompson 1986). The possibility of introducing competition by making the market contestable either through franchising or by adopting common carrier status where industries are perceived to have natural monopoly characteristics is considered in section 6.6. Here the system of regulation adopted in the United Kingdom is outlined.

As natural monopoly rarely extends to all of the operations of a firm, the government has had to decide what activities need to be regulated, as well as the precise form regulation should take. Common to each of the privatised monopolies has been the introduction of an operating licence for a specific period; in the case of British Telecom (BT) for 25 years (though it is almost certain to be renewed). BT's licence, which contains over 50 conditions, sets out the terms under which the utility must operate and observance is monitored by the industry's regulatory agency, the Office of Telecommunications (OFTEL). OFTEL has a quasi-judicial role similar to that of US regulatory bodies, though compared with its US counterpart, the Federal Communications Commission, it is tiny, having a staff of just over one hundred. The Director General, Professor Bryan Carsberg, may issue orders where he suspects the licence is being breached by BT and the Monopolies and Mergers Commission can introduce modifications to the licence where OFTEL and BT are unable to agree changes.

BT's operating licence prohibits undue preference or discrimination. There must be no exclusive dealing arrangements with suppliers and the company is required to connect any licensed apparatus meeting approved standards to facilitate competition in equipment supplies. BT is also required by its licence to continue to supply social and national security services, including rural services, free 999 emergency services and loss-making public call-boxes, which it provided under nationalisation. This means that despite privatisation, BT must continue cross-subsidisation in the 'public interest' and is not allowed to operate as a purely commercial enterprise. It also means that to prevent rivals competing away BT's most profitable markets, which generate funds to subsidise other services, competition must remain restricted. Cross-subsidisation by a monopoly where there is free entry into the market leads to 'cream-skimming' of profitable business. Rivals will set up to supply only the profitable parts of the BT network which currently subsidise other parts. Therefore, the government has protected BT's monopoly by prohibiting competition. The only exception was the establishment of Mercury Communications in 1982 (a subsidiary of Cable and Wireless) which so far has been primarily concerned with supplying telecommunications services to large business users. Privatisation of telecommunications has not in itself led to more competition. Mercury was set up when BT was state owned and there are to be no other licensed operators until 1990 at the earliest.[2]

Turning to the gas industry, an even smaller regulatory body has been created, the Office of Gas Supply (OFGAS) headed by James MacKinnon with a staff of 15. OFGAS monitors the operations of British Gas, which is regulated like BT mainly by the terms of its operating licence. In the case of gas, as in the case of BT, regulation has to reflect and reconcile the conflicting interests of government, consumers and shareholders, and nowhere is this more apparent than in the way that government attempts to control profits.

A 1982 study of proposals by Professor Littlechild to regulate BT advocated a form of price control through a retail price index minus *X* formula (RPI-X), to apply for five years. Not only did Littlechild think that this would minimise direct interference in BT, thus preventing disincentives from being efficient, he also argued that this form of price control would require less information and monitoring than rate of return regulation, thus reducing the chances of 'regulatory capture'.

Littlechild expected price regulation to be necessary only in some areas of telecommunications and only until sufficient competition developed in all markets supplied by BT, which he estimated, optimistically, to take five years (Littlechild 1983). In the event, the basket of services covered by regulation is a wide one, including home and business line rentals and dialled local and national calls. These services account for around one-half of the company's turnover. After negotiation with BT the government set *X* at 3 per cent until 1989 (4.5 per cent from August 1989), a figure based upon what the company and the government could agree was an acceptable reflection of cost trends in the industry; though some economists have suggested that it is not a severe constraint given the pace of cost-reducing technological advance in telecommunications (Vickers and Yarrow 1985). In principle, unlike the US rate of return regulation, this formula should not distort employment of factor inputs since it is neutral between labour and capital. Also, it should provide BT with incentives to reduce costs because actual cost reductions need not be passed on in lower prices but can raise profits. However, in the future when BT's pricing formula comes up for review, it will be difficult to resist pressure from the company to set *X* according to its own underlying cost trends rather than, for example, cost trends in international telecommunications, which would better reflect the potential for efficiency gains (Sharpe 1984). In this case incentives to lower costs under the formula are reduced and the method of price control suffers from some of the inefficiencies apparent in US regulation.

Also, the government and OFTEL will suffer from the sort of information problems faced by regulators in the United States. If the *X* factor is set too high, BT's profits will be unduly restricted, damaging investment and service quality (and upsetting 1.7 million shareholders in BT, a not insignificant slice of voters). By contrast, if it sets *X* too low profits will be artificially high at a cost to consumers. In either event,

OFTEL will need to ensure that profit reductions in some services are not offset by higher prices elsewhere, either in unregulated charges or within the services covered by the pricing formula. Although the 'RPI-*X*' formula sets a limit to average prices of a basket of services, this still leaves BT freedom to determine prices of individual items in the basket. Prior to privatisation, trunk services cross-subsidised local calls. But now with competition from Mercury in the trunk-call market, BT is busy rebalancing its tariffs, raising charges for local calls and reducing long-distance tariffs, Unravelling such changes which are justified in terms of costs, from those that are not, is currently one of OFTEL's most important functions. Also, the formula does not prevent BT from altering the quality of the services it supplies to lower costs and raise profits.

There is clearly a possibility of disincentives for effective cost control when the 'RPI-*X*' formula is continuous rather than temporary. This is particularly pertinent to recently privatised British Gas and the British Airports Authority and to the proposed sale of the water industry. In these industries the prospects for competition are more limited than in telecommunications, because of natural monopoly characteristics, and price controls are therefore likely to be permanent.

In the case of water, to provide incentives for cost efficiency, Littlechild argued that *X* could be set for each of the ten regional water authorities in England and Wales according to an 'industry yardstick' rather than the authority's own costs. A surrogate form of competition would thus be introduced by penalising those authorities with efficiency gains below the average for the water industry and benefiting through higher profits those which achieve higher than average efficiency. However, critics of this proposal point out that across the industry there are widely varying cost structures, reflecting maintenance of sewers, plant and mains which in some areas are over a century old; costs therefore reflect historical investments (bygones). Owing to the capital-intensive nature of the water industry only around 50 per cent of costs are directly related to changes in the RPI and this share varies widely from authority to authority. Where because of replacement of deteriorating capital an authority's costs rise faster than the average, there is an economic case for higher than average price increases, in some cases *X* might justifiably be negative. Prices limited to an industrial average would unfairly penalise some authorities and be allocatively inefficient. At the present time it is uncertain what type of price control the government will finally impose when the industry is privatised.

In the case of gas, prior to privatisation the chairman of British Gas argued successfully that the industry needed only light regulation because of competition from alternative energy sources (despite the fact that the company accounts for around 60 per cent of the UK domestic energy market and 33 per cent of the industrial market). Pricing regulation based upon the BT formula was introduced to reduce non-gas costs in the industry over five years with *X* set at 2 per cent. The pricing regulation applies, however, only to the 'tariff market' (consumers purchasing under 25,000 therms per annum). The heavy users in the industrial and commercial market will continue to negotiate prices directly with British Gas. The pricing formula has a complex arrangement for relating the efficiency of the company measured in non-gas costs and the beach price of gas to the level of inflation. The idea is that while beach prices paid to North Sea oil companies are outside the company's control, and can therefore legitimately be passed on to gas consumers, consumers must be protected from cost inflation elsewhere. However, this may well reduce the incentive for British Gas to keep down the cost of gas it so purchases, providing a windfall for oil companies at a cost to gas consumers.

Also, prices should be based on long-run marginal cost (LRMC) calculated over the whole range of gas costs; but studies suggest that British Gas has traditionally priced below LRMC and cross-subsidised consumers leading to allocative inefficiency (Hammond, Helm and Thompson 1985). The way in which prices are now regulated does not guarantee a swift movement to economic pricing, while any rebalancing of tariffs will, as in the case of BT, need careful monitoring by OFGAS to ensure that changes are genuinely required and not part of a monopoly-charging strategy. In particular OFGAS will need to be vigilant to prevent monopoly price discrimination or artificial modification of joint cost allocations between the regulated domestic market and the unregulated industrial market, perhaps to inhibit the development of competition in bulk gas supplies. In late 1987, after consideration by OFGAS, BG's method of pricing industrial gas supplies was referred to the Monopolies and Mergers Commission for fuller investigation.

The British Airports Authority, privatised in 1986, has its charges somewhat differently regulated from both BT and British Gas, reflecting the nature of the industry. The BAA controls seven UK airports including the two busiest, Heathrow and Gatwick, and therefore has a localised monopoly over access to air travel. The main feature of price regulation is the imposition by the government of a maximum annual average revenue per passenger from charges at the company's south-east airports as a group and Heathrow and Gatwick individually. This is based upon complex formulae, to be reviewed by the Monopolies and Mergers Commission every five years. However, like the RPI-*X* formula this does not guarantee charges which are allocatively efficient. At the same time, airport commercial services (including duty-free shops) continue to be allocated by competitive franchise ensuring productive but not allocative efficiency. The successful contractors are those which offer the highest percentage of turnover to BAA, encouraging pricing above marginal costs. In the past, BAA's pricing policy has been consistent with sales maximisation subject to a rate of return set by the government (Starkie and Thompson 1985). While privatisation has changed the nature of price control, it is far from apparent that the result is higher allocative efficiency.

This review of the system of regulation of privatised monopolies in the United Kingdom (summarised in Table 6.1) suggests that regulation cannot be relied upon to prevent monopoly abuse. Mandatory price control has been one of the most important innovations of UK regulation in the 1980s and reflects concern about the inefficiencies of rate of return regulation in the United States. The RPI-*X* formula is simple and hence easily understood. But as time passes it may be subject to 'regulatory capture' and come to reflect the industry's costs rather than underlying trends in productivity. Also, when controlling prices the price base selected should best capture the unavoidable industry costs. But the RPI does not meet this requirement since it includes irrelevant costs, e.g., food. Also, the RPI-*X* formula may freeze existing price distortions in BT and domestic gas supplies, thus preventing a speedy move towards allocative efficiency. In the gas industry the ability to pass on all increases in beach prices of gas reduces incentives for British Gas to negotiate for lower-priced gas supplies from oil companies. In the water industry it is difficult to see how an industry average *X* factor could be made to work without penalising areas with special problems in terms of replacing ageing capital stock. In the case of BAA, operating under a somewhat different charging regime, the result is similar concern about continued allocative inefficiency.

Turning to the regulatory agencies, they are small in relation to the companies they have to regulate and highly dependent upon information provided by the monopolies to do their job properly. Nevertheless, OFTEL has shown determination to police BT's activities with commendable independence and OFGAS has similarly made an encouraging start, successfully challenging the reluctance of British Gas to supply important information on the pricing of the company's supplies of North Sea gas. However, these are early days and eventual 'capture' cannot be ruled out. The US evidence suggests that the danger of an over-cosy relationship between regulators and regulated grows over time.

6.6 ALTERNATIVES TO NATIONALISATION AND REGULATION

Both state ownership and private ownership with state regulation appear to introduce inefficiencies in resource allocation. Arguably, the US experience of regulation is as disappointing as the UK experience of nationalisation. Also, it appears that the system of regulation which has been adopted in the United Kingdom in the 1980s cannot guarantee

Table 6.1 UK regulatory structure

Organisation	Main feature of price regulation	Regulatory body	Competition?
British Telecom	RPI–3% (from mid-1989 4.5%) applying to about one-half of turnover	OFTEL	Growing competition from Mercury Communications. Competition in maintenance and sale of apparatus
British Gas	RPI−2% applying to input costs other than North Sea gas and applicable to the 'tariff market' only	OFGAS	Negligible in gas supply. Competition in maintenance and appliance sales
British Airports Authority	Maximum annual average revenue per passenger. Duty-free shops franchised	CAA	Localised monopoly of airports, especially in the south-east
Water (Littlechild proposal)	RPI-X, possibly with X set as an industry average to promote 'yardstick' competition	OFWAT	Localised monopolies

prevention of monopoly abuse. It is, therefore, useful in reviewing the controversy surrounding privatisation of natural monopolies to consider possible alternatives to both public enterprise and private but state-regulated ownership. Below we consider the scope for (1) increasing competition; (2) franchising; and (3) introducing common carrier status.

6.6.1 Competition

Many economists, and particularly the free market Chicago/Austrian schools of economists, argue that the 'dead hand' of government restrictions upon trade are more responsible for monopolies than the 'invisible hand' of markets. Hence governments should concentrate upon removing legislative barriers to trade, in particular regulations and state ownership. Supportive of this argument are empirical studies that suggest that competition introduces incentives to control costs and operate efficiently, which may more than offset any loss of economies of scope under natural monopoly (Primeaux 1977).

Although the Conservative government advocates free market economics, to date the only industry in which privatisation has been accompanied by major trade liberalisation is bus transport. (Sensitive to criticism of the decision not to restructure the gas industry on privatisation, at the time of writing (January 1988) the government is considering ways to introduce competition into a privatised electricity industry.) The notion of introducing competition where there is natural monopoly seems on the face of it problematical. As we saw earlier, if an industry is naturally monopolistic competition will raise costs. Indeed, state regulation or public ownership to prevent entry into the industry might raise welfare if a natural monopoly exists but would in a free market be unsustainable. However, it is probable that a number of the enterprises privatised in the United Kingdom do have activities which could be safely opened up to competition, leading to greater productive and allocative efficiency. Even where competition would not be cost efficient because of natural monopoly, there may still be scope for breaking up what is a national monopoly into regional monopolies or scope for making the market 'contestable'. Splitting a large national monopoly into regional companies would promote comparison of relative performance, thus assisting effective regulation. Also, smaller companies are more vulnerable to take-over by more efficient management.

The possibility of introducing competition even where there is natural monopoly has been reinforced in recent years by developments in the economic theory of 'market contestability' within neoclassical economics. According to this theory, as long as there are no barriers to entry and exit from the industry, the monopolist will have to maximise production efficiency and price according to marginal costs to prevent the loss of some or all of its market to a new entrant (Baumol *et al.* 1982). In particular, the earning of economic rent will attract competitors. Despite being a monopoly, the industry will operate like a firm in a perfectly competitive market because otherwise new firms would set up in the industry and reduce the monopolist's market. Of course, such a high degree of 'contestability' depends upon an assumption that there are no sunk costs (costs not recoverable on exit from the industry) so that 'hit and run' competition is feasible. Also, that the monopolist faced with potential competition will not introduce pricing and other strategies intended to deter rivals in a way which is welfare reducing. In practice these assumptions are unlikely to hold, so that the mere absence of legislative barriers to entry does not guarantee that monopolies will exhibit the welfare properties of perfect competition. None the less, 'contestability theory' has helped create a climate of opinion conducive to deregulation of monopoly, particularly in the United States.

6.6.2 Franchising

Natural monopoly means that provision by more than one firm is more costly than monopoly provision; hence, competition in the field would be welfare reducing. 'Market contestability' theory offers one possible solution, but depends upon restrictive assumptions and is not an answer where natural monopoly minimises costs but is unsustainable. Therefore, recently attention has shifted to introducing incentives for the monopolist to be efficient by creating competition for the field, i.e., competition for the right to be the monopoly supplier, through franchising. A properly constructed franchising scheme fulfils most of the requirements of 'market contestability' and has been described as 'a halfway house between state and private ownership for enterprises with an element of natural monopoly' (*Economist*, 12 July 1986:18). Franchising essentially confers monopoly rights in a given area of economic activity for a prescribed period. It is not unknown in the United Kingdom. For instance, independent television and cable TV services which demonstrate natural monopoly characteristics are already franchised. Also, local authority services where competition in the market raises costs, such as refuse collection, have been subject to contracting out to private suppliers, who then operate the complete service for a given period.

In principle, the franchise (or contract) can be offered to the firm that bids the highest price to run the service, which would capitalise the expected discounted monopoly profits – economic rents – in the bid price accruing to the franchisor (presumably government). However, this would have the disadvantage of imposing monopoly prices on consumers and would be allocatively inefficient. A better alternative is for the franchise to be awarded to the firm which offers to supply at the lowest price to consumers. The latter is often referred to as the 'Chadwick–Demsetz auction' after its nineteenth-century advocate, social reformer Edwin Chadwick, and its more recent proponent, the American economist Harold Demsetz (1968). However, although it benefits consumers over the franchisor, unless the industry is a constant-cost industry it does not guarantee allocative efficiency. Prices are bid down to average costs and not marginal costs. Also, franchising becomes particularly complex in multi-product industries. Where the franchise price relates to average expected revenues there is freedom to establish individual prices within this revenue constraint and hence scope for monopoly price discrimination.

Also, contracts may be costly to negotiate and monitor, which suggests the need for long franchises (Williamson 1976). Contracts have to be drawn up and standards of service under the terms and conditions of the contract policed. Nor is it necessarily the case that the franchise will be highly competitive. For example, potential bidders might collude to reduce competition. Also, the incumbent firm might have special advantages in terms of know-how and capital equipment over other potential contractors when contracts are renewed, thus reducing the level of real competition. Furthermore, contracts cannot usually be complete in the sense of covering every possible contingency during their life. Such contracts would be difficult to write and negotiate. The alternative of incomplete contracts, including for instance revision of prices during the life of the contract to reflect higher costs, creates scope for abuse. A contractor might initially tender at a loss, hoping to win the contract and raise charges later. Also, where prices are renegotiated during the life of a contract as costs rise, the result is a form of cost-plus pricing, with resulting disincentives for franchisees to control costs in a manner similar to inefficiencies found in regulated companies in the United States. Insofar as franchising requires the establishment of a policing mechanism to monitor contract performance and renegotiation of prices and outputs when demands and input prices change, it takes on all the characteristics of regulation. Complete contracts which are frequently recontracted might appear to offer an alternative solution, but usually only by raising contracting costs and by penalising investment. An incumbent will usually be reluctant to undertake investment close to the time of contract renewal lest the contract is lost and the investment wasted.

The existence of sunk costs can also reduce competition when the contract is renewed, just as they reduce market contestability, because they are not an opportunity cost to the incumbent but are relevant to potential franchisees. One way around this sunk-cost problem is for strategic capital equipment to be owned by the state and leased to contractors (as occurs in UK independent television where transmitters belong to the Independent Broadcasting Authority (IBA) and are leased to television companies). However, as the contractors do not own the capital this may lead to excessive wear and tear and inadequate maintenance. Alternatively, there could be a requirement that the winner of a contract must purchase existing capital at a fair valuation from the previous franchisee, assuming that a fair valuation can be agreed.

Recent experience in the United Kingdom of franchising or contracting suggests that there may be appreciable cost savings, especially over public sector provision. Cost savings of around 20 per cent in refuse and cleansing services appear not to be unusual (Hartley and Huby 1985). However, in the United States and United Kingdom, experience of franchising cable and other TV and radio services has not been entirely favourable (Williamson 1976). For the United Kingdom, despite the IBA's ownership of major transmitting assets, Domberger and Middleton (1985) identify a number of serious weaknesses in independent TV franchising relating to over-lengthy contract duration, insufficiently clear performance criteria available to potential franchisees, and appreciable sunk costs in bidding. Thus, franchising may be useful in some but not all cases of natural monopoly. It is likely to be most appropriate for services such as refuse collection, where there are few sunk costs and therefore the costs of entering and leaving the industry are relatively low. But it is probably less appropriate for the operations of the major public utilities which have large capital investments, such as telecommunications, gas and water.[3]

6.6.3 Common carrier status

The introduction of common carrier status is a method of restructuring natural monopolies, which retains the cost savings of monopoly while introducing competition where it is advantageous. Under common carrier status one firm owns and controls the network or local and national transmission grids, depending upon the type of industry, but provision of services on the network or grid is opened up to competition. For example, British Rail, whether in the public or private sectors, would own the rail network, including stations, signals and so on, but rolling stock and passenger and freight services would be operated by separate companies leasing space on the system by competitive bids.[4] Another example could be electricity, where one company might own the transmission system but anyone meeting agreed technical and safety standards could bid to generate electricity to be supplied through the grid directly to consumers or to a further set of independent companies which retail supplies. Recently, the Peacock Report on broadcasting (Report of the Committee on the Financing of the BBC 1987) suggested that BT and Mercury in telecommunications should have common carrier status to allow greater diversity and freedom in communications. And in 1981 the Beesley Report on liberalising the BT network recommended that the government permit the resale of BT capacity to independent suppliers, though the government subsequently rejected this suggestion.

Where there are economies of scope, which means that a sole vertically integrated supplier is most cost effective, this form of industrial restructuring will not be beneficial. However, in other cases common carrier status might offer a means by which competition can be introduced without losing the cost advantages of monopoly. A recent Australian inquiry into telecommunications reported favourably (Report of the Committee of Inquiry into Telecommunications Services in Australia, vol. 1, 1982):

> Separation of system and service would: promote diversity in service supply; facilitate easier market entry by prospective private sector service providers; . . . enable the best use of different types of transmission systems; facilitate more timely introduction of new services; allow simpler regulatory and administrative arrangements, hence minimal government intervention in the market and lower costs to service providers and users.

Already to a limited degree common carrier status exists in the United Kingdom. BT and Mercury currently allow private information and data services on their networks, and the gas and electricity industries since 1982 are required to permit private sector power suppliers access to their transmission systems. These cases, however, highlight some of the problems in implementing common carrier status. If the common carrier continues to provide services in competition this can act to deter new suppliers. The common carrier, as in the cases of British Gas and the Central Electricity Generating Board, can so dominate supplies as to create unacceptable uncertainties about the market and prices for potential competitors. Also, the common carrier can set prices to forestall entry and undertake other forms of predatory action which deter rivals (Hammond, Helm and Thompson 1986).

In most cases there could not be free entry to the system. Presumably British Rail, for instance, would have to select in some way which private operators could use which routes, perhaps through franchising. But given the strategic bargaining advantage of the common carrier with its ownership of the system, usually the method of contracting and prices and outputs would need to be regulated, introducing regulatory inefficiencies. Like franchising, with which it tends to be associated, common carrier status may be a useful method of introducing some competition into a natural monopoly; but it is not free from difficulties and the complexity and costs of the necessary contractual arrangements may swamp any benefits.

6.7 CONCLUSIONS

Natural monopoly arises in multi-product industries where there are economies of scope so that it is most cost efficient to produce the output set in one firm rather than in competing firms. In the post-war period in the United Kingdom the public utilities, often said to be natural monopolies, were publicly owned and protected from competition. However, a combination of the difficulty in operating nationalised industries efficiently and research findings which questioned whether these industries were in fact natural monopolies at all, encouraged many economists to argue for privatisation and liberalisation of markets.

From 1979 the Conservative government introduced a major programme of privatisation which was characterised by state regulation of private monopolies. This policy was pursued despite an extensive literature on regulatory failure, which draws on experience in the United States, and a trend in the United States away from regulation towards promoting competition. In telecommunications, for example, only limited competition was introduced, while the gas industry was privatised with its monopoly power intact.

Privatisation is part of a wider programme to 'roll back the frontiers of the state' pursued by the Conservative government in the 1980s and it would be wrong to see it purely as a response to dissatisfaction with nationalisation as a cure for natural monopoly. The rationale for privatisation is complex and the role of ideology should not be ignored. However, in the privatisation debate natural monopoly raises special issues. These relate to the form of regulation adopted and whether it will duplicate the experience of regulation in the United States; whether private monopoly is superior to state monopoly; and whether the government is overlooking ways of privatising monopolies which introduce competition without raising supply costs. More generally, controversy centres upon whether privatisation has addressed the problem of how best to control monopoly abuse.

To date the government has eschewed radical forms of restructuring on privatisation, preferring to transfer industries to the private sector with their monopoly power largely or wholly intact.[5] This is economically sound where all of the activities in the industry are naturally monopolistic. However, BT and British Gas, and perhaps to a lesser extent the airports and water authorities, are vertically integrated concerns with, it seems, some activities well suited to competition. Even where competition cannot be introduced without cost disadvantages, franchising or common carrier status may offer a solution superior to monopoly regulation (the argument is summarised in Table 6.2). Contrary to the government's apparent expectation, privatisation with regulation appears to provide no simple

Table 6.2 Natural monopoly: possible solutions

Method	Advantages	Disadvantages
State ownership	Combines ownership and regulation to limit conflicts of interest and to promote a flow of information about costs and outputs upon which effective regulation depends	Inadequate incentives for government to use this information to maximise social well-being
Private ownership with state regulation	Efficiency attributes of private ownership combined with state controls to prevent monopoly abuse	State intervention leads to distortion of inputs, outputs and prices, reducing allocative and productive efficiency. Possibility of regulatory capture
Introducing competition	Incentive to produce and price efficiently	Loss of economies of scope. Applicability of 'market contestability' theory is limited by the existence of sunk costs
Franchising	Combines benefits of monopoly with periodic competition for sole supplier status	Possible disincentives to invest plus transaction costs
Common carrier status	Cost savings from monopoly combined with competition where competition is feasible	Transaction costs. Limited applicability where there are economies in vertical integration

solution to market failure under natural monopoly. Indeed, it is unclear whether it is superior to nationalisation, in the sense of being more efficient in the use of resources. Neither theory nor practice suggests that regulated private monopoly is an especially attractive industrial structure.

FURTHER READING

A comprehensive treatment of the theory of natural monopoly can be found in Sharkey (1982). On the distortionary effects of regulation on prices, outputs and investments there is a very detailed account in Bailey (1973), which can be updated by reading Joskow and Noll (1981). For studies of 'regulatory capture' and related theory see Stigler (1971) and Posner (1974). Vickers and Yarrow (1985) provide an interesting account of developments in regulating natural monopolies in the United Kingdom. For a general study of regulation see Utton (1986).

NOTES

1. Note that it is possible for a firm to be a natural monopoly under one set of input prices but not under another as relative factor prices may affect the degree of capital intensity. However, in deriving this cost function fixed input prices are assumed. Thus, the cost function C(q,w) can be written simply as C(q) where q is a vector of outputs and w is a vector of inputs assumed constant.
2. The Monopolies and Mergers Commission is to review the terms and conditions of BT's licence in 1989. Mercury Communication's operating licence does not contain any social obligations or, because the company faces competition from BT, price controls.
3. The use of renewable operating licences in telecommunications and gas means that, in principle, there is scope to introduce competitive tendering to operate these services in the future. However, in practice it is likely to prove politically difficult for any government to divest BT and British Gas of their services.
4. A further possibility would be to allow competitive bids to manage the system. The system operator would then be franchised.
5. Since this chapter was written the government's plans for electricity privatisation have been announced. Conscious of criticism following the failure to restructure the telecommunications and gas industries, the government intends to introduce some competition into electricity generation by dividing the CEGB into two companies – National Power and Power-Gen – and by encouraging new generating companies to enter the market. The distribution of electricity will be handled as now by area boards but these boards will be privatised. Transmission of electricity from the generators to the area companies will be the responsibility of a separate company owning the national grid which will act as a 'common carrier' for the electricity generators. The natural monopoly in electricity supply lies in distribution and transmission, rather than generation, and this is reflected in the government's proposals.

7 · LOCAL GOVERNMENT FINANCE IN CRISIS

Is there a better way?

BOB LEACH

7.1 INTRODUCTION

Local government finance has always been controversial, but never more so than recently. Both the growth and control of local expenditure, and the financing of that expenditure have been the subject of sharp division and heated debate. Moreover, after a decade of significant but still essentially incremental changes, the whole system of local government finance in the United Kingdom faces the most far-reaching and fundamental reform for over a century, a reform which has also and inevitably stirred bitter controversy.

To the layperson the sources of that controversy seem related to abstruse, highly technical issues. It has to be admitted that some topics, such as the annual adjustments of central government grant, are so complex that qualified professionals working in local authority finance departments have difficulty in comprehending them fully. Yet the fundamental source of controversy over local government finance is neither abstruse nor technical. What is at issue is the proper scope and limits of elected local authorities in the United Kingdom. The financing of local government activities is secondary to the question of what those activities should be, and how much autonomy local authorities should have in exercising them. Behind the arguments over controlling local government expenditure, and behind the fierce debate over local government taxation and other sources of revenue lie assumptions about the economic role of government in general and local government in particular. These assumptions in turn reflect conflicting ideological perspectives, which are explored more fully elsewhere. While familiar in other contexts, these competing perspectives are seldom related to controversies over local government finance, which are often treated in a curiously atheoretical way.

This chapter attempts to lay bare the assumptions behind the arguments, and relate these to alternative perspectives. The ordering of topics is, however, fairly conventional. The first part of the chapter examines competing explanations of the growth of local government capital and revenue expenditure, exploring its impact on both the national and local economies (focusing especially on the effect of local spending generally and local economic policy in particular on local employment). The case for central government control of expenditure financed by local taxation is then reviewed. The second half of the chapter switches to an examination of the various sources of local government revenue – central government grants, fees and charges, and local taxation. Assumptions behind past and current practice, and a variety of reform proposals, are then explored. A brief concluding section examines the future of local government finance.

7.2 LOCAL GOVERNMENT EXPENDITURE

The size and more particularly the growth of local government expenditure has been a focus of considerable controversy. Recent estimates suggest that it amounts to some 11 per cent of gross domestic product, and over a quarter of total UK public expenditure (HMSO 1986: 78). A high proportion of this expenditure, around half, is taken by labour costs. Local government employs nearly three million people, or 14 per cent of the country's total workforce.

As with public spending in general, local government expenditure has increased markedly, but irregularly over the last century. The most authoritative study of local government finance (Foster *et al.* 1980: Chapter 4) points out that an average growth rate of current expenditure of 3.4 per cent per annum hides large variations – with sharp falls in local spending during wartime, sharp rises in the immediate post-war years, and two longish periods of very high growth, from 1870 to 1900, and again from 1955 to 1975, when growth rates exceeded 5 per cent per annum. As this was markedly faster than growth in GDP over these two periods, it follows that local government expenditure was then a rising proportion of GDP, but at other times, and notably in recent years, it has declined as a proportion of GDP. Capital spending has not always moved in parallel with current expenditure. There have been periods when it was falling or static while current expenditure was rising steeply. Local authority expenditure as a proportion of total public spending has also fluctuated considerably. It was much higher before the First World War than it is now. Recent trends, particularly the rapid growth in the post-war period until the mid-seventies, and the subsequent record, have been especially controversial (Jones and Stewart 1983; Newton and Karran 1985; HMSO 1986). Concern about the growth of public spending in general in the mid-seventies inevitably focused in part on the record of local government, which was widely held responsible for overspending and extravagance. It was a Labour Secretary of State for the Environment, Tony Crosland, who sternly declared, 'The party's over.' Conservative administrations from 1979 have been particularly critical of local government's spending record, which has been seen as a crucial contributory factor in the rise of total public expenditure which they have been concerned to contain.

Those associated with local government have attributed the rise in spending to a number of factors – the costs of local government reorganisation, inflationary pressures (particularly labour costs and high interest rates), demographic trends and the extra burdens placed on local authorities by central government. It is a frequent local government complaint that town halls are blamed by central government for higher spending that its own policies have made necessary.

Local authorities are not entirely passive agents, however. New services have been pioneered as a result of local initiatives – notably in the economic development and leisure fields – and some established services have been transformed and extended. Local government, like central government, has been subject to electoral and other pressures to increase spending. Both have been affected by the 'revolution of rising expectations'. The rise in spending has also been subject to conflicting theoretical explanations from a variety of ideological perspectives. On the right, Niskanen's (1973) model of bureaucratic oversupply has been utilised to explain increased spending in terms of the vested interests of the local government service. Public choice theory has pointed to poor local accountability as an explanation for the voters' apparent preference for high spending. The local electorate does not bear the bulk of the cost of increased spending, which rational economic behaviour will thus induce it to support. On the left, neo-Marxist analysis suggests that increases in public spending in general, and local government spending in particular, are functional to the needs of capital. However, it is also pointed out that the bulk of local government expenditure does not directly aid the accumulation of capital, but involves services for people, or what is sometimes described as 'collective consumption'. Such social costs are likely to be questioned by capital, particularly in periods of falling profits (Newton and Karran 1985).

Since 1975 total local government spending has fallen as a proportion of total public expenditure, and as a proportion of GDP, but it remains the subject of acute controversy. Jones and Stewart (1983: 12) have contrasted this fall in local spending with the rise in central government spending over the same period, concluding, 'local government spending is not out of control. On the contrary you could say that central government spending is out of control.'

A diametrically-opposed view is given in the Green Paper, 'Paying for Local Government' (HMSO 1986). This argues that while capital spending has fallen, local authority current expenditure has been rising again since 1979, albeit at a much slower rate (0.5 per cent per annum). It is admitted that some reductions in manpower have been achieved, 'but the fall of 4% since 1979 is modest compared with the achievements elsewhere in the public sector' (l. 27). The whole tone of the Green Paper is to suggest that local spending is still far too high. There is 'a concern to contain local government expenditure at affordable levels'. Measures introduced by the government since 1979 to curb spending had proved 'unlikely to bring about the reductions in local authority spending thought necessary'. Moreover, 'throughout a handful of the highest spending authorities have consistently failed to restrain their spending' (l. 24).

There is of course no objective way of determining what the level of local government spending should be, either in total, or in relation to overall public spending, or in relation to GDP or anything else. Comparisons with local government spending in other countries tend to suggest that UK local government expenditure is not excessive or out of line (Newton and Karran 1985: 6–10). However, such comparisons are inconclusive because the structure, responsibilities and traditions of local government vary markedly between countries.

Moreover, it is a fairly meaningless exercise to review local government expenditure in isolation from the activities local authorities are required or permitted to perform. Essentially, local government expenditure is the price-tag for the public provision of a range of services. Significant reductions in local spending can only be achieved if local authorities cut either their range of activities or their service levels. Arguments about local government expenditure are at bottom about the proper economic role of local government. It is this issue which now needs to be addressed.

7.3 THE ECONOMIC ROLE OF LOCAL GOVERNMENT

Little systematic thought has been given this century to the range of functions which should be handled by democratic local government. In practice, functions have been acquired, and sometimes subsequently lost, almost haphazardly, and changes have not been related to any clear idea of the proper scope of local government in a unitary state such as the United Kingdom. There has been no attempt to rationalise the relative spheres of interest of central and local government, or determine the degree of autonomy the latter should enjoy. Nor has there been any systematic effort to distinguish the relative advantages and disadvantages of elected local authorities compared with other public agencies.

Fundamental changes in structure have been undertaken, and equally fundamental changes in finance proposed, without addressing these critical issues (Foster *et al.* 1980: 39–63).

From the professional practitioner viewpoint there was little to be said for entering a theoretical debate on the economic role of local government. The demand for services was largely determined by statute, although influenced to a degree by demographic factors and local pressures. Until recently the legislative framework within which local government operated was apparently reinforced by a broad political consensus on the proper sphere of local authorities. Functions might have evolved without any apparent rationale, but at least there was a general acceptance that local authorities were doing the right kinds of things. Controversy was largely confined to a few specific activities, such as public works, and aspects of financial control and service delivery. That consensus no longer exists. It is now not just the cost of service delivery which is debated, but the whole rationale for local authority intervention in particular fields. On the one hand, local government's role in housing, planning, public transport and even latterly education, has been questioned and sharply reduced or threatened. On the other hand, local authorities themselves have expanded their activities in areas such as leisure services and economic development, and these too have become the centre of controversy. Thus the bundle of services and activities traditionally associated with local government can no longer be simply taken for granted.

Part of the debate is over what sort of public agencies should be providing public services. Control by elected local authorities is only one of a range of options. In practice local government has effectively lost services for which it was previously responsible to other public agencies. Sometimes this was because of technological developments and considerations of scale, arguments which apply perhaps to gas, electricity, trunk roads and possibly water. Sometimes the need for equality of provision and uniformity of standards across the country implicitly ruled out control by local authorities – as in the case of social security payments.

Arguably the whole rationale for elected local authorities involves a degree of discretion and a qualified autonomy. Clearly the freedom enjoyed by local government in a unitary state is heavily constrained. No rights are reserved to local government, and financial, administrative and judicial controls reinforce its constitutionally subordinate position. Yet these limitations are at least partially offset by other characteristics of local government in the United Kingdom. Election gives local authorities a degree of legitimacy not enjoyed by other public bodies. Election implies choice, and choice implies some diversity. Second, local authorities are multi-purpose, unlike most appointed bodies which are single-purpose. Responsibility for a range of functions within a particular area or community implies some scope for determining priorities and allocating resources between as well as within services. Finally, elected local authorities can raise their own taxes. These three characteristics, while conceptually distinct, are heavily mutually dependent, and all imply a qualified autonomy for UK local government (Foster *et al*. 1980: 21–63).

Part of the argument about local authority control over particular services relates to technical problems of administration, and the existence of economies or diseconomies of scale. Another part of the argument hinges on the need for coordination between services. But much of the argument is ultimately based on local choice and discretion. Where, inevitably, local circumstances have to be taken into consideration, and where there is a case for responding to local preferences and permitting a degree of local choice, there is a strong argument for provision by elected local authorities. One major service which is not currently administered by local government, but could be on these criteria, is the National Health Service. It was political constraints rather than any administrative or economic criteria which dictated that first hospitals and then the community health services should be taken out of local authority control (Jones and Stewart 1983).

But much of the debate today is not over what public agencies are most suitable for the regulation and operation of particular public services. It is about whether certain services, many of which have in the past been administered by local government, should be publicly provided in any shape or form. Part of the justification for local authority activities is thus bound up with the wider issue of government economic intervention. Mainstream economics assumes the general superiority of the market in resource allocation, so that any departure from the price mechanism has to be justified in terms of the deficiencies of its operation in specific respects – where there are divergences between social and private costs and benefits, where the benefits of a service are unavoidably general and indiscriminate (e.g., defence, maintenance of law and order) or where there would otherwise be scope for the exploitation of monopoly power, for example (Sandford 1984: 1–19). Such a mainstream approach has been questioned both by radical economists from the Left, who would reject the general presumption in favour of the market, and by the New Right, who would define far more narrowly than customarily the grounds for government intervention.

Of the services traditionally provided by local government, some would be widely viewed as exceptions to the general presumption in favour of market provision – police, fire, highways (perhaps), environmental health and the social control aspects of social services. Others, such as housing, transport, institutional care, education and leisure services could in principle be provided through the market, while in practice there has been some competing private provision in all of them – increasingly so in recent years, as a government influenced by free market economics has sought to extend private sector involvement. Indeed many of those activities in the forefront of the ideological battleground on the public/private sector divide have been within the local government sphere.

Housing, always the most contestable service within the former consensus on welfare provision, has been most affected by the ideological change of climate. The statutory 'right to buy' had already eroded local authority housing provision, even before it was proposed that council tenants should be allowed to opt out of local authority control and choose their own landlords. By the 1990s local government will be left with only a residual housing function.

The deregulation of public transport, and the statutory requirement to contract out cleansing, catering, building and repair, parks, leisure services and other functions is transforming the way in which local authorities operate. The trend is away from direct service provision towards performance-specification and regulation.

The expenditure implications are not entirely clear. The virtual loss of a major service like housing might be expected to reduce expenditure, but in some authorities the separate housing revenue account shows a profit. Deregulation and contracting out may not involve reductions in spending, as local authorities can still maintain subsidies. Greater operational efficiency might produce some marginal savings, but significant reductions would require a change in policy involving a lower level of service provision, and such a policy change could be effected without contracting out. The transfer of a service to another public agency would reduce local government expenditure, but the overall impact on public spending might be relatively slight, depending on the effect of the transfer on policy, resourcing and efficiency.

The crucial point is that arguments over local government expenditure are inseparably bound up with arguments over local government functions and autonomy, and these in turn depend on differing ideological perspectives which can be elucidated but scarcely resolved. Local government expenditure can only be assessed against the job which local government is required to do.

7.3.1 Local government and the national economy

The sheer size and scope of local government clearly has implications for the national economy. Local government expenditure is a significant part of aggregate demand. Any significant change in the level of spending could have marked inflationary or deflationary consequences. Yet before the Plowden Report (1961) there was no attempt to plan public expenditure as a whole, and subsequently central government could influence but not effectively control local spending. While the Keynesian consensus held sway governments lacked the means to manipulate a significant element of aggregate demand. Ironically, only when Keynesianism was abandoned did the Thatcher government acquire the kind of controls which might have been justified in Keynesian terms.

A more fashionable argument over the implications of local government for the national economy is derived from the 'crowding out' thesis of Bacon and Eltis (1978). The growth of what they describe as the non-market sector of the economy has, they argue, crowded out the development of the productive market sector. As local government contributes substantially to the non-market sector, it follows from this analysis that local spending has major and damaging implications for the health of the national economy. Yet the fundamental distinction between the market and non-market sectors, and the underlying assumptions about the nature of wealth creation are so flawed and contestable that no such conclusion can be drawn (Newton and Karran 1985: 20–35). Moreover, the impact of local spending on the national economy depends on what the spending is devoted to, and where it is spent. A clearer indication of the impact of local government expenditure on the economy can only be gained if the expenditure is disaggregated.

7.3.2 Local government and the local economy

The impact of local government spending on local economies is a crucial aspect of any attempt to disaggregate the effect of local government spending. Even if there were no per capita differences in spending between authorities, the impact of that spending on local economies would still be substantial, and because of differences in the levels of local economic activity, varied. In most cities the council is by far the largest employer, with a major influence on the local labour market, and, through the multiplier, on local demand. Council spending inevitably impinges directly on those parts of the private sector supplying it with goods and services and engaged in its capital projects. Particular services, such as highways and transportation, planning, education and environmental health, produce substantial direct and indirect benefits and costs to local business. Revenue raised locally to meet expenditure on local services clearly has some implications for the local economy. Business in particular alleges that non-domestic rates are a significant business cost with substantial implications for local income and employment, although the incidence and economic impact of business rates is contestable (Crawford *et al.* 1985; Bennett 1987).

Discretion and qualified autonomy are (or at least have been) the essence of local government. Service provision and spending patterns differ markedly between authorities, as the government acknowledges when responsibility for 'overspending' is pinned on a small number of local authorities (HMSO 1986: 1. 9). The impact of these marked variations in spending on local economies might be expected to be at least as varied and highly contentious. Radicals suggest that local councils have substantial potential to stimulate economic activity and employment in their areas through their own spending and employment policies in general, and specific economic development policies in particular (Hasluck 1987). On the right it is alleged that ill-advised local council intervention, high spending and high taxation will kill the goose that lays the golden eggs. Economic regeneration is more likely to result from less local government spending and intervention rather than more.

These sharply contrasting viewpoints reflect different assumptions about economic activity. Empirical evidence is inconclusive. Sympathetic commentators suggest that local economic development policies have been far more cost-effective in terms of cost per job created than either government regional policy or the free-market inspired Enterprise Zones (Duncan and Goodwin 1985). Yet because of limitations on powers and spending on economic development, such policies are necessarily severely limited in their impact.

There is rather more scope for using spending and employment on major services if the aim is to achieve a significant impact on the local economy. The quickest way a local authority can reduce unemployment in its area is to employ more staff. It has been suggested that this could be done by meeting perceived needs in the community for domiciliary care for the elderly, nursery education, and the development of services for the young and unemployed (Campbell *et al.* 1987). Free market economists would of course deny that jobs thus created are 'real' jobs, and would further argue that such job creation programmes could 'crowd out' private sector economic activity.

The indirect impact of local spending on local economic activity and employment is more difficult to assess. Local economies are obviously more open and interdependent than the national economy, with 'leakages' a veritable flood. Most estimates of the value of the local multiplier are very low, which suggests little scope for purposeful demand management by individual local authorities acting in isolation. Coordinated changes in local spending by many authorities acting in concert might be more productive, but would probably require at least the tacit support of central government, and would make more sense within a national economic strategy.

A crucial point, often overlooked, is that it is impossible to assess the local economic impact of local government spending, without considering the source of the revenue to meet that spending. Spending may be virtually cost free to the local economy, if it is financed by a 100 per cent grant from central government. At the other extreme the effective bill to the local community for additional spending may be considerably in excess of 100 per cent of the expenditure if, as a consequence of new central government policy – penalties for 'overspending' – a grant which would otherwise have been received is lost. Between these two extremes there is a wide range of possibilities, including partnership schemes in which central and local government share costs on approved urban expenditure programmes. In practice the attractiveness of alternative spending programmes depends considerably on financing arrangements, and such considerations inevitably affect the determination of priorities and resource allocation.

7.4 THE CONTROL AND FINANCING OF LOCAL GOVERNMENT EXPENDITURE

Central government has always sought to influence the level of local government expenditure, through legislation, exhortation, and financial inducements. However, in recent years controls of total local government spending and the spending of specific local authorities have become far more stringent and effective. From the mid-1970s central government has made increasingly strenuous attempts to restrain council spending. The Callaghan government reduced the central contribution to local spending by cutting Rate Support Grant, but otherwise relied on exhortation and consultation. The Conservative government changed the grant system in a way which required central assessment of the spending needs of each authority – the Grant Related Expenditure Assessment (Local Government Planning and Land Act 1980). Increasingly stringent penalties for spending above government-imposed targets were introduced, but without producing the cuts in spending required by central government. Some councils preferred dramatic rate increases to cuts in their spending programmes. As a consequence rate-capping was introduced, with effect from 1984. This allows central government to designate specific authorities as 'overspenders' and fix for them a maximum rate which can not be exceeded. There are also reserve powers for general rate limitation which have yet to be used. Rate-capping is a qualitatively different form of financial control from any central government powers exercised previously. While governments have often sought to influence total local spending, they have not sought direct control over rate-borne expenditure.

The case for such general and specific controls on spending is contested. Jones and Stewart (1983: 11) affirm, 'there is no economic case for any control of local expenditure financed from local taxation.' The impact of such expenditure is neutral on the national economy, they suggest, and it is 'the right and duty of a local authority to decide on the level of its expenditure, if financed from its own local tax'. By contrast the Green Paper 'Paying for Local Government' (1986) flatly asserts there can 'be no question of the Government abdicating its interest in the levels of local authority spending or taxation' (1.17).

Arguments over control rest heavily on analysis of the impact of local government spending on the national economy and local economies, and this is contestable (see sections 7.2 and 7.3 above). More fundamentally, they clearly relate to alternative views of the role and autonomy of elected local authorities in the United Kingdom. If the control of local government expenditure is controversial, the financing of that expenditure is even more so, particularly of late. After decades of resigned acceptance of a system of local government finance which had attracted widespread and bitter criticism (not all of it fair), a radical alternative package was set out in the Green Paper 'Paying for Local Government' (HMSO 1986). Inevitably perhaps, this has tended to narrow as well as intensify the debate, as most of the arguments have concentrated on the rival merits of the traditional system and the government's alternative new system. Yet any investigation of the underlying principles and assumptions behind the arguments must widen the debate beyond the current political agenda to encompass other ideas and reform proposals.

The main sources of local government finance can be quickly summarised. In the first place it is necessary to distinguish between capital and current expenditure (the latter is confusingly called 'revenue expenditure' by accountants in local government). The bulk of capital expenditure is financed by borrowing, although there are some capital grants, and a small part of capital expenditure may be financed out of revenue. A more recent source has been the sale (sometimes forced) of capital assets – principally housing stock. Central government fixes limits to borrowing, but it is up to local authorities to raise loans within this capital allocation. Local government borrowing raises some important issues, but there is not space to consider them at greater length here. This account will therefore concentrate on the sources of current expenditure.

These can be broken down into three main elements – central government grants, fees and charges, and the revenue derived from local taxation. The proportion of revenue derived from these three element has varied considerably over time (Foster *et al.* 1980: 129–51) and may change substantially in the future, yet all three in some shape or form are likely to remain important in any conceivable system of local government finance in the United Kingdom. They will be reviewed in turn.

7.4.1 Grants

Local government has been substantially dependent on central government grants to finance its expenditure since the development of the system in the nineteenth century. Specific grants were given to encourage the provision of a particular service, such as police or highways. In 1958 most specific grants were absorbed into a general grant, known as the Rate Support Grant, which in theory allowed authorities more discretion in determining their own spending priorities. In the post-war period up until the mid-1970s local government's dependence on grant income increased, until twice as much was received in grant as was obtained from rates. Since then the ratio of grant income to rate income has progressively declined. By the mid-1980s rates and rate rebates exceeded the Aggregate Exchequer Grant, although the overall picture conceals considerable variation between authorities, with some remaining highly dependent on grant.

Why is grant needed? Why cannot authorities meet all their spending needs from revenue derived locally? One answer is that there are significant non-local spill-overs resulting from much local authority activity and expenditure. The provision of police services and highways clearly yield benefits outside the immediate locality. Education has national implications. The allocation of responsibilities between central and local government would be relatively simple if services were unambiguously local in their impact. In practice there is a national as well as a local interest in most services currently within the local government sphere. There are thus strong theoretical justifications for grant-aiding local government expenditure. Variations in needs and taxable resources between areas are a major additional practical consideration.

While few would question the need for central government grant, the scale of local government's dependence on central finance has raised some concern. The Layfield Report (1976) drew attention to the implications for local autonomy and discretion. If local authorities were to remain significant decision-making bodies, a larger proportion of their own spending needs would need to be met locally. The emphasis in the 1986 Green Paper is rather different, and echoes public choice theory. If most local spending is met from externally derived sources, the true cost of local policy decisions is not brought home to local electors, which undermines rational economic choice through the ballot box. Ironically, the changes proposed in the Green Paper involved increased dependence on sources of revenue outside the control of individual local authorities.

There is no magic formula for determining the ideal level of exchequer support for local government expenditure, but, as Layfield grasped, the question is inextricably bound up with the degree of autonomy or discretion regarded as appropriate for elected local authorities. If councils are substantially the administrative agents of central government, with little discretion, then dependence on central finance is not a problem. If they are policy-making bodies, determining priorities in accordance with the preferences of the local community, within national constraints and guidelines, they need to raise a substantial proportion of their own revenue from locally derived sources to improve electoral accountability.

Besides problems in determining the aggregate level of exchequer support for local government, there are major problems in distributing grant between authorities. Until 1980 the Rate Support Grant comprised three separate elements – needs, resources, and domestic rate relief. The needs element was supposed to reflect the different spending needs of local authorities, depending on the age structure of the population, and other more complex indicators. The resources element was designed to compensate those authorities with a low rate base. The domestic element was introduced in 1966, essentially for political reasons, to give special relief to domestic ratepayers, thus holding down household rate bills. In 1980, under the Local Government Planning and Land Act, the needs and resources elements were combined into a block grant. Previously 'needs' were calculated in such a way as to reflect, to a degree, past expenditure. This was felt to 'reward' high spending authorities, and was ended in the new formula for determining grant entitlement. This was followed by increasingly severe penalties in terms of loss of grant for authorities which exceeded centrally-determined spending targets. Effectively this involves a dramatic change in the use of grants by central government as a policy instrument. For over a hundred years grant has been used essentially to encourage local government spending. Now it is employed increasingly to deter and punish overspending.

The 1980 Act did not make grant more predictable for individual local authorities, which continues to fluctuate substantially from year to year. Such changes reflect to a degree adjustments in the complex formula for determining grant entitlement, but these owe less to the higher mathematics than to political considerations. Quite simply, governments of all complexions change grant to suit their own political interests. Grant levels have direct implications for local tax levels, and these in turn are reckoned to have electoral consequences. Labour governments thus distribute grant in such a way as to favour the larger urban authorities, which may indeed have more needs, but are also largely Labour-controlled. The Conservatives tend to redress the balance in the direction of the more rural and suburban areas.

The resulting annual changes in grant not only make life inordinately difficult for local finance officers, but also effectively destroy any link between local spending decisions and local tax levels. The average voter finds local government difficult enough to understand without having to unravel a perverse and often inverse relationship between changes in local expenditure and changes in his rate bill. The 1986 Green Paper acknowledges the problem, although there is room for scepticism over the proposed solution. There will be a standard grant 'to provide an additional contribution from national taxation towards the cost of local services' and a needs grant 'to compensate authorities for differences in the cost of providing a standard level of service to meet local needs'. The formula for calculating the needs grant will be reviewed 'with a view to making it less complex and more stable' (HMSO 1986: 10.4). Similar intentions have been expressed before, and it remains to be seen whether they will be realised. It will not be surprising if party political considerations continue to influence grant distribution. The distribution of resources is the essence of politics, and cannot be reduced to some neutral technical formula.

7.4.2 Fees and charges

Local authorities already employ individual user-charges extensively, and the proportion of income derived from such charges has increased markedly in recent years, although the extent of charging varies considerably between authorities. The 1986 Green Paper notes that there are more than 600 local authority services for which charges are made, and that the total income derived from sales, fees and charges amounts to 60 per cent of the yield from domestic rates (HMSO, 1986: 7.4). The most important and widespread charges are for school meals, nursery and adult education, planning applications, recreational facilities, commercial refuse collection and disposal, car parking, home helps and institutional care. Also clearly significant are council house rents, although these now figure in a separate housing account distinct from the general rate fund.

The 1986 Green Paper suggests that 'realistic charging policies help to improve the efficient use of resources', in line with mainstream economic theory. Foster *et al.* (1980: 217) state tersely, 'From the standpoint of economic efficiency no more need be said: charging for services, where feasible, is the most efficient arrangement on economic grounds.' They go beyond anything indicated in the Green Paper, arguing that charging could be introduced for up to 90 per cent of the gross revenue expenditure of local government (page 535). They claim charging is more feasible for most local government services than is generally supposed, as few of them have the defining characteristics of public goods, non-excludability and non-rivalry. They allow streetlighting, most police services, local expenditure on justice, some planning, pollution control and (with reservations) roads as examples of non-excludability. Most of these, with the addition of parks, and possibly museums, are also non-rival (in effect marginal cost is zero or very low). They estimate that altogether these services amount to less than 9 per cent of local gross revenue expenditure. They also argue that externalities are less significant than generally imagined, of more historical than current application, with the important exception of transport.

They conclude that 'various redistributive and paternalistic judgments' are essentially responsible for non-charging. In so far as there is a case for redistribution, they suggest this would be better achieved through national taxation (possibly through Negative Income Tax), or through the use of vouchers or specific grants. Charges would then allow individuals to maximise their own utility by exercising their preferences – a disabled person might choose to spend a disability grant on a colour television or champagne rather than a local authority home help. Any attempt to impose the authority's priorities over the individual's must involve some loss of satisfaction (Foster *et al.* 1980: 509–41).

The argument is provocative. It rests on the common assumption in economics that individuals are the best judge of their own interests. The argument is not normally applied to children, however, and expenditure on education amounts to nearly half of total local government revenue expenditure. Vouchers involve some implicit paternalism, in that they have to be spent on the purpose for which they are designated. Parents are entrusted with a decision over the type of education, but not the need for it. The case for an element of paternalism is stronger still in the child care aspects of social services – battering and abuse involve little scope for the application of market principles.

Some services are provided implicitly to compensate individuals for disadvantages caused by handicap, ill-health or old age. While taxpayers may be content to finance such services as free or heavily subsidised transport and domestic help for those unable or constrained in providing these facilities for themselves, they may be less content to distribute cash bounties to be spent on purposes totally unrelated to the handicap.

Beyond such considerations, the general case for increased charging depends heavily on a substantial and radical overhaul of the whole tax and benefit system. In the absence of such a radical overhaul, there are strong practical reasons for rejecting any dramatic extension of charging for local government services. Without compensation through the tax system, such charges would in most cases involve a substantial redistribution of income away from the poor, the old and the sick.

7.4.3 Local taxation

Local authorities are unique among UK public bodies outside central government in having their own taxing powers. For centuries this has involved rates on various forms of immovable property. In the late nineteenth century what had been described as a 'chaos of rates' was much simplified. In 1929 agriculture was derated, leaving domestic rates, and rates on non-domestic properties, including industrial and commercial premises and government buildings. Responsibility for property valuation shifted from local government to the Inland Revenue in 1950, but otherwise the system has remained substantially unaltered, apart from specific concessions introduced to help domestic ratepayers – domestic rate relief, rate rebates for those on low incomes, and a statutory right to pay by instalments.

The reform or replacement of rates has been long canvassed. Reform has centred principally on rating valuation. At present valuation is on the basis of net annual rental values. The resulting rateable values are incomprehensible to most people, particularly as revaluations, which should take place every five years, are invariably postponed for political reasons. One alternative, taken up in the past by the Liberal Party, is site value rating, another, recommended by the Layfield Report (Cmnd 6453, 1976) is capital value rating. Some form of indexation could surmount difficulties over revaluation. Such a solution may well make rates more comprehensible, but not necessarily more acceptable.

Various new taxes have been proposed to replace or supplement rates – local income tax, local sales tax and most recently the community charge or poll tax. The relative advantages and disadvantages of rates and alternative forms of local taxation have often been listed. Such lists commonly include points which are mutually inconsistent and which derive from fundamentally conflicting assumptions. Sometimes essentially the same point appears on both sides of the balance sheet in slightly different form. Thus rates are condemned for the heavy financial burden placed on poor widows living alone in the family home, and praised as a disincentive to the underoccupation of property. Such an approach to the debate is rather sterile and unproductive. Here the aim is rather to illuminate the underlying themes.

What should a local tax be designed to do? Much depends on prior assumptions about the economic role and autonomy of local government. Many contributors to the debate have had a strong commitment to the values and principles of local democratic institutions. Starting from this assumption the first requirement of any local tax is that it should be clearly under local control. The simple transference of the proceeds of a tax fixed nationally does not answer this requirement – the Victorians tried it, assigning the revenue of miscellaneous taxes and licences to local authorities. Yet these 'assigned revenues' were, in effect, only a highly inflexible form of central government grant, unrelated to local authority needs or resources. The same objection might be levelled at the proposed Uniform Business Rate, which is essentially a national rather than a local tax.

If local authorities are seen as little more than convenient administrative agencies for central government this does not much matter. But if they are seen as representative bodies determining priorities for local communities, they need to raise a substantial proportion of their own revenue from local sources. Preferably any local tax should have a substantial and predictable yield, should be easily adjustable, and unambiguously allocatable to the residents of a local authority. Domestic rates score highly on all these criteria, which is substantially why the local government lobby is so attached to them. Non-domestic rates score highly on every criterion but the last – they are not unambiguously allocatable to authority residents. Their real incidence is not on the industrial and commercial organisations which formally pay them, but on landowners, shareholders, consumers and taxpayers. This is one reason why even some passionate advocates of local democracy have suggested that business rates are unsuitable as a local tax (Jones and Stewart 1983), which also seems to be the majority view among economists who have written on the subject (Hughes 1987; Smith and Squire 1987). A sales tax would fail the same tests and would also be rather more inflexible. Local income tax would only be acceptable if it were based on residence rather than place of work, which in turn would involve high administrative costs. The community charge also substantially meets the criteria, although it may be doubted whether the yield would be substantial enough for local accountability and local choice on the Layfield model.

This is where the 1986 Green Paper departs markedly from the underlying assumptions behind much of the earlier debate. Improving effective local democratic processes was an implicit or explicit premise behind many earlier reform proposals, Layfield admittedly postulated two models, a centralist and localist model, and declared it was up to central government to choose between them, but there can be little doubt over the Committee's preferences. The thrust of the report was the need for additional sources of revenue to enable real responsibility for decisions to be located at local level. Hence the recommendation for the introduction of local income tax as an addition to, rather than replacement for rates. The main thrust of the 1986 Green Paper, by contrast, is the control of local expenditure rather than the promotion of effective local democratic choice. Under the proposals a much smaller proportion of local spending needs would be met from locally derived sources, because although the yield from domestic rates would be substantially replaced by the yield from the community charge, non-domestic rates are effectively transformed into a national tax.

Another major theme in the debate over local taxation has been the notion of fairness. Many of the major critics of rates were not particularly concerned about local democracy. Rates were objectionable because they were held to be unfair. 'Fairness' is a somewhat subjective concept. It is important to distinguish between two very different and conflicting interpretations of what constitutes fairness with respect to local taxation. One is the familiar idea that a tax should be linked to ability to pay. A persistent criticism of domestic rates, given authoritative substance by the research of the Allen Committee (Cmnd 2582, 1965), has been that they are regressive. Rate rebates have somewhat reduced the force of this criticism, but not removed it. A sharply contrasting view is that a local tax should somehow be linked with the use made of local services. Those who pay high rates may make little use of council services, while others who make extensive use of services may pay no rates at all. Some critics would regard this as unfair. Although both criticisms are couched in the same language of 'fairness' they spring from diametrically opposed assumptions. The policy implications are also quite different. Effectively a choice has to be made between the two principles. Most previous reform proposals have regarded the ability to pay principle as paramount. This essentially is the case for local income tax. On these as on other grounds the 1986 Green Paper involves a break with the past consensus. Both the ability to pay principle (described as the redistributive principle) and the beneficial principle (which suggests that local taxation should be related to service provision) are enlisted to attack domestic rates. Yet ultimately, and quite clearly, the Green Paper explicitly rejects the redistributive principle. 'The ideal local tax should fit in with local authorities' role as a service provider . . . That argues in favour of a form of taxation which has some of the characteristics of a charge. It argues against a redistributive tax' (HMSO 1986: 3.31). That is why local income tax is rejected, and the community charge is preferred. Critics have made the obvious point that a poll tax is far more regressive than rates, but the government was clearly not looking for a tax linked to ability to pay, but a tax related to the use of local services. Behind the arguments are conflicting socialist and free market assumptions concerning what constitutes fairness.

A third theme in the debate, largely confined to the academic community has been economic efficiency. Theory suggests that allocative efficiency is reached when no shift in resources could make anyone better off without making someone else worse off. Mainstream economics indicates that this is most easily achieved through the market, or where public agencies are involved in provision, through individual-user charges. There are greater theoretical and practical difficulties in achieving Pareto optimality where services are provided free to the user (or highly subsidised) and the cost met from taxation, which of course is substantially the case for local government.

There are two main ways in which the individual can influence levels of collective provision and taxation in these circumstances, so as to maximize their personal welfare. One is through the ballot box, the other is by moving between local authorities.

The problems of citizens influencing public provision and taxation through voting have been extensively explored by public choice theorists (Green 1987: 92–108). Indeed public choice theory is often employed by free-market economists to demonstrate the superiority of resource allocation through the market, and call for more privatisation of public services. But it is also utilised to minimise what they would see as the inherent deficiencies of public provision, with the ballot box substituting for market choice. Theory suggests that vote-maximising parties will attempt to satisfy the median voter, or appeal to the middle ground. Voters can attempt to maximise their welfare through choosing between the range of policy packages on offer. For a rational choice to be made, the expenditure and taxation implications of policy proposals have to be very clear, and directly related to service provision. Clearly if there were no obvious direct cost to the voter, utility would be maximised by choosing the highest level of service provision on offer. If this line of reasoning is extended, it follows that the best tax to enable citizens to make a rational choice is one which is highly visible, universal and closely linked with service provision. This is substantially the thinking behind the community charge, which meets these criteria. There is a further attraction for the government, for it is clearly anticipated that if the full implications of expenditure proposals are brought home to voters, local government spending will be effectively contained through the ballot box.

There are, however, numerous theoretical and practical problems with public choice theory, and these are probably more marked with respect to local government. Low turnout, voter ignorance, voting on national trends rather than local issues make local elections a dubious testing ground for rational choice models. Additionally, local government services are very heterogeneous. Few are unambiguously beneficial to local residents – there are important spill-overs and national implications. The bulk of services are inevitably redistributional to a degree, both between individuals and households, and over time. The 1986 Green Paper proposals actually involve a distinct weighting of choice against local government expenditure, because revenue from the community charge will only meet around a quarter of the cost of total spending, but marginal increases will have to be met entirely from charge income. This 'gearing effect' is helpfully illustrated in the Green Paper. In the example provided, a 13 per cent increase in a local authority's expenditure requires a 50 per cent increase in the community charge (HMSO 1986: 4.39 and Fig. 14).

A theoretical attraction of local government is that citizens can also move between authorities to maximize their welfare – such an option is clearly available only to a very limited degree if at all at national level. Citizens can 'vote with their feet' with respect to local government, and move around until they find a balance of service provision and local taxation which maximises their utility. The theoretical implications were explored by Tiebout (1956) and subsequent work has elaborated and sought empirical verification for his hypothesis. The practical difficulties are, if anything, greater than with effective rational choice through the ballot box. Voters would require detailed accurate knowledge of service and tax levels in a wide range of authorities, would have to be perfectly free to move, and be uninfluenced by factors not related to local government provision and taxation. Voter ignorance, practical constraints on choice of residence, and the generally greater significance of other factors besides public agency provision limit the scope for welfare maximisation by movements between authorities. There is evidence that very marked differences in provision and taxation between adjoining authorities does have an impact on housing markets, which provides some support for a 'Tiebout effect', but in general such factors do not have an appreciable impact on choice of location. It might be further noted that local government reorganisation in 1974, which involved a reduction in the number and an increase in the size of local authorities, further narrowed the practical scope for choice of residence between different authorities.

Using Tiebout's analysis, Foster *et al.* (1980: 233) suggest that a poll tax is most consistent with economic efficiency for what they describe as beneficial expenditure. However, this endorsement is heavily qualified. They point out that the bulk of local government expenditure is redistributive in effect, and for such expenditure they recommend a land tax, with rates as a second best. Moreover, they conclude (ironically in view of subsequent developments) that 'the equity objections to a poll or per household tax to finance even beneficial services are likely to be overwhelming.' Vickerman (1984) points to the 'relatively neutral' effects of a poll tax, but notes, 'Of course, this neutrality does mean that a poll tax would be strongly regressive.' Showing no greater aptitude for prophecy he observes, 'it has only been seriously suggested in combination with another source of taxation' (page 233).

The difficult and abstract nature of the debate over economic efficiency, coupled with the many practical problems indicated and the somewhat clouded policy implications, have limited its impact on the public discussion of local taxation. Contrasting views of equity, and different assumptions over the role and autonomy of elected local authorities have been more evident in the arguments employed by politicians, lobbyists, the media, and the public. It might seem surprising that two major official publications, the Report of the Layfield Committee (Cmnd 6543, 1976) and the 1986 Green Paper, should reach such diametrically-opposed conclusions. The analysis and recommendations of each cannot be viewed as 'right' or 'wrong' in any objective sense. There is actually little point of contact between the two. Layfield is about central–local relations, while the 1986 Green Paper is about controlling local government expenditure. They are addressing different perceived problems, which in turn reflect different underlying assumptions.

The predictable conclusion is that there is no ideal tax which meets all requirements. Much depends on views of what local government is fundamentally about, and what a local tax should be designed to achieve.

If ability to pay is the prime consideration, local income tax (LIT) is the best solution, followed by domestic rates with a rebate system if the administrative costs of LIT prove a major obstacle. If the link with service provision is seen as critical, then the most obvious implication is an extension of individual-user charges, coupled with central funding of redistributive services perhaps. A poll tax then could be employed to meet residual expenditure, although this would entail an overhaul of the national tax and benefit system, as any system of rebates to offset the palpably regressive nature of a poll tax undermine the economic assumptions on which it rests. Such an approach would also imply a very limited view of the role and autonomy of local democratic institutions. If by contrast the promotion of effective local choice and accountable local government are seen as critical, then a high yield, flexibility, and relation to residence are prime considerations. Here it is difficult to improve on the Layfield recommendations – a reformed rating system based on capital values supplemented by local income tax.

7.5 CONCLUSIONS

The future of local government finance is in the melting pot. Issues, arguments and prescriptions which have loomed large in recent years may prove ephemeral. Four concluding points require emphasis.

First, it is necessary to look at local government finance as a whole. Inevitably attention has focused on specific aspects, particularly local taxation. Yet taxation can only be viewed in relation to other sources of revenue, such as central grants and fees and charges, and these altogether have to be seen in the context of the expenditure needs of local government.

This in turn raises questions about the economic role and autonomy of local government, which leads on to the second major point. The future of local government finance is inseparably bound up with the whole future of local government. Debates about the structure and functions of local government have been conducted independently of debates about local government finance. They need to be considered together.

Third, the debate over local government finance should also be seen in the context of the general questions of public finance. Local government expenditure is an important proportion of total public expenditure. Local taxation is part of general taxation. At one level it is impossible not to have regard for national fiscal policy. At another, justifications for local government activities are in large part bound up with wider arguments over the proper economic role of government, which reflect in turn sharply conflicting ideological perspectives.

Finally, more regard might be paid to the experience of other countries. The protracted public debate over local government finance has been extremely insular. Local democratic institutions are not unique to the United Kingdom, and nor are problems in financing them, yet very little attention has been paid to the way in which other countries have tried to grapple with the problems and issues discussed in this chapter. Whatever the immediate future of local government finance, the controversy will remain, and further change is highly probable. Hopefully such change will take more note of experience elsewhere.

FURTHER READING

For a general guide to UK local government see Byrne (1986) or Hampton (1986). Local government finance has been changing so rapidly in recent years that even the latest editions of standard texts are soon out of date. Hepworth (1984) has long been the most useful guide both for practitioners and academics, but a new edition will be required for the latest developments. Still indispensible for historical background and economic analysis is Foster *et al.* (1980).

Of the many official publications two stand out – the Layfield Report of 1976 and the 1986 Green Paper. The best brief review of the latter and other recent developments is provided by Smith and Squire (1987).

Sandford (1984) looks at local government finance in the context of the economics of public finance, and Vickerman (1984) looks at it in the context of urban economies. For a discussion of the theoretical issues surrounding the growth of local government expenditure see Newton and Karran (1985), Hasluck (1987) has a useful discussion of local economic policy.

8 · THE CHANGING LABOUR MARKET

Interpreting the evidence

JOHN SUTHERLAND

8.1 INTRODUCTION

After over 20 years of 'full' employment, at levels unimagined by the architects of the 1944 White Paper on Employment, 1966 signalled the start of a secular rise in the numbers registered as unemployed. Since then, the absolute total number registered as unemployed has increased tenfold, with temporary downturns in the trend soon overtaken by seemingly inexorable upward pressures. Moreover, as unemployment became more prevalent, the structure of employment changed radically in terms of the economic and employment status of labour market participants and their industrial and occupational distribution.

The first section of this chapter examines the nature and magnitude of these changes. However, economists are divided in their explanations of these changes. In section 8.3, the work of a group expediently described as 'mainstream economists', a group considerably influenced by the methodology of the neoclassicals, is analysed to illustrate how they perceive and investigate economic phenomena, and how they seek to explain issues such as unemployment or changes in the balance between part-time and full-time employment. Integral to this analysis is the possibility of interparadigm conflict. The probability of interparadigm conflict is discussed in section 8.4 where two alternative perspectives are identified. In section 8.4.1, the institutional perspective of segmented labour market theorists is used to illustrate the existence of different methodologies in the investigation of labour market changes. In section 8.4.2, the Marxist perspective is used to illustrate the consequences of adopting an alternative world view.

Table 8.1 The resident population of working age (GB) – (thousands)

	1977	1979	1983	1986*	% change 1977–86
Male	16,801	16,972	17,461	17,748	+5.6
Female	15,309	15,598	15,839	16,143	+5.4
Total	32,110	32,570	33,300	33,891	+5.5

Source: Department of Employment Gazette (May 1987).
*Projected rather than estimated.

8.2 RECENT TRENDS IN THE LABOUR MARKET

The aim of this section is to use statistical data to examine the nature and magnitude of the principal changes that have occurred in the labour market over the last decade. Although supplemented by more specific empirical analyses, in general two conceptually distinct sets of data are employed: stock data, such as the number of employees in employment, which estimate numbers in a given category at a single point in time, and flow data, such as redundancies, which estimate increments and decrements to these stocks over a period of time. The sequence of the material is as follows. First the size of the civilian work force is examined; then the economic status and employment status of the economically active; and finally, the industrial and occupational distribution of the employed are investigated. This is followed by a complementary examination of flow statistics such as labour turnover and redundancies. The section concludes with a brief discussion of some regional and urban statistics to illustrate the point that the pattern of change depicted by national trends does not occur uniformly over space.

The civilian labour force comprises those aged 16 and over who are either in employment or actively seeking employment. Changes in its size are attributable to two factors, demographic forces, principally changes in the age and sex structure of the population, and activity rates, that proportion of the population eligible to participate in the labour market and who do so. The size of the resident population of working age is shown in Table 8.1, the increase over the period reflecting the 'baby boom' of the 1960s. The corresponding activity rates are shown in Table 8.2 and illustrate the marked tendency for male activity rates to decline, and for female activity rates to increase.

It is statistically possible to isolate and estimate the separate contributions made by the population effect and the activity rate effect to changes in the size of the civilian labour force. Between 1977 and 1986, for males the population effect was consistently positive and sufficiently large to offset the consistently negative activity rate effects each year with the

Table 8.2 Civilian activity rates (GB) – (percentages)

	1977	1979	1983	1986	Change 1977–86
Male	90.2	90.0	86.4	85.9	−4.3
Female	63.5	63.7	63.5	67.0	+3.5
Total	77.5	77.4	75.5	76.9	−0.6

Source: *Department of Employment Gazette* (May 1987).

Table 8.3 Economic status – males and females (thousands)

	1977		1986		% change 1977–86	
	M	F	M	F	M	F
Economically active of which:	15,310	9,902	15,531	11,127	+1.4	+12.4
In employment	14,527	9,229	13,806	10,024	−5.0	+8.6
Unemployed*	783	673	1,725	1,103	+120.3	+63.9
On government employment and training schemes			269	130		

Source: *Labour Force Survey*, 1979 and 1986.
*The survey definition of unemployment differs from that used to produce the monthly unemployment count.

exceptions of 1976–7, 1981–3 and 1985–6. For females over the same period the population effect was positive throughout. The activity rate effect was negative in five years (1977–9 and 1980–3). However, so great was the relative size of the population effect that the size of the female civilian labour force increased each year with the exception of 1981–3. When the separate sexes are aggregated, in 1976–7 the positive female activity rate effect more than offset the negative male activity rate effect. In 1977–9 and 1980–3, the negative activity rate effect of one sex reinforced the same of the other. So great was the relative size of the aggregated population effects, however, that only in 1981–3 was the change in the size of the total civilian labour force negative.

Not all those who participate in the labour market do so in the same way. For example, not all those who are economically active are in employment, and not all those who are in employment are full-time employees. Tables 8.3 and 8.4 respectively identify the manner in which economic status and employment status may be classified, and show the change in each classification for the period 1977–86. Most apparent from these tables is the extent to which the following has occurred:

Table 8.4 Employment status – males and females (thousands)

	1979		1986		% change 1979–86	
	M	F	M	F	M	F
Employees	13,105	8,953	11,491	9,214	−12.3	+2.9
of which:						
Full-time	12,866	5,302	11,034	5,070	−14.2	−4.4
Part-time	239	3,651	450	4,138	+88.3	+13.3
Self-employed	1,428	333	2,045	679	+43.2	+103.9
of which:						
Full-time			1,925	356		
Part-time			119	321		

Source: *Labour Force Survey*, 1979 and 1986.
Note: Because of difficulties with classifying responses, the totals presented above do not equate with corresponding statistics in Table 8.3.

1. The size of the civilian labour force has increased, most especially its female component.
2. The numbers of males in employment has decreased.
3. The numbers of females in employment has increased, most especially because of those working on a part-time rather than full-time basis.
4. The numbers of both sexes classified as unemployed have increased.

Those categorised as 'employees in employment' may be further classified according to their distribution by industry and occupation, details of which are presented in Tables 8.5 and 8.6 respectively.

Changes in the pattern of employment by industry reflect factors such as the changing demand for goods and services, itself reflecting changing consumer incomes and tastes; the changing availability of natural resources and their substitutes; the changing technology and organisation of production; the changing perceptions of the role of government; and, for those goods and services internationally traded, the competitiveness of domestic organisations *vis-à-vis* their international rivals. Changes made to the Standard Industrial Classification restrict the period of examination to 1981–6 (and as a consequence ignore the dramatic changes which occurred during the preceding decade. For example between 1974, the year in which the series peaked in that decade, and 1981, the number of employees in employment decreased by 911,000. Furthermore, 1,623,000 jobs were lost in the manufacturing sector in the same period). Table 8.5 illustrates that during the period 1981 to 1986 employment growth was a service sector phenomenon, and although not exclusively, was most significantly female rather than male. Additionally, almost one-fifth of the jobs so created were part-time.

Changes in the industrial distribution of the working population cause

Table 8.5 Industrial analyses of employees in employment (thousands)

	1981				1986				$ change 1981–6			
	Male		Female		Male		Female		Male		Female	
	All	P/T	All	P/T	All	P/T	All	P/T	All	P/T	All	P/T
Agriculture, forestry and fishing	274.4	31.3	91.3	30.7	250.3	33.8	88.1	32.3	−8.8	+8.0	−3.5	+5.2
Energy and water supply	605.4	1.1	90.9	17.8	444.3	1.3	74.5	13.6	−26.6	+18.2	−18.0	−23.6
Other mineral and ore extraction	720.1	6.2	195.4	36.1	592.7	4.1	180.6	28.3	−17.7	−34.9	−7.6	−22.6
Metal goods, engineering and vehicles	2,265.7	23.2	596.0	113.9	1,822.5	16.0	483.3	71.6	−19.6	−31.0	−18.9	−37.1
Other manufacturing industries	1,327.0	39.5	953.8	244.5	1,206.6	34.1	880.3	190.9	−9.1	−13.7	−7.3	−22.2
Construction	965.3	15.4	114.2	48.7	865.2	14.2	118.5	50.1	−10.4	−7.8	+3.8	+2.9
Distribution, hotels, catering and repairs	1,867.3	276.3	2,232.6	1,227.3	1,966.7	304.7	2,355.1	1,322.6	+5.3	+10.3	+5.5	+7.8
Transport and communication	1,127.4	23.6	273.8	55.2	1,053.1	30.2	279.3	61.0	−6.6	+28.0	+2.0	+10.5
Banking, finance, insurance, etc.	894.2	47.8	834.2	208.3	1,135.0	70.2	1,095.8	287.9	+26.9	+46.9	+31.4	+38.2
Other services	2,177.5	253.4	3,702.3	1,798.4	2,349.2	359.0	3,919.3	1,915.3	+7.9	+41.7	+5.9	+6.5
All industries and services	12,224.3	717.7	9,084.5	3,780.9	11,685.5	867.6	9,474.8	3,972.9	−3.4	+20.9	+4.3	+5.1

Source: *Department of Employment Gazette* (February 1987: Historical Supplement Table 14).

Table 8.6 Occupational analysis of persons in employment (1979–83) (thousands)

	1979		1983		% change 1979–83	
	Male	Female	Male	Female	Male	Female
Managerial and professional	3,968	1,894	4,288	2,241	+8.1	+18.3
Clerical and related	968	2,911	782	2,781	−18.1	−4.4
Other non-manual occupations	745	873	819	941	+9.9	+7.8
Craft and similar occupations	4,125	524	3,567	376	−13.5	−28.2
General labourers	420	36	298	33	−29.0	−8.3
Other manual occupations	4,481	3,183	3,613	2,878	−19.4	−9.6
All occupations*	14,706	9,420	13,442	9,290	−8.6	−1.4

Source: *Labour Force Survey*, 1979 and 1983.
*The separate occupations when aggregated do not equal 'All occupations' because of difficulties associated with inadequate job descriptions.

changes to the occupational distribution. Independent of this industry effect, however, there is a simultaneous yet separate intra-industry effect, described as the occupational effect, and attributable to factors such as technical change and job redesign, which change the occupation mix of an industry and therefore occupational structure. Data relating to occupational structure are less easily obtainable than data relating to industrial distribution. Consequently the examination is restricted to the period 1979–83. The most apparent feature of Table 8.6 is the increasing significance of white-collar occupations, their proportion of a decreasing total of those employed increasing from 47 to 52 per cent. Whereas females have proved to be the principal beneficiaries of the increase in white-collar employment, the reduction in manual occupations has been relatively more detrimental to males.

Considerable though all of the aforementioned changes are, any analysis of statistics relating to changes in such labour market stocks underestimates the dynamism of the labour market where activity is continuous as individuals move between different labour market categories and states, and even in and out of the labour market. For example, changes over time to such labour market stocks as employees in employment are the net result of outflows from that stock (separations in this example) and inflows to that stock (engagements in this same example). Changes to these flows are themselves explained by changes to the level of demand for labour and ultimately product demand changes.

Turnover data are restricted to manufacturing industry, where both engagements and separations are seen to move pro-cyclically, with the former leading slightly. The long-run trend of both has been downwards, and during the early 1980s the engagement rate reached unprecedentedly low levels. The cyclical variation of the engagement rate is seen to be greater than that of separations, denoting, in aggregate terms, the relative importance of recruitment policies (i.e., the non-replacement of voluntary quits) rather than redundancy policies to organisations seeking to change manpower levels.

Relative to the number of employees in employment, the number of job changes is considerable. Assuming the manufacturing industry statistics are comparable to those of the employed population as a whole, this implies – using mid-1980s estimates – 4.1 million engagements and 4.8 million separations are made annually. Or restructuring the latter statistic – some 22.75 per cent of the employed labour force quit their jobs each year, implying that the average job is held for four and a half years. This last statistic, however, gives a false picture of the length of job tenure, because it is possible for the length of the average job to be relatively short but for most people to be in jobs which they will hold for some time. For example, Main estimates that the average length of the job held by the currently employed is twenty years for males and twelve years for females (Main 1981).

Although the voluntary quit component dominates the separation statistic creating the pro-cyclical movement, the redundancy component is counter-cyclical. Data relating to confirmed redundancies are available from 1977. At this time the number of redundancies per thousand employees (the redundancy rate) was 7.2. By 1980 it had increased dramatically to 22.1. It peaked in 1981 at 25.1. Since then the trend has been downwards but the rate has not fallen to the 1977 figure.

Job termination may be the result of successful on-the-job search for alternative employment. By contrast it may be involuntary and result in unemployment. Just as separations are not distributed equally among the employed, so too the probability of becoming unemployed is concentrated among particular groups. Nickell's picture of male unemployment in 1972 – female unemployment is less easily examined – showed that the probability of becoming unemployed was related to factors such as age – the young (under 20 years of age) and the old (over 50 years of age) were more prone; socio-economic group – the incidence of unemployment increased dramatically with movement down the skill hierarchy; and family composition – those who were not married had a higher incidence of unemployment than those who were, and among those who were married those who had several children had relatively higher unemployment inflows (Nickell 1980). A noticeable feature of the labour market during the 1970s has been the increasing extent to which males with statistically low probabilities of becoming unemployed have entered the unemployed stock. Hughes and Hutchinson estimate the increase for this group to be as much as tenfold for the period 1972–81 (Hughes and Hutchinson 1986).

When unemployed, the statistical probability of being offered and accepting employment also varies with factors such as age and skill. Historically, for example, skilled males below the age of 45 experienced relatively short unemployment duration spells. According to Hughes and Hutchinson, however, what happened during the 1970s was that the high probability of this group leaving the unemployed stock fell.

Under long-run steady state assumptions, the unemployment count is a function of two components, viz., the rate at which people flow onto the unemployment register, the inflow component, and the average duration of stay on the register, the duration component. Changes in the unemployment count, therefore, are attributable to changes in either or both of these components. In his analysis of these data for 1977–82, Hughes (1982) showed that for males, changes in the unemployment count have been caused largely by increasing duration, a pattern which continues. Indeed, even traditionally short duration groups such as young workers have seen their probability of re-employment rates decrease dramatically. For females the principal component has been the inflow. This, however, appears to be attributable to secular increases in the propensity for females to register as unemployed, a phenomenon which has bedevilled attempts to analyse, statistically, female unemployment.

There are significant inter and intra-regional differences in the statistics examined above, reflecting the fact that the phenomena of job creation and job destruction are not distributed evenly over space.

For example, in the south-east region total employment increased between 1977 and 1987 by 2 per cent. By contrast, over the same period in the West Midlands – a region greatly affected by deindustrialisation – it decreased by 8 per cent and in the north-west it decreased by 13.2 per cent. Over the same period, male unemployment in the south-east rose by 3.3 percentage points. The corresponding increases from higher original rates in the West Midlands and the north-west were 7.3 percentage points and 7.7 percentage points respectively. A similar pattern of regional differences is apparent with respect to female activity rates. Over the same period in the south-east they rose by 3 percentage points from the already relatively high rate of 48.5 per cent. In the West Midlands and the north-west, the increases were marginal, being 0.8 percentage points and 0.9 percentage points respectively. Interregional variations can also be observed in part-time employment (Townsend 1986) and redundancies (Martin 1982).

Owen *et al.*'s (1984) analysis of the components of change in local labour markets have established that variations in economic statistics such as unemployment, activity rates and so on, are sometimes even greater within regions than they are between them. The absence of comprehensive data sets on local labour markets, however, tends to restrict investigations at this level of analysis.

8.3 MAINSTREAM EXPLANATIONS OF CHANGE

Whereas these 'facts' appear to be incontrovertible, as they are organised and reorganised by economists, perceptions of what constitutes 'problems' change, and explanations of what are seemingly objective phenomena differ. The general aim of this and the following sections is to illustrate how and why disagreement may arise when attempting to explain the changes which have taken place in the labour market. In this section we examine the school described as 'mainstream economists' to ascertain not only how and why they may disagree with members of alternative schools but how and why they may disagree with each other.

From the perspective of the mainstream economist, there is unanimity that the common problem is scarcity, a problem not resolved but mitigated by a market system characterised by individuals exchanging and transacting. These markets need not be perfect, nor need they be necessarily clear. What constitutes the specific characteristics of markets is a source of disagreement between mainstream economists. Most assume, however, that market participants are utility maximisers. Therefore all participants exhibit the same behavioural responses of adjusting quantities in accordance with changes in relative prices signalled by the market. From this world view, the mainstream economist proceeds by model-building and model-testing and thereafter uses 'proven' models to examine 'problems'.

In the labour market the individual's decisions to participate or not, and if to participate how many hours of labour to supply, are essentially decisions of constrained maximisation. In the simple neoclassical model (Sapsford 1981) the individual is assumed to have a choice between work and leisure reflected in a map of indifference curves in income and hours space. Attempts to attain the highest possible indifference curve are constrained by a budget line, the slope of which depicts the wage rate the individual faces in the labour market, at a position on the income axis commensurate with the individual's receipt of non-market income. *Ceteris paribus*, increases in the wage rate produce negative income effects and positive substitution effects, with the ultimate impact upon change in hours supplied being dependent upon the relative strength of each effect.

In their development of more sophisticated and complex models, Becker, for example, sees the problem less about the choice between work and play and more about choices relating to the allocation of time between time-consuming activities – which offers the additional possibility of non-market work in activities such as housework and the acquisition of human capital. Lucas and Rapping would see the problem not only as one of substituting between time-consuming activities at a point in time, but one of doing the same over time in what is described as intertemporal substitution. By contrast, however, neo-Keynesians would deny the reality of such choice theoretic frameworks for individuals in a capitalist economy, whose expenditure needs effectively predetermine their need to supply to the market their only asset of potential earnings capacity, viz., their labour power.

Labour demand is modelled in similar fashion (Sapsford 1981). In the short run, when the capital stock is fixed, labour is hired until the product market value of its (decreasing) marginal physical product equals the market wage. *Ceteris paribus* were the wage to decrease, the logic of the model is that additional labour would be hired. In the long run, when capital as well as labour is variable, the entrepreneur has the opportunity of choosing between different factor combinations subject to the constraints imposed by the firm's production function which reflects the possibility of technical substitutability between the factors. Choice of factor combination is partly determined by relative factor prices – and again the logic of the model is that factor quantities employed are assumed to change following relative price changes.

Mainstream economists have different perceptions of the specific nature of the market in which actors supply and demand labour. Following Corina, in his masterful yet now dated survey, some would view it as a 'straightforward extension of more general market theories' (Corina 1972: 5). Others would see it as 'explicable by orthodox market behaviour analysis' (Corina 1972: 5), as long as due allowance was made for such labour market peculiarities as special search and information costs and adjustment processes.

In essence, therefore, there are three elements to each complete mainstream model of the labour market, as follows:

1. A labour supply function.
2. A labour demand function.
3. An adjustment function which identifies the manner in which market disequilibria are corrected.

Thus constructed, the model is then applied to extensive data sets of a cross-section or time-series nature, using statistical techniques such as multiple regression analysis or maximum likelihood. In accordance with the traditions of positivism, some mainstream economists test using the criterion of verification, others test using the Popperian criterion of falsification. Some mainstream economists of an empirical orientation, however, can be observed to do neither.

It has been seen that mainstream economists disagree among themselves, to the extent that they construct alternative models of what they perceive as reality, always subject to their allegiance to a common world view. As they proceed to use these models to explain economic phenomena such as changes in the labour market, the possibilities of further disagreement multiply. These disagreements have their base principally in the employment of different function specifications, different data sets and different statistical techniques of testing. These issues are illustrated in the following paragraphs which describe the manner in which some adherents to this school have examined changes in the labour market.

In the context of labour supply, Joshi provides a good illustration of the application of the utility-maximising individual choice model (Joshi 1986). The problem is to identify the characteristics which distinguish those females who do participate in the labour market from those who do not, and to quantify the effects of such factors which either increase or decrease the probability of participation. The Women and Employment survey data (Martin and Roberts 1984) are used to provide cross-section observations. Participation – several definitions of which are adopted – is the dependent variable, to be explained by independent variables such as the (imputed) wage rate, alternative sources of income and domestic responsibilities. The statistical significance of these and other variables – or their proxies – together with the magnitude of their relative effects are ascertained using multiple regression analysis. Joshi's results show that two variables appear to have important negative effects upon participation, viz., children of pre-school age and non-labour market income, whereas above average earnings power appears to increase the likelihood of participation.

Although cross-section studies such as Joshi's may be used to illustrate the life-cycle effects of female participation such as that associated with children, their number and their age, they cannot examine possible business cycle effects, i.e., the responsiveness of female labour supply, most especially its married women component, to variations in labour market conditions. Theory does not offer unambiguous predictions of the consequences of changes in such conditions. On the one hand, there is the possibility of the pro-cyclical discouraged worker hypothesis in which wage rates are assumed to have been depressed thereby making market work relatively more costly than non-market work and prompting a substitution of time in favour of the latter activity. On the other hand, there is the possibility of the countercyclical added worker hypothesis in which a reduction in household income from other members of the family unit induces women to enter into the labour market. To ascertain which effect is the dominant – because both could occur simultaneously – necessitates a time-series investigation such as that undertaken by Joshi and Owen (Joshi and Owen 1985).

Joshi and Owen use data from *inter alia* the decennial population censuses of 1951, 1961, 1971 and 1981 to construct a model of female labour supply incorporating both life-cycle and cohort variables. Simulations are then made to identify changes in female supply independent of demand variations. The results of these simulations are then compared with actual observed changes in female supply to ascertain the effects of changes in labour demand. The discouraged worker effect is seen to dominate, but over the decades its nature and magnitude appear to have changed. It was most apparent during the 1950s, when females tended to quit the labour force following decreases in demand. By the 1960s, however, only members of the older age cohorts responded in this way. Female labour supply increased during the 1970s, but, according to the authors, 'there is no sign of it shrinking back when growth stagnated or stopped' (Joshi and Owen 1985: i). Apparently modern women are 'more willing to supply their labour for paid work than to withdraw it' (Joshi and Owen 1985: 1).

Compatible though these labour supply explanations may be with the trends in female participation noted in the first section, they are less than adequate in their explanations of changing employment distributions and changing employment patterns. Certainly part-time rather than full-time employment status could be explained by the supply constraints associated with some females' domestic responsibilities (Ballard 1984). As Joshi and Owen themselves suggest, during the last decade of reduced aggregate labour demand, the phenomenon of unemployment in the form of part-time employment may have replaced the historical tendency of females to quit the labour force. However, from the perspective of the mainstream economist, to investigate the possibilities of male–female and/or full-time–part-time substitution – statistically observable in at least some industries if not at the macro level, according to Dex and Perry (Dex and Perry 1984) – requires the addition into the model of a labour demand function in which relative wage and non-wage labour costs are important arguments.

Models incorporating both fully specified supply and demand functions have been applied less to part-time and/or female employees than they have been to other well-identified groups in the labour market, such as young workers, and the labour market as a whole.

In the context of the former, mainstream economists perceive the demand for young workers to be a function of the following:

1. The demand for labour as a whole.
2. The demand for young workers in particular, relative to their substitutes (perhaps part-time females?), a crucial role in this possible substitution being the relative labour costs of the supply inputs.
3. The supply of young workers.

4. The supply of their substitutes.

Lynch and Richardson design and apply a variant of this model to the problem of youth unemployment (Lynch and Richardson 1982). Although a number of factors contribute towards increasing youth unemployment, in this study, most influential for both males and females are relative employment costs. There are, however, two problems with this investigation, each with implications in principle for the authors' results. First, no attempt is made to model the adjustment process between labour supply and demand. Given the institutional factors such as minimum-wage legislation and collective agreements which inhibit wage flexibility in Great Britain, quantity-rationing rather than price-clearing models may be more realistic, but mainstream economists should establish this empirically. Second, in the quantity-rationing model devised and applied by Lynch and Richardson, an assumption is made of the existence of demand constraints throughout the period, whereas the 1950s would appear to be better characterised as a subperiod in which supply constraints existed. In her study of youth unemployment, *inter alia* Rice addresses these two problems (Rice 1986). The quantity-rationing model is established empirically as the preferred alternative. Rice tests for the effect of relative earnings (rather than relative employment costs) and although they are seen to help explain increasing youth unemployment, the assumption of employment conditions switching from a supply-constrained regime to a demand-constrained regime over the period, establishes, most especially for young males, the additional importance of demand-related factors.

In the context of the labour market as a whole rather than one of its subsets, controversy has been dominated by the problem of unemployment. According to the Department of Employment: 'the biggest single cause of our high unemployment is the failure of the jobs market', especially its wage inflexibilities (Department of Employment 1985, Cmnd 9474:13). Academic credence for this contention comes from the Treasury whose simulations suggest an employment elasticity with respect to real wages of −0.75, i.e., a 1 per cent reduction in real wages would result in a 0.75 per cent increase in employment via both substitution and output effects. (HM Treasury 1985).

This result, however, depends upon the model specification and its behavioural interrelationships, and once again it is possible to see how changes in these produce different results – and as an additional consequence, different policy implications. Minford's analysis of the cause of unemployment illustrates this point well (Minford 1985). Minford assumes a two-sector economy. There is a unionised sector, in which unions determine the wage rate, and employers, given their demand for labour function, determine employment levels. There is also a competitive sector, the supply of labour to which consists of all of those unfortunate enough not to obtain employment in the unionised sector. In this competitive sector, other things being equal, the market forces of labour supply and demand determine wage rates. The logic of the model is that successful attempts by unions to increase their wage rates cause employment in the unionised sector to decrease and the supply of labour to the competitive sector to increase, further depressing relative wages in this sector. According to Minford, however, other things are not equal. A social security system provides non-market incomes at levels insufficient to provide work incentives given the wage in the competitive sector and as a consequence unemployment is voluntary rather than involuntary. In this perspective unemployment does not constitute the problem. It is merely symptomatic of such labour market problems as union wage policies and an overly generous social security system. Consequently Minford's policy prescriptions for unemployment include the eradication of union monopoly power and the reform of the tax/benefit system.

Our focus upon supply side models of the aggregate labour market is not to deny either the existence or credibility of alternatives. But it does illustrate how and why even relatively like-minded mainstream economists may disagree in their analysis of unemployment. As would be evident from an equally full discussion of models which assume the existence of involuntary unemployment (e.g., Layard and Nickell 1985) these disagreements about unemployment multiply when the work of less like-minded but still mainstream economists is investigated.

8.4 ALTERNATIVE PERSPECTIVES

Markets, perfect or otherwise, have been seen to dominate the perspective of the mainstream economists, and in those markets the principal actors have been seen to respond to changes in apparently objective circumstances in accordance with unambiguously received signals such as price. The models designed to illustrate and explain these phenomena are manifold but all are variations upon this theme. Even spatial differences, for example in employment growth between regions, are explained in terms of the same variables, if subject to additional lags and rigidities attributable to factor immobilities (Lever and Mather 1986).

The distinction between the mainstream economists and their alternatives is not the dominant tendency of the former to focus upon market forces to the exclusion of other wider social forces. While there are instances of the latter constituting integral elements in mainstream analysis, most frequently their role is either one of short-run effects which are inconsequential in the long run, or one which arises because market forces are weak and anti-competitive forces are strong (Marsden 1986).

In the context of explaining labour market change the dominant mainstream perspective is contested by two alternatives, both with the characteristics of scientific research programmes. One is 'institutionalist' associated with 'segmented' theories of the labour market, the other is 'Marxist'. However, whereas the principal distinction between the institutionalist perspective and the mainstream is the methodological practices of the former, the distinction between the Marxist perspective and the mainstream has its origins in their contrasting world views. In this section we examine change in the labour market using these alternative perspectives.

8.4.1 Segmented markets: an institutionalist perspective

The institutionalists examine the economy at the level of the institution rather than the individual (or class as in the Marxist perspective), describing their nature and behaviour and examining their effects upon the economic system and its principal actors. Segmented theories of the labour market have their origin in empirical investigations of local labour markets in metropolitan areas of the United States where researchers encountered problems – for example, a wide variety of firms of different size and ownership patterns, utilising different technologies and offering contrasting employment conditions and terms – apparently not amenable to neoclassical analysis with its predilections for 'continuity and homogeneity' (Piore 1983: 250). According to one of those researchers, therefore, and contrary to mainstream methodological practice, 'an attempt [was made] to make sense out of the labour market problems as the people in these communities experienced them' and 'to describe the labour market as these people saw it' (Piore 1983: 250).

It was as if two contrasting economies coexisted. One was compatible with mainstream expectations of small competitive owner-managed enterprises with high labour turnover indicative of competitive labour markets. The other was dominated by large mature organisations exercising control over their product markets, often operating in conjunction with employers' federations, and often highly unionised, but always creating internal labour markets which determined the pricing and allocation of labour within the company in accordance with internally generated sets of rules and procedures (Doeringer and Piore 1985).

According to Doeringer and Piore, structured internal labour markets have their origin in factors such as skill specificity – which not only increase training costs absolutely, but increase the employers' proportion of this total – and the skill acquisition process – whereby training is done experientially and informally on the job. Entry into the internal labour market of the organisation from the external labour market is via ports of entry which are restricted in number. Entry criteria are equally restrictive because on entry the individual has future prospects of occupational movement within the mobility cluster.

Doeringer and Piore rationalise the creation of internal labour markets in terms of the savings attributable to reduced labour turnover and technical efficiencies in the recruitment and selection processes. These potential benefits do not accrue to all organisations. Nor may the necessary product market conditions facilitating the development of structured labour markets be present. In its turn, however, the creation of internal labour markets is seen to structure the labour market as a whole, creating, according to dualist theorists, two sectors which display identifiably distinct characteristics. Structured internal labour markets are to be found in the primary sector of the economy, where wages are high, employment is secure and opportunities for advancement exist. Entry into this sector is restricted to those who are perceived to possess the necessary behavioural requirements. Consequently, those who are deemed not to possess those traits – for example, because of their chequered employment histories – or are statistically associated with such stereotypes – for example, members of ethnic minorities and women – are excluded. Considerably less attractive employment conditions are obtained in the secondary sector. Wages are lower; few, if any, on-the-job training opportunities exist; and job insecurity prevails. Indeed there, the employment – and unemployment – experiences tend to engender the very characteristics used to screen out potential entrants to the primary sector. According to this perspective, therefore, factors such as length of job tenure and its concomitant pecuniary rewards, unemployment probabilities and durations are not determined by impersonal market forces. Rather than the outcome of a matching exercise, they are the product of institutional rules and processes.

Establishing the possible existence of labour market dualism (Bosanquet and Doeringer 1973) and ascertaining the benefits of employment within the primary sector (George and Storey 1985) have proved tantalisingly difficult for the mainstream economists. The existence of a segmented labour market – if not a dualist one – and the costs of exclusion from the rewards associated with membership of the preferred segments are more evident in empirical studies compatible with the institutionalist perspective. Manwaring, for example, shows how employers' use of informal rather than formal recruitment channels, principally referrals from existing employees, creates what he terms 'the extended internal labour market', and as a consequence the already existing processes of closure are seen to be extended further into the external labour market (Manwaring 1984). Young adults are especially affected by structured internal labour markets (Ashton and Maguire 1986). The number of ports of entry into employment are reduced, and the particular criteria demanded for entry into primary sector firms effectively discriminate against this group of workers, other than in periods of significant employment expansion.

Whereas this picture of internal labour markets with the subsequent effect of balkanising the labour force, presents an alternative explanation of changing economic status and of what the mainstream economists would describe as the 'rewards' from such, an additional picture of organisation redesign provides a complementary explanation of changing employment status and working patterns. Here, the management of the organisation subdivides the work force into core workers and peripheral workers (Atkinson and Meager 1986). Core workers conduct the key activities of the firm, and are required to undertake functional flexibility as necessary. Peripheral workers are less central to the organisation's needs, and are hired – and fired – as circumstances require. Predominantly married females, they have part-time or temporary contracts of employment. According to this perspective, and in contrast to the supply side hypotheses of mainstream economists, the employment of married females is demand related, necessitated by cost and profit exigencies.

Entry to both Doeringer and Piore's 'structured internal labour markets' and Atkinson and Meager's 'core' necessitates prior screening of candidates to identify those with required productivity levels (and/or requisite attitudes and behavioural traits) given the job specifications. One possible corollary of this is job discrimination, racial and sexual. However, in contrast to mainstream theories of discrimination based on such premisses as 'taste' or 'imperfect information' – and because of which discrimination is assumed to be eliminated in the long run given the free flow of factor inputs and information – the institutionalist's explanation of discrimination both assumes the establishment of processes and rules which exclude certain groups from specific jobs and proceeds to examine the nature of such processes and rules. Exclusion eliminates a number of employment opportunities and has the effect of assigning these discriminated groups, irrevocably, into particular occupation and industries. (For example, data compatible with this phenomenon of 'overcrowding' with respect to female employment can be observed in Tables 8.5 and 8.6, pages 161 and 162. It is less easy to make the same observation with respect to possible racial overcrowding because of data problems, but see Department of Employment (1988).) For the same reason, the incidence of unemployment in these groups would be expected to be disproportionately high.

The employment and unemployment consequences of structured internal labour markets and organisation design have a differential impact over space. Therefore interregional differences, urban–rural drift and inner-city decline ultimately are seen to have a common origin and explanation in organisations' corporate strategy and attendant manpower policies. They are the product of conscious institutional decisions rather than impersonal market forces (Danson 1981).

8.4.2 The Marxist perspective

The distinction between the mainstream school and the Marxist alternative has its origins in contrasting world views, illustrated, for example, in their different perceptions of the market. To the mainstream economists, the market is a neutral system of resource allocation, functioning in the context of the labour market, for example, as a simple matching mechanism. To the Marxist school, according to Ashton: 'the labour market is more adequately seen as an arena in which a series of issues are constantly fought over' (Ashton 1986: 52). Moreover, in this arena, power – in its economic, political and social dimensions – is unequally distributed. Class conflict is endemic.

Markets, therefore, are about processes rather than static equilibria, a difference which has profound consequences for the research methods employed. The accoutrements of extensive research design, such as data classification, trend identification and variable correlation, which typify the work of the mainstream economist, are wholly inappropriate. Indeed, intensive research is required, investigating processes, making use of non-standardised, often qualitative, analytical techniques, often in the context of detailed case studies and always in the context of an overall position of interdependencies which exist between the substructure and the superstructure, compatible with the world views held.

The nature of this perspective and its consequences may be appreciated at the outset by means of examples of work which sought to investigate two significant changes in the labour market, identified in section 8.2, and examined in 8.3, from the perspective of the mainstream economists, viz., female participation, especially of married women working part-time, and unemployment. Following an investigation of part-time employment in Coventry, Beechey and Perkins contend 'that it is invariably women's jobs which have been constructed as part-time jobs; that part-time working is inextricably linked to the existence of occupational segregation: that employers have gender-specific ways of attaining flexibility within their labour forces: that both employers and trade unionists make gender-specific assumptions about what kinds of work are appropriate for women and why married women do part-time work' (Beechey and Perkins 1985: 201). Writing on the unequal distribution of the experience of unemployment, Sinfield maintains: 'the organisation and distribution of work and the allocation of reward, power and social honour among occupations significantly affect who are best protected from unemployment, who are most vulnerable and who are most likely to remain out of work' (Sinfield 1981: 124).

Marxists perceive a competitive process within which, to survive, rival capitals must accumulate. Related to this objective is the strategy of production reorganisation (restructuring) which affects employment indirectly by means of its effects upon labour productivity and output. Production reorganisation is not homogeneous, and in their investigation Massey and Meegan identified three forms and therefore three distinct mechanisms whereby jobs were lost, viz., intensification, investment and technical change and rationalisation (Massey and Meegan 1982). By intensification is meant: 'changes designed to increase the productivity of labour but without major new investment or substantial reorganisation of production technique' (Massey and Meegan 1982: 18). Here output is increased because workers' non-producing time is reduced (achieved following increased job flexibility) and/or the productivity of the work processes is increased (achieved via both mechanisation and task fragmentation). Observed to have been present in industries such as leather, footwear, cycles and textile-finishing, intensification is a cost-reducing measure, and was implemented to increase competitiveness in markets where product demand was decreasing and domestic companies faced threats from foreign low-cost producers. By investment and technical change is meant technical changes to either or both process and product, occasioned by the role innovation plays in the competitive process. Increases in labour productivity result from the increased capital-labour ratio, the ultimate effect upon employment being dependent upon the balance between output change and investment, e.g., the lower the rate of output growth, the greater the probability of job loss. Massey and Meegan found evidence of this form of production reorganisation in industries such as sugar, brewing and malting, iron and steel, textile machinery, jute and carpets. By rationalisation is meant a reduction in capacity achieved via either complete or partial plant closure. Sometimes for small and medium-sized firms, it results in company liquidation. Rationalisation is attributable to excess capacity, an inevitable outcome in the accumulation process. Massey and Meegan observed it in industries such as electrical machinery, woollen and worsted, iron and casting, and paper and board.

Job loss consequent of production reorganisation is not distributed equally across occupational groupings. Sometimes the unskilled are most affected; sometimes, following de-skilling, jobs are created for those who possess no obviously recognisable labour market skills.

Change to employment levels within organisations is sometimes achieved by means of natural wastage, for example, nil replacement of voluntary quits. Sometimes redundancies are declared. Massey and Meegan's perspective of and interindustry analysis of redundancy, however, contrasts vividly with that of Metcalf's cross-sectional statistical analysis, where redundancy rates are explained in typical mainstream fashion using four sets of variables, viz., 'cyclical variation in employment, variables to capture trend rates of employment, labour force composition variables' and two policy variables (Metcalfe 1986: 167).

According to the Marxist perspective, in the capitalist mode of production, labour is alienated. Consequently, to realise fully the potential of labour's contribution to the production process, capital via its managing agents must implement, additionally, labour control strategies at the point of production (Braverman 1974). Post Braverman, it is recognised in principle, that these strategies may take several forms. 'Simple' control may operate via the adoption of piecework wage payment systems; 'technical' control may operate when the pace of work is 'machine' determined; and 'bureaucratic' control may operate when employees are incorporated into elements of the decision-making via formal collective bargaining procedures. Alternatively, management may operate such 'person-related' policies as 'open-door' or quality circles.

Choice of control strategy is influenced by the nature of labour to be controlled, most especially the extent of perceived worker resistance. Consequently, to stereotype, whereas unionised males may be more suitably managed by a process of collective bargaining which would institutionalise conflict, part-time females, traditionally not union members, may be more amenable to policies associated with human resource management. Choice of control strategy is influenced also by the external economic and political environment. High levels of unemployment associated with reduced union 'power' and the emasculating labour and union legislation of the Thatcher administrations, for example, reduce employee resistance to managerial control initiatives manifest in the increasing prevalence of concession bargaining. In this Marxist perspective, however, the dynamics of work place power relationships can only be investigated further within their framework in a concrete historical context.

Control strategies may change therefore as these circumstances change. Additionally, however, capital has the option of adopting labour substitution policies, such as changing the technology to facilitate the employment of a more tractable labour force, even changing the location of production if necessary to greenfield sites where labour may be more susceptible to control. Hence geographical areas as well as human skills become redundant to capital's needs.

In this perspective therefore, changes in employment and unemployment levels in industrial and occupational distribution, in the creation and destruction of jobs over space, are explained ultimately by capital's inexorable drive to accumulate and the changing balance of class forces.

8.5 CONCLUSIONS

When examining change in the labour market, the terrain is contested principally by three perspectives which have been termed a mainstream perspective, an institutionalist perspective and a Marxist perspective.

According to the mainstream perspective, individuals are assumed to exchange and transact in markets, freely making decisions in accordance with relative changes in the constellation of prices which they face. Therefore change, no matter of what or where, is attributable to the aggregate net effect of these decisions. This particular world view has been seen to be distinguished from others. However, within this perspective, controversies have been identified, for example, about the manner in which markets operate, how they or their component parts should be modelled, and how these models should be tested.

The institutionalist perspective has been seen to have its origins in a methodological reaction to the mainstream perspective. As a consequence, its adherents address different puzzles and offer different explanations. What they do not necessarily offer is a distinct world view. Their controversies with the mainstream school are principally methodological. In this way the institutionalist perspective contrasts with the Marxist perspective whose adherents do offer a distinct world view based upon the class conflict inherent in capitalist society. As a consequence, adherents to the Marxist perspective have distinct views as to what constitutes 'problems' as well as alternative theoretical and methodological frameworks.

If the mainstream perspective appears to dominate this as well as other areas of the literature – apparent for example in the ubiquity of phraseology such as 'the labour market' – it does so more because of the organisation of academia than any intrinsic superiority of its frame of reference, methodology or adherents. Here too there is no algorithm of truth, merely a plurality of perspectives with all that that entails.

FURTHER READING

Although the applied work to which it refers is now somewhat dated, Sapsford (1981) remains a comprehensive and popular exposition of the dominant mainstream paradigm. Rice (1986) is a fine example of the application of this analysis. Doeringer and Piore (1985) – cooriginators of what is now known as the dualist/segmented perspective – is a classic of this genre. Their United States reference material is integrated with British studies by Marsden (1986) who evaluates this perspective in the context of mainstream analysis. Ashton's survey is more comprehensive in its coverage of perspectives (1986) as is Routh (1987) although their focus upon unemployment is more narrow. Massey and Meegan (1982) provide an excellent illustration of the Marxist perspective, although this needs to be complemented by a reference on the labour process (such as Thompson (1983)). Also using a perspectives approach, Hasluck (1987) provides a concise survey of spatial themes.

9 · PUBLIC EXPENDITURE

Master or servant?

TERENCE KARRAN

9.1 INTRODUCTION

The modern welfare state, and the high level of government expenditure it necessitates, are of comparatively recent vintage, being specific to the twentieth century. However, public expenditure, and its fiscal prerequisite taxation, have always been the defining characteristics of governments. The still-extant Domesday Book (quite correctly known as the Book of Judgement!) was compiled in 1086 as part of the legitimising process of a new ruler of England demonstrating his right to extract levies from the populace to pay for the services of the state. Echoing sentiments which would not be out of place today, the Anglo-Saxon Chronicle records that 'the land was vexed with many calamities arising from the collection of the royal money' (Wood 1987:21). Hence controversy about the desirability of government spending predates the welfare state, and has probably been voiced for as long as governments have extracted taxes to pay for state services.

Clearly the role of the state has increased markedly from that of 'night watchman' of Norman times, which was concerned with little more than internal security and external relations. Today the modern British state acts as universal benefactor funding a vast array of services, to give 'cradle to the grave' welfare coverage. The greatest increase in the state's invention has come in the post-war period. Undoubtedly this growth was occasioned by many unique historical and political factors, including the need to repair war damage and the election of a Labour government. Additionally at this time there was consensual acceptance by both the major political parties and the electorate of increased public spending to achieve two particular policy goals. First, the recognition that the state ought to provide certain social services for all up to a universal standard – education, health, housing, pensions, etc. Second, in addition to the belief that the state ought to spend money to alleviate poverty and social distress, there was a realisation that such intervention ought to be tied to the use of Keynesian macroeconomic techniques, so that the state could manage the economy to prevent a recurrence of the unemployment problems of the interwar years.

Up until the late 1970s there was a marked basic broad consensus between the two major British political parties about the desirability of state spending – epitomised by the use of the term 'Butskellism'. However, recent years have seen the degree of contention associated with this function of the state increasing, as the level of public spending has risen. Indeed today arguments are vigorously pursued about the desirable level and effects of public expenditure, and the appropriate role of governments in altering taxation and spending levels.

The controversy surrounding public expenditure is of particular interest to students of economics, but has an impact which stretches further than purely academic debate. At an academic level the veracity of economic theory is continually being tested and subsequently refined. This affects the workings of government within which politicians assess the practical efficiency of newly refined macroeconomic policy instruments. The impact of these policy instruments generates changes in public opinion, to which those in the political domain may respond, and shifts in economic indicators which are scrutinised by politicians and economic theorists alike. At an academic level recent years have seen the central role ascribed by Keynesian macroeconomic theories to public spending come under attack from monetarist and neoclassical doctrines. Economic theorists in the Keynesian camp continue to advocate the primacy of public expenditure as a means of controlling the economy, while those in the monetarist and neoclassical schools espouse the view that sustaining high levels of public expenditure can cause both macroeconomic instability and an erosion of personal freedom.

This academic dichotomy about the role of public expenditure and the shift in the intellectual climate have been paralleled at a political level. Governments of both the right and the left used macroeconomic techniques derived from Keynesian theory with ever-diminishing efficacy during the 1960s and 1970s. Failure by governments to secure high economic growth rates and conquer both inflation and latterly, unemployment, lead to a search for more effective policy instruments from within previously discredited pre-Keynesian doctrines. This resultant shift away from Keynesianism was more marked in parties of the right than the left, giving rise to a political cleavage in marked contrast to the post-war consensus about the nature and role of public spending. Right-wing parties, returning to their old pre-Keynesian roots, now advocate a minimalist role for public expenditure as a macroeconomic tool while stressing the consequent increases in individual freedom and choice that result from tax cuts. Parties of the centre and left continue to advocate an active role for public expenditure as a policy tool within an amended but essentially Keynesian framework, while also stressing the welfare benefits of state intervention.

The extent of the difference in the approaches to public spending taken by the political parties can be illustrated by the appeals made to the voters in the 1987 British election. The Conservative manifesto stated: 'we are engaged in reducing the share of the nation's income taken by the state . . . . Our aim is to ensure that public expenditure takes a steadily smaller share of our national income' (Conservative Party 1987:29). This was in marked contrast to the Labour Party's policy priority of creating a million jobs in two years at the cost of £6 billion, to be funded by 'the money that would be used up by the Thatcher government in its 2p income tax bribe. . . (and . . . by prudently borrowing three billion pounds' (Labour Party 1987:5).

However, in spite of these apparently diverse party stances, careful analysis (Rose and Karran 1987) reveals the taxation and spending policies of British governments of varying parties to be determined more by the inertia of previous decisions, than by strong political commitments to radical policies. A wider cross-national study (Rose and Karran 1984) suggests that the strong impact of previous decisions is not unique to Britain but has been instrumental in raising public spending in most western industrialised nations in the post-war period.

Governments select policy instruments to secure political goals in the light of prevailing academic and intellectual opinion about the efficacy of these instruments. Additionally they respond to swings in electoral support and popular opinion as expressed inside the political parties, in the media and through the ballot box. The ascendancy of governments of the right in western democracies in the 1980s is in part a reflection of changes in public opinion about the desirability of increased state spending. In 1987 Britain's inherently disproportionate electoral system lead to the election of a right-wing government committed to public expenditure cuts but the majority of those voting supported parties with contrary policies. Consequently the public debate about the desirability of state spending has continued, and become more heated as the impact of expenditure cuts on public services is being felt by the majority of electors who voted against the government which is implementing these policies.

Hence in sum the controversy about public spending can be seen to be long-standing rather than recent, though contemporary times have seen the debate grow more heated both in academic circles and in the political and public domains generally. Similarly, though the impact of public spending is of great interest to economic theorists, its far-reaching effects make it of concern to a wider audience whose everyday lives it influences. Its continuing degree of controversy clearly makes public expenditure a worthy topic of consideration, and it is the purpose of this chapter to look at some facets of that controversy. The high level of interest in state spending is reflected in a vast literature on the subject. However, the aim of this chapter follows the general theme of the book, which is to focus on particular areas of controversy. First, the question of what exactly is public expenditure and how big it is will be examined. Following from this, cross-national data will be used to provide a comparative context for subsequent debates about the impact and desirability of high spending levels. Finally, an examination will be made of theories which attempt to explain the apparently universal growth in public spending.

9.2 HOW BIG IS PUBLIC EXPENDITURE?

The phrases 'public expenditure' or 'government spending' seem self-explanatory – obviously they relate to money spent by the government on services for the general public. However, to analyse the impact of state spending, to chart trends in its growth and to make cross-national comparisons, we need to know more exactly what these expenditures involve. It is difficult to measure the size of the government's slice in the national cake as first, there is no agreed universal definition of public expenditure, and second, there are various ways of measuring the cake itself. Moreover, as Heald (1987: 11) has demonstrated, disagreement about the correct definition of the public sector has done much to fuel misleading speculation about the overwhelming burden of the public sector.

OECD definitions of 'general government' spending, which include the expenditure of central and local government are not problematic. Difficulties arise when deciding whether to include nationalised industries, which in some nations, notably Britain, are substantial, under the aegis of the public sector. This is reflected in the alteration of the treatment of the nationalised industries in the British national accounts. Until the late 1970s British national accounts included the spending of the nationalised corporations when calculating public spending. In 1977 the Treasury brought the national accounts into line with international accounting practices by excluding expenditure by nationalised industries which the industries funded internally. This adjustment had considerable ramifications for the perception of the size and growth of the public sector, as Leo Pliatzky's 'inside' account of the workings of the Treasury relates (Pliatzky 1982: 106).

There is considerable cross-national variation in the definitional criteria for nationalised industries. State ownership or control seems the most appropriate criterion, however, in Britain this presents difficulties.

Following the extensive privatisation programme, the government's ownership of nationalised industries and public corporations has declined, though it may still exercise ultimate control in certain areas. In addition categorisation of expenditure by bodies on the fringe of government is difficult. Furthermore this criterion of ownership seldom corresponds exactly with that used in other countries, say France, which would place only the major nationalised industries in the public sector.

In addition, even if public spending is restricted to the narrower OECD definition, Pathirane and Blades (1982: 273) demonstrate that other discrepancies can occur. The most common measure of public spending is that of total expenditure on services on the current account, plus capital outlays. However, this would exclude transfer payments, such as those in social security programmes, and hence would therefore tend to understate the size of the public sector share in the national economy. However, as Pathirane and Blades point out, this is countervailed by the fact that the government purchases a wide range of goods from the private sector: hence the measure overestimates the resources within the public sector.

The problems associated with measuring the public sector can be readily illustrated by referring to the British national accounts statistics. As Table 9.1 shows, in 1986 money spent by central and local government on current goods and services and capital items totalled £162.2 billion. To calculate the total public sector, money spent by the nationalised industries has to be added. After 1977 only the portion of nationalised industries' capital spending financed by government loans or grants was included in state expenditure. Estimation of these additional monies brings the public sector share to £167.3 billion. To assess the share of public expenditure in the national economy, there are two possible measures of the latter. The first, gross domestic product at factor cost, excludes expenditure taxes but includes subsidies, hence it is smaller than the other GDP measure which is calculated at market prices. The choice of the appropriate measure of the national economy is as arbitrary as that for public spending, but may have considerable impact on the perception of public spending as Table 9.1 demonstrates.

If general government expenditure is chosen to represent the public sector and GDP at market prices of the whole economy, then the state's share is 43.3 per cent. By contrast, if a wider view is taken of the state's activity and nationalised industries are included, but expenditure taxes excluded by using factor cost GDP, the government's stake rises to 52.4 per cent. Hence by varying the measures used, the public expenditure share itself can vary by 20 per cent. Given the contentious nature of public expenditure, the choice of classification used in calculating the state's share may be as dependent on political priorities as on purely technical accounting practices.

Table 9.1 The public sector share of the UK economy 1986

(A)	General government expenditure	= £162.191 million
(B)	Public sector adjustment (estimated nationalised industry entries)	= £5.129 million
(C)	(A) + (B) = Estimated public sector	= £167.320 million
(D)	Gross domestic product at factor cost	= £319.089 million
(E)	Gross domestic product at market prices	= £374.895 million
	(A) as % of (D) = 50.82%	
	(A) as % of (E) = 43.26%	
	(C) as % of (D) = 52.43%	
	(C) as % of (E) = 44.63%	

Source: CSO, *UK National Accounts 1987* (London: HMSO, 1988, Tables 1.2, 6.1, 6.3, 6.4, 9.4).

Table 9.2 Total outlays of government as % of GDP 1966, 1986

Nation	Outlays as % GDP 1966	1986	% Increase in public sector share
Sweden	38.3	63.5	65.8
Netherlands	40.7	59.1	45.2
Denmark	31.7	55.4	74,8
Italy	34.3	50.4	46.9
Belgium	33.5	53.2	58.8
Austria	38.3	51.9	35.5
Norway	34.8	52.0	49.4
Germany	36.7	46.6	27.0
Canada	29.5	46.2	56.6
UK	35.3	46.2	30.9
Finland	32.0	42.3	32.2
USA	28.5	36.9	29.5
Iceland	28.4	36.6	28.9
Japan	19.1	33.1	42.3
Mean	32.9	48.1	44.6

Source: OECD, *Economic Outlook* (June 1987: 163).

Assessments of whether the state's share is too large in Britain are clearly dependent on what is included. In addition, though the appropriate size for the state's spending level may be a matter for political debate, any assessment requires some comparative yardstick. The oft-made suggestion that Britain's economic problems arise from too large a public sector can be appraised by seeing if nations with a comparable or greater public sector share similar economic problems. Different national accounting systems create difficulties for such appraisals. However, using the OECD standard accounting methods minimises these cross-national differences. Table 9.2 shows the share of total outlays of government as a percentage of GDP for OECD nations for 1966 and 1986.

As the table shows, the state's stake in the economy varies considerably cross-nationally. Hence at the top of the table in 1986 Sweden devoted nearly two-thirds of the nation's resources to public spending. By contrast the state's portion of the economy in Japan is only 33.1 per cent – virtually half of that of Sweden. When viewed in an international context, the UK public sector does not appear to be large. In 1986, of the 14 nations listed, only four allocated a smaller proportion of their domestic product to state spending than Britain, and all of Britain's European neighbours have a larger public sector.

Two further features are apparent from the table. First, the data are not suggestive of any particular definitive relationship between public sector size and economic performance. A cursory examination reveals that Japan, whose economic growth rate exceeds that of other nations, has a small public sector. However, the United States also has a comparatively small public sector but has sluggish economic growth and a massive government budget deficit. Similarly, on various economic measures of standard of living, Sweden performs better than the United Kingdom, however Sweden has a public expenditure share a third as great again as that of Britain.

The final feature discernible from Table 9.2 concerns the growth of the public expenditure share in the economy. During the period 1960–85 Britain suffered comparatively low economic growth, initially high inflation and growing unemployment in spite of the efforts of government of both parties. If the public sector represented a burden on the economy as a whole, this burden was growing less fast in Britain than elsewhere. In 1966 Britain had the fifth largest public sector to GDP ratio, but 20 years later it had fallen to the tenth. Consequently the growth rate of the public sector in Britain was the fourth lowest among all the other nations listed.

However, in every nation shown in Table 9.2, the share of the economy taken by public spending has risen in the 1966–86 period. The average increase over the 20 years has been virtually a half. For some nations the growth has been very rapid – Denmark, for example, saw the public sector share grow by three-quarters, while in Iceland the increase was less than a third. It is to the reasons for this growth that we now turn.

9.3 WHY DOES PUBLIC EXPENDITURE INCREASE?

The data in Table 9.2 show that recent times have seen a universal increase in public expenditure. However, this contemporary increase is merely part of a longer-term trend present in industrialised nations, which can be well illustrated for the first industrial nation – Britain. Table 9.3 shows the growth in public spending in Britain as a fraction of the whole

Table 9.3 Growth of public spending in Britain 1790 to 1987

Year	Spending as % GNP at factor cost
1790	12
1800	24
1820	17
1840	11
1860	11
1880	10
1900	15
1920	26
1938	30
1960	41.2
1980	52.2
1985	51.5
1987	50.1

Sources: Peacock and Wiseman (1967: Tables 1 and 2).
CSO, *1971 National Income and Expenditure* (London: HMSO, 1971, Table 1.1).
CSO, *1986 UK National Accounts* (London: HMSO, 1987, Tables 1.2, 9.4).
CSO, *1987 UK National Accounts* (London: HMSO, 1988, Tables 1.2, 9.4).

economy since the eighteenth century. Until this century public spending was comparatively low. Although unique historical circumstances, such as the Napoleonic Wars against the French, did force up spending levels, once the emergency was over spending returned to the old pre-war level. Hence by 1900 the state's claim on the economy was only marginally greater than it had been in 1790. The great increase in public spending followed in the wake of the two world wars. From 1900 to 1920 the public expenditure share in GNP nearly doubled, while the period after the Second World War witnessed spending by the government rise from 30 to 41 per cent of GNP. By 1980 the state's share of the national economy was four times what it had been two hundred years before. Recent years have seen a slight decline in the public sector, but even in 1987 it still exceeded half of GNP. This upward trend in government expenditure was not unique to Britain – though it may have been more marked here – but was experienced in most other industrialised nations.

How might we explain this apparently universal growth in public spending? The literature on the theories of growth of public expenditure is considerable. In an attempt to link the common strands and perspectives of this disparate work, Tarchys (1975) devised a matrix of nine modes of explanation. These nine cells are the product of three levels of analysis (socioeconomic, ideological-cognitive and political-institutional) and three perspectives (consumer, financial and producer). Tarchys admits that these categories are neither discrete nor exhaustive but merely serve to illustrate the diverse approaches that could be used to explain public expenditure growth.

Different academic disciplines provide different theoretical perspectives, and thus different answers, to the question of how and why public expenditure has grown. It is impossible to cover the multitude of theories even within the particular discipline in a chapter such as this. However, to gain an appreciation of the scope of such theories attention will be paid to three different perspectives. First, economic theories of expenditure will be considered, after which political theories that take account of the political process will be appraised. Finally, bureaucratic theories of expenditure increase will be considered.

9.4 ECONOMIC THEORIES OF EXPENDITURE GROWTH

9.4.1 Wagner's law of increasing state growth

Although the acceleratory trend in government spending is a recent phenomenon, its previous steady growth had attracted the attention of economists. One of the earliest analyses was by Adolphe Wagner who saw that the growth in industrial output was accompanied by a rise in state spending. On the basis of this empirical evidence Wagner postulated a 'Law of Increasing State Activity' whose 'explanation justification and cause is the pressure of social progress and the resulting changes in the relative spheres of private and public economy, especially compulsory public economy' (Wagner 1890:16). In positing this causal relationship between industrialisation and public spending, Wagner adopted what would today be seen as a 'demand side' explanation for increased expenditure and identified three pressures making for greater state intervention.

In the first instance increasing urbanisation and industrialisation cause greater social and economic diversity and complexity in society. This necessitates greater spending on the traditional functions of government to facilitate more extensive systems for revenue collection and to continue to maintain law and order. Second, Wagner thought that growing industrialisation necessitated larger capital units which could be more effectively provided and managed by the state through public corporations than by private investment. Finally, Wagner pointed to the need for particular services which cannot be adequately provided by the private sector, but which are necessary both to sustain economic growth (such as education) and to combat its deleterious effects (social services expenditure).

The logical extension of the relationship outlined by Wagner was that government would encroach unchecked on the national economy until all expenditure was in the public sector. However, Wagner recognised that there was 'a proportion between public expenditure and national income which may not be permanently overstepped . . . . For in the last resort, the state's fiscal requirements covered by taxation figure as expenditure in the household budget of the private citizen.' Hence, as Alt and Chrystal (1983) point out, Wagner's Law may be interpreted as saying that government expenditure is a proportion of national income, or in proportion with national income. The first presupposes a rising share for public expenditure in the national income; the second a constant share. Alt and Chrystal (1979) suggest an interpretation accommodating both – with an accelerating share in the economy for government expenditure during initial industrialisation followed by a stable share which increases in line with the national economy.

Rapid growth in public expenditure in the post-war era, both in absolute terms and as a percentage of the national economy, stimulated attempts to test Wagner's Law empirically. Time-series analysis of modern industrialised nations such as Sweden (Hook 1962), Germany (Andic and Veverka 1964), France (André and Delorme 1975) and America (Ganti and Kolluri 1979), and developing nations like the Caribbean (Goffman and Mahar 1971) and Mexico (Mann 1980) provide qualified support for Wagner's basic tenet of rising government spending but also emphasise cross-national variation in the relative importance of factors causing this growth. Gandhi's (1971) survey of such cross-sectional studies of 'Wagner's Law' draws attention to its imprecision, which has given rise to five different versions of the Law. Gandhi concludes that the empirical studies provide contradictory evidence, some supporting and others negating the theorem about rising public expenditure.

In addition the theoretical context for Wagner's Law has been open to criticism. Schumpter (1954: 851) questioned both the originality and the theoretical competence of Wagner's work. More recently Peacock and Wiseman (1967) suggest that the assumedly technical reasons Wagner gives for expenditure growth relate particularly to his views on the desirable role of the state. In essence they note that the proof of the law of increasing state expenditure is dependent on acceptance of the organic theory of the state that Wagner accepted but did not prove. More critically Burton (1985) finds the reasoning behind Wagner's Law unsatisfactory and his underlying theory of the state discredited.

Wagner's major contribution was to identify that growth in the economy was concomitant with rising public spending, and to provide an explanation for this relationship, which he assumed to be causal. In the century since Wagner's initial study many empirical analyses have been undertaken, which confirm that public spending tends to rise as the economy expands.

However, controversy and disagreement still exist about the nature and causes of this growth.

9.4.2 The displacement effect hypothesis

Wagner's study of the nineteenth century assumes that the level of government spending will rise as a result of the demands made on the state during industrialisation. However, the first systematic empirical investigation of the growth of state expenditure in Britain for the period 1890 to 1955 by Peacock and Wiseman (1967) adopts a contrary approach which concentrates on the supply side of the public expenditure equation and looks at the burden of taxation. Their analysis focused on the residual impact of necessary increases in taxation in times of national emergency.

Peacock and Wiseman argue that during times of stability decisions regarding the size and rate of growth of the public sector are likely to be influenced more by beliefs about the acceptable level of taxation that will be more influential than ideas about assumedly desirable increases in state expenditure. Prospective increases in spending will be constrained by perceptions of what are tolerable and acceptable levels of taxation. During times of national emergency, notably wars, taxpayers will acquiesce to higher levels of taxation, considered unacceptable in times of peace. Hence exceptional circumstances necessitate exceptional fiscal sacrifices by taxpayers. However, rises in expenditure (and by extension, taxation) levels, once implemented, quickly become the accepted status quo. Hence once the national emergency is over and stability returns, both taxation and public expenditure will remain at the new higher level.

As well as making tolerable higher levels of taxation and spending, social upheavals will impose public service obligations on governments. Some of these will relate to the social upheaval itself (such as war pensions, for example), others will relate to the resultant alterations in public perceptions of the role of governments. Peacock and Wiseman consider that through this inspection effect, social upheavals make known to both voters and governments previously unrecognised problems.

In support of Peacock and Wiseman, Crowley's (1971) analysis of western Europe over the very long term (AD1000 to 1959) suggests a cyclical incidence of wars which occasioned first an increase and then a decline in the growth of government spending. Further work by Marr (1974) confirms the cyclical nature of government involvement. However, Burton (1985) makes the point that cross-sectional studies may be inappropriate given that the displacement hypothesis relates specifically to Britain. More importantly he suggests that whereas British wars in the nineteenth century occasioned increases in public spending, there was a return to pre-war spending levels when the conflict ceased. Moreover the hypothesis fails to account for the inexorable growth in spending since hostilities ended.

9.4.3 Other economic models

Prominent among various other economic theories advanced to account for public expenditure increases are those which concentrate on economic growth.

Rostow (1971) explains public expenditure growth in terms of the developmental stages of a nation's economy. In underdeveloped countries a high level of investment is needed to establish the economic infrastructure necessary to reach the threshold for economic take-off. The national communications network of road and rail, the generation and supply of power, the provision of adequate sanitation, which are all prerequisites for a modern industrial state, have to be provided for from the public purse. Once economic take-off has been achieved the role of public investment is complementary with that of private investment. When the nation reaches a mature state of economic development, repeated market failures prompt further public expenditure.

Baumol (1967) adopts a different stance, approaching the phenomenon of rising government expenditure in terms of unbalanced growth between public and private sectors. Baumol divides the economy into progressive and non-progressive sectors. In the progressive private sector economies of scale and technological advance permit greater productivity of labour and increased output of goods and services. In the non-progressive service-intensive public sector, labour is part of the output. Though public sector productivity is lower than that of the private sector, wage rates are set at a similar level in both. Productivity rises only in the private sector but wage rates rise in both, hence public expenditure rises. Moreover as public services are more labour intensive, and as employees in them have no incentive to improve productivity, the increase is acceleratory.

Spann (1977), estimating productivity growth for six state and local services, found some empirical support for Baumol's analysis. On average productivity gains in these public services were either zero or negative for the period 1962–7. Moreover 20 to 25 per cent of the growth in local and state expenditures were due to low productivity gains in the public sector.

9.5 POLITICAL THEORIES OF EXPENDITURE GROWTH

The previous analyses of Wagner, Peacock and Wiseman, Baumol, and Rostow all have a theoretical framework grounded in economics. However, it has long been recognised that public expenditure determination is a function of political influences as well. At the turn of the century Knut Wicksell's (1896) work on public finance had analysed public sector decision-making in terms of political and collective choice. Lindahl (1919) followed Wicksell's analysis by examining the part played by the political bargaining process in budgetary determination. More recently Buchanan (1978) has indicated that taxation and public expenditure must be considered within the political process determining them, i.e., public finance theory cannot be divorced from a theory of politics. Similarly in his study of the growth of government, Rose (1984) demonstrates that it is the combined impact of various social, economic and political influences that have lead to an increased role for the state.

Public expenditure determination is a function of government which, in democratic nations, acts on behalf of and in response to the wishes of the electorate. Theories of the impact of the political process on public expenditure concentrate on the actions of voters and of politicians and parties seeking electoral support, as well as the manner in which decisions are made.

Most voter models find their lineage in Downs' (1957) study which applied an economic theoretical framework to micropolitical analysis. Thus Downs saw the political parties as operating like competing firms but attempting to maximise electoral support rather than profits. Within this scenario public expenditure decisions are made by electors casting their votes in favour of the political party whose fiscal policy comes nearest to maximising their own individual utility. Within any population there will be voters wishing for high, medium and low levels of public spending. The level preferred by the median voter will eventually prevail, as those wanting low spending will be outvoted by those who favour high and moderate spending, while those who wish for high spending will be outvoted by those desiring low or moderate spending levels.

Building on Downs' work, Macpherson (1961) develops a model of political equilibrium, derived from the economic theory of the price mechanism, market operation and marginal utility. In this analysis the central mechanism is the party system which produces political equilibrium by both combining the diverse needs of electors, enabling political decisions to be made, and allowing competition between the political parties to produce sets of decisions that citizens are willing to pay for.

Considering further the impact of politics on spending decisions, Black (1958) extended the analysis to look at the process of determination of majority decisions. Black starts from a similar base to Downs, that of a utility function, i.e., an individual set of preferences. Reconciliation of different preferences necessitates a process of exchange, compromise and mutual adjustment. Black showed that simple majority voting can produce continuous cycling rather than positive outcomes. Hence the outcome may be determined by when the vote is taken, and voting rules and agenda setting may be important. Similarly Tullock (1959) studied decisions on highway spending in the United States and demonstrated that the sequence of majority votes on spending projects could overextend the budget and make every one worse off than they would be without collective action.

How might these theories about the actions of voters and parties explain growth in spending? Metzler and Richard (1978) point to the fact that whereas each elector has the same voting power, they may have disproportionate financial resources. Hence median voters may favour reallocative policies made possible by higher public expenditure funded by higher taxes, as their net benefits will increase while those of their richer counterparts decline. Hence, as the franchise was extended via the abolition of property qualifications to vote, the new electors voted for reallocative policies and forced up public expenditure. In what has come to be known as the 'paradox of collective action' Olson (1965) develops a similar argument. Taxpayers and recipients of government benefits are not the same people. Hence, since the two roles are divorced, individuals will demand increased government spending via the ballot box without realising the costs or without having to pay for it themselves. Eventually, Olson argues, this paradox can give rise to an irresponsible demand for a growth in the bureaucracy and public expenditure.

A further theme on similar lines is developed by Courant, Gramlich and Rubinfield (1979) who argue that voter preferences on public expenditure will vary in accordance with whether the elector is employed in the public or the private sector. Public sector employees who vote for increased public spending accrue direct benefits in the form of increased salaries and indirect benefits through increased service provision. Dunleavy (1980) provides positive evidence that employment in the public sector is now more important than class in determining whether an elector will vote for the Labour Party which traditionally supports increased public spending.

These explanations of public expenditure growth assume that the impact of the voter in determining policy is paramount. However, the process of political bargaining is two-way: politicians do not respond passively to electors' demands but actively attempt to secure support by offering the voter fiscal incentives. As Buchanan and Tullock (1962) suggest, the benefits of public expenditure are enjoyed by particular groups but paid for by taxes on everyone. Vote-maximising politicians who are lobbied by minority groups will tend to secure their support by increasing the financial benefits to such groups, thus raising public expenditure. Additionally politicians may seek support in order to maximise any financial advantages they may enjoy as legislators. Crain and Tollinson (1976) examining the record of legislatures in the USA found that politicians do respond to economic incentives and hence legislative decisions tended to reflect individual financial advancement.

The application to the political process of models derived from economics clearly offers substantial insight into the process of public expenditure determination. However it is not without its critics. Dunleavy and Ward (1981), for example, critically challenge its underlying assumptions and rationale. Median voter analyses like that espoused by Downs assume that voters' preferences are fixed and hence invariant in response to party competition. However, Dunleavy and Ward demonstrate that this assumption is highly unrealistic as both the state and the parties can alter or affect individual voters' preferences. Hence the state can alter the social and spatial structure of society through building council house estates; can exploit social tensions, for example through trade union legislation; and can alter the rules of party competition, for example by reforming local government or insisting on a political levy from their members. Similarly parties can support or aggravate levels of social tensions and enhance the salience of cleavages, for example over race; can control the mode of competition, for example by opposing proportional representation; and can control the political agenda by focusing on particular issues, for example nuclear weapons or the NHS.

These criticisms serve to indicate that although political parties' processes affect public expenditure determination, like purely economic theories they provide only a partial answer. Public expenditure policies are determined through the political process, but these policies are implemented by bureaucrats, who can exercise considerable influence over the outcome. It is their impact we will now consider.

9.6 BUREAUCRATIC THEORIES OF EXPENDITURE GROWTH

Weber's original work on bureaucracy viewed the bureaucrat as a meritocratic expert carrying out administrative duties unstintingly and unthinkingly. Applying theories of economic rationality to the bureaucrat's role, Tullock (1965) challenged existing Weberian ideas of bureaucracy and saw bureaucrats as utility-maximisers and not faceless officials passively following orders. Similarly Niskanen (1971) views purposive behaviour by individuals as the essence of social behaviour, with bureaucrats like everyone else maximising their personal utility. Hence bureaucrats will be motivated by salary, public reputation and prestige, power and patronage, all of which can be seen as a function of the total budget of the bureaucracy.

Both public sector employees and sponsoring departments of bureaucratic services will influence a bureaucrat's tenure. Unless he can provide increasing budgets and salaries for his staff, and unless he proposes aggressively more activities and higher budgets, he will come under pressure from both employees and sponsors. Niskanen considers that legislators cannot reduce a bureau's budgets because motions on budgets are denied or approved, rather than amended. Moreover bureaucracies are invariably monopsonies, in that they offer the only source of administrative and legislative advice, so legislators are denied an alternative supply. In addition the review of each bureau's proposed budget is undertaken by specialised government committees, which are dominated by representatives of groups with an interest in maintaining a high level of services. Thus politicians with a background in or knowledge of medicine are more likely to attend committees determining the size of health service budgets. Niskanen's work suggested that bureaucrats could extend budgets to twice the size necessary to meet the genuine demands for public goods and services with the eventual result that all the benefits of public goods are absorbed by the bureaucrats.

Noll and Fiorina (1978) take a different view of the respective pressures of legislators and bureaucrats on the growth of the budget. Essentially politicians are seeking to maximise the budgets of bureaucracies, while the bureaucrats aim to increase the number of staff employed. By maximising budgets, politicians can maximise electoral advantage through the promise of greater benefits to the electorate. Some of these benefits will take the form of straight transfer payments which bureaucrats have little incentive to increase. However both bureaucrats and politicians may have a vested interest in increasing the delivery of public services, which necessitates a growth in bureaucratic size. Thus they suggest that both politicians and bureaucrats are motivated, but in different ways, though with the same result, that of increasing the size of the public expenditure bill.

These arguments have a persuasive logic. However, it is questionable whether they have universal applicability. Peacock (1978), for example, suggests that Niskanen's bureaucrat has little in common with the British civil servant, but could be approximated by the Minister in charge of a government department. However the Minister does not normally seek budget maximisation, since the unpopularity of resulting tax increases act as a constraint. Civil servants also, Peacock suggests, do not behave as Niskanen's model indicates, in that they are concerned with the formulation and execution of policy, neither of which presupposes budget maximisation.

9.7 CONCLUSIONS

The three theories of public expenditure growth considered above provide equally plausible explanations at different levels. However, as we have seen, these theories contradict each other and for this reason the topic of public expenditure remains controversial in academic circles. What can we therefore say about these different theories, and the degree to which they increase our understanding of state spending?

The problems about determining the primacy of any one of these theories are not peculiar to the phenomenon of public spending, but relate to the social sciences generally. In the first place, it is possible that these explanations are not mutually exclusive, and hence it is clearly feasible that more than one theory could be correct. Furthermore, it is clear that the determination of public expenditure is a complex procedure involving many actors and processes. In the social sciences, unlike the natural sciences, it may be possible to hold the effects of any one factor constant or eliminate the impact of any particular process, so that the contribution of other factors can be assessed. Indeed, actually measuring the effects of different elements may not be feasible. Hence, for example, we can not remove the effects of bureaucrats in the budgetary process to assess how great a part legislators may play. Moreover, even if this were possible, what units could be used to measure the influence of legislators? However, even if it were possible to remove the effects of any one element, it is conceivable that the impact of the total elements acting in unison is greater than the sum of the effects of the individual elements, so a reductionist exercise could be counterproductive. Also, unlike scientific experiments, social science phenomena are time specific and hence do not allow for repeatable tests. For example, it is not possible to create the NHS in the 1930s in order to test what effect health improvements might have had on pre-war economic output. Allied to this is the problem that the effects of the crucial factors in the process of public expenditure determination may themselves be altering over time, so that one theory may be appropriate during one period but not in the next.

The nature of social science phenomena hence create difficulties with respect to the testing of hypotheses. In addition there are other fundamental problems, which are hinted at above and which will continue to make public expenditure a controversial issue. Foremost among these is that choices about public expenditure are not only technical, economic decisions, but are also a function of particular political beliefs and ideologies, held by both academics and the general public alike, which are essentially subjective. Whether someone believes that a high level of public expenditure is desirable will be a reflection of their particular subjective view of the world. This is well illustrated at a national level. Thus in certain nations (notably the Scandinavian countries) a level of public spending of over half the domestic product is regarded by citizens as 'normal' and 'proper'. However, such a share in the economy for the state purse would be considered as 'excessive' by the populace in other nations like Britain, the United States and Japan. Consequently, provided that differences in political opinion about public expenditure continued to be voiced, it will remain an oft-debated and highly controversial issue.

FURTHER READING

For students who wish to pursue some of the issues raised in this chapter, the following texts are recommended: Heald (1987) offers a thorough appraisal of a wide range of issues concerned with public expenditure, including accountability, efficiency and privatisation. Brown and Jackson (1982) provide a discussion of public expenditure definitions and theories of growth. A useful introduction to voter models of public expenditure can be found in Breton (1974), while Niskanen's (1971) study of the impact of bureaucrats makes interesting reading. Gough (1981) reviews theories of the role of public expenditure from both the right and left, as do Newton and Karran (1985).

10 · HAS MONETARISM FAILED?

Conflicting results from the UK inflation laboratory

NIGE HEALEY

10.1 INTRODUCTION

As an intellectual force, monetarism came to the fore with the apparent breakdown of 'Keynesian' demand management policies and the acceleration in world inflation in the mid-1970s. In contrast to the Keynesian orthodoxy it superseded, monetarism is a relatively simple theoretical structure. Although, like Keynesianism, it is far from a monolithic body of thought, in the final analysis monetarism is founded upon three central postulates (see, for example, Mayer 1978; Purvis 1980; or Laidler 1981):

1. That the money supply is exogenous and can be controlled by the monetary authorities.
2. That the demand for money is a stable function of a few key variables, including most notably nominal income (the money value of GNP).
3. That the private sector is inherently stable, automatically tending to its 'natural rate' of employment and real output in the long term.

Monetarists, most notably Friedman, have been amongst the fiercest advocates of the positivist tradition in economics and monetarism has been subjected to rigorous empirical analysis over the years. The specification and estimation of the demand for money function, in particular, has probably attracted more econometric attention than any other behavioural relationship in economics. Yet despite the massive volume of empirical work, monetarism continues to divide the economics profession.

Ostensibly, one of the main reasons for this is the well-known difficulty of empirical testing in social science. Because economists cannot perform controlled experiments, they are limited to passively observing events in the real world. As a result, the interaction of the variables with which the testers are concerned is clouded by interactions with extraneous factors. In seeking to clean the data of such disturbances and isolate the nature of the underlying relationships, economists therefore have considerable scope for, consciously or subconsciously, finding the verification or falsification of the hypotheses they are seeking.

Unusually, however, in 1979 the UK government implemented a textbook monetarist policy, which was widely viewed as the closest approximation to a 'monetarist experiment' yet seen. Uniquely, it appeared, the economics profession was to witness a 'laboratory' experiment in which Britain had 'volunteered to be the Friedmanite guinea pig' (Galbraith 1980). The Bank for International Settlements (1980: 9) claimed that 'economists and policy-makers have for once been offered the possibility of observing an experiment', a view confirmed by Tobin (1981: 280) who described the government's medium-term financial strategy (MTFS) as 'a very interesting and . . . risky experiment in macroeconomic policy'. This view was widely shared by many other economists (see, for example, Pratten 1982; Miller 1982; Artis and Bladen-Hovell 1987).

Whether or not this episode of UK policy can be said truly to constitute a 'monetarist experiment' is not at issue here. The key point is simply that the UK government did attempt to follow monetarist policy prescriptions much more closely between 1979 and 1982 than either it or any other western government had done before or since, and that in so doing it generated a substantial new body of evidence about the validity of the postulates which underpin monetarism. This chapter examines these results and concludes that, although this experience has dealt the credibility of practical monetarism a serious blow, the underlying theoretical issues which divide economists remain as far from resolution as ever.

10.2 THE NATURE OF THE 1979–82 'MONETARIST EXPERIMENT'

In May 1979 the Conservative Party was returned to power with the declared intention of implementing a textbook monetarist programme designed to 'squeeze inflation out of the system'. Developed with the assistance of eminent monetarist economists over a number of years (Keegan, 1984), the new Conservative strategy gave overriding priority to the attainment of predetermined monetary targets, eschewing all other non-market restraints on the price level:

> the Government considers that a progressive reduction in the rate of growth of the money stock is essential to achieving a permanent reduction in the rate of inflation.
>
> (Treasury 1980: iii)

The new government's disinflation programme accordingly involved a steady reduction in the rate of monetary growth with target ranges preannounced for each of the four years ahead, aiming for price stability by the final year. To the extent that entrenched inflationary expectations were slow to adapt, the government anticipated adverse real side-effects in the short term, but hoped that widely publicising its monetary targets would accelerate adjustment:

> monetary targets, openly proclaimed and explained, can have a crucial effect in reducing inflationary expectations . . . [and] can help ease the return to realistic collective bargaining.
>
> (Conservative Party 1977: 6)

The central elements of the 'monetarist experiment' were brought together for publication in the shape of the 'Medium Term Financial Strategy' (see Table 10.1). The new strategy was warmly welcomed by monetarists:

> I strongly approve of the general outlines of the monetary strategy outlined by the Government: taking monetary growth as the major intermediate target; stating in advance targets for a number of years ahead; setting targets that require a steady and gradual reduction in monetary growth; and stressing the Government's intentions of strictly adhering to those targets.
>
> (Friedman 1980: 56)

In the event, the experiment lasted only from the General Election in June 1979 to March 1982. During this period, short-term interest rates were raised to record levels and fiscal policy severely tightened in an attempt to keep monetary growth within its target band. The exchange rate appreciated sharply and employment and output fell quickly, with the greatest losses being concentrated in construction and the tradeables sector of manufacturing. After initially rising, inflation also fell after 1980 (see Table 10.2).

Towards the end of 1981, the government began to address its interest rate changes to the behaviour of the exchange rate, which had previously been allowed to float cleanly in accordance with orthodox monetarist prescriptions.[1] Consequent overshooting of the £M3 target range was officially sanctioned by revising upwards all the future targets in the 1982 MTFS. 'It was less a question of moving the goalposts than laying out a new pitch' (Smith 1987: 106). The monetarist experiment was effectively over.

In the next three sections (10.3–10.5), the evidence generated by the

Table 10.1 The medium-term financial strategy 1980–8

MTFS targets	1980	1981	1982	1983	1984	1985	1986	1987	1988	Outturns
PSBR (% GDP)										
80/81	3.75									5.70
81/82	3.00	3.00								3.50
82/83	2.25	2.25	3.50							3.30
83/84	1.50	1.50	2.75	2.75						3.25
84/85			2.00	2.50	2.25					3.10
85/86				2.00	2.00	2.00				1.60
86/87					2.00	2.00	1.75			1.00
87/88					1.75	1.75	1.75	1.00		−0.75
88/89					1.75	1.75	1.50	1.00	−0.75	
89/90							1.50	1.00	0.00	
90/91								1.00	0.00	
91/92									0.00	
£M3 (% pa)										
80/81	7–11									20.0
81/82	6–10	6–10								14.5
82/83	5–9	5–9	8–12							10.0
83/84	4–8	4–8	7–11	7–11						9.8
84/85			6–10	6–10	6–10					9.5
85/86			5–9	5–9	5–9	5–9				14.8
86/87					4–8	4–8	11–15			18.0
87/88					3–7	3–7		****		
88/89					2–6	2–6				
89/90										
M1 (% pa)										
82/83			8–12							11.0
83/84			7–11	7–11						11.0
84/85			6–10	6–10	****					
85/86				5–9						
PSL2 (% pa)										
82/83			8–12							9.0
83/84			7–11	7–11						12.3
84/85			6–10	6–10	****					
85/86				5–9						
MO (% pa)										
84/85					4–8					5.5
85/86					3–7	3–7				3.5
86/87					2–6	2–6	2–6			4.0
87/88					1–5	1–5	2–6			5.0
88/89					0–4	0–4	1–5	2–6	1–5	
89/90							1–5	1–5	1–5	
90/91								1–5	0–4	
91/92									0–4	

Source: Medium Term Financial Strategy, published in HM Treasury, *Financial Statement and Budget Report* each March; CSO Financial Statistics (various).
**** = Target range abandoned.

Table 10.2 Selected economic indicators 1979–86

	1979	1980	1981	1982	1983	1984	1985	1986	1987
PSBR (£bn)	12.7	11.8	10.6	5.0	11.6	10.1	7.6	2.4	−1.4
Cyclically-adjusted* PSBR (£bn, 1979 base)	12.7	6.2	−0.8	−7.0	1.0	0.0	−0.5	1.2	n/a
Real† PSBR (£bn)	1.6	1.4	1.3	2.9	−6.3	−3.5	−1.2	0.7	n/a
Increase in £M3 (%)	13.4	18.8	13.4	9.3	10.9	10.0	13.3	18.0	22.8
Increase in MO‡ (%)	8.2	4.1	2.6	3.5	6.0	5.8	4.2	5.4	4.2
Short-term interest rates	16.5	13.6	15.4	10.0	9.0	9.3	11.5	11.0	8.4
Exchange rate ($)	2.12	2.33	2.03	1.75	1.52	1.34	1.30	1.47	1.63
Inflation (RPI %)	13.4	18.0	11.9	8.6	4.6	4.9	6.1	3.4	4.2
Increase in nominal GDP (%)	15.6	15.9	10.6	10.2	8.0	7.3	9.7	6.5	8.6
Increase in real GDP (%)	2.2	−2.1	−1.3	1.6	3.4	2.4	3.6	3.1	4.4
Unemployment (%) (excl. school-leavers)	4.8	6.1	8.5	9.9	10.8	11.1	11.3	11.5	10.3

Sources: Bank of England Economics Division, *Bank of England Quarterly Bulletin*, Economic Trends.

*The cyclically-adjusted PSBR is the PSBR which would obtain, given government spending plans and tax rates, at a given point in the economic cycle (usually 'full-employment', here the point on the cycle reached in 1979). It therefore measures deliberate policy changes in the fiscal stance, abstracting from those which arise naturally due to changes in employment, output and inflation.

†The inflation-adjusted PSBR is the deficit after allowance has been made for the 'inflation tax', i.e. the fall in the real value of outstanding public sector debt due to inflation. It therefore measures changes in the public sector's real indebtedness.

‡MO is the broad measure of the monetary base.

1979–82 period, and the very different interpretations of these results by different groups of economists, are examined with respect to each of the three postulates which lie at the heart of monetarism (see section 10.1 above).

10.3 THE MONEY SUPPLY

Monetarist theory actually makes two fundamental, closely related propositions about the money supply. The first is that the supply of money is exogenous with respect to the demand for money, in the same way that the supply of cars is, in an analytical sense, distinct and separate from the demand for cars. The second is that the authorities can, if they so choose, control the rate at which new money is supplied to the economy.

10.3.1 The exogeneity of the money supply

This first proposition ensures that the ultimate holders of money must respond to an exogenous increase in the supply of money (e.g., by spending it) in such a way that one or more of the arguments in their demand function changes (e.g., real income or the price level), so increasing demand and eventually restoring equilibrium. In this view of the world, monetary growth can therefore be seen as an exogenous 'shock' to the economy, which causes temporary disequilibrium in the money market as economic agents find themselves with excess real money balances. Friedman, for example, has frequently used the metaphor of scattering newly-printed money from a helicopter to capture the exogenous spirit of the money supply process. The changes in nominal income, and eventually prices, which later follow an initial increase in the money supply, are the result of economic agents seeking to restore portfolio equilibrium by spending these excess balances on real and financial assets.

Many economists have long been hostile to this approach. As Davidson (1972: 106) points out: 'in the real world, money is not created as the manna from heaven of a Patinkinesque world or dropped by helicopter as in Friedman's construction.' Any observed statistical correlation between changes in the money supply and changes in nominal income might therefore equally be interpreted as evidence that the latter causes the former, rather than the reverse as monetarists postulate. As Kaldor (1980: 90) argues:

> Under a 'credit-money' [as opposed to a commodity-money e.g., gold] system such unwanted or excess amounts of money could never come into existence; it is the increase in the value of transactions [nominal income] – whether it is due to a rise in costs or in the volume of production or both – which calls forth an increase in the 'money supply'.

Under the institutional arrangements which obtain in the United Kingdom, the relationship between broad monetary growth (i.e., the increase in the outstanding stock of notes and coin in circulation and sterling bank deposits) may be expressed in terms of the various financial transactions which bring about this increase (see Table 10.3).

Expressed in this way, it is not difficult to see how monetary growth might be endogenous to the system. Suppose the private and overseas sector find themselves with insufficient money balances because nominal income has risen. One solution is to borrow from the banking system; another is to switch from foreign currency assets into sterling, which may force the authorities to undertake open-market sales of sterling on the foreign exchange market. A third solution is to reduce net purchases of public sector debt, both by cutting down on new purchases and allowing existing securities to mature. All three adjustment mechanisms have the effect of increasing the money supply; that is, of making the money

Table 10.3 The supply-side identity

Increase in money supply	=	Public sector borrowing requirement (PSBR)
		less
		Net sales of public sector debt to the non-bank private and overseas sector
		less
		Net sales of foreign exchange reserves (i.e., open-market purchases of £ by the public sector)
		plus
		Increase in £ bank lending to private and overseas sectors

supply endogenous to the system, so that it passively adjusts to changes in nominal income, rather than exogenous, so that it causes these changes.

This issue of exogeneity is crucial to monetarism. If the money supply is indeed demand-determined, then 'controlling' its growth is pointless. To the extent that the authorities can exercise any influence over its rate of growth at all, this is only because the main instruments of monetary policy, namely changes in the size of the PSBR and the level of short-term interest rates, also have a direct impact on nominal income. Deflating the economy through high interest rates and fiscal contraction may therefore succeed in reducing monetary growth, but this will be primarily because the demand for money has been reduced by a prior fall in nominal income, rather than because the rate of monetary growth has been cut directly.

Traditionally, monetarists have relied on the existence of time lags between changes in the rate of monetary growth and (subsequent) changes in nominal income to provide evidence of a causal relationship running from (exogenous changes in) the former to the latter (e.g., Friedman and Schwartz 1963). The difficulties with such a crude methodology are well known and need not be rehearsed here. Moreover, everyday experience throws up countless examples of prior events (e.g., the purchase of wedding rings) being caused by later events (e.g., marriage services), rather than causing them. Yet despite the myriad problems of establishing the exogeneity of monetary growth using time lag techniques, economists have continued to contribute to a growing literature on this subject.

The experience of the 1979–82 monetarist experiment simply serves to highlight the limitations of this approach. While monetarists argue that in terms of monetary aggregates like the monetary base, monetary growth was reduced sharply between 1979–81, so curbing the growth of nominal income, Table 10.2 above confirms that over the same period the fiscal

Table 10.4 £M3 targets and outturns

Target period	Target range	Outturn	Overshoot from target mid-point
4.76– 4.77	9–13%	17.7%	+6.7%
4.77– 4.78	9–13%	16.0%	+5.0%
4.78– 4.79	8–12%	10.9%	+0.9%
10.78–10.79	8–12%	13.3%	+3.3%
6.79– 4.80	7–11%	10.3%	+1.3%
6.79–10.80	7–11%	17.8%	+8.8%
2.80– 4.81	7–11%	18.5%	+9.5%
2.81– 4.82	6–10%	14.5%	+6.5%
2.82– 4.83	8–12%	11.0%	+1.0%
2.83– 4.84	7–11%	9.7%	+0.7%
2.84– 4.85	6–10%	12.2%	+4.2%
2.85– 4.86*	5– 9%	16.6%	+9.6%
2.86– 4.87	11–15%	18.4%	+6.0%

Source: Financial Statement and Budget Reports; *Bank of England Quarterly Bulletin*.
*Target temporarily suspended in October 1985.

stance also became extremely contractionary with the underlying structural surplus rising as high as 5–6 per cent at the nadir of the recession; at the same time, short-term interest rates and the exchange rate were both rising sharply. All three factors were strongly deflationary in their own right and it is notable that, measured in terms of £M3, monetary growth only began to slow after the growth of nominal income began to fall. In other words, the period 1979–82 can be used to support the interpretation of an exogenously-determined monetary contraction driving down nominal income or equally a fiscally-led deflation reducing the rate of growth of a demand-determined money supply.

10.3.2 The control of the money supply

Even if the exogeneity of money is accepted for the sake of argument, the history of targeting the money supply in the United Kingdom appears to cast considerable doubt on the related monetarist proposition that the monetary authorities can actually control its growth. Table 10.4 sets out the actual target ranges for £M3 which were in force for each policy period 1976–87.

It is interesting that for the three target periods of the monetarist experiment, the average overshoot was 8.3 per cent on an average target mid-point of only 8.7 per cent, compared with 4.0 per cent on 10.5 per cent under the 1974–9 Labour government and 4.3 per cent on 9.4 per cent after 1981–2. In other words, although the targets themselves were rather more restrictive between 1979–82, the authorities' performance in achieving these targets was considerably worse.

There are two possible conclusions which could be drawn from these figures. The first, favoured by monetarists, is that despite the government's rhetoric, the Bank of England flinched from properly using its power to control the money supply. The second, favoured by, *inter alia*, the Bank itself, is that the recent acceleration in financial innovation and the globalisation of financial markets has made it technically impossible for a central bank to identify and control the growth of 'money'.

The first of the possible interpretations of the Bank's demonstrable inability to control £M3 is that the Bank in fact never genuinely tried. Brunner, for example, has argued that, despite rhetoric to the contrary, the Bank's 'strategy and tactics remain[ed] far removed from monetarist ideas' (Brunner 1983: 53). Friedman (1980: 57) similarly claims that:

> Central banks throughout the world have rendered lip-service to the control of monetary aggregates by announcing monetary growth targets. However, few have altered their policies to match their professions of faith . . . . The United Kingdom is . . . an egregious example.

The monetarists' major grievance concerns the method by which the Bank of England controls monetary growth. In principle, monetary growth may be controlled either by influencing the demand for bank credit (which creates new deposits) or by acting directly on the supply of bank credit, in the sense of limiting the banks' ability to satisfy any given level of demand. Throughout the period 1979–82 (and beyond), the Bank relied on the former approach, despite the advice of many monetarists to move over to the latter on grounds of technical efficiency.

Table 10.3 relates monetary growth to the different sources of demand for bank credit, where the demand for bank credit by the public sector is simply the difference between its total borrowing needs (the PSBR) and funds raised from non-bank sources (by the sale of public sector debt and official foreign exchange reserves). Under the present arrangements, the Bank controls monetary growth by manipulating short-term interest rates in order to influence (a) the volume of public sector debt sales, so altering indirectly the public sector's demand for bank credit for any given PSBR and level of foreign exchange market intervention; and (b) the private and overseas sectors' demand for bank credit, which is believed to be interest-sensitive.

The logic of the MTFS was that the rate of monetary growth and the size of the PSBR were predetermined (see Table 10.1) and the exchange rate clean-floating (so that official sales and purchases of foreign exchange would not compromise domestic monetary control). The Bank was then to adjust interest rates to whatever level was necessary to achieve the monetary target. This it does by passively supplying the reserves (the monetary base assets) that the banks need to underpin their increasing loans and deposits, but at an interest rate of its own choosing. At the outset of the monetarist experiment, many UK monetarists, notably Brian

Griffiths, Roy Batchelor and Allan Meltzer, were highly critical of the Bank's procedures for monetary control, arguing that it was technically deficient and that, by implication, the Bank's declared preference for the status quo augured badly for monetarism. Friedman (1980) was particularly harsh in his assessment. Commenting on the Green Paper jointly published by the Bank and the Treasury to promote discussion of monetary control techniques, he wrote:

> I could hardly believe my eyes when I read . . . 'The principal means of controlling the growth of the money supply must be fiscal policy – both public expenditure and tax policy – and interest rates.' Interpreted literally, this sentence is wrong. Only a Rip Van Winkle, who had not read any of the flood of literature during the past decade and more on the monetary process, could possibly have written that sentence.
>
> (Friedman 1980: 57)

The alternative procedure widely favoured by monetarists is monetary base control. This involves rigidly controlling the volume of reserves supplied to the banks and so, through the credit multiplier, the total volume of new credit the banking system is able to create. In this system, it is claimed, rather than interest rates being adjusted in a hit-or-miss affair to achieve the monetary target, the monetary target is guaranteed and interest rates are simply the market mechanism by which the available bank credit is rationed between competing customers in the public, private and overseas sectors. In other words, the supply of bank credit is controlled at source, rather than by the Bank 'guesstimating' the level of interest rates at which the target amount will be demanded.

The monetarists' case is thus that the Bank deliberately chose not to move to the system of monetary control which would have ensured the government's MTFS targets were realised. Instead it maintained its traditional 'Heath Robinson system' (Congdon 1982: 96) of influencing monetary growth indirectly through changes in short-term interest rates. There have been a number of reasons offered for this intransigence: the Bank's innate conservatism; the potential conflict between the Bank's historic role as 'lender of last resort' and monetary base control; and a bureaucracy's dislike of the imposition of performance targets and the greater scope for flexibility offered by the existing *modus operandi*. With regard to the last point, it is notable that the Bank consistently played down the importance of £M3 targets throughout the period – in sharp contrast to the government:

> A monetary target . . . provides a necessary discipline. But in the short term, our actions need to be guided by a range of considerations.
>
> (1981 Mansion House speech (Bank of England 1984: 54))

Many monetarists, however, go beyond this and argue that the Bank's refusal to adopt monetary base control was symptomatic of a deep-seated hostility to monetarism. There is some evidence for this view as well.

The 1973–83 Governor of the Bank, Sir Gordon Richardson, was frequently openly sceptical of the ability of monetary targets alone to produce inflation-free economic growth, arguing, for example, that:

> This spirit of disillusionment with demand management is justified up to a point, but it is capable of being carried too far . . . . One should recognise that the blame for inflation rests not on any simple cause, but rather on a multitude of political and economic pressures.
>
> (Bank of England *op. cit.*: 53–4)

It is widely known that relations between the government and the Bank were severely strained between 1979–82, the former concerned about the persistent overshooting of their monetary targets and the latter alarmed at the impact of the interest rate rises on the exchange rate (Riddell 1983). The monetarists complain that by retaining control over interest rates, the Bank was able to prevent them rising to the heights necessary to bring £M3 under control. They also point to the Bank's attempts to hold down the exchange rate by open-market sales of sterling. Such intervention had been explicitly rejected by the government and caused further tension between the Prime Minister and the Governor.

The second interpretation of the £M3's wayward behaviour, and the one favoured by the Bank of England itself, is that in an open, capitalist economy precise control of the money supply may actually be beyond the capacity of the authorities. Even ignoring the acute problems experienced by the government in limiting its own contribution to monetary growth (the PSBR is highly sensitive to the business cycle and hence difficult to target in the short to medium term – see Tables 10.1 and 10.2), there remains the knotty issue of circumventive financial innovation by the banks themselves.

In principle, banks may be analysed using the same tools of microeconomics as industrial firms, the nature of their business being that they 'buy' money in the form of deposits and 'sell' it in the form of loans, making a profit from their mark-up. Like their industrial counterparts, banks seek to maximise profits subject to various constraints, for example, legislative restrictions on their deposit-taking and lending transactions and the competitive behaviour of their rivals. Such constraints on profit maximisation can be eased by innovating, that is, by diversifying into new markets and introducing new financial products (Aktar 1983). The parallels with industry are so close that this process has been dubbed 'financial engineering' (Podolski 1987: 110).

The implications of such innovation for the ability of the authorities to control the growth of defined monetary aggregates like £M3 are far-reaching. Most obviously, rapid financial innovation quickly renders official controls on specific activities cosmetic, as banks find new ways to circumvent such restrictions. The government's decision to abolish all direct bank controls, including the 'corset', in 1980 was taken in the light of this consideration. However, the structural changes in the financial system during the 1980s also blunted the edge of the authorities' only remaining weapon of short-term monetary control, interest rate adjustments. As the commercial banks moved aggressively into new areas of business (e.g., mortgage lending, high-interest current accounts, etc.), at the same time other innovations, especially the growing importance of 'off-balance-sheet' activities like interest rate hedging (see Chapter 11), reduced the sensitivity of larger, corporate borrowers to changes in short-term interest rates. The expected, inhibiting effects of the 1980–1 interest rate hikes on the growth of bank credit were thus swept aside by the momentum that rapid financial innovation had built up in the system.

From the Bank of England's point of view, the monetary base debate was essentially a red herring in the context of these developments. Both its chosen *modus operandi* and monetary base control ultimately act on the demand for bank credit (and so the supply of money) through changes in interest rates. Financial innovation appeared to have so weakened this policy instrument that monetary control over the period 1979–82 proved unattainable at a level of short-term interest rates which was economically and politically acceptable. Far from deliberately undermining the government's monetarist experiment, as monetarists claim, the Bank's view is that this episode confirmed the enormous difficulties, if not impossibility, of tight monetary control in a rapidly changing, increasingly integrated financial environment (Fforde 1982).

10.4 THE DEMAND FOR MONEY

Taken in conjunction with an exogenously-determined money supply, a stable demand for money function provides the basis of the monetarist case for postulating a causal link running from changes in the money supply to changes in nominal income. A stable demand for money function 'guarantees that some, or all, of the factors [of which nominal income is the most important] determining the demand for money will shift in a systematic way in response to a change in the supply of money' (Treasury and Civil Service Committee 1981a: 58). Another way of expressing the same point is to assert that the income velocity of circulation (nominal income/money supply) is stable and predictable over time (see Table 10.5)

In fact, the dramatic decline in the £M3 income velocity of circulation since 1979 appears to conflict sharply with this second postulate of monetarism. It certainly provides prima-facie evidence for a demand for money function which is inherently unstable, a conclusion confirmed by

Table 10.5 £M3 income velocity of circulation 1979–88

	Jan.–Mar.	Apr.–Jun.	Jul.–Sep.	Oct.–Dec.
1979		3.77	3.90	3.90
1980	3.92	3.91	3.82	3.76
1981	3.71	3.65	3.57	3.57
1982	3.23	3.23	3.21	3.24
1983	3.29	3.12	3.19	3.17
1984	3.16	3.10	3.10	3.10
1985	3.06	3.01	2.94	2.94
1986	2.88	2.73	2.68	2.63
1987	2.57	2.48	2.44	2.37
1988	2.33			

Source: Bank of England Quarterly Bulletin, various.

a number of recent studies. Following Grice and Bennett (1981) who characterised the history of empirical work on the demand for money as the 'years of hope' (1966–71), the 'years of despair' (1972–8) and the 'years of Hendrification' (1979–80), Taylor (1987: 225) has brought the nomenclature up to date with the 'years of uncertainty' (1981–7).

As with the behaviour of the money supply, there are, of course, conflicting interpretations of this evidence too. Broadly speaking, opinion is divided between those who consider that the demand for money function is inherently stable and have therefore sought to rationalise its apparent breakdown since 1980, and those who view the post-1980 episode as further confirmation of the deep-rooted volatility of the demand for money.

10.4.1 Is the demand for money stable?

It is important to note that monetarist theory does not postulate a constant, irrevocably fixed velocity of circulation, nor even one which is invariant with respect to monetary impulses. To quote Friedman (1980: 59):

> the initial effect of a change in monetary growth is an offsetting movement in velocity, followed by changes in the growth of spending . . . . The initial offsetting movement in velocity is misleading, since it simply reflects the lags in reaction.

Modern versions of monetarism have attempted to embrace an important new development in monetary theory, the 'buffer stock' or disequilibrium money' approach. In monetarist guise, the buffer stock approach extends Friedman's notion of 'lags in reaction'. The argument is that, faced with sudden, unexpected increases in the money supply, economic agents in a monetary economy have no choice other than to absorb these excess balances into their portfolios while they decide how best to reallocate their assets; that is, money acts as a 'shock absorber' or 'buffer stock', temporarily insulating the real economy from disturbances in the financial sector.

As Laidler (1984: 29) concludes:

> we have here an obvious starting point for an explanation of why . . . short-run demand functions have been less successful in recent years. It is well known that the transmission mechanism of monetary policy is complex and subject to long and variable time lags, and yet in the case of single equation 'demand for money' studies, the buffer stock approach implies the mechanism is embedded in a constant parameter. Would it be surprising if such a procedure proved satisfactory enough when dealing with periods of monetary tranquillity, but turned out to be inadequate when faced with . . . unstable money supply behaviour?

Laidler's argument, in other words, is that the apparent fragility of previously estimated demand for money equations reflects not any inherent instability, but 'is rather a statistical artifact generated by inadequate modelling of the transmission mechanism' (Laidler *op. cit.*: 29). An alternative defensive response also starts from the same basic presumption that the underlying function is stable, but seeks to explain the apparent breakdown of the demand for money function in terms of deficiencies in earlier empirical studies rather than in the basic theory itself. In essence, this view assumes that past equations have been wrongly specified, but that it has taken recent monetary developments to expose these weaknesses.

The basic equation of the traditional demand for money study is:

$$M_{dt} = a + bPY_t + cr_t$$

where PY = nominal income, and r = rate of interest on non-money financial assets (e.g., long-term rate of interest). This basic equation can be made more sophisticated by entering non-interest rate variables as logarithms, building in lag structures and incorporating other explanatory variables (e.g., financial wealth, different rates of interest, etc.). Various recent studies have suggested, however, that the current failure of this approach to explain monetary behaviour in the 1980s stems from the widespread omission of certain key variables whose importance has increased of late.

One candidate is the rate of inflation. Most studies assume that by including nominal interest rates, the operation of the Fisher effect (i.e., that nominal interest rates are equal to real interest rates plus expected inflation) ensures that inflation effects are implicitly captured. Where nominal interest rates are institutionally sticky, this assumption may be invalidated. A recent study by two well-known UK monetarists, Budd and Holly (1986), suggests that incorporating the rate of inflation explicitly may offer a way of improving the performance of estimated equations.

Another key variable widely omitted from earlier studies is the 'own rate of return' on money. In a world where money is predominantly non-interest bearing (e.g., notes and coin and zero-interest current accounts), the rate of interest on alternative financial assets (e.g., the long-term rate of interest on government securities) serves as a useful proxy for the opportunity cost of holding money. One of the most dramatic effects of financial innovation has been to blur the distinction between money and non-money, by making some forms of money (e.g., cheque accounts) interest-bearing and some forms of interest-bearing non-money more liquid (e.g., building-society deposits) since it is presumably the differential between the rate of return on money and non-money which affects the demand for money, incorporating an estimate of the own rate of return on money into the equation is one way of allowing for these changes.

In a wide-ranging review of recent work to find new specifications of the demand for money function which exhibit stability, Taylor (1987: 237) concludes:

> the effects of financial innovation (operating through the opportunity cost of holding money) and the effects of inflation are important determinants of both the short- and long-run demand for broad money . . . if proper account is taken of [these factors] . . . the evidence for the stability of the demand for broad money is at least as strong as the evidence for instability.

10.4.2 Is the demand for money inherently unstable?

Arguably, one of the most important contributions of Keynes was to move economics out of the neoclassical world of perfect certainty into one characterised by uncertainty. 'Uncertainty', unlike risk, implies a future which cannot be predicted with a mathematical probability, thereby rendering expectations about the future necessarily subjective and changeable. In Keynes' words, he sought to construct a theory of output and employment that was capable of 'analysing the economic behaviour of the present under the influence of changing ideas about the future' (Keynes 1936: vii).

In a constantly changing world, such expectations, formed subjectively on the basis of imperfect information, will therefore tend to be highly volatile. In Keynes' (1937: 217) words: 'opinions . . . are themselves subject to sharp fluctuations . . . [due to] the flimsiness of the basis of the knowledge on which they depend.' In such a world, money plays a crucial role in the operation of the economy. It provides a 'temporary abode of potential purchasing power' and thus allows what would otherwise necessarily be simultaneous barter transactions to be split and spread over time; hence 'money, in its significant attributes, is above all a subtle device for linking the present to the future' (Keynes 1937: 294). As Davidson (1972: 101) notes: 'In the absence of uncertainty, neoclassical theory had no room for the store of value function in its definition of money; nor would money play any more important role than peanuts in a neoclassical world.' Once uncertainty is introduced, money provides a perfect hedge: spending on goods, services and capital-uncertain financial assets can be deferred by accumulating money balances.

The concept of uncertainty is therefore assigned pride of place in Keynes' theory of the demand for money. Of the familiar trinity of motives for holding money – transactionary, precautionary and speculative – the last two are intimately bound up with expectations of an uncertain future: expectations of future income, expenditure, inflation and interest rates. Speculative balances, for example, are held with 'the object of securing profit from knowing better than the market what the future will bring forth' (Keynes 1937: 170). It follows as a direct consequence that the demand for money will tend to be highly unstable, waxing and waning with every change in market sentiment.

In Hutton's (1986: 112–13) words: 'Liquidity-preference is at the heart of the market economy . . . The whole point of liquidity-preference is that there is no stable relationship between a given interest rate, the classes of financial asset held, the level of saving, and the level of investment.' Commenting on the way in which Keynes has subsequently been interpreted and taught, Hutton (*op. cit.*: 113) writes: 'to box [liquidity-preference] into the IS/LM approach and to assume that expectations are given . . . is to traduce Keynes to the point of betrayal.'

This approach has traditionally underpinned the Keynesian case against monetary targeting. Twenty years before Mrs Thatcher first took office, the Radcliffe Committee (1959: para. 391) concluded that they could not 'find any reason for supposing, or any experience in monetary history indicating, that there is any limit to the velocity of circulation'. The 'LM' curve has often been described as a 'straw in the wind of uncertainty', since volatile expectations would cause it to shift its position in the absence of accommodating changes in the money supply. Although Keynes himself conceded that, *ceteris paribus*, changes in the money supply might cause changes in interest rates (and so nominal income), he pointed out that 'there were several slips between cup and lip' (Keynes 1936: 173), the most fundamental being the instability of expectations in an ever-changing, unpredictable world. For many orthodox Keynesian economists, therefore, the behaviour of the income velocity of circulation since 1979 is conclusive evidence that the demand for broad money is inherently unstable.

10.5 THE STABILITY OF THE PRIVATE SECTOR

Controversy over the authorities' ability to control the money supply and the existence of a stable demand for money function continues to rage. The final monetarist proposition, namely that the economy is self-stabilising at its natural rate of output and employment in the long run, also continues to divide the economics profession. Indeed, the tempo of this particular debate has, if anything, increased in recent years. That this should be so is puzzling, for it is in this context that the evidence generated by the monetarist experiment appears most unequivocal. Between 1979 and 1982 registered unemployment more than doubled to over three million and despite nearly 20 definitional changes to the official statistics over the last six years, all but one of which reduced the recorded total, registered unemployment today remains only slightly below its 1982 figure.

Underpinning the monetarist proposition of stability is the theoretical concept of a 'natural rate of unemployment' to which the economy naturally tends in the absence of destabilising monetary policy. To quote Friedman (1968: 8):

> At any moment of time, there is some level of unemployment which has the property that it is consistent with equilibrium in the structure of real wage rates . . . . The 'natural rate of unemployment', in other words, is the level that would be ground out by the Walrasian system of general equilibrium equations, provided there is embedded in them the actual structural characteristics of the labour and commodity markets, including market imperfections, stochastic variability in demands and supplies, the cost of gathering information about job vacancies and labour availabilities, the costs of mobility and so on.

It is clear that the hypothesis of private sector stability, and the related concept of a natural rate of unemployment, contrast sharply with 'the fundamental practical message of the General Theory: that a private enterprise economy . . . needs to be stabilised, can be stabilised, and therefore should be stabilised by appropriate monetary and fiscal policies' (Modigliani 1977: 1). Unsurprisingly, those hostile to monetarism have seized on the persistently high levels of unemployment suffered by the United Kingdom as further evidence of its failure.

Proponents of the natural rate hypothesis, however, have provided a strong defence, to the extent that their policy prescriptions have inspired the government to move on from a counterinflationary strategy based on monetary control to an employment-creating programme based on supply-side reforms. The essence of the monetarist case is that a variety of factors has raised the natural rate of unemployment in recent years.

10.5.1 Has the 'natural rate of unemployment' increased?

It is important to note that, to quote Friedman (1968: 9), the 'natural rate of unemployment [is not] immutable and unchangeable. On the contrary, many of the market characteristics that determine its level are man-made and policy-made.' Various economists, most notably Minford (1981), have offered a number of reasons why these 'man-made' and 'policy-made' factors may have changed to force the natural rate of unemployment from between 1.5 and 2.5 per cent in the 1960s to 6 per cent in the 1970s and 10 per cent in the 1980s. These so-called 'supply-side' factors all turn on an intensification of atrophy in market forces.

The operation of the housing market is one suggested area in which recent developments have contributed to a rise in the natural rate of unemployment by reducing the geographical mobility of labour (one of the structural characteristics 'embedded' in Friedman's natural rate). Private rented accommodation in many areas has become increasingly scarce since the early 1960s and local authorities have accordingly experienced growing waiting lists for council houses; owner-occupation has also increased rapidly over the same period, but moving between areas has been made increasingly difficult by the growing gulf between house prices in north and south. Minford *et al.* (1987) lay the blame for all these ('policy-made') factors, and the unemployment they cause, squarely at the door of government:

> The housing market in Britain is subject to massive government intervention in four main ways: the Rent Acts, the subsidies to council-house rents, the subsidies to owner-occupiers through mortgage tax relief [and the abolition in 1961 of Schedule A, the former tax on the notional value of home ownership], and the system of planning restrictions on land for housing . . . . The British housing market is a mess because it is over-regulated and this has serious effects on mobility and so on unemployment.
>
> (Minford *et al.* 1987: 1, 121)

Another source of upward pressure on the natural rate of unemployment is the operation of the tax and social security systems. The Liverpool Group argues that political pressure to raise the level of social security benefits relative to income tax thresholds has created 'poverty' and 'unemployment traps' which catch increasing numbers of people (the 'poverty trap' reduces the incentive to take better-paid jobs, so inhibiting labour mobility, while the 'unemployment trap' deters individuals from taking registered jobs at all). Minford claims that every 10 per cent rise in real social security benefits has raised the natural rate of unemployment by over 2 per cent, or half a million.

Finally, growing monopoly power on the part of trade unions is frequently cited by monetarists as contributing to the continuing high levels of unemployment. Although Friedman denies that, in themselves, trade unions cause higher unemployment, since the higher real wages gained by organised labour simply puts downward pressure on real wages in the competitive, non-unionised sector of the labour market, if social security benefits set a floor below which real wages cannot fall, union activity could work to raise the natural rate in this indirect fashion. More generally, trade unions could use their monopoly power to impose a range of restrictions on occupational and geographic labour mobility.

The government has been particularly concerned that developments in the labour market have contributed to the rise in the natural rate of unemployment. A series of new employment acts since 1979 has been aimed at reversing the concessions granted to the union movement in the 1970s. The government has also addressed other alleged imperfections in the labour market, including the Wages Councils, the 1946 Fair Wages Resolution and public sector pay bargaining procedures based on the notion of 'comparability'.

10.5.2 Is the private sector inherently unstable?

Economists hostile to the neoclassical concept of a natural rate of unemployment typically interpret events since 1979 as confirmation of its invalidity, regarding the attempts by monetarists to explain the rise in the natural rate as mere ex-post rationalisation. A central element in the rejection of the natural rate hypothesis is the way in which the labour market interacts with the goods and money markets. The essential message of Keynes is that employment is determined by the level of aggregate demand, with real wages determined in turn by the level of employment. This turns monetarist theory on its head, by reversing the direction of causality between changes in employment and changes in real wages. More importantly, it implies that the economy will settle at whatever level of unemployment is consistent with the prevailing level of aggregate demand. Again, as with the issue of the exogeneity of money, the debate turns on inferring the direction of causality from observed movements in economic variables.

A number of economists (e.g., Pratten 1982; Reddaway 1982; Neuberger 1985) take the view that, by assigning overriding priority to defeating inflation at a time when prices and wages were already accelerating and world demand falling, the government imposed an unduly severe deflationary shock on the economy. While this has succeeded in bringing down inflation, through 'disinflation by fear' (Matthews and Reddaway 1980: 12), the short-run trade-off between unemployment and inflation – and the surprising ease with which the electorate has accepted mass unemployment – now prevents the authorities from anything more than modest reflation.

Such economists are dismissive of the opposing argument that the natural rate of unemployment has increased. As Neuberger (*op. cit.*: 18–19) points out:

> the conclusion that government action [to expand demand] can only be rejected if the Keynesian analysis is rejected in total and the whole explanation is cast in terms of supply-side factors . . . . This is not to say that supply-side factors cannot play a role in output and jobs [but] the case that they have done so in the recession of the last five years remains to be demonstrated. The Keynesian analysis remains as relevant today as [ever].

A separate view denies that there is any relationship between unemployment and inflation at all in the United Kingdom. Beckerman (1985) has shown that the decline in price and wage inflation since 1979 can be statistically explained entirely in terms of the fall in international commodity prices. It follows that 'there is no particular level of unemployment [i.e. the natural rate] which keeps inflation stable' (Beckerman 1985: 9). Beckerman's interpretation of the 1979–82 monetarist experiment is that the upturn in inflation caused by the 1979 OPEC oil price rise misled the government into sharply deflating demand and forcing up unemployment. Because unemployment and inflation are unrelated, there existed no feedback mechanism to halt the deflation, which continued until import prices began to ease, by which time unemployment had risen to unprecedented levels. Once inflation stabilised at around 5 per cent, the logic of the monetarist theory dictated that the economy must have lodged at a new, higher natural rate – hence, any reflation of demand was deemed to be futile since it would lead to renewed inflationary pressures.

10.6 CONCLUSIONS

> Economists cannot experiment to test their theories. The nearest approach to an experiment occurs when a Government adopts new policies . . . Mrs Thatcher's policies, which are based . . . on monetarist theories of how the economy operates are therefore of special interest to economists.
>
> (Pratten 1982: 36)

These words, written shortly before the end of the 1979–82 monetarist experiment, convey something of the way many economists viewed the anti-inflationary strategy launched by the Conservative government in 1979. Among supporters and opponents alike, there was a general air of expectancy and a feeling that this experience would answer important theoretical questions about the design of macroeconomic policy and the underlying robustness of the economic models, hypotheses and theories which buttress them.

In the event, the experiment has proved, or rather disproved, nothing. Monetarists have denied that an experiment ever took place at all; and they have developed new theories to explain the behaviour of the income velocity of circulation or blamed external shocks for structural shifts in the demand for money and the natural rate of unemployment. Anti-monetarists, in contrast, have interpreted the government's failure to execute its strategy as planned as evidence that the money supply cannot be controlled; the gyrations in the velocity of circulation have been taken as further proof that the demand for money is inherently unstable and the coincidence of continuing mass unemployment and stable inflation has been used to attack the natural rate hypothesis.

In a political sense, the 1979–82 experiment certainly did provide a test of practical monetarism and, if nothing else, it established that rigid monetary rules are not the panacea for inflation-free growth in a dynamic, open economy that the government originally hoped. But in the economic sense of testing key macroeconomic theories, the experiment merely served to illustrate once again the difficulties and limitations of theory appraisal and choice through empirical testing and to highlight the fact that the sources of controversy in economics run far deeper than many of its practitioners would like to believe.

FURTHER READING

For well-informed and highly readable accounts of the execution of the monetarist experiment, see either Riddell (1983) or Keegan (1984). The Treasury and Civil Service Committee's investigation of the strategy, summarised in Treasury and Civil Service (1981), provides a fascinating insight into the views of a wide range of eminent economists, both pro- and anti-monetarist, on the whole question of disinflation through monetary restraint. For a general discussion of the lessons of the monetarist experiment, see Smith (1987).

NOTE

1. The Bank of England raised short-term interest rates, first from 12 to 14 per cent in September 1981, and then to 16 per cent in October 1981, in a concerted attempt to arrest a run of the pound – in direct contravention of the government's declared policy which was to allow the exchange rate to float cleanly.

11 · THE DEREGULATION OF THE FINANCIAL SYSTEM

For better or worse?

ROGER HENDERSON

11.1 INTRODUCTION

Financial deregulation involves the opening up of financial markets and systems to encompass new participants and products. It results from initiatives to improve market efficiency and attract new business, classified according to whether the aim is to remove constraints on diversification, to improve competitiveness, to liberalise capital flows, to open up domestic markets to foreigners or to encourage financial innovation (Dale 1986). Whilst the process is popularly associated with the 'Big Bang' at The Stock Exchange, this event should be judged within a broader context and time horizon covering the expansion of UK banks, building societies and institutional investors, the 'internationalisation' of lending and the 'securitisation' of financial instruments and technological innovations to improve communications and financial transactions.

Given such fundamental changes, financial deregulation, not surprisingly, is subject to many controversies of the nature outlined in Chapter 1. These include: *terminology* (is deregulation or reregulation the appropriate concept?); *objectivity* (perceptions of the City affect the gathering of information, judgement and decision-making); *ideology* (between proponents of decentralised free-market systems and those who favour centralised government regulation, epitomised in the Securities and Investments Board (SIB) debate); and *efficiency* (economic and financial costs of deregulation, resource use and appropriate structures including the issue of financial conglomerates).

This chapter discusses the background to such controversies by considering the major changes to the financial system, and the theoretical and practical aspects of financial services regulation. Thereafter specific regulatory, macroeconomic and microeconomic controversies are examined prior to evaluation of deregulation in terms of the economy, risk and the small investor.

11.2 THE CHANGING FINANCIAL SYSTEM

11.2.1 The background

Financial liberalism is not new. A century ago capital flowed freely in response to risk and reward criteria: British capital built Argentinian and Indian railways; Argentinian wheat destined for Europe was traded, insured and financed in London, the fulcrum of an open system with few distinctions between commercial and investment banking, insurance and investment advice.

Gradually this open trading scenario was replaced by widespread protectionism and by 1945 many nations had isolated large parts of their financial services industries. In the United Kingdom the Bank of England sought to allay fears of inadequate investor protection and systematic risk by encouraging the emergence of oligopolistic self-regulating clubs, such as the Accepting Houses Committee (AHC), Committee of London and Scottish Clearing Banks (CLSCB), and the Building Societies Association (BSA). For members, such clubs provided benefits of restricted membership and control of competition (via interest rate agreements). The dominance, if not efficiency, of such cartels was impressive. By 1955, the clearers held three times the deposits of the building societies and fixed borrowing and lending rates by collective agreement linked to base rate. Competition from newly-emerging finance houses was stifled by the 1963 Protection of Depositors Act and lending ceilings became commonplace.

The period 1969–71 represented the first significant phase of financial deregulation. Mergers reduced the number of clearing banks and in 1971 direct credit controls and the interest rate cartel were abolished under Competition and Credit Control (CCC), which placed greater reliance on market guidance. In addition the US administration decided to abandon the dollar's peg to gold, which signalled a move towards floating exchange rates and freer capital flows (McMahon 1987).

The 1970s was a decade of change which threatened the traditionally demarcated UK financial system. Declining rates of return on capital forced the corporate sector to supplement internal funding with more bank finance. Moreover, high and volatile levels of inflation, uncertain interest rates and the expanding wholesale markets furthered the shift to bank finance on a floating rather than fixed rate basis. For the individual customer retail banking offered little by way of interest-bearing accounts despite high nominal interest rates. Consequently an increasing proportion of personal savings went to the building societies, which, benefiting from the housing boom and tax concessions, had experienced extraordinary growth. By 1980 their liabilities had reached a level 20 per cent higher than those of the clearers (Fforde 1983).

These domestic changes were dwarfed by the expansion of international finance, spurred by the 1973/4 energy crisis. McMahon (1987) comments:

> It is almost impossible to over-estimate the effects of this financial earthquake, whereby a quintupling of the oil price overnight created massive balance of payments imbalances and inflicted on the world a painful combination of price inflation and demand deflation. The need to finance the surpluses and deficits was a major factor – perhaps the major factor – in creating an international banking system where previously there had only been a collection of national banking systems.

London was particularly affected. OPEC oil revenues on deposit were recycled to governments needing to borrow their way out of the crisis. However, the lack of controls over wholesale markets was highlighted by the 1974 secondary banking crisis which, together with European Community (EC) directives on banking law, eventually encouraged the 1979 Banking Act and thus an overhaul of banking supervision.

11.2.2 Developments under the Thatcher government

Although significant the events of the 1970s were insufficient to break the dominant segmented 'club' structure of the UK financial system. However, a second major wave of deregulation started in 1979 with the abolition of exchange controls and coincided with indigenous oil production and the election of a very pro-market Conservative government. Goodhart (1987) argues that the ending of exchange controls was decisive in that UK financial transactions became subject to international competition and domestic credit controls could be circumvented by offshore operations. Thus a surge of overseas investment by UK institutional investors began in 1979, supplementary special deposits ('corset') became ineffective and were abolished in June 1980, and consumer instalment credit controls in July 1982.

Competition between clearing banks and building societies intensified in the early 1980s. The latter faced various threats: the clearers free from 'corset' restrictions successfully attacked the mortgage market; the government, needing to fund a large PSBR soaked up personal sector savings via gilts and national savings issues; and various financial institutions used innovations to offer combined money transmission and savings facilities. The building societies' response was constrained by their restrictive legislative framework, their excessive reliance on retail deposits, the concentrated industry structure, their dominance in personal sector mortgages, and the pricing cartel which effectively benefited borrowers at the expense of depositors (Llewellyn 1985).

Given such constraints the building societies' success in gaining personal sector deposits is remarkable. As their international earnings have fallen, the clearers have sought more personal sector custom, introducing money market accounts and flexible bank charges in an effort to boost retail performance. Other responses have involved investment in cost-saving technologies like BACS (Bankers Automated Clearing Services), offering interbank electronic funds transfer, and CHAPS (Clearing House Automated Payments) for cheque handling, while the 1980s have also witnessed the rapid spread of automated teller machines (ATMs) and 'after-hours' machine-run service centres in branch foyers to counter the longer opening hours of building societies.

Such innovations in cash management have brought the deposit and investment markets closer together (Carter *et al.* 1986). However, an equally significant integrating factor with far-reaching implications for financial services is 'securitisation', the process whereby trading in securities replaces bank lending. For banks securitisation offers opportunities to earn fee income, to alter asset portfolios by trading securities rather than wait for loans to mature, and, moreover, to shift risk to non-bank investors provided they are willing to hold traded securities. However, it also implies the exchange of traditional corporate lending business for newer, riskier investment banking activities. For major borrowers, security issues can be cheaper than bank borrowing, and the risk of being locked-in to unfavourable rates can be alleviated by refinancing or by swapping fixed for variable rate obligations.

Securitisation has encouraged various new instruments, including convertibles, options, straight and floating rate bonds. UK firms have borrowed actively on the eurobond markets, raising £4 billion in 1986 (Johnson 1986), making these markets as significant as the stock market or bank lending for corporate finance. Such developments are really part of the 'internationalisation' of financial markets. Whereas in the inflationary environment of the 1970s syndicated eurocurrency-lending dominated international finance, the 1982 debt crisis, pressures on bank capital ratios, the improvement in inflation and falling margins all reduced the attraction of such loans. The subsequent switch in the pattern of lending in favour of OECD-based customers has furthered securities trading, market integration and innovation.

Such financial innovations assisted by technological advances and pressures for deregulation have helped to integrate formerly discrete markets: finance has flowed directly between borrower and lender; a wider range of institutions has participated in long-term finance; and computer technology and communications developments have made information a strategic resource readily accessible in diverse locations. The convergence between domestic and euromarkets is evidenced by the narrowing of yields and greater use of interest rate and swap techniques. These processes of change reached a climax in October 1986 with the 'Big Bang' at The Stock Exchange. The developments there were partly a reaction to securitisation and an attempt to enhance the international competitiveness of the capital market.

11.2.3 Deregulation of the UK capital markets

The UK Stock Exchange is the central market in transactions in shares, domestic corporate bonds of UK-listed and selected foreign companies, in gilts, and in public sector and certain overseas government securities. Prior to 'Big Bang' its 4,582 members formed 209 firms, mostly partnerships, and were organised on a strict separation of function basis into 192 broking and 17 jobbing firms. Under 'single capacity', brokers, acting as agents for customers, negotiated deals with jobbers for a minimum commission, managed portfolios and provided investment advice. Jobbers, as principals, traded securities on a competing market-maker basis, although the system was highly concentrated with only five jobbing firms handling deals of institutional size, and two dominating the gilts market (Jackson 1985). Members had limited capital needs: brokers acted as agents, whereas jobbers handled large volumes with modest sums because of order-flow concentration, namely, brokers fed orders to relatively few jobbers.

Pressure for reform has come from various environmental forces. First, institutional investors seeking to diversify and 'internationalise' their portfolios are attracted to efficient markets to trade large volumes of stock. Second, technological developments allow information dissemination and distant trading thus encouraging market integration. Third, corporate treasurers have become more sophisticated in their financing methods, hence promoting 'securitisation', and fourth, the 'climate' of deregulation has altered capital markets elsewhere, notably in New York since May 1975.

Rose (1986) suggests such internationalisation and securitisation fuelled 'Big Bang' in several ways. First, deregulation enabled the New York stock market to gain business from London as the main dealings in over 20 major UK equities shifted there to be traded in American Depository Receipt (ADR) form (see 'Glossary of Terms' below). Second, the eurobond market expansion had been outside the realm of The Stock Exchange. Third, UK securities firms had been too small to compete globally. Fourth, overseas firms had been established in London, not to participate in UK securities transactions, rather to exploit London's location and expertise.

In addition to such external factors, internal rules covering commissions, duties and capital needs, constrained Stock Exchange member firms' competitive capacities. The proximate cause of the 'Big Bang' was the Office of Fair Trading (OFT) investigation in 1983, which identified various rules contrary to the 1956 Restrictive Practices Act. In June 1983, Cecil Parkinson, then Secretary of State for Industry, agreed with The Stock Exchange chairman, Nicholas Goodison, that the government would exempt The Stock Exchange from legal action provided it abolished its minimum fixed commission scales by the end of 1986.

Internal pressures also arose from restrictions on outside ownership, which left members poorly capitalised and technologically backward. Outsiders could hold only a maximum 10 per cent shareholding (raised to 29.9 per cent in 1982), and membership of wider corporate bodies was effectively stopped. Any move to dual capacity implied adequate capitalisation and thus greater outside participation. Thus the pressures for reform are interrelated, and whereas the original perception of 'Big Bang' related to the abolition of fixed commissions, later the emphasis switched to London capturing a leading role in the global securities market.

The new structure came into effect in 1986. A 'Little Bang' on 1 March allowed outsiders to fully own member firms and establish new firms from scratch. Many banks and financial institutions had taken participation in anticipation of the rule change, and thereafter deals were consolidated. By February 1987, 65 outside entities held stakes in member firms together with several new direct entrants, including subsidiaries of large overseas investment houses, such as Merrill Lynch (USA) and Nomura (Japan).

The main reforms occurred on 27 October in a single 'explosion', hence 'Big Bang'. Fixed commissions and single capacity were replaced by a 'dual-capacity, quote-driven, market-maker system'. Members may now act as dual-capacity broker/dealers, either as dealer (buying from and selling to clients from their own book) or as broker (arranging a deal in return for a negotiated commission). Members may also register as market-makers, which implies maintaining an active, continuous and liquid market in specified stocks.

Technological innovation is central to the new system. The Stock Exchange automated quotations (SEAQ) system displays share price information 'on screen', which, relayed via TOPIC, The Stock Exchange videotext information system, provides 'real time' prices for over 3,500 securities. Market-makers input prices from their offices and share deals are arranged between participants by phone, then promptly reported to SEAQ for price-updating and surveillance purposes, thus trading is more visible and independent of the old trading-floor.

The 'Big Bang' also involved reform of gilt-edged security dealings. Formerly the Bank of England, as issuer and manager of government debt, dealt through the government broker with only two jobbers. Now dealing is direct with 27 market-makers, who in turn may use several interdealer brokers (IDBs) to hedge their positions. This system is seen to be more open and compatible with overseas markets, yet, with investor protection in mind, guidelines have been established for the duties and capitalisation of market-makers (Bank of England 1985).

The aforementioned structural changes inevitably require accompanying adjustments to the regulatory framework, since 'Big Bang' broke down the compartmentalised club structure on which UK regulators had relied. As The Stock Exchange developments are part of wider changes affecting the financial system, there has been much debate as to the appropriate regulatory framework for the industry as a whole.

11.3 REGULATION, DEREGULATION OR REREGULATION?

11.3.1 Regulatory frameworks, risk and ideology

Through its structure and regulatory framework, the financial system plays a vital role in enabling the economy to carry risk, an activity central to the spread of innovation and growth. Rybczynski (1985) suggests the structural evolution of the financial system occurs in three phases: initially bank intermediaries dominate; then market-orientation (capital markets channel savings directly); finally strong market-orientation (institutions trade their assets). However, this process is modified by the regulatory framework. If this imposes obstacles to charging market prices for savings, hinders financial innovation or restricts the operations of institutions then the evolutionary process may be hampered.

What then determines the prevailing regulatory framework? Is it solely a function of the existing financial system or of wider economic and political influences? Deregulation appears popular with governments of varying political persuasions, and McMahon (1987) sees shifts in the underlying political climate towards greater emphasis on the allocative forces of competition as a significant influence. Stigler (1986) favours economic explanations and cites the abolition of interest rate ceilings, minimum commissions, and growth of non-bank financial intermediaries in the United States as responses to inflation, high interest rates, institutional investment and computerisation rather than revulsion against public regulation. Such parallels appear in the United Kingdom where the breakdown of fixed commissions reflected institutional pressures and, moreover, external competition was diverting business from The Stock Exchange, thus hastening the need for reform.

Many critics argue the term 'deregulation' is misleading. Jack (1986) suggests the 1986 Financial Services Act creates a wider-reaching regulatory system than previously existed. Moran (1986) talks of the 'reconstruction of regulation through tightly disciplined "corporatism"' and Goodhart (1987) argues the new regulations 'turn the clock back towards the old self-regulating, compartmentalised clubs'. Certainly the plethora of recent financial legislation, plus present City demands for 'compliance officers' seem at odds with the concept of deregulation.

Llewellyn (1987) argues that since the UK regulatory mix is changing, 'reregulation' is a more appropriate term. He identifies alternate forms of regulation: environmental (e.g., economic policy restraints such as credit restrictions to effect monetary policy); legal; self-imposed (e.g., restrictive practices as per old Stock Exchange); moral suasion (e.g., Bank of England directives); self-regulation (i.e., a designated agency oversees its own industry); and external agency (i.e., an independent body imposes explicit regulations).

Such forms are then combined with the areas over which regulation applies to produce a regulatory matrix. The areas of regulation are: functional (e.g., demarcation between insurance, investment banking, etc.); ownership (i.e., interlocking ownership control); price (e.g., restrictions on interest rates); entry barriers; and operations (e.g., balance sheet covenants on banks). Thus, financial deregulation is really about the changing mix of legal, self-regulatory, self-imposed and moral forms covering various areas of regulation.

Within the United Kingdom, financial services industry regulation is moving from self-imposed cartels to more formal use of regulatory bodies, and is increasingly based on *functional* rather than *institutional* criteria, with more explicit control over each business sector. Thus, opposing regulatory trends are apparent. Competition has encouraged deregulation of many self-imposed rules, while the Financial Services Act imposes stringent and far-reaching legislation on a wide range of activities in the industry.

11.3.2 Regulation of financial services

The traditional regulatory focus in the securities industry was investor protection via the Prevention of Fraud (Investments) Act 1939 and amendments, which required securities dealers to be licensed or members of a recognised association. However, the failure of the Act to cope with innovations, such as commodity futures and unit-linked life assurance, and the greater integration of the industry together with failures of individual firms (e.g., Norton Warburg in 1981), prompted the Gower Report on investor protection and the regulatory system. Gower (HMSO 1984) envisaged a body to oversee the industry, whilst leaving daily operational control to self-regulatory organisations. A subsequent White Paper (HMSO 1985), the precursor to the Financial Services Act, made it clear that although the legislation aimed primarily to improve investor protection, there was equally a need to enhance the efficiency and competitiveness of the industry.

The Financial Services Act received Royal Assent on 7 November 1986. Its central objective is to form a regulatory structure based on the Secretary of State's powers to authorise and regulate investment businesses. These powers are delegated to the Securities and Investments Board (SIB), which is responsible for the authorisation of firms and individuals undertaking investment business, either directly or via their membership of a recognised self-regulatory organisation (SRO) or professional body. The SIB is unique as a private company empowered to prosecute offenders under the Act, notably for conducting unauthorised investment businesses. It will vet applications for authorisation, promulgate rules, discipline offenders, use intervention powers to protect investors (e.g., prohibit firms from disposing of assets), and oversee a compensation fund.

Most practitioners will probably belong to an SRO to whom delegated authority is given by the SIB. Five SROs are envisaged: The Securities Association (TSA); Financial Intermediaries, Managers and Brokers Regulatory Association (FIMBRA); Investment Managers Regulatory Organisation (IMRO); Association of Futures Brokers and Dealers (AFBD); and Life Assurance and Unit Trust Regulatory Association (LAUTRO). The most significant is TSA, the outcome of a merger between The Stock Exchange and the International Securities Regulatory Organisation (ISRO), which was formed in 1985 to oversee institutions involved in bond and equity dealing in London. The new regulatory structure is practitioner-based, self-regulation within a statutory framework. This is to ensure the SROs do not revert to 'clubs and cartels' (Berrill 1986). The shift in the regulatory matrix shows deregulation is more about reorganisation of controls rather than their reduction.

11.4 ISSUES ARISING FROM FINANCIAL CHANGE

11.4.1 Regulatory issues

The Financial Services Act is subject to much controversy, ranging from the general philosophy of regulation to its specific rules. The fundamental dilemma is the need to change the United Kingdom's highly segmented financial markets and make them competitive, yet deny access to unsuitable practitioners. There is also the business conflict between the desire to trade with less capital, to lower prices to be competitive, and to seek aggressively market share, and the opposing desire of regulators to see non-aggressive, adequately-capitalised businesses making steady profits (Redwood 1986).

Such conflict is inherent in the new legislation which Goodhart (1987) argues shows little regard for economic analysis of social costs and benefits. He contends that the Act partly derived from public reaction to the old 'clubs', which was countered by establishing a quasi-public regulatory body, which in turn promotes self-regulatory clubs! Much debate has centred on what powers the non-statutory SIB can enforce without becoming accountable to Parliament, as per a statutory commission. The government sees the SIB as essentially a self-regulatory body funded and staffed by practitioners, whereas the Opposition argue it is effectively a statutory body, and, to maintain its independence of the City, should be publicly financed (Dudley 1987).

Concern has also been expressed over the relationship between the SIB and the SROs. Equality in standards of business conduct and investor protection is fundamental to the legislation, yet the SROs differ widely in their operations and self-regulatory experience. The Stock Exchange feels it may be at a competitive disadvantage *vis-à-vis* less mature SROs (Jack 1986). FIMBRA has warned that harsh rules regarding capital adequacy could reduce the numbers of independent investment advisers and is sceptical of SIB claims that better regulation will generate sufficient business growth to offset extra compliance costs. However, FIMBRA has supported the SIB over 'polarisation', the controversial ruling that life assurance and unit trust salesmen must either be completely independent or represent one company, not both.

Polarisation is central to the regulation versus competition issue. The SIB argue it is essential to determine the status of salesmen or intermediaries to ensure prudent behaviour and minimise conflicts of interest. In contrast, the OFT contends polarisation reduces the independent advice available from banks and building societies. Traditionally bank managers have responded to customer requests for advice ('independent intermediary') but as such might have sold one of the bank's own policies ('company representation'), a dual role no longer tenable. The issue may be circumvented by distinguishing generic advice on the investment options for a capital sum and specific advice related to in-house products, but will require separate subsidiaries providing investment management facilities authorised by an appropriate SRO (Hanson 1986).

The existence of several SROs and diverse financial conglomerates raises issues of overlapping supervision. Firms involved in futures and eurobonds might be members of both the AFBD and TSA, hence creating duplication of control and excessive compliance costs. Overlaps are also likely with outside regulators. For example, banks will be authorised by the Bank of England and an SRO or the SIB itself. A potentially more disturbing situation is where supervisors adopt a narrow regulatory stance and thus no overall control is exercised. Recent proposals envisage the exchange of information gathered under various statutes by regulators and a 'lead' regulator for monitoring conglomerates.

The crucial practical test of the regulatory system is how it deals with scandals and failures. If authorities disclose they are investigating a market-maker, few people will wish to deal with that firm and the authorities may precipitate the very crisis they wish to avoid. In finance, the problem is compounded by the risk of contagion, since when one bank or building society falters there is a massive outflow from the industry unless intervention occurs. However, failure to investigate equally weakens public confidence as do fraud, 'inside dealings' and the lack of publicised prosecutions of offenders.

11.4.2 Microeconomic issues

In theory deregulation away from cartel-determined charges should produce efficiency gains and social benefits. Tobin (1984) suggests financial market efficiency has four meanings. First, 'information-arbitrage' efficiency refers to the efficient markets hypothesis that only insiders can consistently outperform the market, and most academics in financial management concur that securities markets are efficient in this context.

Second, there is 'fundamental-valuation' efficiency, the accuracy with which market valuations reflect future earnings expectations. However, take-over activity, motivated by the undervaluation of assets, indicates market failure since target companies' share prices are pushed closer to their fundamental asset values. Moreover, the October 1987 share price collapse had little to do with underlying UK corporate performance and asset values, but rather external market influences.

Third, 'full-insurance' efficiency occurs when economic agents can insure themselves against future contingencies. For example, earnings in productive years are traded for consumption in retirement, futures markets allow hedging, capital markets risk-taking or avoidance. In practice the financial system is not fully efficient regarding the time profile of income – borrowing against future earnings is difficult and the contingency of inflation is relatively uninsured.

The fourth form of efficiency ('functional') refers to the functions performed by financial markets. Critics argue that The Stock Exchange, as mainly a secondary market, is inefficient in raising new finance and funds for real investment. Goodhart (1987) believes such secondary trading adds nothing to the earnings prospects of the firms whose assets are traded and, hence, nothing to wealth creation. Tobin (1984) also argues that the financial system absorbs increasingly scarce resources, notably intelligent, managerial-quality young labour, into activities disproportionate to their social productivity.

A further controversy surrounds the financial costs of deregulation. Lomax (1987) estimates this at £100 million, considerably more than public losses through fraud. However, defenders argue that the necessary standards cannot be costed, that such sums are minute in relation to the City's earnings, and that few firms are establishing systems from scratch. This is no comfort to the smaller investment intermediaries whose compliance costs may amount to 12 per cent of turnover (Pointon 1986). He cites professional indemnity insurance, membership fees of SROs, funding of compensation funds, higher accounting and legal fees, plus staff retraining costs as seriously compromising the profitability of smaller operators.

Conglomeration and concentration pose another potential problem. Bevan (1985) identifies various incentives for such conglomerate growth: the internationalisation of markets; the lifting of controls on bank lending; the greater sophistication of instruments and operators; increased consumer demands for wider services; and information technology innovations. To these should be added the capital needs of the new securities markets.

A prime objective of the 'Big Bang' was to allow capital injections into member firms and to facilitate vertical integration as opposed to the horizontal mergers between brokers, characteristic of the New York deregulation. Unfortunately, UK banks found problems in financing and integrating acquisitions. For example, Midland Bank bought brokers W. Greenwell, but Greenwell's equity business did not convince Midland's top management and failed to gain sufficient financial backing. Eventually in March 1987 Midland withdrew from equity market-making, the core of the new Stock Exchange, leaving Greenwell as an old-style agency broker. Such problems encourage the attraction of horizontal integration to secure the critical size for successful operations, for example, Hill Samuel's links with the Union Bank of Switzerland (Pagano and Rodgers 1987).

The emergence of conglomerate structures highlights the fundamental regulatory issues of overlapping supervision, functional or institutional controls and the risk of contagion whereby a loss of confidence in one company spreads to others within the group structure. Such fears can also generate overrestrictive reaction by the authorities. Llewellyn (1987) argues that the 1986 Building Societies Act contains onerous limitations on the societies' capacity to diversify and undermines the concept of 'competitive neutrality' in regulation, namely, societies will have less freedom to compete in the business of banks than vice versa.

The growth of financial conglomerates raises the spectre of potential conflicts of interest. Where investment advice, market-making and fund management are provided, there may be a temptation to promote in-house funds as opposed to more suitable investments for the client, to generate commissions via many unnecessary switches of investments and to place unsuccessful underwriting issues into in-house funds. Institutions are supposed to erect 'Chinese Walls' between their corporate finance and investment management businesses, so that merger/take-over bids planned by client companies will not be leaked to investment managers and used to gain unfair advantage. However, recent scandals concerning 'insider trading' highlight the dangers inherent in the new system.

11.4.3 Macroeconomic issues

The changes to the UK financial system are indicative of greater international market integration. Securities dealing is now a footloose industry with limited ties to specific national centres. Major currencies are traded hourly worldwide and liberalisation fosters inward and outward capital flows. However, deregulation has not arisen from specific international cooperation, rather from anticipated domestic benefits. Accordingly, such international integration can conflict with national regulators' desires to control their markets.

A broader problem is that deregulation and market integration encourage the international substitution of financial assets and currency swaps. Hence, increasingly, interest rates are determined in global rather than domestic markets, and so policies to curb the PSBR and lower interest rates become less viable under such conditions. Policy decisions on capital flows are similarly affected by deregulation. The 1986 EC decision to liberalise cross-border capital movements raises sensitive issues as to how less prosperous members can prevent outflows and the impact on capital formation and supervision (Peel and Nicol 1986). In the United Kingdom net cumulative capital outflows have amounted to £27.8 billion since 1979, leading to pressure for the reinstatement of exchange controls. However, Chrystal and Dowd (1986) contend that investment flows in part reflect expectations of returns by investors, such that even effective controls on foreign investment will not guarantee the displaced funds will go directly into the UK economy.

The extent to which markets have now become interdependent was clearly illustrated on 19 October 1987 ('Black Monday') when New York's 22 per cent fall in the Dow Jones stock market index was followed by a 15 per cent decline in the Tokyo market, the suspension of Hong Kong trading, and a 11 per cent fall in the London FT–SE 100 index. Various domestic factors compounded the London crash including Salomon Brothers' announcement on 12 October of 150 redundancies in its London office, disclosure of a sharp rise in bank lending in September, the hurricane which paralysed the UK markets on Friday 16 October and, ironically, the enhanced capacity of the SEAQ computerised trading system to deal with vast numbers of transactions. However, the overriding reasons for the crash were international and the relative strength of UK companies and the economy counted for nothing in the face of US market volatility.

The proximate cause was massive market disappointment with the huge US trade deficit coinciding with 'sell' messages from leading US analysts. The underlying causes were based on a realisation that the US Administration was unwilling to act to cut its vast budget and trade deficits by raising interest rates, but instead would allow the dollar to fall further, thus hastening fears of inflation. Moreover, this implied a final failure of international economic policy coordination, notably the February 1987 agreement ('Louvre Accord') to stabilise the dollar and promote expansion in Japan and West Germany. Rising interest rates there and the worsening Gulf crisis exacerbated the problem. Eventually a general disbelief in the 'bull' markets phase occurred, culminating in the share slump. Thus, the intervention versus liberalisation issue is still central to economic controversy. By intervening to stabilise foreign-exchange markets, central bankers destabilised their own money and bond markets. By raising interest rates to stabilise these, they destabilised their equity markets. As Reading (1987) comments, 'in today's inter-connected markets if you interfere anywhere, you affect everywhere.'

Finally, the growing presence of foreign, multinational institutions carries with it special dangers. Riley (1986) distinguishes various American entrants: commercial banks building international securities businesses (e.g., Citicorp, Chase Manhattan); large global trading investment banks (e.g., Goldman Sachs, Merrill Lynch, Salomon Brothers); and smaller securities firms, often with a significant eurobond business (e.g., Kidder Peabody, E. Hutton). The Japanese are also becoming major participants. Nomura Securities, with a market valuation of £13 billion some five times greater than NatWest, was the first of several Japanese firms to join The Stock Exchange and various continental banks are also developing their UK operations. The Union Bank of Switzerland, for example, maintained the long Swiss tradition of investment banking by acquiring brokers Phillips and Drew, and market-maker Mousdale and elsewhere Crédit Suisse and Banque Paribas have made small acquisitions.

Although such multinationals may increase liquidity and trading volume, they also provoke fears that they might uncompetitively exploit their dominance in integrated markets. Much will depend on The Stock Exchange's ability to develop and regulate the SEAQ international system, a formalised market with over 60 market-makers offering prices in more than 600 stocks. This represents a step towards an international equity system, but also adds an international dimension to deregulation issues.

11.5 FOR BETTER OR WORSE? THE IMPLICATIONS OF DEREGULATION

Discussion of the many issues surrounding deregulation highlights the major changes, for example, the emergence of financial conglomerates, the increasing foreign influence in the City, and the new working practices at The Stock Exchange. The issues bring into focus the value of such changes, namely, will they be for better or worse for the economy, financial system and individual investor?

The financial system is undoubtedly a crucial cog in the modern economy. Between 1979 and 1985 GDP grew by £17.2 billion (at 1980 prices) of which £7.2 billion was attributable to the financial sector, and, moreover, the City's receipts from services undertaken overseas have proved a major source of invisible earnings. However, critics argue that any gains are from position-taking, not real wealth creation, thus fuelling impressions that financial services are less productive than manufacturing and benefit from downturns elsewhere in the economy, especially when interest rates are high. Although deregulation may not dispel criticisms that the UK financial sector is uninterested in industry, nevertheless large businesses should encounter wider financing options as competition, securitisation and market access is enhanced. However, the smaller corporate sector may be disadvantaged since here The Stock Exchange is less significant than bank finance, and, in recent years the banks have focused upon regaining personal sector business, a move given further impetus by deregulation.

The employment impact of deregulation appears concentrated. In recent years frenzied recruitment drives have aimed at systems analysts, lawyers, accountants, dealers and experienced managers capable of integrating the new conglomerates. This surge in vacancies has been accompanied by salary increases disproportionately higher than in other occupations, thus furthering the drift of able graduates and computer experts away from industrial jobs and regions. However, the market downturn since October 1987 has left many firms with trading volumes too low to sustain overheads. Westwell (1987) cites NatWest Investment Bank as insisting its top managers take 20 per cent cuts in salaries, while several American banks have begun redundancy programmes. Possibly this shake-out is overdue since firms have grabbed staff in the vain hope of competing with the likes of Nomura and Merrill Lynch, but may now be forced into defensive mergers and further staff cuts.

Earlier reference was made to Rybczynski's belief that an evolving financial sector helps the economy carry risk. Undoubtedly deregulation is associated with innovation and competition, but Rose (1986) argues that greater risk is apparent and cites abuses from insider trading and inconsistent supervision. Moreover, uncertainties created by new instruments have left authorities unsure as to the stability of their policies. Few regulators now know how to define money, how to control it or, indeed, whether it needs control! Elsewhere, sophisticated products such as options and futures do not offer genuinely new ways of lowering risk, whilst complex technological systems leave firms vulnerable to decisions undertaken by their specialist, yet relatively junior employees. Indeed, the events of 'Black Monday' have brought the issues of financial innovation, risk and the individual investor sharply into focus. The reported £20,000 losses by a Derbyshire schoolboy on a £100,000 share portfolio and debts of over £1 million incurred by a trainee accountant through options trading expose loopholes in the City regulations, especially regarding member firms' 'knowledge' of their clients, and, indeed the understanding required by customers of market operations (Hughes 1987).

The clearing banks' involvement in the new markets illustrates that although risk can be diversified via acquisition, it is redistributed, not eliminated, within the system. Whilst losses on such acquisitions may be minimised by capital increases, if they coincide with foreign currency exposure or similar strains, then problems arise. For example, Midland Bank announced in July 1987 a £1.1 billion capital increase, combining asset sales and a rights issue, to cover bad debt provisions and poor performances by subsidiaries. Of the doubtful loans 40 per cent had been inherited from Crocker National Bank of California, acquired to give Midland a US presence. In the subsequent sale of Crocker to buyer Wells Fargo, Midland was forced to retain Crocker's bad debt portfolio and institutional pressure urged Midland to consider disposing of assets such as Clydesdale Bank, Thomas Cook and Samuel Montagu. The poor performance of these subsidiaries shows the problems of building diverse operations when the maintstream business is under pressure. Cane (1987) refers to heavy expenditure by Midland in technology, yet problems with settlement and dealing systems in Samuel Montagu. His comment that these problems are 'serious but hardly unique among London's financial institutions' implies further risks may be inherent in the emerging financial system.

Rightly or wrongly, the impact of deregulation is often associated with the individual investor. Critics argue that the institution-dominated pattern of share ownership will remain, and, in a world of conglomerates and self-regulated 'clubs', the individual seems vulnerable to biased advice, conflicts of interest and rising costs. The abolition of fixed commissions will provide markedly lower charges only for large-scale investors and heavy expenditure on technology may need to be recouped from the ultimate consumer via higher charges. With regard to quality of service, investors may prefer to 'shop' in a 'financial supermarket' and Terry (1985) envisages customers entering a branch, obtaining a share quote via computer screens and dealing immediately. Indeed, Redwood (1986) argues that the investor should benefit from wider choice and information, a clearer statement of costs and retail access. However, conglomerates have hitherto conducted their disparate activities from separate premises and thus efficiency and service gains from complex multipurpose operations may be difficult to realise.

Recent increases in share ownership among small investors are often cited as effects of deregulation and government attempts to encourage an enterprise culture, yet share ownership still covers only approximately 20 per cent of the population and, moreover, much of the growth has come from attractive privatisation issues and favourable employee share-schemes. However, the current institutional dominance is significant only if it makes the capital market less efficient as a source of funding. Critics argue that institutions are risk-averse, deal only in small quantities of shares, and create volatility in share prices and the cost of capital to borrowers (Ball 1984). Much of the evidence surrounding such arguments is inconclusive, given the wide range of influences on real investment, risk, the cost of capital and availability of funding. Nevertheless, deregulation seems unlikely to alter radically the balance between institutional and individual initiative, and thus such debate will continue.

11.6 CONCLUSIONS

Deregulation should enable London to remain a leading international financial centre at a time when its traditional oligopolistic structures and practices together with pressures from 'securitisation', 'internationalisation' and technological innovation threatened to take business elsewhere. The 'Big Bang' is thus part of a wider trend away from specialisation in the UK financial system, epitomised by the emergent financial conglomerates adding securities-trading and investment banking to their existing operations.

Deregulation is beset by controversy. At the operational level, debate about effective regulation covers many issues: statutory or non-statutory control; overlapping and underlapping responsibility; 'equivalence'; 'polarisation'; and immunity. At the philosophical level, deregulation raises questions about market efficiency, conglomerate growth and market structure, the costs of change and national economic policy. These are central to the core free-market versus interventionist controversies of modern economics and again illustrate how difficult it is for economists to agree. Defenders of The Stock Exchange see it as the axle on which the whole financial system turns, and whose efficiency depends upon the free play of market forces, others argue that because it is so crucial intervention is necessary. Indeed, Keynes (1936), in reference to The Stock Exchange, once commented:

> when the capital development of a country becomes the by-product of the activities of a casino, the job is likely to be ill-done.

Above all, the term deregulation is itself controversial, especially as the regulatory mix within the financial system is undergoing change. Indeed, reregulation may be a more appropriate concept since the authorities, for better or worse, are seeking a philosophical and practical balance between intervention and liberalisation.

FURTHER READING

Given the relatively recent nature and diversity of the changes to the UK financial system, much of the relevant literature is to be found in bank reviews, publications by The Stock Exchange and journals such as the Bank of England Quarterly Bulletin, Journal of Banking and Finance, Journal of Political Economy, Banking World and Financial Weekly. On the 'Big Bang' see Thomas (1986), Hamilton (1986) or Riley (1986). On deregulation Dale (1986) provides a series of specialised conference papers. On the UK financial system established texts include those of Peasnall and Ward (1985), Wilson (1983) and Bain (1981), together with some commendable recent publications dealing with changes to the financial services environment, notably Lewis and Davis (1987), Carter *et al.* (1986) and Howcroft and Lavis (1986).

GLOSSARY

ADR	American Depository Receipts – issued by US depository banks once the registered shares which they represent are lodged at a branch overseas. ADRs can then be freely traded and for UK stocks have proved popular with US investors.
AFBD	Association of Futures Brokers and Dealers – SRO to be mainly responsible for dealers on the London International Financial Futures Exchange.
AHC	Accepting Houses Committee.
ATM	Automated Teller Machine – cash dispenser and information source regarding a bank account.
BACS	Bankers Automated Clearing Services – a clearing system for direct debits, standing orders and credit transfers between the major clearers.
Big Bang	27 October 1986 when new Stock Exchange regulations took effect.
Black Monday	19 October 1987, when a sharp fall was experienced in UK (and US) share prices.
BSA	Building Societies Association.
Broker (also broker/dealer or stockbroker)	Member of the Stock Exchange providing advice and dealing services to the public. Can now act in a dual capacity.
CHAPS	Clearing House Automated Payments System for electronic sterling payments transfers between UK banks.
Chinese Walls	Refers to internal divisions or controls that firms deem necessary to prevent abuses under the new dual-capacity

	operating system. These controls should be insurmountable obstacles as per the Great Wall of China.
CLCB	Committee of the London Clearing Banks.
Clearing bank	A bank through which the cancellation of offsetting indebtedness as evidenced by cheques, notes, etc. occurs ('clearing').
Compliance officers	Personnel recruited to ensure their banks or other institutions comply with the terms of the new financial services legislation.
Conglomerate	Organisational structure involving a group of companies with few common threads and operating in diverse industries and markets. However, also applied to banks which are expanding into various areas of financial services – financial conglomerate.
Convertibles	Bonds giving the investor the option to convert them into equity at a fixed conversion price and between specified dates.
Dow Jones index	A price-weighted share index and guide to the US market.
Dual capacity	Stock Exchange members are now able to act as broker/dealers as both principal and agent.
Eurobond	A bond underwritten by an international syndicate of banks.
Eurocredit	A loan denominated in a currency other than that of the country of the bank office extending the credit.
FIMBRA	Financial Intermediaries, Managers and Brokers Regulatory Association – the largest SRO covering diverse forms of investment business, e.g., general insurance broking.
FRN	Floating Rate Note – security or bond with interest reset at regular intervals against a reference rate.
FSA	Financial Services Act 1986 – the new investment legislation in the United Kingdom.
FT–SE 100 Index	Real-time stock market index covering the 100 largest companies by capitalisation. A guide to the market mood.
Futures contract	Standardised contract covering sale or purchase of set quantity of commodity, financial instrument, etc. at future date.
Investment bank	Bank engaged in securities issue, distribution and underwriting.
ISE	The International Stock Exchange of the United Kingdom and Republic of Ireland – namely, The Stock Exchange.
Jobber	Principal who deals in shares. Now no longer a separate function after 'Big Bang'.
LAUTRO	Life Assurance and Unit Trust Regulatory Organisation – an SRO linking unit trust and life assurance business.
Market-maker	New name for broker/dealer who after 'Big Bang' specialises in ensuring a continuous market in shares.
NIF	Note Issuance Facility – enables borrowers to issue short-term paper in own name. Banks may guarantee the availability of funds to the borrower by purchasing unsold notes at rollover dates or arranging standby letters of credit.
Option	The right, not the obligation, to buy a share at a set price within a set period.
SEAQ	Stock Exchange Automated Quotations System for UK securities. A database giving quotations and information for trading UK securities.
Securitisation	The process whereby financial institutions, instead of lending

direct, help companies to raise funds by the issue of securities, often via eurobond issues.

SIB — Securities and Investments Board – statutory body under the FSA charged with control over the various investment bodies registering under the Act.

SRO — Self-Regulatory Organisation – although the FSA means securities legislation will occur within the framework of law, much of the regulation will be conducted by various regulatory bodies responsible for their members' conduct.

Swap — A given currency is simultaneously bought and sold but with different maturities.

TOPIC — The Stock Exchange's own videotex terminal network used for distributing SEAQ and SEAQ International information to subscribers.

TSA — The Securities Association – an SRO to oversee broker/dealers, market-makers and other members of the Stock Exchange. Also covers non-Stock Exchange firms active in international securities dealing.

Underwriting — An agreement whereby securities houses, banks or other financial concerns guarantee to buy a proportion of a new issue, if necessary, to ensure the issue is fully subscribed.

12 · CRIME AND ECONOMICS

Lessons to be learned?

TOM BURDEN

> With adequate profit, capital is very bold. A certain 10% will ensure its employment anywhere; 20% will produce eagerness; 50% positive audacity; 100% will make it ready to trample upon all human laws; 300% and there is not a crime at which it will scruple.
>
> (Karl Marx *Capital*, vol. 1: 760)

12.1 INTRODUCTION

Crime is big business. A single criminal act may involve a profit of millions of pounds. Crime is also widespread. A substantial section of the population supplements its income by illegal means. The involvement of most people with crime takes two forms. In addition to those who benefit from it there are also those who are likely to be victims of it. Crime is obviously a matter of major personal significance.

Undoubtedly also, crime is a matter of major economic significance. It is reasonable to suggest that an account of the modern British economy which ignored the role of crime would be seriously lacking. However, with few exceptions, the accounts given by economists ignore the issue of crime altogether or assign to it a marginal significance or, more rarely, apply the standard neoclassical toolkit to its analysis. For example, no mention of it can be found in the tables of contents, or even the indexes, of major introductory texts such as Lipsey or Begg; it does, however, receive three-quarters of a page in the eleventh edition of Samuelson! To read these and most other economics texts one would think that crime had little or no place in economic life.

In recent years, public awareness of the scale of illegal economic activity has undoubtedly increased. In part this has been due to the publicity given to major financial scandals in the City. Another important factor has been the apparent growth of the 'black' or 'shadow' economy, involving 'moonlighting' and the provision of services such as household repairs on a cash-only basis in order to evade tax. At the same time recorded crime, much of it undertaken for personal gain, has increased at an average rate of 6 per cent p.a. over the last 30 years.

Although some economists have attempted to address the issue of crime, notably Becker (see Anderson 1976) and Burrows and Veljanovkski (1981), theirs remain isolated contributions. More generally, its almost complete neglect by 'respectable professors of the dismal science' suggests that crime does not fit easily into the explanatory framework of standard economics. This in itself requires explanation. Indeed, as this chapter will show, the attempt to incorporate crime into the discipline of economics casts doubt on the usefulness of some of the underlying assumptions of conventional economic analysis.

In order to explore the issues raised for economics by the question of crime this chapter will be organised in the following way. Section 12.2 will examine the development of classical thought in order to show how and why crime has been excluded from the purview of economics. Section 12.3 will examine the range and significance of criminal economic activity. Finally, Section 12.4 will attempt to assess briefly the implications for economics of giving a central place to the understanding of crime.

12.2 CRIME AND THE CLASSICAL TRADITION

The analysis of crime played little or no part in the classical economic tradition which crystallised in the late eighteenth and early nineteenth century in the work of Smith, Ricardo and their contemporaries. This classical tradition was part of a broad movement which established recognisably modern modes of thought in a number of areas of study. This occurred in the study of crime where a 'classical' tradition was established in the new science of criminology. Thus, at the outset the topic of crime was separated from the developing discipline of economics. The academic division of labour formed at this time was never subsequently overcome and the two areas of study have remained apart ever since. We can learn something about the fundamental nature of both economics and criminology if we consider the origins and general characteristics of classicism (Barber 1967; Young 1981).

12.2.1 Classicism and industrial capitalism

In Britain the classical mode of thought grew up alongside a historic process of change involving the development of industrial capitalism. This period is often known as the industrial revolution, but it was more than just industry which was revolutionised. In fact a whole new way of organising economic, social and political life came about. The classical mode of thought had a major effect on the new patterns of life that were emerging. However, classicism itself was also strongly influenced by these broader changes that were taking place throughout society.

It is important to remember that classical thought, whether in economics or criminology was used as a weapon in the struggle to determine the principles on which society should operate. Far from being neutral, dispassionate and disinterested commentators, the thinkers who put these ideas into a systematic and organised form were themselves passionately concerned to change society. Broadly speaking, the classical thinkers sought to establish ways of organising society in which individuals could pursue their own material interests in a 'rational' way. The key element which gave classical thought its immense appeal, especially to the better off, was the demonstration that by giving free play to the pursuit of self-interest, the interests of society would also be safeguarded. In economics this meant organising the economy so as to give free reign to the pursuit of self-interest, to private property rights and to the market. In criminology this meant designing a legal system which ensured the apprehension of offenders, which rested on a carefully graded tariff of penalties adjusted to outweigh the prospective benefits of crime, and which used imprisonment to reform as well as to punish those who broke the law.

These new ideas were taken up by those who sought the changes in government policy necessary to make them the organising principles of society. Classical economics provided the arguments for a range of movements seeking the establishment of the principles of the free market. These included the movement to reform the 'poor law' so as to abolish cash benefits to the poor, and the Anti Corn Law League which sought to remove all restrictions on the freedom of trade in corn.

Classical criminology provided arguments for the establishment of an organised and full-time police force, for the reform of the law to make punishments proportionate to crimes and for the setting up of a carefully regulated prison system to rehabilitate offenders and return them to society as rationally motivated citizens who would support themselves lawfully. Leading figures in the development of classical thought in economics (such as Nassau Senior) and criminology (such as Jeremy Bentham) also played a major role in movements seeking political change.

The vision of the society classicism sought to create tells us a great deal about the sort of theory it was. This vision was based on free individuals lawfully pursuing their own interests under some form of constitutional government. Legal equality based on civil rights, the rule of law, individualism and representative political institutions were its cornerstones of this vision. It was put forward as an alternative to the 'absolutist' or semi-feudal arrangements which dominated Europe in the eighteenth century. The classicists sought an end to feudal privileges and to state-granted monopolies, to archaic and unpredictable legal arrangements, to restrictions on the free pursuit of self-interest and to aristocratic or monarchical government.

Classicism envisaged an orderly and prosperous society with effective legal and political institutions in which everyone would have a place. It would be a society in which no one need have good reason for opposing the overall principles on which it was based. The belief that this 'utopia' could be brought into being lay behind every manifestation of the classical mode of thought. Classicism, both in criminolgy and in economics, went to considerable lengths to demonstrate that if only certain basic principles were followed then everyone would benefit or at least there would be, in the words of a key classical thinker, Bentham, 'the greatest happiness of the greatest number'.

12.2.2 Dealing with the deviant

The classical vision had another and darker side however. Since a society based on classical principles would be the embodiment of all that was rational and indeed truly human, it followed that those who individually or collectively opposed or rejected this kind of society were themselves irrational or at least misguided. It was therefore necessary for these people to be dealt with. They could either be remade into adequate citizens or they would have somehow to be excluded from it. Thus, classical thought, which was viewed by its supporters as a great instrument for promoting freedom, was at the same time the basis for a series of 'reform' movements which sought to incarcerate those whose behaviour deviated from the classical ideal.

Undoubtedly this period saw a major reduction in the tolerance of those in power for disorderly behaviour of all kinds. The first half of the nineteenth century, which was the heyday of classicism, saw successful movements for the development of a wide range of these institutions: lunatic asylums for the insane; prisons and reformatories for those who violated the law; and workhouses for those who failed to maintain themselves and their families by wage labour. Thus deviants were to be isolated from public view where their activities might be 'contagious' and worked upon by agents of the new order until they were 'remoralised'. In addition, the level of surveillance was to be increased by the establishment across the country of full-time police forces to replace the ancient system of parish constables.

Leading economists played their part in promoting these ideas. Alfred Marshall, for example, the author of 'Principles of Economics' (1890), probably the first major economics textbook, proposed that the poor should be forced into labour colonies (Stedman Jones, Part III).

Paradoxically, the people could only be freed to enjoy the benefits of the classical utopia if it was underwritten by a substantial increase in the coercive capacity of the state. Because the institutions dear to classical thought, such as private property, the free market, the workhouse and the restriction of the franchise to property owners, were believed to be the embodiment of rationality itself, those enemies of reason who opposed them, such as trade unionists, factory reformers, opponents of the workhouse and Chartists, could without difficulty be treated as criminals or at least deviants.

Classicism was a remarkably successful movement. In a few decades the overall direction of state policy was shifted substantially and a new kind of society based on industrial capitalism and urban life came into being. While classicism did not create the institutions of this new society it can justly be viewed as the inspiration of its most articulate exponents and apologists. Classicism attained its resonance with the age because it presented an idealised view of changes in economy and society that were already taking place. The ideas of Adam Smith, for example, had a considerable appeal to commercially-inclined eighteenth-century landowners who were seeking more and more to reduce the costs and increase the profits of agricultural enterprise.

As industrial capitalism began to develop, Smith's ideas were also taken up by the new class of industrial capitalists and by those who sought to protect their interests. Along with industrial capitalism came the rapid growth of an urban industrial working class. Many members of this class attempted to resist various features of industrial capitalism, including the destruction of traditional cottage or domestic industries, the long hours of work in the factories, the use of child labour, the insecurity of employment and the power of the factory owners and their agents. This resistance posed a threat to the interests of the new class of industrial capitalists and indeed to everyone whose wealth rested on the rapid expansion of investment, trade, commerce, construction, the provision of professional services and all the other activities which went along with economic change. The ideas of classicism provided a rationale for dealing with resistance and for pushing forward towards a fully capitalist society.

Classical economics cleary demonstrated the futility of opposing the determination of wages by the market and the futility of collective bargaining and trade unionism which would simply drive away capital and reduce employment if successful. It demonstrated that crucial economic decisions on investment, working conditions and employment practices should be the sole concern of the owners of firms. Classical criminology showed how the legal system could be used to support the precepts of classical economics. It showed that those who violated the law or who proved unable to maintain themselves should be placed in institutions designed to turn them into useful members of society.

12.2.3 The legacy of classicism

From the start, therefore, both economics and criminology closely identified themselves with capitalism and with the dominant class of Victorian society. An intimate linkage with policymaking was established, which has remained in existence ever since. While these close links with the powerful have enhanced the prestige of the two subjects, they have also helped to imprison them within the confines of important classical assumptions. Some of these, such as the assumption of 'rational' motivation and the use of a deductive approach to theory construction, are methodological, but others are 'political' in the sense that they involve a view of how society should be organised. In particular, the orthodox traditions of both economics and criminology share a number of 'political' assumptions:

1. Each sees the role of the 'discipline' as providing a guide for state policy.
2. Society is implicitly assumed to rest on a consensus on the desirability of economic, political and social arrangements based on individual freedom and especially on free markets.
3. The content of the law where it supports these arrangements is not viewed as a legitimate matter for academic examination: it is simply taken as a given.
4. The state is viewed as a neutral force standing above society and operating in the interests of all.
5. Crime, deviance, resistance and other forms of political and social dissent are seen as the activities of a minority of irrational, misguided or malevolent individuals.

It is this 'political' attachment to the existing economic order and legal framework which is partly responsible for a corresponding inability to engage critically with it except in very limited terms. Contemporary mainstream economics, for example, largely confines its criticism of capitalism to the notion of 'market failure' at both micro and macro-levels, which itself implies 'market success' as the norm. In a similar vein, conventional criminology views the administration of the law as sullied only by 'miscarriages of justice'. Crime itself is seen as a product of atypical social conditions or of individual psychological or even biological deficiencies rather than as being a normal product of the social order of capitalism.

In some technical respects economics rather more than criminology has remained close to the model laid down in the classical period. The assumption of rational individualism ('rational economic man') and a deductive approach are still mainstays of economic analysis. However, criminology quite quickly diverged from the assumption that crime could be eliminated by organising a system of penalities so that no rational person would take part in it. It also moved away from the belief that imprisonment could be used to remake criminals into rational members of society. The reasons why these assumptions of the classical tradition were abandoned was simply that they proved to be incorrect. Crime showed no signs of disappearing despite the reform of the system of penalties. And despite the considerable effort and ingenuity put into the design of regimes of imprisonment, these failed to have any noticeable rehabilitative effects. Partly as a result, criminology then moved away from the purely deductive approach of the classical tradition and adopted a succession of 'positivist' models in pursuit of an effective explanation of crime.

What came to be called positivism in criminology involved the abandonment of the deductive method; instead it sought direct knowledge of the subject in question. It involved the empirical study of criminals and/or the social circumstances in which crime seemed to flourish. The psychological variant involved the search for the 'criminal type' who is inherently predisposed to crime. The later sociological variant involved a search for the social conditions which produced crime. In particular this tradition sought to identify criminal neighbourhoods or areas and to seek the mechanisms of family and community life which led to crime.

However, criminological positivism proved as unsuccessful as classicism as a means of providing effective guidelines for the elimination of crime. In large part this was due to the fact that positivism still retained the 'political' assumptions of classicism. Probably the most damaging assumption was that society was fundamentally harmonious and that criminal activity was some peculiar species of behaviour carried out by abnormal people. What modern research has demonstrated conclusively is that crime is an activity undertaken by very large numbers of people and that to a large extent the reasons that explain crime are no different from the reasons that explain any other type of behaviour (Box 1983).

In contrast, though major changes took place in analytical techniques the subsequent development of economics remained true to the precepts of classicism. The discipline developed without any major shift in either the 'political' or the methodological assumptions of the classical era. Of course there were important changes in economics such as the development of marginalism, welfare economics, Keynesianism, econometrics and even monetarism. However, all these were essentially technical changes in how economic analysis was to take place. They did not involve a shift in what was to be studied or in the attitude taken to it. The market and a strong 'political' commitment to it remained central to the discipline.

Systematic empirical study was a much later development in economics than in criminology and it never came to occupy a dominant position in the subject in the sense of becoming the primary basis for the formulation of theory. In fact there has been a remarkable continuity in the approach and in the definition of the subject matter of economics since the classical period. The dominant economic tradition has retained an attachment to the view of society as a harmonious unity and to the conception of economic activity as the rational pursuit of individual interests through the market. In effect, although it has not normally been stated, economics has continued to concern itself until very recently almost exclusively with legal and contractual economic activities. Mainstream economics has remained blind to the entire range of activities which involve the production and distribution of services outside the legal and contractual sphere, such as crime and unpaid domestic labour. As such it offers a view of the British economy which is seriously misleading.

12.3 THE SCOPE OF CRIMINAL ECONOMIC ACTIVITY

This section of the chapter will examine the forms taken by illegal economic activity in Britain and assess their overall significance. The category 'crime' is itself a rather difficult one for what counts as crime can be changed by state action. The law may be changed to 'criminalise' an activity that was previously legal or vice versa. The period of prohibition in the United States, which criminalised the production and sale of alcoholic drinks, is an example of the former. Similarly what counts as a legal activity in one society may be a crime in another. For example, various quite legal forms of financial speculation in the United Kingdom would be serious criminal offences in the Soviet Union.

Crime, therefore, is not a fixed and universal category but a matter of social definition. In order to understand crime we need to ask why it is that some activities are 'criminalised' while others are not. For crimes of gain (economic crimes) we are really looking at how those in power draw the boundary between legitimate and illegitimate methods of acquiring wealth. What is to count as crime, therefore, is reflection of the distribution of power in society. Given a set of laws, the extent to which they will be violated will depend on the existing opportunities for lawbreaking. For example, the increase in personal wealth resulting from the industrial revolution led to increased opportunities for theft from households. Similarly, the increased use of electronic financial transfers widens the opportunities for crimes such as computer fraud. New patterns of crime therefore develop which correspond to the changes in technological and economic conditions.

12.3.1 Corporate crime

Throughout history entrepreneurs have availed themselves of opportunities for illegal acquisition under the cover of running a legitimate organisation. However, the era of industrial capitalism has consideraby increased the importance of business crime. The economic significance of the development of the limited liability joint-stock company is important here. From the mid-nineteenth century this gradually became the normal form of ownership of larger-scale industrial and commercial capital in the United Kingdom.

Crimes committed by companies cannot be policed in the same way as crimes committed by individuals. The company can be treated in law as a 'legal personality' but unlike an ordinary individual it cannot be punished in the same way. A company cannot be imprisoned; fines of a kind which threaten the economic viability of the company are unlikely to be levied. In effect the legal sanctions available against illegal company activities are relatively weak. In addition, it is extremely difficult to discover whether corporate crimes have been committed because of the secrecy in which commercial transactions often take place. Further, the extraordinary complexity of some of the relevant statutes, particularly those relating to company law, make it very hard for the prosecution to prove a case. Where enterprises operate multi-nationally the jurisdiction within which offences take place may be difficult to establish. All these factors increase the likelihood of corporate crime.

Corporate crime can be a feature of various aspects of company operations. The range of crimes that corporations can commit has been enormously increased by the growth of detailed regulation of company activities which has criminalised many previously legal activities. For our purposes the following areas will be examined:

1. Dealings with consumers (such as quality of the product and credit arrangements).
2. The employment of labour (such as equal pay, minimum wages, health and safety and discrimination).
3. Commercial operations (such as restrictive trade practices, insider dealing and bribery).

To deal first with consumer law: protection of consumers began in the nineteenth century with laws against the adulteration of food. However, prior to the Sale of Goods Act of 1893 the onus was generally put on consumers to establish the quality of the goods they purchased. Since that time the scope of consumer protection has gradually been widened to cover a number of other areas such as attempts by producers to limit their legal liability, false trade descriptions, and restrictions on the marketing of financial products such as loans and insurance policies.

It appears that violations of these laws is much more common among small firms than among the large corporations that dominate the markets for consumer goods. This is probably because prosecution would lead to unfavourable publicity and to enormous costs resulting from the need to reorganise production. This is not to say that consumers are effectively protected – numerous 'Which' surveys demonstrate the extent to which they may be exploited by firms such as garages or jobbing builders – simply that this can normally take place without any criminal offence being committed. It is impossible to estimate the extent to which criminal laws governing consumer protection are violated. As with other areas of business law, enforcement is not primarily the job of the police. Instead it is largely a function of other bodies such as the Office of Fair Trading or Local Authority Public Health Departments, which rarely initiate prosecutions.

A rather greater body of evidence on the extent of corporate crime exists in relation to the employment of labour. These crimes cover the following areas: violation of wages laws; violation of health and safety regulations; and violation of the laws on sex and race discrimination. As with laws relating to consumer protection, criminal law relating to employment is not generally enforced by the police.

Since their initial establishment in 1909 Wages Boards have set the minimum wages for a number of industries. In 1960 the number of workers covered by these provisions reached 3.5 million. The Wages Act 1986 has reduced the scope of the system of wage regulation and the number covered now is about 2.7 million. The number of 'outdoor inspectors' has been cut by 60 per cent since 1979 and each employer is visited on average only once every 15 years. One-third of all firms visited by inspectors are found to be breaking the law, but prosecutions are almost unknown. The enforcement of health and safety laws has also been studied. The findings show that there are a very large number of criminal offences committed by firms in this area. Industrial accidents alone account for about 600 deaths and over 18,000 major injuries every year. Many other workers, and sometimes members of their families, are harmed by dangerous substances in the workplace. Despite the potential seriousness of the criminal violation of regulations, very few prosecutions take place. In 1983 1,366 cases were heard in court. The average fine imposed was £252. The attitude of firms often seems to be that the benefits of breaking the law may well outweigh the likely costs.

The laws relating to discrimination by sex and race in employment are enforced in another fashion. When someone believes that they have been discriminated against they take their complaint to the Community Relations Commission (for race cases) or the Equal Opportunities Commission (for sex cases). Attempts at 'conciliation' are then undertaken. Only if these fail is a prosecution undertaken. The number of successful prosecutions for race and sex cases is minute. In 1982 only 26 cases of sex discrimination were upheld. Of 273 cases relating to race discrimination in employment only 19 were upheld. Evidence however suggests that discriminatory practices of both kinds are very widespread. Experiments involving sending equally qualified job applicants of different sexes (for sex discrimination) or races (for race discrimination) have demonstrated this. In individual cases, however, it is extremely difficult to prove since some other factor can almost always be found to justify an employer's preference for one applicant over another.

Finally, we turn to commercial operations, the category which covers the range of activities where firms deal with one another and with the state. Financial rather than manufacturing enterprises appear to be most likely to engage in criminal activities simply because greater opportunities present themselves (Levi 1981). An interesting example is what is now referred to as 'insider dealing' (see also Chapter 11). This offence involves the use of confidential information relating to company affairs to buy or sell shares for profit.

As a form of crime, insider dealing has some distinctive characteristics. It is hard for those involved (and for outsiders) to see why it is any more culpable than other, perfectly legal, financial speculations which yield very large profits. Also, in contrast to say, robbery or fraud, it is hard to identify clearly the victims of this practice. Its extent is unknown. A few prosecutions have taken place but it is likely that these by no means represent the scale on which the offence is committed. The reason is that this offence is extremely unlikely to be reported and the authorities have no power to seek out violations without evidence being first presented to them.

A recent case involving Guinness demonstrated a number of features of the UK financial system relevant to understanding the role of crime within it. In 1987 Guinness arranged for up to £100 million of company funds to be used to pay third parties who were contracted to arrange purchases of Guinness shares in order to increase their market price in the attempted take-over of Distillers. This operation resulted in an increase in the Guinness share price from 280p to 353p. What went on was only revealed as a result of a 'tip off' from the US Securities and Exchange Commission. All the money used for this purpose was used illegally and many individuals and organisations benefited by six-figure sums. At the time of writing (October 1987) only the Chairman of Guinness has been arrested. Interestingly, he has been charged with attempting to pervert the course of justice, not with an offence specifically concerned with the mechanics of the take-over bid.

From a criminological standpoint what is most significant about these offences is the very large scale of the sums of money involved. The vast majority of personal crimes for gain which lead to custodial sentences, often very long ones, involve sums which are a tiny fraction of those which are common in large-scale City crimes. Major financial institutions such as The Stock Exchange or Lloyds (the insurance market) are subject only to the minimum of state regulation. There is no requirement for detailed records of financial transactions to be registered or recorded with public authorities so that evidence is very hard to come by. No competent independent body exists to investigate and prosecute City crime. The Bank of England, which has the overall task of regulating the City, is more concerned to 'maintain confidence in financial institutions' than to seek the prosecution of offenders when there is a major scandal. Finally, the treatment of convicted offenders by the courts is hardly such as to constitute a major deterrent to others.

The systematic use of bribery as a means of facilitating economic transactions is usually depicted in the British press as a practice largely confined to foreigners: when evidence of British participation is discovered this is invariably viewed officially as a case of 'one rotten apple'. On average only about a dozen people each year are imprisoned in the United Kingdom for corruption and bribery. However, evidence exists that it takes place on a very wide scale in British business and in the public sector. Indeed business dealings involving the public sector are a particularly common focus for corrupt activity. This was most clearly illustrated in the Poulson case (Doig 1984: Chapters 5–10). This kind of activity is unlikely to be reported for several reasons. The people most likely to know of it are often colleagues of those involved and strong pressures exist not to 'wash dirty linen in public'. Documents which might be used as evidence are very hard to come by. The police have no special powers to search commercial premises for them and neither are they allowed access to information in bank accounts. The Poulson case only came to light as a result of enquiries made in the course of public bankruptcy proceedings.

Criminal actions by multinational companies are particularly difficult to uncover since they operate in a complex environment where what may be legal in one national sphere of operations may be illegal in another. The legality of various widely-used practices such as 'transfer pricing' is a case in point (see Chapter 4). Transfer pricing involves fixing the prices at which components or services are bought and sold between branches of the firm in different countries so that profits are allowed to accrue to branches in nations with low taxes on profits. The borderline between crime and such 'creative accounting' is often hard to draw. Bribery is also a feature of the operation of multinational companies. Its use by British companies has been well documented, particularly in the DTI investigation into Lonrho.

12.3.2 Illegal businesses

The category 'illegal business' covers the range of activities where organisations (firms and even industries) exist whose purpose is primarily to accumulate profits illegally. These 'firms' range from small temporary partnerships, established to undertake a particular crime such as an armed robbery, after which they are dissolved, to giant multinational enterprises like some of those involved in the international drugs trade (Henman *et al.* 1985). Some attempts have been made to use economic theories of the firm and sociological theories of business organisation to help explain why criminal 'firms' adopt a particular form of organisation and pursue particular strategies (McIntosh 1975).

The existence of illegal business organisations results to a large extent from legal prohibitions or controls on the production and/or distribution of certain products or services for which a market exists. These restrictions may be temporary. An example would be wartime controls involving rationing which can lead to the development of a black market. However, it is usually the case that illegal businesses result from less transient restrictions on the scope of free-market activity. Prohibitions often involve recreational activities such as drug-taking, certain sexual services, some types of gambling, and some blood sports. This situation allows criminal entrepreneurs to set up in business to meet the unmet demand. The situation where buyer and seller freely transact (illegal) business has been said to involve crimes without victims (Schur 1965).

Probably the largest and most complex criminal business involves the illegal supply of drugs. In the cases of cocaine and heroin, a vast international network links the farmers who grow the crops from which the drugs are manufactured to the eventual consumers, many of whom live in the West. The international drugs business illustrates some of the consequences of illegal business. In those countries where the drugs are purchased for illegal use numerous crimes are committed by consumers in order to provide funds to purchase the drugs, while the enormous profits made by those who control the supply lead to bribery and to the corruption of law enforcement and other state officials in the various countries involved.

Another important area of illegal business involves gambling, which is likely to be found when the state restricts the scope for legal gambling. This may involve a large number of small locally based firms. For example, in the United Kingdom prior to the legalisation of betting shops, very large numbers of people took part in illegal off-course gambling on horse races and dog races and a large network of 'bookies' runners' were employed to carry bets from punters to bookmakers. Illegal gambling clubs also existed to cater for those wishing to play a variety of games such as roulette or *chemin de fer*.

On a smaller scale some illegal gambling clubs operate in order to evade taxation. The provision of illegal or semi-legal sexual services is organised in a rather similar way. Here there also tend to be sole proprietorships and small-scale businesses. Because of the localised nature of the market the advantages of internal economies of scale are not usually evident though external economies of scale generally lead to a clustering of activities of this kind in 'red light districts'. Even where these activities are not themselves forbidden by law the firms may continue to operate illegally in order to evade both tax and publicity.

A development that is sometimes found in areas of provision such as drugs, gambling and prostitution is the development of firms that deal in all these as a kind of criminal conglomerate. In the United States the term 'organised crime' is used for this and the best-known example is the 'mafia' though this is not a unified organisation. Due to the scale of these firms and the integration of their activities, other developments often occur such as a process of cartelisation by which geographical areas are divided between firms to prevent competition. In addition owing to the vulnerability of such large and complex organisations they frequently seek to guarantee their immunity from prosecution through bribery of law enforcement officers and even politicians.

12.3.3 Personal crime

Very large numbers of those who are normally thought of as law-abiding people regularly commit offences for material gain. The three most common contexts in which these offences take place involve being an employee, paying personal taxation and receiving social security benefits.

Employees of many kinds regularly or opportunistically steal from their employers (Mars 1982). The way in which incomes are supplemented by crime varies from occupation to occupation. The variation is partly related to differences in the opportunities available for theft. Office workers, for example, normally have access to telephones and to items of stationery. Many may also have the opportunity to 'fiddle' expenses paid by their employers. Many manual workers in manufacturing have access to equipment and finished products or components which may be stolen. Those working in firms involved in transportation, warehousing or retailing may have access to a wide range of products which can be stolen.

Such theft may sometimes be viewed as part of the customary perquisites of a particular job and employers often collude in their commission. Large retailers, for example, often expect a degree of theft by staff, which is referred to euphemistically as 'stock shrinkage'. So long as it remains within certain limits no strenuous efforts are made to prevent it. Managements often turn a blind eye to these practices both because they have customarily been tolerated and because they are ways in which employees can increase their incomes without management having to pay higher wages. As a result few of these cases are reported and even fewer result in prosecution. In addition, the places where the offences take place are not ones to which the police normally have access so the offences do not come to their attention by that route. Thus, in this as in many other cases, the criminal statistics bear little relationship to the true extent of criminal activity.

Personal direct taxation is another sphere of widespread criminality (Field *et al.* 1977). This is not true of those who are taxed by PAYE which is very tightly controlled with the tax being deducted before payment of wages or salaries. However, the self-employed not only enjoy a more lax set of tax regulations, they also have many more opportunities for tax evasion. Tax crime among the self-employed takes two main forms. It may involve falsely claiming business expenses so that a larger proportion of income remains untaxed, or it may involve 'cash' transactions which do not exist for tax purposes and through which both income tax and VAT may be evaded.

There is evidence that these activities are widespread. It has been found, for example, that the standards of consumption of self-employed people are often much higher than their declared incomes would permit. Despite their limited and declining resources, substantial numbers of cases come to the notice of the Inland Revenue which is also the relevant prosecuting authority. However, prosecution is very rare. Cases are seldom publicised in the media unless they involve some well-known public figure and the stigma of a criminal label is not normally attached to offenders. Indeed, those who have committed these crimes are usually invited to discuss them with the Inland Revenue and some kind of a deal is normally struck concerning paying back part or all of the unpaid tax without prosecution.

Social security payments are another area where criminal behaviour is evident. Crimes of this kind usually result from misinformation given to the authorities about personal circumstances or from failure to reveal changes in circumstances (Field 1983). Very rarely claimants may be claiming benefit at more than one office. Most of the money which is spent on social security is unlikely to be the subject of any kind of criminal misappropriation. Well over 60 per cent goes to pensioners and about another 10 per cent goes on child benefit – in both these cases fraud is very rare. Accusations of widespread fraud generally involve unemployed men and unsupported women, particularly those claiming Supplementary Benefit (now Income Support).

On occasions media campaigns against social security fraud take on the appearance of a witch hunt or 'moral panic'. In one such instance in 1977 a full investigation of cases reported to the MP Ian Sproat revealed that the amount lost through fraud was 30p for every £1000 paid in benefit.

It needs to be remembered that the DHSS employs a large and periodically expanded army of special investigators to pursue fraud. In addition, those who are apprehended are very likely to be prosecuted. In fact, the total value of unclaimed benefits is around one hundred times greater than the value of fraudulently obtained payouts from the cash benefit system.

The crimes involved with employment, personal taxation and social security vary in terms of their public visibility and in terms of the disapproval which is earned by those who commit them. Probably the greatest contrast is between the treatment accorded those who claim state benefits to which they are not entitled and that given to those who defraud the tax authorities. These offences also vary in the degree to which they are listed in the official crime figures. It seems likely that the extent of unrecorded crime in the case of social security is less than that for crimes at the place of work or in personal taxation.

12.4 CONCLUSIONS

Criminal economic activity appears to be a major feature of the British economy. The extent of this illegal activity at any one time depends in part on where the boundaries of legality are drawn. The dividing line between legal and illegal business activity is never one that is clear-cut. Normal business practice frequently involves actions, such as giving 'gifts' to customers or lavish entertaining or the provision of trips abroad, which in some contexts are legal and in others illegal.

The more complex and wide ranging the scope of legal regulations, the more crimes are created. 'Ordinary people' not normally thought of as criminals take part in crime as a matter of course with little compunction. They are aided in this by commonly understood conceptions of crime in which people are able to view their own violations of the law as 'technical offences', 'perks' or 'fair game'. In addition, crime is encouraged by the enormous variations in the rigour with which the law is enforced. The mechanisms of enforcement are often weak and sometimes partly controlled by those likely to commit the offences. The scale of punishment is low compared to that meted out for 'ordinary' crimes such as robbery or burglary. As a result some of those who commit offences which yield them substantial personal gains run little risk of prosecution and almost no risk of heavy punishment. All these features increase the likelihood of criminal behaviour. However, it is difficult to give even a rough estimate of its overall extent since most offences are not reported because there is no directly affected victim to make a complaint.

In recent years the concept of the 'black' or 'shadow' economy has been used to describe the provision of goods and services outside the taxed and recorded sector of economic activity. It seems that this concept needs to be broadened to include the very wide range of criminal economic activity that appears to be a normal feature of our economic arrangements. The implications for economic theory and analysis of a thoroughgoing recognition of the role of what might be called 'the illegal sector' are wide ranging. They raise a number of 'technical' issues concerning the adequacy of conventional economics.

First, economists need to develop a more critical view of official statistics since it is evident that these do not portray a valid picture of the extent and forms of economic activity. Figures for national income which only include declared incomes or the declared value of output of legally constituted firms, are certainly misleading. Some of the deficiencies of national income figures as a measure of economic activity are well known, particularly the absence of unpaid domestic labour. However, the absence of unrecorded criminal transactions further vitiates the validity of these figures.

Second, the use of economic analysis as a basis for determining or advising on economic policy in a number of areas needs to be reviewed in the light of the importance of the criminal sector. One area is personal taxation. Knowledge of the extent of access to untaxed illegal gains would certainly give proposals on the structuring of personal taxation greater grounding in reality. Another area involves incomes policies. Attempts to control personal incomes are unlikely to have the desired macroeconomic effect if substantial income opportunities are available outside the legal economy which the authorities have no control over or accurate knowledge of.

Policies aimed at modifying the distribution of income and wealth also require more accurate data on the current position which can only be guessed at if the official figures are the sole source of information. Detailed industrial planning might also be rendered more difficult by the widespread use of resources outside the legal sector. However, this is perhaps not such a major problem since a feature of much of the illegal economy is the low value of capital invested in it. Indeed this relative lack of fixed capital assets such as large factories partly accounts for its lack of visibility.

Third, the processes involved in understanding the nature of change in the criminal sector require analysis. The extent and form of criminal economic activity in the longer term is affected by the general pattern of economic, technological and social development, which determines the overall structure of criminal opportunities. In the shorter term it is affected by the normal process of economic fluctuation which periodically increases the numbers unable to maintain themselves by wage labour. As a result, certain types of crime, particularly those committed by poorer people, are likely to increase. Other crimes, however, such as those requiring buoyant financial markets, may increase in times of boom.

Finally, economists might also consider whether direct study of criminal economic activity should be undertaken. The theory of the firm might well be enriched by empirical study of criminal enterprises. Similarly, industrial economists might find they had something to learn from the close examination of patterns of organisation and integration found in large-scale crime. Certainly a knowledge of these areas would provide economists with a great deal of interesting material for example and comparison.

The points covered so far in this conclusion deal with ways in which the existing practice of economic analysis might be enhanced by a focus on the illegal economy. However, it can be argued that its existence raises some rather more fundamental issues about the character of economics.

One major part of the 'political' legacy of classicism is the assumption that society rests on a consensus and that those who do not accept this are somehow irrational and thus beyond the scope of normal economic analysis. From this follows the exclusion of crime from mainstream economic analysis. However, this assumption also has other damaging consequences. It prevents economics from realistically conceptualising politics and the economic role of the state, which have assumed such great importance in the twentieth century.

Economists have always tended to deal with policy issues as if policymaking could be treated as a largely technical matter on which they could simply advise without in any way taking sides. This might be referred to as the 'mandarin' conception of the role of economics. Its clearest example is Keynesianism, which views itself as a kind of intellectual toolkit for the Chancellor of the Exchequer. In reality of course, this kind of activity does involve taking sides because of the hidden 'political' assumptions which classicism inserted into the basic theoretical structure of the subject. Essentially, mainstream economics stands for the maintenance of the power of private property and the continued existence of free markets on which it largely rests. The state is not a neutral body which stands above society and acts in the interests of everyone and neither is the economics profession.

The second key part of the classical legacy is the emphasis on legitimate market activities as defining the scope of the subject. A great deal is left out because of this. Feminists have criticised the neglect of the role of women in a number of disciplines. In economics this is most clearly seen in the failure to make the activity of domestic labour part of the focus of the subject since it does not take place in the public realm of markets. Just as domestic labour is excluded because it lacks a market context, so crime is excluded because it is not a legitimate economic activity.

The final legacy of the classical tradition lies in the imagery which is incorporated in its portrayal of the capitalist economy. It is only those on the outer fringes of the neo-Austrian school, such as Murray Rothbard, who have followed the logic of the free market to the point of total nihilism. They propose a society where no legal prohibitions exist on the use of violence, blackmail, and the production and consumption of pornography and psychotropic drugs. The mainstream tradition of economics, however, evokes a different image. It is based on the classical vision of a peaceful, prosperous, law-abiding competitive utopia ('perfect' competition).

This is, of course, a thoroughly one-sided vision. Crises, unemployment, industrial decline, alienation from work, and exploitation do not play much part in it, and neither does the illegal economy. Classicism presented us with the picture of the entrepreneur and the worker dealing with one another on an equal basis and being rewarded in proportion to their contribution, while private property and the market ensured prosperity and social justice. It would, however, be no less unrealistic to portray our economy and society as dominated by criminal forms of acquisition, bribery and corruption, the breaking of employment law, huge fortunes criminally made and vast illegal businesses. Along with this it would be possible to lay emphasis on the way in which the classical ethos of the 'rational' pursuit of self-interest tends to break through any restraints and leads inexorably to the nightmare of a predatory society dominated by the war of all against all. To portray the modern British economy in these terms would no doubt be a travesty; but to ignore this side of economic reality is equally misleading.

FURTHER READING

On the classical tradition see Barber (1967) for economics, and Young (1981) for criminology: Young also examines positivism in criminology. Neoclassical approaches to crime and law are developed in Anderson (1976) and Burrows and Veljanovski (1981). Heertje *et al.* (1982) examine the black economy. On the scope of criminal activity Box (1983) is outstanding. For detailed accounts of particular areas of crime see Henman *et al.* (1985) on drugs, Mars (1982), Kinnersley (1979) and Levi (1981) on crime at work, and Doig (1984) on bribery and corruption. Schur (1965) examines crimes without direct victims, such as gambling.

13 · CONTROVERSY IN CONTEXT

MIKE CAMPBELL, MIKE HARDY AND NIGE HEALEY

13.1 INTRODUCTION

It should be clear that applied economics, that is, the use of economic theories in trying to understand and explain real-world phenomena, is no easy task. We are faced with many philosophical, methodological and operational difficulties in seeking to expand our knowledge. Indeed, such knowledge as we already have is provisional and contested. For both these reasons, there is widespread controversy in applied economics – controversies reflected in the wide variety of course structures and curricula available in higher education and in the miles of shelves of books, journals, pamphlets and reports providing different interpretations of, and insights into, the economic world around us. Contests for the minds of economists, economics students and the public at large range over a raft of issues: the problems to be analysed; the methods to be used in the analysis; the results obtained from the analysis; the policy implications of the results; and the degree of certainty to be attached to the conclusions reached.

Economists, then, disagree. Despite at least two hundred years of the existence of the subject, first as political economy and latterly as 'economics', despite a prodigious output of both economists and publications and despite an enormous volume of both theoretical and empirical work, there remains a fundamental lack of unanimity on the causes of, and solutions to, the great economic problems of society. In this book we have examined a wide range of such issues in applied economics – from enterprise to crime, from mergers to regulation, from the City to the labour market, from macroeconomic policy to health policy, from multinational companies to public spending and local government finance.

In this context, we have attempted to do three things:

1. To show that agreement on these issues does indeed remain elusive.
2. To demonstrate that the treatment of applied economics as a 'contested terrain' is a valuable, if sometimes salutary, approach to the study of applied economics.
3. To examine the reasons for the existence and continuation of controversy in applied economics.

The first chapter of the book identified the major sources of controversy in applied economics, whilst the eleven subsequent chapters examined key areas of applied economics as fields of controversy. Whereas each of these chapters provided an examination of a distinctive field of applied economics through a lens, this final chapter by contrast provides a brief examination of the major reasons for continued controversy in turn, using illustrations from the thematic chapters. It then, finally, offers some tentative remarks on the future of applied economics as seen from the perspective of the approach adopted in this book.

13.2 WHY DO ECONOMISTS DISAGREE?

Why do economists disagree? From the contested terrain of applied economics, the different chapters of this book each selected a particular, localised skirmish for closer examination. The subsequent discussions of controversies as varied as merger activity and monetary control all sought to highlight the fundamental disagreements between economists working in these areas. Each chapter also revealed that, despite the wealth of empirical research and the massive investment of intellectual capital, there appears to be little tendency for these disagreements to be systematically eliminated over time.

As Chapter 1 foreshadowed, the ultimate cause of perpetually unresolved controversy is that the economics profession finds it so difficult to choose between competing explanations, theories, models and perspectives. Partly this is because there is no consensus on the appropriate methodology for choosing. But even to the extent that the majority of economists nominally subscribe to the positivist approach, it is far from clear that they follow its prescriptions rigidly and impartially in their day-to-day researches. The purpose of this section is to explore both these explanations of why economists disagree in the context of the material covered by this book. It broadly follows the structure of Chapter 1, seeking to illustrate many of the methodological issues previously raised, with examples culled from Chapters 2–12.

13.2.1 The subject matter of economics

A social science like economics has greater difficulty in establishing a secure, established knowledge base than the natural sciences because its ultimate subject matter comprises conscious human actors, rather than passive (in the sense of being purely reactive, rather than proactive) physical elements. Not only is knowledge about human behaviour more difficult to obtain and more probabilistic, it is not immutable. One of the enduring contributions of the rational expectations school has been to remind the profession that estimated relationships are likely to break down whenever policymakers seek to exploit them – precisely because policy intervention may alter the trade-offs rational individuals face, so inducing them to utility-maximise in a different way from the past.

Chapter 2, for example, highlighted the independent nature of human behaviour, emphasising the impact and role of individuals as entrepreneurs who adopt a proactive stance. In examining the phenomenon of corporate merger activity, Chapter 3 similarly stressed the importance of innovative behaviour on the part of both institutions and financial intermediaries. Chapter 11, which examined the changing regulation of the UK financial system, further developed this theme confirming that financial institutions are not passive agents in this process either, but rather that they constantly innovate to overcome regulatory constraints on their behaviour. Hence, the reaction of the system to a given change in the regulatory framework is extremely difficult to predict, so making the design of an optimal policy highly contentious.

13.2.2 Induction

Observing and collecting data, and then seeking to construct theories by generalising from this evidence, carries with it serious methodological deficiencies. Not only are some data not directly observable (e.g. labour bargaining power), but the inductive process of generalising from the particular is widely acknowledged to be logically flawed. None the less, despite widespread protestations to the contrary, it is induction and not deduction (see 13.2.3) which underpins a significant amount of economic research.

Chapter 4 on multinational corporations (MNCs) highlighted both the extent and dangers of induction in economics. Detailed case studies of the effects of a particular MNC, or of MNCs in general in a particular economy, constitute the dominant method of investigation in this field. Yet the very different results obtained from different studies confirm the problems inherent in generalising from the particular. Chapter 9 also showed how some of the most influential theories in the area of public expenditure determination have been developed inductively from empirical observation (e.g. 'Wagner's Law' of expanding state activity).

Chapter 3 revealed that much of the economic literature on merger activity employs the case study approach, similarly attempting to infer general principles from specific experiences. This chapter, like Chapter 2 on enterprise, illustrated too that much of the data which is in principle needed to build theories of merger behaviour, is unobservable. Pursuing this theme, Chapter 5 examined the economics of health and health care and showed that despite broad agreement among economists working in this field on basic theoretical issues, controversy rages at an operational level largely because of difficulties with data. By definition, the 'outputs' of health care are not directly observable. Hip replacement operations produce a longer, and better quality of life for the patients treated, but rational decision-making requires some means of quantifying this output in order that it can be costed and compared with competing health care programmes. The estimation of health outputs is thus one of the most clear-cut areas of applied economics where data problems divide even like-minded economists.

13.2.3 Verification versus falsification

Scientific method involves constructing theories, not from observable facts, but from the application of a deductive logic to assumptions to generate hypotheses (or predictions) about economic behaviour, which can then be tested against the facts. The purpose of such testing is not to 'prove' that the theory is empirically 'true', since logically that is impossible, but rather to falsify it. A theory which survives repeated attempts at falsification can thus be regarded with increasing confidence over time, even though its validity can never be completely established. However, despite paying lip service to this notion of scientific method, many economists do not aggressively seek to falsify theories, but instead search for data which are consistent with their predictions. This bastardised version of the scientific method, known as verification, is clearly evident in many of the areas examined in this book.

Chapter 4, for example, showed how many case studies in the field of MNOs appear to be motivated by a desire to find data that are consistent with certain hypotheses, rather than by a rigorous attempt to falsify predictions. Chapter 7 confirmed that research by economists preaching falsificationism, but practising verificationism, is predictably widespread at the interface of economics and politics. In the debate about the role and size of local government, both opponents and proponents alike have selectively sought evidence which supports (i.e., verifies) their view of local government, rather than that which challenges it. Particular councils which 'overspend' are cited to reinforce the view that local government is inherently prone to profligacy; particularly harsh examples of the redistributive effects of the 'community charge' are found to promote the proposition that a poll tax is unacceptably regressive.

13.2.4 Ceteris paribus

In economics, controlled laboratory experiments, in the sense of focusing attention on the variables being studied and isolating the effects of all extraneous factors, are rarely possible. Indeed, in contrast to most research in the natural sciences, the economist is normally forced to test hypotheses by passively waiting for the real world to throw up evidence of behavioural relationships. The fundamental problem is, therefore, that apart from the key independent variables in which the economist is interested (say, monetary growth), the real world may also be exerting all sorts of other forces (changes in oil prices, wages, the exchange rate, etc.) on the putative dependent variable (inflation). In reality, the hypotheses being tested are conditional predictions of the form: *ceteris paribus*, an increase in the rate of monetary growth will lead to an increase in the rate of inflation; yet *ceteris* are seldom *paribus*.

When econometric techniques for screening out the effects of extraneous variables – that is, trying to create artificially the relationship between independent and dependent variables, which would have been observed had *ceteris* remained *paribus* – are continually being refined, this feature of economic testing remains a major cause of the persistence of controversy. Despite the mathematically scientific gloss, isolating the link between X and Y from the surrounding 'noise' is still arguably an art. More importantly, the scope this art offers for interpreting events in different ways means that the apparent falsification of a theory may always be repudiated on the grounds that the extraneous factors have been incorrectly handled in the analysis.

In relation to the growth of public expenditure, Chapter 9 graphically illustrated this difficulty, demonstrating that it is almost impossible to isolate empirically the particular effect of bureaucrats on public spending as distinct from the influences exerted by City institutions or pressure groups. Chapter 10 examined the so-called monetarist experiment, a classic example of the '*ceteris* were not *paribus*' immunising stratagem in operation. When faced with apparently incontrovertible evidence that, contrary to the central monetarist hypothesis, the demand for money is demonstrably unstable, monetarists have invoked the sudden acceleration of financial innovation, *inter alia*, to explain its recent behaviour. To rationalise the present high levels of unemployment which, since inflation is now relatively stable, must by definition be the 'natural rate' that monetarists originally claimed was stable in the longer term, monetarists have argued that external shocks have served to drive the rate up from its 1979 value.

Chapter 11 also illustrated the same point. In a rapidly changing, innovative financial system, unexpected economic developments which follow a change in the regulatory framework may be explained by reference to some exogenous shock which was not, and could not, have been anticipated at the time the regulations were devised. Hence, the satisfactory establishing that a particular regulatory approach has or has not been successful is highly problematic.

13.2.5 Econometrics

Statistical methods of scientific inquiry in economics serve several purposes. Not only does 'econometrics' provide the tools needed to analyse and interpret statistical data, but also sets out guidelines for accepting the results as falsifying the hypothesis under scrutiny. The problems associated with testing conditional predictions are such that occasional contradictory observations must be weighted against the mass of supporting evidence before a theory is finally rejected. Econometrics is, however, only as strong as the weakest link in the chain of hypothesis-testing. Impeccable mathematical precision is worthless when applied to data of questionable reliability, for example. Moreover, despite recent advances, the econometric techniques which exist for identifying such basics as the direction of causality between correlated variables remain crude. But perhaps the key point is that when economists continue to disagree for deep-rooted empirical, philosophical and methodological reasons, econometrics cannot by itself apply more than a superficial, scientific sheen to the process of hypothesis testing.

Chapter 4 revealed that a wide range of statistical examinations of the impact of MNCs has been undertaken, but that results are claimed in support of rival theories and perspectives. Rather than pointing unambiguously in one direction, case studies using different periods, countries, scales of investigation, definitions and data, all throw up different and often conflicting results. Chapter 4 also illustrates the deep empirical problem in attempting to establish the 'counterfactual' (i.e., what would have happened to variable X in the absence of Y), a problem echoed by Chapter 3 in its review of pre and post-merger profitability studies, and the importance of data problems in work of this nature, where official reporting practices and data coverage vary widely from country to country.

Chapter 8 on labour markets showed how research design (i.e., the nature of empirical investigation) differs between perspectives, in this case according to whether the focus of attention is on equilibria (using qualitative, intensive methods) or processes (typically employing quantitative, extensive techniques). Chapter 8 also demonstrated that different data sets, statistical techniques and model specifications (e.g., in relation to employment functions) could produce a variety of conflicting results, with the results varying from country to country and from period to period.

Chapter 12 illustrated clearly the data problems inherent in many areas of economic investigation. With regard to crime, the extent and scope of such activity is largely unknown, and so access to accurate, meaningful data is almost impossible. Moreover, even defining what constitutes illegal activity is very much a function of the prevailing boundaries of legality, which are far from historically, cross-culturally or internationally rigid.

Chapter 9 similarly showed how controversial the measurement of public expenditure can be, with a variety of conflicting definitions favoured by different economists. Chapter 9 also highlighted how difficult it can be to isolate causality, even in the absence of data problems, calling to mind the old econometrician's adage: 'if you torture the data long enough, you make it confess to anything.' This point was taken up by both Chapter 5 (the economics of health) and Chapter 10 (the 'monetarist experiment'). Health status is a complex function of a wide range of social and economic factors – income, diet, education, housing, etc. – hence isolating the effect of any one 'independent' variable is a hazardous task. Similarly, inflation is codetermined by a variety of factors – monetary growth, interest rates, the exchange rate, world prices, productivity, wage costs, etc., many of which are interrelated in complex ways. As a result, establishing, to quote Beckerman (1985), 'how the battle against inflation was really won', is as contentious as statistically 'proving' the cause of a fall in the incidence of cervical cancer.

13.2.6 Assumptions

Instead of testing conditional predictions, with all the attendant problems, one alternative is to test a theory's assumptions against empirical data. If these are not falsified, and the deductive reasoning is not logically flawed, then the theory's predictions can be confidently accepted without the need to test the predictions directly. However, the acceptance of realistic (i.e., empirically accurate, but necessarily more complex) assumptions makes the process of deduction and prediction less easy and precise. More significantly, certain assumptions are unfalsifiable in principle (e.g., individual rationality). The Austrian school's solution is to develop assumptions a priori by subjective introspection, so that no empirical contest is required.

Chapter 2 highlighted this difference between 'realistic' and a priori assumptions, focusing on the role of enterprise in the Austrian school, which follows from assumptions established by introspection, and its essentially peripheral nature in neoclassical tradition. In contrast, Chapters 3 and 5 showed how the (unfalsifiable) assumption of rationality pervades many explanations of merger activity and monopoly behaviour respectively.

13.2.7 Economists and paradigms

One further approach to explaining the relative permanence of 'contest' in economics argues that controversy grows when the 'dominant' paradigm faces an either internally or externally-induced crisis, and rivals appear to offer challenge. This is because different paradigms embody different techniques, methodologies and values. A contest for intellectual supremacy is not just between rival theories, but between rival paradigms. Such contests cannot be resolved by falsification or indeed by any other 'rational' process for they are 'incommensurable'.

The main 'contests' discussed in Chapter 2 on 'enterprise' and Chapter 3 on 'mergers' reside in growing crises in the 'dominant' paradigm. Both reflected the development of rival paradigms within the theory of the firm. Chapter 2 illustrated the effects of contrasting assumptions about 'perfect information', whereas Chapter 3 considered the challenges of 'managerialism' and of interdependence within oligopoly rivalry. In both cases, a crisis has developed within the dominant paradigm of perfect competition.

In a similar vein, Chapter 7 focused on the terrain currently bitterly contested by rival paradigms in the study of local government. One view starts from the assumption of individual rationality and a belief in the efficiency of universal market forces, arguing a minimalist role for local government. The opposing position stresses the limitations of the market in areas where information is imperfect and externalities, both positive and negative, are rife.

In Chapter 12 on crime, it was argued that there has not yet been a 'revolution' in economics; it remains dominated by the legacy of 'classicism' and by a methodology of rational individualism and deductive reasoning. This focuses economics on harmonious market relationships as the single organising force. As a result, the structure of the economy portrayed in economics is unrealistic to the extent that crime is a major element in economic and social organisation.

Such paradigm battles make debate relatively sterile, with few points of genuine contact. The adversaries argue past each other, in terms which are often mutually incomprehensible.

13.2.8 The economics profession

Among students of the history of economic thought there is a saying that 'the Keynesian revolution succeeded because the classical economists got old and died.' It crudely expresses the idea that economists are rarely persuaded to abandon ideas once acquired, so that new theories only become established by proving themselves to be more attractive than the old to those newly entering the profession. There are good illustrations of this throughout the chapters of this book. In Chapters 2, 3 and 5 which examine, in different contexts, the conduct and performance of firms and consider appropriate government policy, the intellectual 'old guard' continue to prop up theories even where the policy so derived abjectly fails. The neutrality of contemporary merger policy discussed in Chapter 3, and the continued search by economists for the scale of economies and profit performances expected with post-merger enterprises, reflect the continued belief in the predictions of neoclassical theory of the firm.

Certainly, Chapter 10 demonstrated that monetarists, with their theories under increasing attack, have generally proved reluctant to part with cherished beliefs, clinging to them in the face of mounting contradictory evidence. We have seen a rate of legitimate and illegitimate immunising stratagems employed to protect such theories and thereby maintain controversy. Additionally, the hierarchies of the profession, and the unwillingness to discard acquired intellectual capital, help to maintain 'old' ideas.

13.2.9 Scientific research programmes

The acknowledgement of the coexistence of rival paradigms requires then a consideration of their relative merits. However, as we have seen, their 'hardcore' elements are not open to testing and thus choosing between research programmes on this basis. Nevertheless, their 'protective belts' are subject to testing, and choice between scientific research programmes (SRPs) can be made on the basis of which is the more progressive.

It seems clear, however, that little applied economics in the areas we have investigated is undertaken within a common SRP. It is thus difficult to choose which research programmes are the more progressive. Indeed in some areas, for example, the discussion of natural monopoly in Chapter 5 perhaps, rival SRPs appear not to exist at all – or at least are not widely communicated within the profession or to students. Chapter 2 illustrated the consequences of adopting alternative SRPs – both Austrian and neoclassical – for the study of enterprise. Both are founded on respective 'hardcores' of ideas which cannot be challenged – the psychology of decision-makers in this case. The controversy over public policy follows directly, with the neoclassical tradition justifying state intervention and the Austrian approach prescribing a clinical, anti-trust stance.

Chapter 9 showed that there is a very wide range of research programmes inside and outside mainstream economics, examining the causes of public expenditure growth: supply-side theories; demand-led explanations; explanations focusing on voters and political parties; and explanations based on the behaviour of bureaucrats. The discussion of public expenditure confirms that it is not fully clear which, if any, of these programmes is degenerative or progressive, and further, that there is little evidence that economists are 'switching' between the different hardcores, a condition necessary if contention is to be diminished.

Chapter 10, in discussing the position of monetarists, suggested that it may indeed be impossible to judge between hardcores, as the criteria upon which judgements are made are themselves theory-dependent. Ultimately theory choice is an ethical matter.

13.2.10 Values and competing perspectives

Chapter 12 on crime argued that economics is not neutral. With reference to the treatment (or lack of it) of crime, in economics, it was argued that economic thought relates to the specific character of the economy and society within which it is embedded and that, as a result, economics has not treated crime as a 'normal' product of capitalist societies. Chapter 9 illustrated the difficulties of separating applied economics from the prevailing political climate and from contested political viewpoints, in the context of the major debate over the appropriate volume, nature and economic effects of public spending. Indeed, different theories of the effects of public spending are often grouped as 'right wing' and 'left wing' – and there are few economists holding one set of political views who accept the economic arguments of the other. Ultimately the choices over public expenditure cannot be reduced to technical economic decisions but are instead a function of political beliefs and ideologies, and thus subjective. How possible, or sensible, is it then for economists to separate consciously such considerations from their purview?

Thus assumptions, theories, methodologies and problem choice in the different paradigms or research programme approaches, it can be argued, are value impregnated; as values cannot be eliminated through falsification, a range of value-laden positions can coexist. Chapter 3, for example, showed how fundamentally different positions can be held on the impact of big business, and Chapter 2 discussed how competing views on enterprise and equilibrium were not resolvable.

A range of schools of thought, as well as the mainstream, contest the terrain of economic debate. They are distinguishable from each other and from the mainstream both by their world view and their methodological position, *inter alia*.

We saw in Chapter 4 on multinational companies that the theoretical perspective which is adopted is a crucial determinant in the evaluation of the impact of MNCs on the balance of payments, employment, technology and industrial relations and that the prerequisites for any serious analysis that goes beyond description is a theoretical framework.

In orthodox approaches the internationalisation of market imperfections provides the theoretical framework whereas in Marxist approaches corporate behaviour is treated as being structured by the dynamics of capitalist economies. Each approach asks different questions and, perhaps more importantly, interprets empirical evidence through a different theoretical lens. For example, one can interpret the employment effects of the spread of MNCs in terms of its positive job generation *or* as a search for docile, compliant labour. One can interpret the technological effects as the beneficent transmission of new technology-generating increased competitiveness and growth *or* it can be interpreted as a mode of increasing dependency, as inappropriate and increasing the control of management over the labour process. The interpretation of *given* effects of MNCs may then be assessed as beneficial *or* detrimental depending on the perspective. As pointed out in Chapter 4, 'How one looks at problems and how one values the various points' is an important influence on the conclusions reached.

Chapter 8 on labour markets examined the mainstream institutional and Marxist perspectives in attempting to understand the operation of labour markets and to explain empirical changes in the market for labour. We saw how their methodologies, 'world views' and foci for study differ. The mainstream focuses on the construction of labour supply, labour demand and adjustment functions, often within an individual framework of free choice, whilst institutionalists as represented by segmented labour market approaches, focus on institutions and how they actively structure labour markets. Marxists, instead, focus on power and conflict in markets and how institutions are in turn structured by the wider forces of accumulation. So, for example, with regard to female participation in the labour force, the underlying conceptualisations are quite different.

13.3 CONCLUSIONS

It is to be hoped that this examination of the myriad reasons for the existence and continuation of controversy in applied economics enables us to understand better why economists disagree; how *some* of them either cannot be resolved or only with considerable difficulty. Empirical research, the *sine qua non* of applied economics, is much more difficult, contentious and problematic than is often considered in many textbooks, articles and courses. Even then it can usually be employed only to resolve disagreements, internal to a particular paradigm/research programme/perspective ('intra' paradigm disputes) rather than those between different paradigms/research programmes/perspectives ('inter' paradigm disputes), for it must be remembered that methodologies vary between such different approaches as do 'world views'. Moreover, economists, and thus economic research, are influenced by the external environment in which they operate, so that the academic profession, and the institutions and organisations for which they work, together with the 'peculiarities' of the particular economics education they have undertaken, will influence their *modus operandi*.

The search then, for an ultimate, objective, universally agreed truth in economics is a chimera. The scope for reducing, let alone eliminating, controversy and disagreement is limited. Indeed one implication of the approach adopted in this book is that 'the problem' is not the existence of controversy but rather the lack of it in communicating the subject matter of economics to generations of students. Economics is a rich, heterogeneous subject which deals with some of the most interesting, complex, fundamental and intractable problems facing humankind. In such a situation it would not only be surprising but misleading and indeed dangerous to give the impression that there is a body of uniquely correct knowledge agreed by all reasonable people, which is readily available to resolve economic problems. The claims of economics need to be both more modest and more realistic. In this light, controversy is not only inevitable but positively desirable. A more pluralist and heterodox approach to the study of economics is required in order to provide its communicants with both a more holistic understanding of the economic world and of the potential of economics in resolving its problems. Only in this way can we be truly 'free to choose' between the array of theory and evidence that confronts us. Such choices, however, it should now be clear, are both difficult to make and provide ample scope for the continuation of controversy in applied economics.

BIBLIOGRAPHY

Aaronovitch, S. and Sawyer, M.C. (1975) *Big Business: Theoretical and empirical aspects of concentration and mergers in the United Kingdom*, London: Macmillan.

Aktar, M. (1983) 'Financial innovations and their implications for monetary policy: an international perspective', *BIS Economic Papers* (Bank for International Settlements), no.9, December.

Akehurst, R., Brazier, J. and Normand, C. (1980) 'Internal markets in the National Health Service', *Centre for Health Economics Discussion Paper 40*, University of York.

Alt, J.E. and Chrystal, K.A. (1983) *Political Economics*, Brighton: Wheatsheaf Books.

Allen, J. (1965) *Report of the Committee of Inquiry into the Impact of Rates on Households*, Cmnd 2582, London: HMSO.

Anderson, R.W. (1976) *The Economics of Crime*, London: Macmillan.

Andic, S. and Veverka, J. (1964) 'The growth of government expenditure in Germany since the unification', *Finanzarchiv*, 23.

André, C. and Delorme, R.J. (1975) 'The long-run growth of public expenditures in France', *Public Finance*, 33.

Arrow, K.J. (1963) 'Uncertainty and the welfare economics of medical care', *American Economic Review*, 53.

Arrow, K.J. (1974) 'Gifts and exchanges', *Philosophy and Public Affairs*, 1.

Artis, M. and Bladen-Hovell, R. (1987) 'The UK monetarist experiment, 1979–1984', *International Review of Applied Economics*, vol.1, no.1, January.

Ashton, D.N. (1986) *Unemployment under Capitalism: The sociology of British and American labour markets*, Brighton: Wheatsheaf Books.

Ashton, D.N. and Maguire, M.J. (1986) 'Young adults in the labour market', *Department of Employment Research Paper*, no.55.

Atkins, R. (1988) *Financial Times*, 13 January.

Atkinson, J. and Meager, N. (1986) 'Is flexibility just a flash in the pan?', *Personnel Management*, September.

Averch, H. and Johnson, L.L. (1962) 'Behaviour of the firm under regulatory constraint', *American Economic Review*, vol.52, December.

Bacon, R. and Eltis, W. (1978) *Britain's Economic Problem: Too few producers*, London: Macmillan.

Bailey, E.E. (1973) *Economic Theory of Regulatory Constraint*, Lexington: D.C. Heath.

Bailey, E.E. and Malone, J.C. (1970) 'Resource allocation and the regulated firm', *Bell Journal of Economics and Management Science*, vol.1.

Bain, A.D. (1981) *The Economics of Financial Systems*, Oxford: Martin Robertson.

Ball, J. (1984) 'Institutional investment', *Lloyds Bank Review*, October.

Ballard, B. (1984) 'Women part-time workers: evidence from the *1980 Women and Employment Survey*', *Employment Gazette*.

Bank of England (1984) *The Development and Operation of Monetary Policy 1960–83*, Oxford: Clarendon Press.

Bank of England (1985) 'The future structure of the gilt-edged market', *Bank of England Quarterly Bulletin*, June.

Bank of England (1986) 'Developments in international banking and capital markets in 1985', *Bank of England Quarterly Bulletin*, March.

Bank for International Settlements (1980) *Annual Report*.

Barber, W.J. (1967) *A History of Economic Thought*, London: Penguin.

Baumol, W.J. (1967) 'Macroeconomics of unbalanced growth: the anatomy of urban crisis', *American Economic Review*, vol.57.

Baumol, W.J., Bailey, E.E. and Willig R.D. (1977) 'Weak invisible hand theorems on the sustainability of multi-product natural monopoly', *American Economic Review*, vol.67, June.

Baumol, W.J., Panzar, J.C. and Willig, R.D. (1982) *Contestable Markets and the Theory of Industry Structure*, New York: Harcourt Brace Jovanovich.

Beckerman, W. (1985) 'How the battle against inflation was really won', *Lloyds Bank Review*, no.155, January.

Beechey, V. and Perkins, T. (1985) 'Conceptualising part-time work', in Roberts, B. *et al.* (eds) *New Approaches to Economic Life*, Manchester: Manchester University Press.

Beesley, M.E. (1981) *Liberalisation of the Use of British Telecommunications Network*, London: Department of Trade and Industry.

Beesley, M.E. and Littlechild, S. (1983) 'Privatisation: principles, problems and priorities', *Lloyds Bank Review*, July.

Bennett, R.J. (1987) 'Local business taxes: theory and practice', *Oxford Review of Economic Policy*, vol.3, no.2.

Berle, A.A. and Means, G.C. (1932) *The Modern Corporation and Private Property*, New York: Commerce Clearing House.

Berrill, K. (1986) 'Regulation in a changing City: bureaucrats and practitioners', *Midland Bank Review*, Summer.

Bevan, T. (1985) 'Banking conglomerates: revolution or evolution?', *Barclays Review*, vol.60, 3 August.

Birch, D.L. (1983) 'The job generation process', in *MIT Study on Neighbourhood and Regional Change*, Cambridge, Mass.: MIT Press.

Birch, D.L. and Maynard, M. (1988) 'The RAWP review: rawping the United Kingdom', *Centre for Health Economics Discussion Paper*, no.19, University of York.

Black, D. (1958) *The Theory of Committees and Elections*, Cambridge: Cambridge University Press.

Black Report – see Townsend and Davidson.

Blaug, M. (1980) *The Methodology of Economics: Or how economists explain*, Cambridge: Cambridge University Press.

Boland, L. (1982) *The Foundations of Economic Method*, London: Allen & Unwin.

Bolton, J.E. (1971) *Small Firms: Report of the Committee of Inquiry on Small Firms*, London: HMSO.
Borrie, G. (1987) 'Merger policy', Paper 6, *Institute of Fiscal Studies*, June.
Bosanquer, N. (1983) *After the New Right*, London: Heinemann.
Bosanquet, A. and Doeringer, P.B. (1973) 'Is there a dual labour marker in Great Britain?', *Economic Journal*, vol.83.
Box, S. (1983) *Power, Crime and Mystification*, London: Tavistock.
Braverman, H. (1974) 'Labour and monopoly capitalism: the degradation of work in the 20th century', *London Monthly Review Press*.
Brech, M. and Sharp, M. (1984) *Inward Investment: Policy options for the United Kingdom*, London: Routledge & Kegan Paul.
Brenner, M.H. (1977) 'Health costs and benefits of economic policy', *International Journal of Health Services*, 7.
Breton, A. (1974) *The Economic Theory of Representative Government*, London: Macmillan.
Broome, J. (1985) 'The economic value of life', *Economica*, 52.
British Business (1986) June.
Brown, C.V. and Jackson, P.M. (1982) *Public Sector Economics*, Oxford: Martin Robertson.
Browning, P. (1983) *Economic Theory and Policy in the UK*, Oxford: Martin Robertson.
Brunner, K. (1983) 'Has monetarism failed?', *Cato Journal*, no.3, Spring.
Buchanan, J.M. (1978) 'From private preferences to public philosophy: the development of public choice', in *The Economics of Politics*, London: Institute of Economic Affairs.
Buchanan, J.M. and Tullock, G. (1962) *The Calculus of Consent: Logical foundations of constitutional democracy*, Chicago: University of Michigan Press.
Buckley, P. (1982) *Management Bibliographies and Reviews*, Bradford: MCB Publications Ltd.
Buckley, P. and Casson, M. (1976) *The Future of the Multinational Enterprise*, London: Macmillan.
Budd, A. and Holly, S. (1986) 'Economic viewpoint: does broad money matter?', *London Business School Economic Outlook*, 1985–89, vol.10, June.
Burden, T. and Campbell, M. (1985) *Capitalism and Public Policy in the UK*, London: Croom Helm.
Burton, J. (1983) *Picking Losers. . . ?*, London: Institute of Economic Affairs.
Burton, J. (1985) *Why No Cuts*?, Hobart Paperback 104, London: Institute of Economic Affairs.
Burrows, P. and Veljanovski, C.G. (1981) *The Economic Approach to Law*, London: Butterworth.
Business Monitor (1981).
Byrne, T. (1984) *Local Government in Britain*, Harmondsworth: Penguin.
Caldwell, B. (1982) *Beyond Positivism: Economic Methodology in the 20th Century*, London: Allen & Unwin.
Campbell, M. (1981) *Capitalism in the UK*, London: Croom Helm.
Campbell, M., Hardy, M., Healey, N., Stead, R. and Sutherland, J. (1987) *Economic Sense: Local Jobs Plans: A national perspective*, Manchester: Centre for Local Economic Strategies.
Cane, A. (1987) 'A Moses to lead Midland out of the wilderness', *Financial Times*, 15 July.

Carter, R.L., Chiplin, B. and Lewis, M.K. (eds) (1986) *Personal Financial Markets*, Oxford: Philip Allan.

Chalmers, A.F. (1982) *What is this Thing Called Science?* Milton Keynes: Open University Press.

Chrystal, K. and Dowd, K. (1986) 'Two arguments for the restriction of international capital flows', *National Westminster Quarterly Review*, November.

Chrystal, K.A. and Alt, J.E. (1979) 'Endogenous government behaviour: Wagner's Law or Gotterdammerung?', in Cook, S.T. and Jackson, P.M. (eds) *Current Issues in Fiscal Policy*, Oxford: Martin Robertson.

Clarke, R. (1985) *Industrial Economics*, Oxford: Basil Blackwell.

Clarke, R. and McGuinness, A. (1987) *The Economics of the Firm*, Oxford: Basil Blackwell.

Cobham, D. (1984) 'Popular political strategies for the UK Economy', *Three Banks Review*, no. 143, September.

Cole, K., Cameron, J. and Edwards, C. (1983) *Why Economists Disagree: The political economy of economics*, Harlow: Longman.

Collard, D. (1978) *Altruism and Economy*, Oxford: Martin Robertson.

Congdon, T. (1982) *Monetary Control in Britain*, London: Macmillan.

Conservative Party (1977) *The Right Approach to the Economy*, London: Conservative Central Office.

Conservative Party (1987) *The Next Moves Forward*, London: Conservative Central Office.

Cooper, M.H. (1975) *Rationing Health Care*, London: Croom Helm.

Cooper, M.H. and Culyer, A.J. (1973) *Health Economics*, Harmondsworth: Penguin Books.

Corina, J. (1972) *Labour Market Economics*, London: Heinemann Educational Books.

Courant, P.N., Gramlich, E.M. and Rubinfield, D.L. (1979) 'Public employee market power and the level of government spending', *American Economic Review*, vol.69.

Cowling, K., Stoneman, P., Cubbin, J., Hall, G., Domberger, S. and Dutton, P. (1980) *Mergers and Economic Performance*, Cambridge: Cambridge University Press.

Cowling, K. and Sugden, R. (1987a) *Transnational Monopoly Capitalism*, Brighton: Wheatsheaf Books.

Cowling, K. and Sugden, R. (1987b) 'Market exchange and the concept of a transnational corporation', *British Review of Economic Issues*, vol.9, no.20.

Crain, W.M. and Tollinson, R.D. (1976) 'State budget sizes and the marginal productivity of government', *Public Choice*, vol.27.

Crawford, P., Fothergill, S. and Monk, E. (1985) *The Effect of Business Rates on the Location of Employment*, University of Cambridge, Department of Local Economy.

Crowley, R.W. (1971) 'Long swings in the role of government: an analysis of wars and government expenditures in Western Europe since the eleventh century', *Public Finance*, vol.26.

Cullis, J.G. and West, P.A. (1979) *The Economics of Health*, Oxford: Martin Robertson.

Culyer, A.J. (1983) (ed.) *Health Service Indicators*, London: Martin Robertson.

Culyer, A.J. (1987) 'The future of health economics in the UK', in Teeling-Smith (ed.) (1987) *Health Economics: Prospects for the future*, London: Croom Helm.

Culyer, A.J. and Cullis, J.G. (1976) 'Some economics of hospital waiting lists', *Journal of Social Policy*, vol.5.
Culyer, A.J. and Simpson, H. (1980) 'Externality models and health: a rueblick over the last twenty years', *Economic Record*, vol.56.
Curran, J. (1986) *Bolton Fifteen Years On*, London: Small Business Research Trust.
Dale, R. (ed.) (1986) *Financial Deregulation*, Cambridge: Woodhead-Faulkner.
Danson, M.W. (1981) 'The industrial structure and labour market segmentation: urban and regional implications', *Regional Studies*, vol.16.
Davidson, K.M. (1985) *Megamergers: Corporate America's billion dollar takeovers*, Cambridge, Mass.: Ballinger.
Davidson, P. (1972) 'Money and the real world', *Economic Journal*, vol.82, no.325, March.
de Jonquieres, G. (1987) 'Japanese industry', *Financial Times*, 7 December.
Demsetz, H. (1968) 'Why regulate utilities?', *Journal of Law and Economics*, vol.11, April.
Department of Employment (1985) *Employment: The challenge for the nation*, Cmnd 9474, London: HMSO.
Department of Employment (1988) 'Ethnic origins and the labour market', *Gazette.*
Department of Trade and Industry (1984) *The British Telecom Licence*, London: HMSO.
Department of Transport (1986) *Economic Regulation of the British Airports Authority PLC*, London: HMSO.
Dex, S. and Perry, S.M. (1984) 'Women's employment changes in the 1970s', *Employment Gazette.*
Dicken, P. (1986) *Global Shifts, Industrial Change in a Turbulent World*, London: Harper & Row.
Doeringer, P.B. and Piore, M.J. (1985) *Internal Labour Markets and Manpower Analysis* (2nd edn), Boston: M.E. Sharpe.
Doig, A. (1984) *Corruption and Misconduct,* London: Penguin.
Domberger, S. and Middleton, J. (1985) 'Franchising in practice: the case of independent television in the UK', *Fiscal Studies*, vol.6, no.1.
Douglas, G. and Miller, J.(1974) *Economic Regulation of Domestic Air Transport: Theory and policy*, Washington, DC: The Brookings Institution.
Dow, S. (1985) *Macroeconomic Thought: Methodological approach*, Oxford: Basil Blackwell.
Downs, A. (1957) *An Economic Theory of Democracy*, Oxford: Oxford University Press.
Doyal, L. and Pennel (1979) *I: The political economy of health*, London: Pluto Press.
Drummond, M.F. (1980) *Principles of Economic Appraisal in Health Care*, Oxford: Oxford Medical Publications.
Drummond, M.F., Ludbrook, A., Lowson, K.V. and Steele, A. (1986) *Studies in Economic Appraisal in Health Care*, vol.2, Oxford: Oxford University Press.
Dudley, K. (1987) 'Taking a gamble on self-regulation', *Banking World*, June.
Duncan, S. and Goodwin, M. (1985) 'Local economic policies: local regeneration or political mobilization', *Local Government Studies*, Nov./Dec.
Dunleavy, P. (1980) 'The political implications of sectoral cleavages and the growth of state employment', *Political Studies*, vol.28.
Dunleavy, P. (1984) 'The limits to local government', in Boddy, M. and Fudge, C. (eds) *Local Socialism*?, London: Macmillan.

Dunleavy, P. and Ward, H. (1981) 'Exogenous voter preferences and parties with state power: some internal problems of economic theories of party competition', *British Journal of Political Science*, vol.11.

Dunning, J.H. (ed.) (1971) *The Multinational Enterprise*, London: Allen & Unwin.

Dunning, J.H. (1976) *US Industry in the UK*, London: Wilton House.

Dunning, J.H. (1979) 'Explaining changing patterns of international production, in defence of economic theory', *Oxford Bulletin of Economics and Statistics*, no.41.

Dunning, J.H. (1981) *International Production and the Multinational Enterprise*, London: Allen & Unwin.

Dunning, J.H. (1985) *Multinational Enterprises, Economic Structure and International Competitiveness*, London: John Wiley.

Dunning, J.H. and Pearce (1981) *The World's Largest Industrial Enterprises*, Farnborough: Gower.

Eatwell, J. (1986) 'Economics seems to have lost its nerve and retreated into a cocoon of intellectual irrelevance', *The Listener*, 11 September.

Edwards, C. (1985) *The Fragmented World: Competing perspectives on trade, money and crisis*, London: Methuen.

Eichner, A. (ed.) (1983) *Why Economics is not yet a Science*, London: Macmillan.

Enderwick, P. (1982) *Labour and the Theory of the Multinational Enterprise: Organisation of the firm and ownership of subsidiaries*, Harlow: Longman.

Enthoven, A.C. (1985) *Reflections on the Management of the National Health Service*, London: Nuffield Provincial Hospital Trust.

Feldstein, M. (1967) *Economic Analysis for Health Service Efficiency*, Amsterdam, North Holland: Van Nostrand.

Feyerabend, P. (1975) *Against Method: Outline of an anarchist theory of knowledge*, London: New Left Books.

Fforde, J. (1982) 'Setting monetary objectives', *Federal Reserve Bank of New York*, Conference Paper, May; reprinted in Bank of England (1984), *op. cit.*

Fforde, J. (1983) 'Competition, innovation and regulation in British banking', *Bank of England Quarterly Bulletin,* September.

Field, F. (1983) 'Fraud and scrounging in the welfare state', in Coates, D. and Johnson, G. (eds) *Socialist Arguments*, Chapter 8, Oxford: Martin Robertson.

Field, F., Meacher, M. and Pond, C. (1977) *To Him Who Hath*, London: Penguin.

Department of Trade and Industry (1985) *Financial Services in the UK: A new framework for investor protection*, Cmnd 9432, London: HMSO.

Fine, B. (1975) *Marx's Capital*, London: Macmillan.

Fine, B. (1979) 'World economic issues and inflation', in Green, F. and Nore, P. (eds) *Issues in Political Economy*, London: Macmillan.

Fine, B. (1980) *Economic Theory and Ideology*, London: Edward Arnold.

Fine, B. and Harris, L. (1985) *The Peculiarities of the British Economy*, London: Lawrence & Wishart.

Finsinger, J., Hammond, E. and Tapp, J. (1985) *Insurance: Competition or regulation*?, London: Institute for Fiscal Studies.

Flanders, A. (1964) *The Fawley Productivity Agreements*, London: Faber & Faber.

Forsyth, D. (1972) *US Investment in Scotland*, New York: Preager.

Foster, C.D., Jackson, R. and Perlman, M. (1980) *Local Government Finance in a Unitary State*, London: Allen & Unwin.

Freeman, C. (1974) *The Economics of Industrial Innovation*, Harmondsworth: Penguin.

Friedman M. (1953) *Essays in Positive Economics*, Chicago: University of Chicago Press.

Friedman, M. (1962) *Capitalism and Freedom*, Chicago: University of Chicago Press.

Friedman, M. (1968) 'The role of monetary policy', *American Economic Review*, vol.58, no.1, March.

Friedman, M. (1980) in Treasury and Civil Service Committee (1980), *op. cit.*

Friedman, M. and Schwartz, A. (1963) *The Monetary History of the USA*, Washington: National Bureau of Economic Research.

Galbraith, J. (1980) *The Observer*, 31 August.

Gallagher, C.G. and Stewart, H. (1984) 'Jobs and the business life cycle in the UK', in *Research Report No.2*, Dept of Industrial Management, University of Newcastle.

Gandhi, V.P. (1971) 'Wagner's law of public expenditure: do recent cross-section studies confirm it?', *Public Finance*, vol.26.

Ganti, S. and Kolluri, B.R. (1979) 'Wagner's Law of public expenditure: do recent cross-section studies confirm it?', *Public Finance*, vol.34.

Gapper, J. (1988) 'Livingstone looks to the young and skilled', *Financial Times*, 18 January.

Gennard, J. (1972) *Multinational Corporations and British Labour: A review of attitudes and responses*, New York: British–North American Committee.

George, K.D. and Storey, J. (1985) 'Manual workers, good jobs and structured internal labour markets', *British Journal of Industrial Relations*, vol.23.

Godfrey, C. (1986) 'Factors influencing the consumption of alcohol and tobacco: a review of demand models', *Centre of Health Economics Discussion Paper*, University of York.

Godfrey, C. and Powell, M. (1987) 'The confusion of economic costs in studies of alcohol and tobacco', *Proceedings of the International Conference on Economic Costs of Alcohol, Tobacco and Drug Use*, December, Rotterdam: Erasmus University.

Goffman, I.J. and Mahar, D.J. (1971) 'The growth of public expenditures in developing nations: six Caribbean countries 1940–65', *Public Finance*, vol.26.

Goldberg, W.H. (1983) *Mergers: Motives, modes, methods*, Science Centre Berlin, International Institute of Management: Gower.

Goodhard, C.A.E. (1987) 'The economics of "Big Bang"', *Midland Bank Review*, Summer.

Gort, M. (1969) 'An economic disturbance theory of mergers', *Quarterly Journal of Economics*, 83.

Gough, I. and Hogarty, T.F. (1970) 'New evidence on mergers', *Journal of Law and Economics*.

Gough, I. (1981) *The Political Economy of the Welfare State*, London: Macmillan.

Gower, J. (1984) *Review of Investor Protection – The Gower Report*, Cmnd 9125, London: HMSO.

Green, D.G. (1985) 'Which doctor? a critical analysis of the professional barriers to competition on health care', *Research Monograph 40*, London: Institute of Economic Affairs.

Green, D.G. (1986) *Challenge to the NHS*, Hobart Paperback 23, London: Institute for Economic Affairs.

Green, D.G. (1987) *The New Right*, Brighton: Wheatsheaf Books.

Green, F. and Nore, P. (eds) (1979) *Issues in Political Economy: A critical approach*, London: Macmillan.

Green Paper (1978) *A Review of Monopolies and Mergers Policy*, Cmnd 7198, London: HMSO.

Grice, J. and Bennett, A. (1981) *The Demand for Sterling M3 and Other Aggregates in the United Kingdom*, HM Treasury Working Paper, no.20, London: HMSO.

Grossman, M. (1972) 'On the concept of health capital and demand for health', *Journal of Political Economy*, vol.80.

Hamill, J. (1984) 'Multinational corporations and industrial relations in the UK', *Employee Relations*, vol.6, no.5.

Hamilton, A. (1986) *The Financial Revolution*, New York: Penguin.

Hammond, E.M., Helm, D.R. and Thompson, D.J. (1985) 'British Gas: options for privatisation', *Fiscal Studies*, vol.6, no.4.

Hammond, E.M., Helm, D.R. and Thompson, D.J. (1986) Competition in electricity supply: has the Energy Act failed?', *Fiscal Studies*, vol.7, no.1.

Hannah, L. (1974) 'Mergers in British manufacturing industry 1890–1918, *Oxford Economic Papers*, vol.26.

Hannah, L. (1976) *The Rise of the Corporate Economy*, London: Methuen.

Hannah, L. and Kay, J.A. (1977) *Concentration in Modern Industry*, London: Macmillan.

Hanson, D. (1987) 'A statutory system of control?', *Banking World*, June.

Harrison, J. (1978) *Marxist Economics for Socialists*, London: Pluto.

Hartley, K. and Huby, M. (1985) 'Contracting-out in health and local authorities: prospects, progress and pitfalls', *Public Money*, September.

Hasluck, C. (1987) *Urban Unemployment*, Harlow: Longman.

Hayek, F. (1933) 'The trend of economic thinking', *Economica*, May.

Hayek, F. (1962) *The Road to Serfdom*, London: Routledge & Kegan Paul.

Heald, D. (1984) *Public Expenditure*, Oxford, Martin Robertson.

Heald, D. (1987) *Public Expenditure: Its defence and reform*, Oxford: Basil Blackwell.

Heathfield, D. and Hartropp, A. (1983) 'What economists do', *Economics*, Summer.

Heertje, A., Allen, M. and Cohen, H. (1982) *The Black Economy*, London: Pan.

Henman, A., Lewis, R. and Malyon, T. (1985) *Big Deal: The politics of the illicit drugs business*, London: Pluto.

Hepworth, N.P. (1984) *The Finance of Local Government* (7th edn), London: Allen & Unwin.

Herzel, L. and Katz, L. 'Insider trading: who loses?', *Lloyds Bank Review*, 165.

Hindley, B. (1972) 'Recent theory and evidence on corporate merger', in Cowling, K. (ed.) *Market Structure and Corporate Behaviour*, London: Gray-Mills.

HMSO (1944) *A National Health Service,* Cmnd 6502, London: HMSO.

HMSO (1986) *Paying for Local Government*, Green Paper, Cmnd 9714, London: HMSO.

HM Treasury (1980) *Green Paper on Monetary Control*, March, London: HMSO.

HM Treasury (1985) *The Relationship between Employment and Wages*, London: HMSO.

HM Treasury (1986) *The Government's Expenditure Plans 1986/87 to 1988/89*, vol.2, Cmnd 9702, London: HMSO.

HM Treasury (1987) *The Government's Expenditure Plans 1987/88 to 1989/90,* vol.2 Cmnd 56–11, London: HMSO.

Hood, N. and Young, S. (1976) 'US investment in Scotland: aspects of the branch factory syndrome', *SJPE* 23.

Hood, N. and Young, S. (1979) *The Economics of the Multinational Enterprise*, Harlow: Longman.

Hood, N. and Young, S. (1982) *Multinationals in Retreat: The Scottish experience*, Edinburgh: Edinburgh University Press.

Hook, E. (1962) 'The expansion of the public sector: study of the development of public civilian expenditure in Sweden during the years 1913–1958', *Public Finance*, vol.17.

Houston, T. and Dunning, J. (1976) *UK Industry Abroad*, London: The Financial Times Ltd.

Howcroft, J.B. and Lavis, J. (1986) *Retail Banking*, Oxford: Basil Blackwell.

Hughes, A. and Singh, A. (1980) 'Mergers, concentration and competition in advanced capitalist economies', in Mueller, D.C. (ed.) *The Determinants and Effects of Mergers*, Cambridge: Oelgeschlager, Gunn and Hain.

Hughes, G.A. (1987) 'Fiscal federalism in the UK', *Oxford Review of Economic Policy*, vol.3, no.2.

Hughes, M. (1987) 'Pitfalls in the financial rulebook', *The Guardian*, 1 November.

Hughes, P.R. (1982) 'Flaws on and off the Unemployment Register', *Department of Employment Gazette*.

Hughes, P.R. and Hutchinson, G. (1986) 'The changing picture of male unemployment in Great Britain 1972–1981', *Oxford Bulletin of Economics and Statistics*, vol.48, no.4.

Hutchinson, T.W. (1978) *On Revolutions and Progress in Economic Knowledge*, Cambridge: Cambridge University Press.

Hutton, W. (1986) *The Revolution That Never Was: An assessment of Keynesian economics*, Harlow: Longman.

Hymer, S. (1972) 'The multinational corporation and the law of uneven development', in Bhagwati, J. (ed.) *Economic World Order from the 1970s to the 1990s*, New York: Collier Macmillan; reprinted in Radice, H. (ed.) (1975) *International Firms and Modern Imperialism*, Harmondsworth: Penguin.

Ignatieff, M. (1978) *A Just Measure of Pain*, London: Macmillan.

Ingham, D.H.A. (1987) 'Change in The Stock Exchange and regulation of the City', *Bank of England Quarterly Bulletin*, February.

Inland Revenue Statistics (1985, 1986) London: HMSO.

International Labour Organisation (1976) *Multinationals in Western Europe: The industrial relations experience*, Geneva: ILO.

Jack, R.B. (1986) 'A review of legal problems', in Dale, R. (ed.) *Financial Regulation*, Cambridge: Woodhead-Faulkner.

Jackson, P.D. (1985) 'Changes in The Stock Exchange and regulation in the City', *Bank of England Quarterly Bulletin*, December.

Jackson, P.M. (1980) 'The public expenditure cuts: rationale and consequences', *Fiscal Studies*, 1.

Johnson, C. (1986) 'Securitisation of credit', *Lloyds Bank Economic Bulletin*, vol.91, July.

Jones, G.W. and Stewart, J.D. (1983) *The Case for Local Government*, London: Allen & Unwin.

Jones-Lee, M.W. (ed.) (1982) *The Value of Life and Safety*, Amsterdam, North Holland: Van Nostrand.

Joshi, H. (1986) 'Participation in paid work: evidence from the Women and Employment Survey', in Blundell, R. and Walker, I. (eds) *Unemployment, Search and Labour Supply*, Cambridge: Cambridge University Press.

Joshi, H. and Owen, S. (1985) 'Does elastic retract? The effect of recession on women's labour force participation', *Discussion Paper*, no.64, London: Centre for Economic Policy Research.

Joskow, P. and Noll, P. (1981) 'Regulation in theory and practice: an overview', in Fromm, G. (ed.) *Studies in Public Utility Regulation*, Cambridge, Mass.: MIT Press.

Kahn, A.E. (1983) 'Utility regulation revisited', in Danielson, A.L. and Kamerschen, D.R. (ed.) *Current Issues in Public Utility Economics*, Lexington, Mass.: D.C. Heath.

Kaldor, N. (1980) in Treasury and Civil Service Committee (1980), *op. cit.*

Karran, T.J. (1984) 'The local government workforce: public sector paragon or private sector parasite', *Local Government Studies*, vol.10.

Katouzian, H. (1980) *Ideology and Method in Economics*, London: Macmillan.

Katouzian, H., Mayes, C. and Thompson, D. (1986) *Privatisation and Regulation: The UK experience*, Oxford: Oxford University Press.

Katouzian, H. and Thompson, D.J (1986) 'Privatisation: a policy in search of a rationale', *Economic Journal*, vol.96, March.

Keat, R. and Urry, J. (1982) *Social Theory as Science*, London: Routledge & Kegan Paul.

Keegan, W. (1984) *Mrs Thatcher's Economic Experiment*, Harmondsworth: Penguin.

Keynes, J. (1936) *The General Theory of Employment, Interest and Money*, London: Macmillan.

Keynes, J. (1937) 'The general theory of employment', *Quarterly Journal of Economics*, vol.51.

Khun, T. (1970) *The Structure of Scientific Revolutions*, Chicago: University of Chicago Press.

Killick, T. (1982) 'Employment in foreign-owned manufacturing plants', *British Business*, 26 November.

Kilpatrick, A. and Lawson, T. (1986) 'On the nature of industrial decline in the UK', in Coates, D. and Hillard, J. (eds) *The Economic Decline of Modern Britain*, Brighton: Wheatsheaf Books.

Kinnersley, P. (1979) *The Hazards of Work*, London: Pluto.

Kirzner, I. (1973) *Competition and Entrepreneurship*, Chicago: University of Chicago Press.

Kirzner, I. (1979) *Perception, Opportunity and Profit*, Chicago: University of Chicago Press.

Kuehn, D. (1975) *Takeovers and the Theory of the Firm*, London: Macmillan.

Labour Party (1987) *Britain Will Win*, London: Labour Party.

Laidler, D. (1981) 'Monetarism: an interpretation and an assessment', *Economic Journal*, vol.91, no.361.

Laidler, D. (1984) 'The "Buffer Stock" notion in monetary economics', *Economic Journal Supplement Conference Papers*, vol.94.

Latsis, S. (ed.) (1976) *Method and Appraisal in Economics*, Cambridge: Cambridge University Press.

Layard, R. and Nickell S. (1985) 'The causes of British unemployment', *National Institute Economic Review*.

Layfield, F. (1976) *Local Government Finance*, Cmnd 6453, London: HMSO.

Lees, D.S. (1961) *Health Through Choice*, London: Institute of Economic Affairs.

Lees, D.S. (1967) 'Efficiency in government spending: social services, health', *Public Finance*, vol.22.

Le Grand, J. (1978) 'The distribution of public expenditure: the case of health care', *Economica*, vol.45.

Le Grand, J. and Rabin, M. (1986) 'Trends in British health inequality 1931–1983', in Culyer, A. and Johnson, B. (eds) *Public and Private Health Services: Complementarities and Conflicts*, Oxford: Basil Blackwell.

Lessnoff, M. (1976) *The Structure of Social Science*, London: Allen & Unwin.

Lever, W. and Mather, F. (1986) 'The changing structure of business and employment in the conurbation', in Lever, W. and Moore, C. (eds) *The City in Transition: Policies and agencies for the economic regeneration of Clydeside*, Oxford: Clarendon Press.

Levi, M. (1981) *Phantom Capitalists*, London: Heinemann.

Lewis, M.K. and Davis, K.T. (1987) *Domestic and International Banking*, Oxford: Philip Allan.

Lichtenheim, P. (1983) *An Introduction to Post-Keynesian Theories of Value and Price*, London: Macmillan.

Lindahl, E. (1919) 'Just taxation: a positive solution' reprinted in Peacock, A. and Musgrave, R.J. (eds) *Classics in the Theory of Public Finance*, New York: St Martin's Press, 1958.

Lipsey, R.G. (1979) *An Introduction to Positive Economics* (5th edn), London: Weidenfeld & Nicolson.

Littlechild, S.C. (1983) *Regulation of British Telecommunications' Profitability*, London: Department of Trade and Industry.

Llewellyn, D.T. (1985) 'The changing structure of the UK financial system', *Three Banks Review*, vol.145, March.

Llewellyn, D.T. (1987) 'Competition and the regulatory mix', *National Westminster Quarterly Review*, August.

Lloyd, T. (1986) *Dinosaur and Co.*, Harmondsworth: Penguin.

Loasby, B. (1982) 'The entrepreneur in economic theory', *Scottish Journal of Political Economy*.

Lomax, D. (1987) 'Risk asset ratios: a new departure in supervisory policy', *National Westminster Quarterly Review*, August.

Lynch, L.M. and Richardson, R. (1982) 'Unemployment of young workers in Britain', *British Journal of Industrial Relations*, vol.20.

McDermott, P.J. (1979) 'Multinational manufacturing firms and regional development: external control in Scottish electronics industry', *Scottish Journal of Political Economy*, vol.26, no.3.

McGuire, A., Henderson, J. and Mooney G. (1988) *The Economics of Health Care: An Introductory Text*, London: International Library of Economics.

McIntosh, M. (1975) *The Organisation of Crime*, London: Macmillan.

McMahon, K. (1987) 'Market forces and official responses', *Midland Bank Review*, Spring.

Macpherson, C.B. (1961) 'Market concepts in political theory', *Canadian Journal of Economics and Political Theory*, vol.27.

Machlup, F. (1978) *Methodology of Economics and Other Social Sciences*, New York: Academic Press.

Main, B.G.M. (1981) 'The length of employment and unemployment in Great Britain', *Scottish Journal of Political Economy*, vol.28, no.2.

Mann, A.J. (1980) 'Wagner's Law: an econometric test for Mexico, 1925–1976', *National Tax Journal*, vol.33.

Manwaring, T. (1984) 'The extended internal labour market', *Cambridge Journal of Economics*, vol.8.

Margolis, H. (1982) *Selfishness, Altruism and Rationality*, Cambridge: Cambridge University Press.

Marr, W.L. (1974) 'The expending role of government and wars: a further elaboration', *Public Finance*, vol.29.

Marris, R. (1964) *Economic Theory of Managerial Capitalism*, London: Macmillan.
Mars, G. (1982) *Cheats at Work*, London: Allen & Unwin.
Marsden, D. (1986) *The End of Economic Man? Custom and competition in labour markets*, Brighton: Wheatsheaf Books.
Martin, J. and Roberts, C. (1984) *Women and Employment Survey*, London: HMSO.
Marx, K. (1970a) *Capital*, vol.I, London: Lawrence & Wishart.
Marx, K. (1970b) *The German Ideology*, London: Lawrence & Wishart.
Massey, D. and Meegan, R. (1982) *The Anatomy of Job Loss: The how, why and where of employment decline*, London: Methuen.
Matthews, R. and Reddaway, W. (1980) 'Can Mrs Thatcher do it?', *Midland Bank Review*, Autumn.
Maule, C.J (1986) 'A note on merger and the business cycle', *Journal of Industrial Economics*, vol.16.
Mayer, T. (1978) *The Structure of Monetarism*, New York: W.W. Norton.
Maynard, A. and Ludbrook, A. (1981) 'Thirty years of fruitless endeavour', in van der Gaag, J. and Perlman, M. (eds) *Health, Economics and Health Economics*, Amsterdam, North Holland: Van Nostrand.
Metcalfe, D. (1986) 'Employment subsidies and redundancies', in Blundell, R. and Walker I. (eds) *Unemployment, Search and Labour Supply*, Cambridge: Cambridge University Press.
Metzler, A. and Richard, S.F. (1978) 'Why government grows (and grows) in a democracy', *Public Interest*, vol.52.
Miller, M. (1982) 'The medium term financial strategy: an experiment in co-ordinating monetary and fiscal policy', *Fiscal Studies*, vol.3.
Millward, R. (1986) 'The emergence of gas and water monopolies in 19th century Britain: why public ownership?', *Salford Papers in Economics*, 86–4.
Millward, R. and Parker, D. (1983) 'Public and private enterprise: comparative behaviour and relative efficiency', in Millward, R., Parker, D., Rosenthal, L., Summer, M. and Topham, N., *Public Sector Economics*, London: Longman.
Minford, P. (1981) 'The economic outlook', *Liverpool Occasional Paper*, no.1.
Minford, P. (1985) *Unemployment: Cause and cure* (2nd edn), Oxford: Basil Blackwell.
Minford, P. *et al.* (1987) *The Housing Morass: Regulation, immobility and unemployment*, Hobart Paperback 25, London: Institute of Economic Affairs.
Mishan, E.J. (1971) 'Evaluation of life and limb: a theoretical approach', *Journal of Political Economy*, vol.79.
Modigliani, F. (1977) 'The monetarist controversy or should we forsake stabilisation policies?', *American Economic Review*, vol.67, no.1.
Mooney, G.H. (1986) *Economics, Medicine and Health Care*, Brighton: Wheatsheaf Books.
Moran, K. (1986) 'Corporatism resurrected: economic interests and institutional change in the City of London', paper presented to the Annual Conference of the UK Political Studies Association University of Nottingham, 8–10 April.
Morris, R. (1964) *The Economic Theory of Managerial Capitalism*, London: Macmillan.
Mueller, D.C. (1969) 'A theory of conglomerate mergers', *Quarterly Journal of Economics*, vol.8.
Mueller, D.C. (ed.) (1980) *The Determinants and Effects of Mergers*, Cambridge, Mass.: Oelgeschlager, Gunn and Hain.
Myrdal, G. (1958) *Value in Social Theory*, London: Allen & Unwin.
Navarro, M. (1976) *Medicine Under Capitalism*, London: Croom Helm.
Nelson, S. (1959) *Merger Movements in American Industry, 1895–1956*, National

Bureau of Economic Research, General Series 66, Princeton: Princeton University Press.
Neuberger, H. (1985) 'Why is unemployment so high?', *National Westminster Bank Quarterly Review*, May.
Newbould, G. (1970) *Management and Merger Activity*, Liverpool: Guthstead.
Newton, K. and Karran, T.J. (1985) *The Politics of Local Expenditure*, London: Macmillan.
Nickell, S.J. (1980) 'A picture of male unemployment in Britain', *Economic Journal*, vol.90, no.360.
Niskanen, W.A. (1971) *Bureaucracy and Representative Government*, Chicago: University of Chicago Press.
Niskanen, W.A. (1973) *Bureaucracy: Servant or master?*, London, Institute of Economic Affairs.
Noll, R. and Fiorina, M. (1978) 'Voters, bureaucrats and legislators', *Journal of Public Policy*, vol.7.
O'Connor, J. (1973) *The Fiscal Crisis of the State*, New York: St Martin's Press.
OECD (1987) *Financing and Delivering Health Care*, Paris: OECD.
Olson, M. (1965) *The Logic of Collective Action*, Cambridge, Mass.: Harvard University Press.
Owen, D.W. *et al.* (1984) '"Job shortfalls" in British local labour market: a classification of labour supply and demand trends, 1971–81', *Regional Studies*, vol.18, no.6.
Pagano, M. and Rodgers, P. (1987) 'Moving horizontally to the second "Big Bang"', *The Guardian*, 16 July.
Panzer, J.K.C. and Willig, R.D. (1981) 'Economies of scope', *American Economic Review, Papers and Proceedings*, vol.71, May.
Panic, M. and Joyce (1980) 'UK manufacturing industry international integration and trade performance', *Bank of England Quarterly Bulletin*, March.
Pathirane, L. and Blades, D.W. (1982) 'Defining and measuring the public sector', *Review of Income and Wealth*, 28.
Pauly, M.V. (1968) 'The economics of motal hazard', Comment in *American Economic Review*.
Pauly, M.V. (1980) *Doctors and Their Workshops: Economic models and physical behaviour*, Chicago: University of Chicago Press.
Peacock, A. (1978) 'The economics of bureaucracy: an inside view' in *The Economics of Politics*, London: Institute for Economic Affairs.
Peacock, A. and Wiseman, J. (1967) *The Growth of Public Expenditure in the UK* (2nd edn), Oxford: Oxford University Press.
Peasnall, K.V. and Ward, C. (1985) *British Financial Markets and Institutions*, Englewood Cliffs, NJ: Prentice Hall.
Peel, Q. and Nicol, A. (1986) 'Symbolic step towards deregulation', *Financial Times*, 19 November.
Peltzman, S. (1976) 'Toward a more general theory of regulation', *Journal of Economics of Law*, vol.19.
Penrose, E.T. (1959) *The Theory of the Growth of the Firm*, Oxford: Basil Blackwell.
Pheby, J. (1988) *Methodology and Economics: A critical introduction*, London: Macmillan.
Piore, M.J. (1983) 'Labour market segmentation: to what paradigm does it belong?', *American Economic Association Proceedings*, pp.249–53.
Pliatzky, L. (1982) *Getting and Spending*, Oxford: Basil Blackwell.
Plowden, W. (1961) *Control of Public Expenditure*, Cmnd 1432, London: HMSO.
Podolski, T. (1987) 'Financial change and monetary policy in the 1990s',

Conference Paper, *Economics Association Annual Conference*, April; reprinted in *Economics*, vol.xxiv, part 4, no.100, Winter.

Pointon, G. (1986) 'Bill could mean ruin for small brokers', *Financial Weekly*, 14 August.

Posner, R.A. (1974) 'Theories of economic regulation', *Bell Journal of Economic and Management Science*, vol.5.

Prais, S.J. (1976) *The Evolution of Giant Firms in Britain*, Cambridge: Cambridge University Press.

Prais, S.J. (1981) 'The contribution of mergers to industrial concentration: what we do know?', *Journal of Industrial Economics*, vol.29.

Pratten, C. (1982) 'Mrs Thatcher's economic experiment', *Lloyds Bank Review*, January.

Price, K. (1986) 'The global financial village', Special Report, *Banking World*, Autumn.

Primeaux, W.J. (1977) 'An assessment of x-efficiency gained through competition', *Review of Economics and Statistics*, vol.59.

Purvis, D. (1980) 'Monetarism: a review', *Canadian Economic Review*, vol.13, no.1.

Radcliffe Committee (1959) *Committee on the Working of the Monetary System*, Cmnd 827, May, London: HMSO.

Rapaport, C. (1986) 'Japanese investment in Europe', *Financial Times*, 13 November.

Reading, B. (1987) 'How current policy paved the way for crash', *The Guardian*, 15 November.

Reddaway, W. (1982) 'The government's economic policy: an appraisal', *Three Banks Review*, no.136, December.

Redwood, J. (1986) 'How to protect the investor', *Lloyds Bank Review*, April.

Reid, S. (1968) *Mergers, Managers and the Economy*, New York: McGraw Hill.

Report of the Committee of Inquiry into Telecommunications Services in Australia (1982) vol.1.

Report of the Committee on the Financing of the BBC (1986) Peacock Committee, London: HMSO.

Report of Her Majesty's Customs and Excise (1986) London: HMSO.

Rice, P.G. (1986) 'Juvenile unemployment, relative wages and Social Security in GB', *Economic Journal*, vol.96.

Riddell, P. (1983) *The Thatcher Government*, Oxford: Martin Robertson.

Riley, B. (1986) 'Okay till the bears return: the City revolution', *Financial Times*, 27 October.

Robbins, L. (1935) *An Essay on the Nature and Significance of Economic Science*, London: Macmillan.

Robinson, R. (1988) 'Efficiency and the NHS: a case for internal markets', *Health Unit Paper*, no.2, London: Institute for Economic Affairs.

Rose, H. (1986) '"Big Bang": how far will the shock waves go?', *Barclays Bank Review*, vol.61, 4 November.

Rose, R. (1984) *Understanding Big Government*, London: Sage.

Rose, R. and Karran, T.J. (1984) 'Inertia or incrementalism? A long-term view of the growth of government', in Groth, A.J. and Wade, L.L. (eds) *Comparative Resource Allocation: Politics, performance and policy priorities*, London: Sage.

Rose, R. and Karran, T.J. (1987) *Taxation by Political Inertia*, London, Allen & Unwin.

Rosser, R. (1983) 'Issues of measurement in the design of health indicators: a review', in Culyer, A.J. (ed.) *Health Indicators*, Oxford: Martin Robertson.

Rostow, W.W. (1971) *Politics and the Stages of Growth*, Cambridge: Cambridge University Press.

Routh, G. (1986) *Unemployment: Economic Perspectives*, London: Macmillan.

Rowthorn, R. (1980) *Capitalism, Conflict and Inflation*, London: Lawrence & Wishart.

Russell, L. (1986) *Is Prevention Better Than Cure?*, Washington, DC: The Brookings Institute.

Rybczynski, T.M. (1985) 'Financial systems, risk and public policy', *Royal Bank of Scotland Review*, vol.148, December.

Sandford, C. (1984) *Economics of Public Finance*, Oxford: Pergamon Press.

Sapsford, D. (1981) *Labour Market Economics*, London: Allen & Unwin.

Saunders, P. (1985) 'Public expenditure and economic performance in the OECD countries', *Journal of Public Policy*, vol.5.

Sawyer, M.C. (1985) *The Economics of Industries and Firms* (2nd edn), London: Croom Helm.

Schumpeter, J. (1952) *Capitalism, Socialism and Democracy* (4th edn), London: Allen & Unwin.

Schumpeter, J. (1954) *History of Economic Analysis*, Oxford: Oxford University Press.

Schur, E.M. (1965) *Crimes Without Victims*, Englewood Cliffs, NJ: Prentice Hall.

Scouller, J. (1987) 'The United Kingdom boom in perspective', *National Westminster Bank Quarterly Review*, May.

Seckler, H. (1978) *Thorsten Veblen and the Institutionalists*, London: Macmillan.

Sen, A. (1984) 'Description as choice', *Oxford Economic Papers*.

Sen, A. and Williams, B. (eds) (1982) *Utilitarianism and Beyond*, Cambridge: Cambridge University Press.

Shand, A. (1984) *The Capitalist Alternative*, Brighton, Wheatsheaf Books.

Sharkey, W.W. (1982) *The Theory of Natural Monopoly*, Cambridge: Cambridge University Press.

Sharpe, T. (1984) 'Privatisation, regulation and competition', *Fiscal Studies*, vol.5.

Sinfield, A. (1981) 'Unemployment in an unequal society', in Shower, B. and Sinfield A. (eds) *The Workless State*, Oxford: Martin Robertson.

Smith, D. (1987) *The Rise and Fall of Monetarism: The theory and politics of an economic experiment*, Harmondsworth: Penguin.

Smith, S. and Squire, D. (1987) *Local Taxes and Local Government*, London: Institute of Fiscal Studies.

Solomon, R.F. and Ingham, K.P.D. (1977) 'Discriminating between multinational subsidiaries and indigenous companies: a comparative analysis of the British mechanical engineering industry', *Oxford Bulletin of Economics and Statistics*, vol.39, no.2.

Spann, R.M. (1977) 'Rates of productivity change and the growth of state and local government expenditures', in Bocherding, T.E. (ed.) *Budgets and Bureaucrats: The sources of government growth*, Boston: Duke University Press.

Starkie, D.N.M. and Thompson, D.J. (1985) 'The Airport Policy White Paper: privatisation and regulation', *Fiscal Studies*, vol.6, no.4.

Stedman-Jones, G. (1971) *Outcast London*, London: Penguin.

Stern, J. (1983) 'The relationship between unemployment, morbidity and mortality in Britain', *Population Studies*, vol.37.

Steuer, M.D. and Gerrard, J. (1971) 'Industrial relations, labour disputes and labour utilization in foreign owned firms in the United Kingdom', in Dunning, J.H. (ed.) *The Multinational Enterprise*, London: Allen & Unwin.

Stigler, G. (1971) 'The regularities of regulation', in Dale, R. (ed.) *Financial Regulation*, Cambridge: Woodhead-Faulkner, 1986.

Stigler, G. (1971) 'The theory of economic regulation', *Bell Journal of Economics and Management Science*, vol.1.

Stopford, J.H. and Turner, L. (1986) *Britain and the Multinationals*, Chichester: John Wiley.

Storey, D.J. and Johnson, S. (1987) *Job Generation and Labour Market Change*, London: Macmillan.

Storey, D.J., Keasey, K., Watson, R. and Wynarcyk, P. (1987) *The Performance of Small Firms*, London: Croom Helm.

Tarchys, D. (1975) 'The growth of public expenditure: nine models of explanation', *Scandinavian Political Studies*, 10.

Taylor, M. (1987) 'Financial innovation, inflation and the stability of the demand for broad money in the United Kingdom', *Bulletin of Economic Research*, vol.39, no.3.

Teeling-Smith, G. (ed.) (1987) *Measuring the Social Benefits of Medicine*, London: Office of Health Economics.

Teeling-Smith, G. (1984) *A New NHS Act for 1996?*, London, Office of Health Economics.

Teeling-Smith, G. (ed.) (1987) *Health Economics: Prospects for the future*, London: Croom Helm.

Terry, N. (1985) ' "The big bank" at The Stock Exchange', *Lloyds Bank Review*, vol.148, April.

Thomas, L. (1977) 'On the science and technology of medicine', in Knowles, J.H. (ed.) *Doing Better and Feeling Worse: Health in the United States*, New York: W.W. Norton and Co.

Thomas W.A. (1986) *The Big Bank*, Oxford, Philip Allan.

Thompson, P. (1983) *The Nature of Work*, London: Macmillan.

Tiebout, C. (1956) 'A pure theory of local expenditure', *Journal of Political Economy*, vol.64, no.5.

Titmus, R.M. (1982) *The Gift Relationship*, London: Allen & Unwin.

Tobin, J. (1981) in Treasury and Civil Service Committee (1981b), *op. cit.*

Tobin, J. (1984) 'On the efficiency of the financial system', *Lloyds Bank Review*, vol.153, July.

Torrence, G.W. (1986) 'Measurement of health utilities for economic appraisal', *Journal of Health Economics*, vol.5.

Townsend, A. (1986) 'Spatial aspects of the growth of part-time employment in Britain', *Regional Studies*, vol.20, no.4.

Townsend, A. and Davidson, M. (eds) (1988) *Inequalities in Health: The Black Report*, Harmondsworth: Penguin.

Treasury, HM (1980) *Monetary Control*, March, London: HMSO.

Treasury and Civil Service Committee (1980) *Memoranda on Monetary Policy*, HC–720, Session 1979–80, July, London: HMSO.

Treasury and Civil Service Committee (1981a) *Report*, HC 163–I, Session 1980–81, February, London: HMSO.

Treasury and Civil Service Committee (1981b) *Minutes of Evidence*, HC 163–II, Session 1980–81, February, London: HMSO.

Trippier, D. (1984) 'Major share of job generation is by small firms', *British Business*, 13 July.

Tullock, G. (1959) 'Problems of majority voting', *Journal of Political Economy* vol.67.

Tullock, G. (1965) *The Politics of Bureaucracy*, Washington: Public Affairs Books.

US Tariff Commission (1973) *Implication of Multinational Firms for World Trade and Investment*, Report of the Committee of Finance of the US Senate, Washington: US government printer.

Utton, M.A. (1979) *Diversification and Competition*, Cambridge: Cambridge University Press.

Utton, M.A. (1986) *Economics of Regulating Industry*, London: Basil Blackwell.

Van der Gaag, J. and Perlman, M. (eds) (1981) *Health, Economics and Health Economics*, Amsterdam, North Holland: Van Nostrand.

Veatch, R. (1980) *A Theory of Medical Ethics*, New York: Basic Books.

Vickerman. R.W. (1984) *Urban Economics*, Oxford: Philip Allan.

Vickers, J. and Yarrow, G. (1985) *Privatisation and the Natural Monopolies*, London: Public Policy Centre.

Von Mises, L. (1960) *Epistemological Problems of Economics*, New York: Van Nostrand.

Wagner, A. (1890) *Finanzwissenschaft, Pt II*, Leipzig.

Wagstaff, A. (1987) Econometric studies in health economics: a survey of British literature', *Centre for Health Economics Discussion Paper*, no.32, University of York.

Warner, K.E. and Luce, B.R. (1982) *Cost-Benefit and Cost Effectiveness Analysis in Health Care: Principles, practice and potential*, Ann Arbor, Michigan: Health Administration Press.

Weidenbaum, M.L. (1981) *Business, Government and the Public*, 2nd edition, Englewood Cliffs, NJ: Prentice Hall.

Westwell, J. (1987) 'Yuppies in the firing line', *The Sunday Times*, 8 December.

Whynes, D. (ed.) (1983) *What is Political Economy*?, Oxford: Basil Blackwell.

Wicksell, K. (1896) 'A new principle of just taxation', in *Finanztheoretische Untersuchungen*, Jena, East Germany.

Williams, A. (1978) 'Need: an economic exegesis', in Culyer, A.J. and Wright, K.G. (eds) *Economic Aspects of Health Services*, London: Martin Robertson.

Williams, A. (1979) 'One economist's view of social medicine', *Epidemiology and Community Health*, vol.33.

Williams, A. (1981) 'Welfare economics and health status measurement', in van der Gaag, J. and Perlman, M. (eds) *Health, Economics and Health Economics*, Amsterdam, North Holland: Van Nostrand.

Williams, A. and Anderson, R. (1975) *Efficiency in the Social Services*, Oxford and London: Basil Blackwell and Martin Robertson.

Williamson, O.E. (1976) 'Franchise bidding for natural monopolies: in general and with respect to CATV', *Bell Journal of Economics*, vol.7, no.1.

Wilson, J.Q. (ed.) (1980) *The Politics of Regulation*, New York: Basic Books.

Wilson, K.K. (1983) *British Financial Institutions*, London: Pitman.

Wiseman, J. (ed.) (1983) *Beyond Positive Economics*?, London: Macmillan.

Wolff, R. and Resnick, S. (1987) *Economics: Marxian versus neo-classical*, Baltimore: Johns Hopkins University Press.

Wood, M. (1987) *Domesday: A search for the roots of England*, London: BBC Books.

Young, J. (1981) 'Thinking seriously about crime', in Fitzgerald, M., McLennan, G. and Pawson, J., *Crime and Society*, London: Routledge & Kegan Paul.

Young, S. and Hood, N. (1980) 'Recent patterns of foreign direct investment by British multinational enterprises in the United States', *National Westminster Bank Review*, May.

INDEX